Sunday's Child?

On board the Kindertransport, 1 December 1938.

Sunday's Child?

A MEMOIR

Leslie Baruch Brent

First published in the United Kingdom in 2009 by
Bank House Books, PO Box 3, New Romney, TN29 9WJ

www.bankhousebooks.com

British Library Cataloguing in Publication Data
A catalogue entry record for this book is available from the British
Library.

ISBN 9781904408444

Typesetting, design and origination by Bank House Books
Printed by Lightning Source

I dedicate this memoir to my dear parents, Arthur and Charlotte Baruch, to my sister Eva-Susanne; and to my wife Carol

Why is it we want so badly to memorialise ourselves? Even while we're still alive. We wish to assert our existence, like dogs peeing on fire hydrants . . . At the very least we want a witness. We can't stand the idea of our own voices falling silent, like a radio running down.

The only way you can write the truth is to assume that what you set down will never be read. Not by any other person, and not even by yourself at some later date. Otherwise you begin excusing yourself.

Margaret Atwood, *The Blind Assassin* (Bloomsbury, 2000)

Contents

CONTENTS

List of Illustrations

Acknowledgements

I gladly acknowledge the help of the following: Raymond Bar von Hemmersweil, Antony Barnett, Philippa Bassett (Archivist, Special Collections, University of Birmingham), Prof. Emeritus J.R. Batchelor, Eric Bourne, Carol Brent, Gerald Browton, Capt. Robert and Mrs Ruth Durrant, Barbara Fletcham Smith, Thilde Fraenkel, Kathleen Goff, Andy Kenny, Martin Lubowski, David Martin, Henry and Patricia Mayer, Prof. Konrad Messmer, Hans and Susanne Meyer, William Mills (Librarian and Keeper, Scott Polar Research Institute), Ruby Monnet, Gerd Nathan, Dr Ray D. Owen, Dorle Potten, Zdzislaw Pacholski, Dr Heinz Redwood, Peter and Anita Rich, Dr Paula Sells, Dr Hermann Simon, Prof. Emeritus Elizabeth Simpson, Prof. Emeritus Michael Trede, Ernest and Ingelore Weinberg, Helen Williams.

My special indebtedness is to my wife Carol, who has not only put up patiently with my preoccupation whilst writing this book but has acted as a friendly critic throughout.

I also wish to express my gratitude to my editor, Simon Fletcher, without whose enthusiastic support and encouragement these memoirs would still be languishing in my computer.

Foreword

Privileged to provide a foreword to Leslie Brent's *A History of Transplantation and Immunology* (Academic Press, 1997), I noted of the author: 'As to his contributions, the reader can glean from the text and citations that he has been a leader in transplantation research and immunology over the whole period of its history. As to his life, an account of it would be inspiring as any in his collection. Happily, it isn't over yet.'

Now, a decade later, I have the privilege of drafting a foreword to that account. It is, in part, a deeply reflective history of a life that began happily in pre-war Germany, where he encountered early gathering clouds of Hitler's madness. He escaped as a boy with the first Kindertransport to England, was fortunately taken into a very unusual boarding school there, served in the British army, entered a university, studied and gained stature in an exciting field of science, and became a worldwide leader in that field. But the memoir is not strictly, or perhaps even mainly, an autobiography. True, it abounds in personal thoughts and events along the way, many of them sure to be fascinating to a variety of readers. They carry the personal to broader contexts - academic, cultural, societal. But in large part the book reflects an extraordinary sensitivity to the people whose lives interwove with his. There are many examples - of others who shared the exodus from Germany, their backgrounds, experiences, what happened to them - and those they had to leave behind, like the author's own family; who taught at the first school in England, where did they individually come from, what were their characteristics? Colleagues, and experiences in the army, at university, in the distinguished research group he joined and people in his later life - all receive painstaking respect.

SUNDAY'S CHILD?

The book is a series of essays rather than a continuous autobiographical narrative; essays ranging widely and interestingly to include reflections, for example, on 'the new anti-Semitism', on the atomic bombs, on 'falling in love', on Vichy France, Zionism, Iraq, art, literature, sports, people and politics. Anyone who reads this foreword has access to the extensive table of contents and an invitation to browse. This foreword is not a review, only an appreciation.

Leslie's father described him as 'Sunday's Child', one of good fortune. Throughout there is an emphasis on how 'lucky' he has been. This is true compared with many others less fortunate. But it is in his ability to recognise opportunities, to generate admirable accomplishments, to value and understand associates, and to communicate it all in clear, interesting writing that this Sunday's Child excels. From beginning to end he gives us a 'good read', meanwhile offering historians invaluable insights into important periods and aspects of our history.

Ray D. Owen
Emeritus Professor
California Institute of Technology
July 2008

Preface

The reader is entitled to know what drove me to write this book, which is not so much an autobiography as a group of essays focusing on certain periods of my life. Other chapters are devoted to extraordinary people who were important to me in my personal and scientific development; others still to institutions with which I have been involved - from the Jewish orphanage in Berlin, Bunce Court School in Kent, the British Army, the University of Birmingham and University College London, St Mary's Hospital Medical School, my life as a local politician and campaigner, to my membership of Crouch End Festival Chorus. One chapter deals with several important scientific discoveries to which I have contributed, and another - arguably the most troublesome - discusses the possible motivation of Adolf Hitler in forcing me, together with many thousands of others, to become a refugee from Nazi oppression. In this context my attitude to Judaism and Zionism needs to be considered, as must the question of identity of one who came to England without his family at the age of thirteen. I also try to grapple with the Holocaust and with the disastrous attack on Iraq and its consequences.

It would be presumptuous of me to claim that my life has been particularly exceptional. Plenty of accounts have recently been published of the lives of people who went through childhood experiences not dissimilar to mine. Harking back to another era, the African Olaudah Equiano, who came to England in the eighteenth century as a slave and who achieved great distinction as a writer and campaigner for human rights, was truly unique and I would not dream of comparing his extraordinary experiences and achievements with my own. It may nonetheless be apposite to quote from his book *The African* (1789,

1

republished by X Press, 1998) because it expresses very elegantly some of my own feelings in submitting this book to a readership that extends beyond the immediate circle of my family and friends:

> I believe it is difficult for those who publish their own memoirs to escape the imputation of vanity. Nor is this the only disadvantage under which they labour: it is also their misfortune, that whatever is uncommon is rarely, if ever, believed, and from what is obvious we are apt to turn with disgust, and to charge the writer of it with impertinence. People generally think those memoirs only worthy to be read or remembered which abound in great or striking events; those in short, which, in a high degree, excite either admiration or pity; all others they consign to contempt or oblivion.
>
> It is therefore, I confess, not a little hazardous in a private and obscure individual, and a stranger too, thus to solicit the indulgent attention of the public; especially when I own I offer here the history of neither a saint, a hero, nor a tyrant. I believe that there are few events in my life which have not happened to many. It is true the incidents of it are numerous; and did I consider myself a European, I might say my sufferings were great; but when I compare my lot with that of most of my countrymen, I regard myself as *a particular favourite of Heaven*, and acknowledge the mercies of Providence in every occurrence of my life.

To this I say 'amen'! It was my parents who, in one of their last Red Cross messages sent in the middle of the Second World War and shortly before they were sent to their deaths, reminded me that I was, after all, 'ein Sonntagskind' and that I would surely make my way. (This German expression implies good fortune rather than its meaning in the old English nursery rhyme, according to which a child born on Sabbath's Day 'is fair and wise, and good and gay'.)

Chapter One: A Tombstone

Its discovery

In July 1999 I received a fax from Zdzislaw Pacholski, a Polish photographer living in Koszalin near the Baltic Sea. He wrote: 'Thank you very much for your letter – it's really sad story. But I have good message for you (I hope). I think I found tombstone of your family. *David Baruch*, born 1840, granite, inscriptions in German and Hebraic languages. Maybe he is your grandfather?'

This news came like a bolt out of the blue. Koszalin had been called Köslin before the Second World War, and that is where my family had lived until 1938. My family name had indeed been Baruch. Apart from an uncle and a cousin my whole family was killed by the Germans during the war. When I revisited Koszalin for the first time in 1989 I found a town that had been largely rebuilt following widespread destruction during the fighting between the German and Soviet armies towards the end of the war. The German market town of Köslin had become the wholly Polish Koszalin. The huge domed synagogue had been burnt to the ground by the Nazis during the Kristallnacht (the night of the broken glass) pogroms on 9 November 1938, the 'new' Jewish cemetery had given way to the Technical University and as far as I could make out there wasn't a single Jew left. Yet suddenly it appeared that a family relic had survived.

I was wildly excited, and rushed to my study to check the name on a family tree my 'American' cousin, Warren Munroe (formerly Wolfgang Münzer), had sent me years ago. Yes, there he was: David Baruch – not my paternal grandfather, but his younger brother whom I had never known. I immediately faxed Zdzislaw (Zibi for short) to ask all the obvious questions, but especially where the gravestone had been

3

found – and whether it was small enough to be carried back to London in our car!

It turned out that Zibi had discovered the tombstone in the local museum, but it had been found by a friend of his, lying in a shallow stream that flows through the lower reaches of the town. It is a stream in which I used to look for sticklebacks in my early childhood. One point puzzled me greatly. I well remember the Jewish cemetery, a small well-kept enclave with graves surrounded by low box hedges, which we visited occasionally to tend to the graves of our family members; but it was on a hill, well away from the stream. Surely vandals wouldn't have taken the trouble to carry it all that way? My cousin Warren soon solved this riddle for me: although the 'new' cemetery had been on the hill, the old one had indeed been situated in the valley near the stream.

Because my great-uncle's gravestone appeared to be the only Jewish artefact left in this Polish town, I suggested to Zibi the possibility of using it as a memorial to the Jewish community, together with a suitable plaque, perhaps near the site of the synagogue. I did this with some trepidation, knowing about the anti-Semitism that had been a feature of Polish life before the war, and I did not think that Zibi would regard it as workable idea. I did, however, offer to help with the costs of erecting such a memorial. Zibi replied at once: the same thought had occurred to him and he would be discussing it with 'some good friends' in the town. Some years later it was, in fact, returned to its original resting place (see Epilogue, p. 287).

I owe the reader an explanation of how Zibi and I became friends even though we had never met. In 1997 I received a letter from him together with a brochure for an Anne Frank exhibition he had helped to organise in Koszalin. He had been given my name and address by a neighbour who, with his wife and two sons, had inhabited the flat in which my family had lived until they were forced to flee the town in 1938.

First visit to Koszalin

On my first visit to Koszalin in 1989 my former wife Joanne and I had knocked on the door of this third-floor flat, the building having survived the war with not so much as a scratch. Even the ceramic tiles in the entrance hall, each with a sea shell or some other marine creature, were intact. We had armed ourselves with a note written in Polish by someone in our hotel. This explained that I had lived in the flat before the war, and asked whether the present occupants would greatly mind if we had a look at it for auld lang syne. Andrzej and Malgorzata Michalek spoke neither English nor German, but somehow they managed to convey to us that they would prefer us to return on the following afternoon, which we did.

By that time Malgorzata had baked a delicious cake and brewed a pot of coffee. This was before the end of Communism in Poland and conditions were still harsh – so a special effort had been made for us. I entered the flat with beating heart and very mixed emotions. Yes, there was the tiled stove at one end of the sitting room against which we used to sit to warm our backs, and with the small cavity in which we baked apples. And yes, there was the little balcony outside the kitchen window on which I had spent many an hour pretending to sail the seas in my ship – perhaps to England? With bits of English and German, and with the help of a dictionary and dramatic gestures, we managed to convey to our hosts the reason for this rather extraordinary visit. We have exchanged Christmas cards ever since and have become good friends.

A year after our visit Andrzej and Malgorzata left the flat to move into a house built by themselves as part of a cooperative, some way out of town, and that is where they found themselves to be Zibi's neighbours. They had told (Malgorzata 'with tears in her eyes') Zibi and his wife Janina about me, and were therefore indirectly implicated in the revelation of the tombstone.

Whilst my first visit to Koszalin with Joanne and my son Simon had been painful and cathartic, my later trips, accompanied by my second wife Carol, proved to be pleasurable and exciting, for now I had good friends there who were always welcoming.

Zibi is a man of parts, as well as a man with his heart in the right place, and his photographs have been exhibited in Germany as well as Poland. In the year 2000 he published a pictorial history of Koszalin and asked me to write a review of it, which I gladly did. It was highly complimentary, but made the point that, though it showed pre-war scenes, there was no direct reference to the fact that before the Second World War Koszalin had been a typical German market town; and I expressed the view that Koszalin in the Nazi era would have been well worth discussing. Had this omission been deliberate so as to spare the feelings of Polish readers? (The text in the book was in Polish, German and English.)

I have returned to Koszalin three times, each time accompanied by Carol. The visit in 2001 was purely private, and my friends in the town made it a very rewarding, interesting and enjoyable experience. Having travelled there by car, we were able to explore the town and its environment more extensively than was possible in 1989, and at last I began to comprehend the new layout of the city and to recognise remnants of a past era. The pain of returning to the town in which I had spent my childhood had largely gone, and we were overwhelmed by the friendliness and empathy of Zibi and his wife Nina, Malgorzata and Andrzej.

The visit in 2005 was the result of an official invitation by the Lord Mayor and the city council, and the extraordinary week in Koszalin, in which I was extravagantly honoured in a number of ways and which proved to be one of the highlights of my life, is briefly described in the Epilogue. It set in train a sequence of events that are continuing – events that I think have to do with a need to recognise the not always palatable past of the Polish people in relation to their Jewish neighbours, and with a strong desire on the part of some people in Koszalin – principally Zibi and a Catholic priest, Henryk Romanik – to encourage the community to act in ways that lead to reconciliation. I regard my role in all this as catalytic and emblematic. Our visit to Koszalin in 2006, this time as guests of the University of Technology, was equally momentous, and again I have covered this in the Epilogue. It seems that I have been 'adopted' by the city in a strange and heart-warming way, and that I shall always be welcomed there – an extraordinary inversion of what happened in 1938, when I was forced to leave the German town of my birth in disarray and under severe duress.

Chapter Two: A Childhood by the Baltic

My family; happy years

Jwas born Lothar Baruch on a summer Sunday in Köslin, Germany, in 1925, the year that Margaret Thatcher and Pierre Boulez were born, England cricketers won their first test match against Australia since 1912, and General Hindenburg was sworn in as Germany's new president. Adolf Hitler, having been released from the fortress of Landsberg where he had been placed for his treasonable activities, had persuaded the Bavarian authorities to lift a ban on his party and its newspaper with a promise of good behaviour and the renunciation of force in his quest for political power. In prison he had written a book, dictated to his close supporter Rudolf Hess, with the title of *Four Years and a Half of Struggle Against Lies, Stupidity and Cowardice*. Friends having advised him to find a shorter title, it became his notorious manifesto *Mein Kampf*, the implications of which the world unfortunately chose to ignore.

Until Hitler and his National Socialists turned life for German Jews upside down in the early to mid-thirties I had a pretty normal childhood insofar as any childhood can ever be described as normal. My parents Arthur and Charlotte were German Jews, or Jewish Germans, who were comfortably off without being wealthy, and who practised their religion with conviction though without orthodoxy. They were well respected in the Jewish community, which comprised about 150 people, and they were at the same time integrated into German social and cultural traditions. Their families had lived in Köslin for several generations, certainly from the beginning of the nineteenth century and probably well before, and like so many others in their position they could not conceive that they might one day be deprived of their 'Heimat'. This attitude prevented them from seeing the writing on the wall until it was too late.

My father became a travelling salesman for some large firms selling children's and women's clothes after his father-in-law, who owned a haberdasher's shop in the middle of town, could no longer employ him. This meant that he was absent from home for varying periods, visiting shops in different parts of Pomerania. Our last flat was located in the street leading to the railway station, and meeting my father off the train is one of my joyful memories. Carrying in each hand a heavy suitcase containing not only his clothes but also his many samples, he was invariably the first to emerge from the platform and was proudly escorted home by me.

He was tall and quite good-looking – at least I thought so and I still do – with an aquiline if somewhat semitic nose and an almost bald head that had been a feature from early adulthood. He always wore a grey Homburg with a ribbon around it and later I attributed his baldness to it, probably wrongly. Whilst not especially athletic, he was an excellent swimmer who sometimes frightened me by swimming a long way into the Baltic Sea, and I found his expectation of me in that respect rather overpowering. He also enjoyed walking: regular walks into the local forest, with our friends the Lewins, were *de rigueur* on Sunday afternoons whenever he was at home. Once we had reached the top of a densely wooded hill (the Gollen), the adults tended to gravitate to the café whilst I and my sister Eva Susanne, who was two and a half years older, roamed in the woods, got toy aeroplanes stuck high up in trees and, to our eternal shame, persecuted our friend Ingelore Lewin who, as a single child, was being brought up with far greater decorum than the Baruch children. She later married my best friend from school days in Kent, Ernst Weinberg, and she has remained a very dear friend, so the persecution could not have been too serious! Between the Lewins and the Baruchs there was a family whistle which provided instant recognition, so that when collecting the Lewins from their house *en route* to the Gollen, for example, we were able to let them know that we were outside without verbal communication or ringing the bell. The notes were a phrase from a popular song, I believe ('Die Sonne geht auf', the sun is rising). It became, and remains, my own family's whistle.

My father (Va) played the piano rather well and the *Songs without Words* by Mendelssohn remain a nostalgic memory. He also had a good voice – he sang in a men's choir – and liked to sing Schubert songs at home. He and I occasionally sang simpler songs together, one of them with the refrain 'Und wir fahren, und wir fahren, g'en Engeland' (And we sail, and we sail, towards England). Whenever possible he played the organ at religious services in the synagogue whilst my mother, Eva and I

8

sang in the choir. An abiding memory is of the hand-operated pump of the rather grand organ. Usually an elderly and feeble-looking man, presumably not Jewish, was employed to do the pumping. However, every now and again his strength failed him, the sound became flatter and flatter, and I had to rush over to save the day.

Va had a way with words, and he followed what I perceive to be an old German tradition of composing poems for special family occasions such as birthdays. The only poem I have in my possession was sent to me when I was already in England. They were always well rhymed, witty and to the point. I like to think that this gift has been passed on to me to a degree, as I too tend to write poems, sometimes quite lengthy but of inferior quality. Birthdays, retirements and other celebrations, such as the publication of my book *A History of Transplantation Immunology*, and the occasional after-dinner speech given at annual scientific meetings in a Tyrolean ski resort, to which I have been privileged to be invited for the last thirty-odd years, have been marked in this way.

Va was well disposed towards the English and admired them. On one of our walks into the local woods he admonished me for walking with my toes pointing outwards; English sportsmen, I was told, always walk with their feet parallel. He seemed to be unable to follow his own advice and, thanks to heaving his heavy suitcases around on his travels, was flat-footed.

He had been a soldier during the First World War and had served as a medical orderly. Having rescued an injured soldier under fire he was awarded the Iron Cross, Second Class, and I am pretty certain that he later felt this would afford him some protection during the Nazi regime. It must have added to his false sense of security, and it certainly failed to save him and his family, in common with many others who had served their country during that war. Va didn't talk much about those years, though it was clear that food was in very short supply: when eating a slice of sausage for breakfast he gave us a demonstration of how that was eaten during and just after the war. It was placed near the front of a slice of bread and then gradually pushed further back, to be consumed only at the very end! This method was called 'Schiebebrot' (push-bread).

(My father was one of 100,000 German Jews who had served in the German army in the First World War, and many of them distinguished themselves in battle. According to S.C.J. Nicholls, about 25,000 Jews became officers in the Austro-Hungarian army, including twenty-five generals – although admittedly all but three had converted – and three field marshals. One of the latter was deported from Vienna in 1943 and perished in Auschwitz.)

My mother (Mu) was a lovely, warm woman (well, whose mother wasn't?), tall and with an ample figure, on whose lap I loved to snuggle. Whilst Va could at times be a trifle stern, Mu was the embodiment of maternal softness and love. Earlier in her life she had acted as book-keeper for her father's business but I remember her as a full-time mother and housewife. She too was musical but her piano playing was less accomplished than my father's. She must have had quite a hard time of it thanks to my father's frequent absences. Occasionally a certain tension was evident between them – I suspect that there may have been some marital infidelity, probably on my father's part if my cousin's opinion is anything to go by. Be that as it may, I know that I felt jealous on my father's behalf because of the attention paid to Mu by her brother-in-law (my cousin's father). On one occasion when he visited my mother during one of Va's absences, I was sent to the dark and dank coal and potato cellar in the basement to fetch a bucket of coal – I thought to get me out of the way. I rushed breathlessly down the four flights of stairs and up again so as not to leave these two together on their own longer than I could help! I am sure that psychologists will draw their own conclusions; the whole episode may have been, and probably was, perfectly innocuous.

It was my mother who sang Brahms's lullaby 'Guten Abend, Gute Nacht' to us on many evenings immediately before we fell asleep and who taught us the prayer 'Lieber Gott ich bitte Dich, führe und beschütze mich, daß ich einst, als großer Mann, anderen Menschen helfen kann' (Dear God, I beg you to lead and protect me, so that when I am a grown man I can help others). This simple prayer has stayed with me all my life and has acted as a guide far more powerfully than any formal prayer. Another bedtime song Mu often sang with us was 'Sandmännchen kam geschliechen . . .' (The little sandman came stealing by . . .). On Sunday mornings Eva and I were allowed to join our parents in their vast double bed and getting up was invariably resisted for as long as possible. My father therefore adopted the ruse of quoting a bard (which?): 'Auf, auf, sprach der Fuchs zum Hasen, hörst du nicht den Jäger blasen?' (Away, away, said the fox to the hare, have you not heard the hunter's horn?). And after several abortive attempts to jump out of bed we were eventually persuaded by the fox. I perpetuated this little ritual with my children, who found it as engaging as my sister and I had done.

Mu had a tendency towards rheumatism and her knees were sometimes swollen and painful; from time to time she went to a spa like Baden-Baden in the hope of improvement. She struggled valiantly with corsets and stays – mysterious and wondrous gadgets for a young lad like me – and she was not averse to wearing her fox fur in the winter to protect her from the icy north-east wind.

My sister Eva seems, in retrospect, to have been far more mature and sophisticated than her little brother. One of my many huge regrets is that I did not have the opportunity to know her as an adult. She and I led separate lives much of the time, but inevitably there was some sibling rivalry in the early years, largely I think on her part because she may have thought that it was I who was the apple of my mother's eye. This, whether true or not (and it probably was), engendered some jealousy. I had 'replaced' an earlier brother, Heinz Günther, who had died soon after birth, and this may well have made me seem especially precious to my parents. As youngsters Eva and I certainly managed to fight at times, yet at others she was the dear older sister who, for example, when I was four or five, entranced me with her imaginative twilight stories of the mysterious 'mandarins' whom she claimed to have spotted across the valley in some lit-up windows, and who invented a secret language. She once woke me up in what seemed to me to be the dead of night and persuaded me to leave my cot in order to listen at and look through the keyhole of the door leading to my parents' bedroom. I didn't know what to make of the grunts and cries and I doubt that she did, but I found it quite disturbing. Deliciously unsettling were the spooky stories told to us in the dark – the only light coming from the stove – by a much-loved elderly woman who did some sewing for my mother and who baby-sat from time to time.

Unlike me, placid to a fault, Eva was highly strung and in her adolescence, before I was taken away from Köslin, she threw some spectacular tantrums, the nature of which I did not understand. I remember trying to act as peacemaker on one occasion when she stormed out of the flat threatening never to return, with my parents and me in hot pursuit. On another occasion she threatened to throw herself out of the window. I don't know whether these tantrums were part of her adolescence or brought about by a far greater understanding than I had of the seriousness of the political situation and the declining economic and social status of my family. Or there may have been other family problems that had passed over my head.

Eva had piano lessons and showed great promise; she too had a good voice. To this day I have feelings of guilt towards her – not because of any shortcomings in our relationship but because on a sweltering summer's day I stole ten pennies from her purse so that I could buy myself an ice-cream. I must have been six or seven at the time. Of course, far weightier feelings of guilt derive from the fact that she was left behind, at her own insistence I believe, when I escaped to England in a Kindertransport.

Yes, on the whole I had a pretty happy and normal early childhood, for my parents managed to hide from me their ever more straitened circumstances and the significance of what went on around us once the Nazis had gained power.

The large flat that I remember from my earlier years had a spacious drawing room with a grand piano, and sliding doors leading into a smoking room and library, in which I browsed illicitly from time to time – looking at forbidden books. The grand piano, together with much furniture and some valuable objects, was sold when we had to move into a smaller flat (the one not far from the railway station). This is the time when Millais' *The Gleaners* disappeared, though I doubt that it was the original! My father and his male friends enjoyed smoking cigars, and on one occasion I collected a number of cigar butts, which I took, together with a friend, into the roof-space of our block of flats. There we smoked them, and I soon became very green round the gills. The experiment was never repeated and it probably put me off smoking for life, though I dabbled with a pipe when I was in the army and at university.

I spent much time on innocent pleasures – endlessly whipping my wooden spinning top on the pavement outside our block of flats, cruising up and down on my scooter, sitting on our tiny kitchen balcony pretending to be sailing the seas, and reading adventure stories like *Emil and the Detectives* and an abridged version of *The Last of the Mohicans*, which fired my imagination – though I cannot remember whose side I was on. One book from my early childhood comprised Jewish stories from the East, Poland or Russia I think, and one of them, which involved wolves howling in the forest, left a particularly vivid impression on me. There was a great deal of visiting other members of our family and friends, which I regarded as something of a trial and tribulation. In the mornings I enjoyed watching my father shave with an old-fashioned cut-throat, which was ceremoniously sharpened on a leather strap. One of the joys of walking to school on a Monday morning was to call in at the Konditorei (patisserie), where for ten pennies one was able to buy, if in luck, a conical bag of bits and pieces of cakes and confectioneries left over from the previous Sunday. The delectable taste of this Monday morning treat has stayed with me most vividly. We made our own yoghurt by leaving uncovered bowls of unpasteurised milk in the open until it set and a skin formed – delicious with sugar or, when available, bilberries that we had picked in the woods. In the winters we baked apples on the shelf of our tiled oven, which also provided the flat with heat.

Not far from our flat in the Bahnhofstrasse was what I assume must have been a knacker's yard, to which I sometimes gravitated to watch horses being fed and led around the yard by a somewhat disreputable-looking elderly man. On one occasion he invited me to sit on an old nag whilst he was leading it round the yard and I managed to fall off. My right wrist was extremely painful and my mother was greatly alarmed when she saw me, looking as white as a sheet. Naturally she wanted to know how I had hurt myself, but out of a sense of loyalty to the old man – whom I thought might get into trouble if I told the truth – I steadfastly refused to say. I was taken to the local hospital, where I was X-rayed and found to have a fracture of the wrist. This was reset under what I think must have been chloroform anaesthesia, a highly disagreeable experience.

Subsequently I was taken to my uncle and aunt, the Münzers, where the interrogation continued, but I refused to spill the beans despite all kinds of inducements. I don't think that a sense of loyalty - in this case probably mistaken - has ever been my problem.

Our summer holidays were almost invariably spent in a small village on the Baltic Sea - Grossmöllen, or Mielno as it is now called - some 10km from the town. My parents always rented a small cottage from a farmer, and the three to four weeks by the seaside were utter bliss. A tram ran between Köslin and the seaside, and if one was lucky one stood on the platform behind the tram driver, watching him operate the control lever, apply the brakes and strike the strident bell with his foot. The countryside in that part of Pomerania is flat and the farmhouses were generally thatched. Many of their chimneys were occupied by stork nests, and one of the excitements of the journey was to count the number of black and white storks along the way. (The thatched houses were largely destroyed during the war but, to encourage the migrating storks to go on nesting, tall poles with small platforms have been erected by the Polish authorities, and these seem to be sufficiently attractive to the storks though rather less romantic to the viewer.) One year, when I had been given a gleaming new bicycle for my birthday, my father and I pedalled to Grossmöllen, leaving the women to make their way by tram with all the family clobber. I shall never forget the exterior toilet of our little cottage; it consisted of a long bench with three circular holes, each with a bucket containing some strong-smelling disinfectant. Fortunately I cannot remember ever sharing this toilet, and the amount of time spent in it was, not surprisingly, minimal.

The summers were usually hot, and when making my way to the beach I had to run very fast in order to prevent the soles of my feet from being blistered by the sand of the dunes. It was indeed a simple and innocent life. The days were spent on the beach with all the usual seaside pleasures of sandcastles (endlessly defeated by the incoming tides), handball and of course swimming. One or two small basketwork shelters were hired for the season to enable the women to undress with some degree of privacy and to provide shelter when the wind blew hard, which it did quite often. Whilst my mother and the children often swam out to the first sandbank, my father had the audacity to swim as far as the third and I considered this to be a great feat of daring. My father also occasionally accompanied a fishing boat under sail on an overnight trip, fishing being a major industry before the Baltic became seriously polluted after the war. Scanning the horizon the next morning, spotting his boat, helping to haul it on to the beach and welcoming the heavily tanned hero was a great joy. Some parts of the beach were occupied by the fishermen's wives, dressed in black and accompanied by the older men, mending fishing nets: the smell of creosote, used to protect the nets and the boats, still remains nostalgically in my nostrils. Our friends the Lewins were often in Grossmöllen at the same time and spent many happy hours with us on the beach. Sunsets over the Baltic Sea could be spectacular, as could the odd thunderstorm with its aftermath of prolonged silent lightning.

Other assorted memories from that happy period of my childhood? I was once sent to a holiday camp in Denmark, but all I remember of that is my first exposure to porridge, which is an acquired taste that came to me much later in England. I enjoyed accompanying my mother to the open market in the town square and to the fish market in a side street, where the fishermen's wives displayed their menfolk's latest catch and sang its praises in raucous voices. (The sight of a live eel taken home to be killed there was not a pretty sight!) I much enjoyed skating on a lake, together with my friend Ingelore Lewin (known as Inge). Skating towards a hole in the ice into which a skater had allegedly disappeared, and sledging down a hill into a partly frozen-over bog, added to the excitements of the winter activities. The winters were hideously cold and the summers pleasantly hot.

A less than pleasurable memory is having an abscess below my ear lanced by the town's dentist, Dr Cohn, who happened to be a friend, a good doctor and therefore deemed to be qualified to undertake this minor surgery.

'Cultural' highlights included some magic lantern and film shows at a friend's house and being taken to see *San Francisco*, starring Clark Gable, at the local fleapit in 1936.

My Jewish upbringing

Judaism, though not of the orthodox kind, played an important part in our life. We regularly attended the Friday evening services in the absurdly grandiose synagogue and my mother lit the two Sabbath candles on returning home, with my father breaking the traditional bread and singing the short Hebrew prayers blessing the bread and the sweet wine sipped from a silver goblet. By Friday evening the flat had to be spotless, and the wooden kitchen table and the kitchen floor were well and truly scrubbed, often by me as I enjoyed helping my mother in the house. All surfaces in the kitchen, in which we took our meals, were covered with freshly washed and ironed fitted and embroidered cloths bearing Dutch motifs in blue on white. On Saturday mornings I often accompanied my father and grandfather to the morning service. Services were predominantly conducted in Hebrew, and as my knowledge of Hebrew was strictly limited to say the least I tended to be bored. My maternal grandfather was a deeply religious man and, like others, he was sometimes accorded the honour of reading passages from the Torah, the decorated Holy Scrolls topped by their gilded crowns, and it would have been considered disloyal of me not to have sat by his side. He was a serious and solemn man, without a discernible sense of humour, and I felt rather in awe of him. (My relationship with my grandchildren is so utterly different!) Although it was a liberal synagogue the men were separated from the women, who sat in the balconies on either side.

All Jewish festivals were celebrated with gusto and I harbour the most pleasant and nostalgic memories of them, from Sukkoth to Passover. For Sukkoth, a kind of harvest festival, a hut symbolic of the temporary shelter used by the Israelites during their time in the wilderness was created in the open space behind the synagogue, and from its flimsy beams hung vines, bunches of grapes and palm leaves. The Jewish capacity of celebrating with a glass of sweet wine, duly praised in song, is a rather endearing feature. The Passover feast was always memorable, not only because of its traditional and symbolic food but because the youngest male child present is expected to ask the questions from the Hagadah referring to the purpose of the celebration. And every year we intoned the symbolic words 'See you next year in Jerusalem' with due solemnity, though I had no idea what this signified.

As I grew older I was allowed to fast with the adults on Yom Kippur, the Day of Atonement, and the twenty-four-hour fast ended with yet another sumptuous feast. Food is an important ingredient in Jewish ritual, which is none the worse for it. Simchat Torah, the Celebration of the Law, was very much a child's event, for after the service children paraded and danced round and round the synagogue having sweets and sometimes coins thrown towards them, sometimes from the upper galleries. This tended to lead to rather undignified scrambles, with the most agile child garnering the largest hoard. Chanukah, the Festival of Lights, celebrates the rededication of the desecrated Temple in the second century BC and the miraculous survival of a single unpolluted vessel of oil, enough for one day only – though it lasted for eight. We lit the candles of the Minorah on successive evenings and sang the Chanukah song recounting the stirring events of the past. I doubt that there is a Jew who has forgotten the traditional tune. And then there was Purim, a day of jubilation at the saving of the ancient Jews in Persia by Esther, the Jewish wife of King Xerxes, who outwitted the evil Haman's plot to destroy the Jewish population. We children sometimes performed a play telling the Purim story.

Although I am now an agnostic I have a sense of nostalgia for these religious activities with their rituals and pleasurable activities. From a child's viewpoint they seem to be unrivalled by other religions for the sheer excitement and fun, as well as gravitas, they generated. Although my parents insisted on Eva and me getting some Hebrew lessons, together with a few other children in the town, the rather weird little red-haired man who travelled weekly from a neighbouring town to teach us completely failed in his feeble endeavours, and this educational initiative was eventually terminated. I am afraid that we gave this man rather a hard time and I wonder what became of him. We spoke Hochdeutsch (the German spoken by educated people) and no Yiddish, though a few Yiddish words were used, such as 'rischis' for anti-Semitism, 'nebbich' for pathetic and 'goy' for Christians.

We had a young cantor for many services, especially on high holidays, and he sang the traditional prayers in a mellifluous tenor voice. One of them, a prayer sung on the Day of Atonement, still haunts me. My mother wanted me to become a cantor but, alas, her ambition was not to be fulfilled, though I took up singing late in life.

After all this it may come as a surprise to the reader that we used to have a Christmas tree and that my father was not averse to dressing up as Father Christmas when delivering presents to people living in our block of flats.

The rise of Nazism: early consequences

I was friendly with a non-Jewish boy living a floor below us in the Bahnhofstrasse. His father having been an officer in the First World War, there were several swords on the premises. My friend and I once staged a mock fight in which I represented (with great prescience) the English, and during the course of it I fell off a chair and finished up with a huge bump above one eye. This was expertly treated by the boy's mother with a lump of raw steak. Not very long after, with the assumption of power by the National Socialists and my friend's father's membership of the SA (the notorious brown-shirted Sturmabteilung), this friendship was abruptly and without explanation terminated.

From here on my family's life and that of all German Jews, which up to then had been so normal, began to disintegrate in ways that could not have been predicted, and which many people, despite mounting evidence, chose to ignore or minimise – my parents included. Paradise was irretrievably lost.

Chapter Three: Gathering Storm Clouds

By 1932 the Weimar Republic – that great experiment in German democracy – had collapsed. Hitler followed Hindenburg as chancellor, having established his National Socialist party as a potent force by dint of political machinations and sheer thuggery and intimidation, aided and abetted by inflation, unemployment and poverty. In the following year's elections his party managed to gain control of the Reichstag and now the abuse of power was truly under way. These events have been described and analysed in numerous books, among them those by Martin Gilbert (*A History of the Twentieth Century, vol. 1: 1900-1933*) and Michael Burleigh (*The Third Reich - a New History*).

Rabid anti-Semitism, as well as a loathing of Communism, was a central plank of Hitler's philosophy as foreshadowed in *Mein Kampf*, and life for German Jews began to be precarious from the moment that Hitler assumed power in 1932. However, the enshrinement of anti-Jewish measures in the German constitution did not come about until 1935, with the promulgation of the so-called Nuremberg laws. By depriving them of citizenship, German Jews were declared to be an underclass: many professions were barred to them, marriage and sexual relationships between 'Aryans' and 'Non-Aryans' were strictly forbidden, female non-Jewish servants under the age of forty-five could no longer be employed by Jewish families and, rather ludicrously, Jews were prohibited from flying the German flag. All this gave licence to Germans and to the SA in particular to persecute individuals and Jewish businesses with impunity. How did this impinge on life in Köslin?

17

SUNDAY'S CHILD?

Life in Hitler's Germany

In economic terms it meant that Jewish shops like my grandfather's and my uncle's steadily lost customers, though in a small town like Köslin – distant from Berlin and Munich – the changes probably came about more slowly than in the large cities. My father began to struggle making a living, losing one sales commission after another. The move to a much smaller flat reflected this loss of earning power.

The Jewish community became more and more isolated, and stones were thrown through the synagogue windows during services, eventually forcing the dwindling congregation to conduct its services in the home of the Arndts, one of the synagogue's wealthier families. I remember the sense of shock among the adults when one Jewish man was sentenced to several months' hard labour for having a relationship with an 'Aryan' woman. At school we were subjected to Nazi propaganda, and on one occasion we were shown a film about Horst Wessel, a young Nazi who had been shot by a Communist, apparently in a sordid quarrel; despite this, he was raised to the status of hero and martyr to the Nazi cause. I tagged along but felt deeply uncomfortable. By that time most boys and girls had been inducted into the Hitler Youth and were wearing uniforms, an experience from which we Jews were fortunately debarred. Yet I felt strangely excluded.

A marching song was named in honour of Wessel – the Horst Wessel Song – which begins with 'Die Fahne hoch, die Reihen fest geschlossen, SA marschiert, in ruhigen festen Schritt . . . (Raise the flag and, in tightly closed ranks, SA men march with calm and firm tread . . .). This was sung with fervour on all marches and at demonstrations, rallies and ceremonies and it became Germany's second national anthem. To hear it now in documentary films of that period still sends shivers down my spine. At the same time the cult of the Nazi flag was developed to a fine art, so that streets in the town were festooned with the swastika at every possible opportunity. Jewish homes and shops naturally did not fly this flag and therefore stood out. A thoroughly oppressive atmosphere ensued. Virtually every week money was collected at street corners for good causes, such as the Winterhilfe (aid to the poor in winter) or less noble causes, and when the wearing of a swastika badge became routine this again pointed a finger at Jews, who declined to wear them. Friends and acquaintances began to greet each other with the Hitler salute, accompanied by the cry 'Heil Hitler!' and although my father persisted in raising his hat and uttering the usual greeting this aberrant behaviour marked us more and more as outsiders. Non-Jewish Germans who had been friends, or at the very least had been friendly, began to melt away, and it was a common occurrence that they would cross the street rather than cope with the embarrassment of coming face to face with us and having to greet us with the Hitler salute or ignore us altogether. The Hitler cult, which raised him to a god-like figure, became very frightening indeed.

One disturbing memory is of the day (probably in 1934 or 1935) that my father was asked to report to the local police station for questioning. I don't know what it was all about but my mother grew increasingly restless as the day wore on. As dusk approached she asked me to go to the police station to try to find out when he would be sent home. I was told to wait outside and another hour or two went by. I distinctly remember the smell and hiss of the carbide lamp that swung in the wind outside the building as it got dark. Eventually my father emerged, to great mutual rejoicing, and my reward was a Schokoladenbombe, an extra special chocolate-covered ice cream, on the way home.

A frightening experience

Soon after the Nazis came to power I had my first truly frightening experience; I must have been seven or eight at the time. My sister and I had been left alone with my maternal grandmother (Meta Rosenthal) in a first-floor flat in the main street, the Bergstrasse. (My grandfather had already died, luckily for him from natural causes.) Oma was a truly tragic figure. She was not only stone deaf so that one had to shout loudly into an ear trumpet, but she suffered from a condition that made her skin unbearably scaly and itchy. The only available treatment for what I assume must have been a particularly fulminating case of psoriasis was, it seems, the application of large amounts of Vaseline. The smell of slightly rancid Vaseline and shedding epithelium made Oma very unappealing to us children, even though she always brought out a tin of enticing sweets whenever we visited.

It was evening and already dark when Eva and I heard the sound of feet marching in step, a drum-beat and the Horst Wessel Song. This was the local SA on the march, in a show of strength, each uniformed man carrying a flaming torch. Numerous large swastika flags were borne aloft. One other song, sung in typically brutal Nazi fashion, each word viciously spat out, went like this: 'Und wenn das Judenblut from Messer spritzt dann geht es gar so gut' (And when Jewish blood spurts from the knife then all is really well). Eva and I watched from behind the closed curtains with a strange mixture of fear and fascination. This incident made an indelible impression on me, and I remember the tune as well as the words only too well. It should have set alarm bells ringing for my parents. Perhaps it did, for I remember that some time later – I don't know exactly when – they wrote rather desperately to a famous namesake in America (the financier Bernard Baruch, who was an adviser to President Roosevelt and almost certainly no relation!) in the hope that he might help them to emigrate. I don't think they ever received a response.

I find it astonishing that, so far as I am aware, my parents did not take any interest in the emerging Zionism; the notion of emigrating to Palestine was never aired in my presence. They were rooted too deeply in German culture to consider this to be an option, and by the time that they might have done so it was too late. That they held Hitler in contempt right from the beginning is clear from an amusing episode concerning the parting of my hair, which had always been on the right because of a stubborn whorl on the left that made the parting there difficult. As anyone who has watched documentary films of that period knows, Hitler's parting was on the right side; and so it was decreed that, despite my protests, my parting would forthwith be on the left. A small and futile protest of sorts, but a protest all the same.

The only member of our extended family to own a radio was my uncle Louis Münzer, who had a shop selling men's clothes in the market square. He stocked hats of all kinds, including silken top hats, and I remember particularly well rows and rows of nautical caps that sailors and fishermen liked to wear. His radio was in his office, and we sometimes gathered there to listen, despite much crackling of the crystal set, to the demented voice of the Führer pronouncing on Germany's future, the state of the world and his hatred for Bolsheviks and Jews, two groups who were closely associated in his mind. In 1935 Mussolini invaded Abyssinia, overcoming fierce resistance by dint of greatly superior weapons; but we cheered every time a short-lived Abyssinian victory was announced, and we were deeply disappointed when the Emperor Haile Selassie had to flee the country in 1936. He had become my great hero, David fighting Goliath; I was not to know that in later years he himself was to become something of a tyrant.

Persecution; and a fateful decision

At the age of ten, in 1935, I moved from the Volksschule (primary school) to the Mittelschule, a secondary school that, unlike the Gymnasium (or grammar school), taught English and French instead of Latin and Greek. This was a deliberate decision by my parents because they felt in their bones that I might soon be in need of a modern foreign language, and in this they were so right. My form master - I believe his name was Dr Gaul - was a committed Nazi and a member of the SA, who sometimes taught in full uniform. It was he, ironically, who taught me English, and it went strongly against his grain that I proved to be one of his best pupils. I was the only Jewish boy in the class if not in the school and was soon subjected to some isolation and abuse, which by 1936 had become physical in that snowballs and stones were thrown at me on my way home, clearly with intent. On several occasions when in full flight I sought shelter with our friends the Lewins, whose flat was halfway home, and until their daughter Inge reminded me some years ago I had completely forgotten, probably suppressed, that I was in a pretty distressed state on one or two occasions and bleeding from minor scalp wounds. My Nazi teacher was visibly upset when I won a 75m sprint on a sports day organised in grandiose Nazi fashion, with lots of flags, on the outskirts of the town; it seems astonishing that I was allowed to participate at all. However, this relative tolerance was not to last much longer.

My position in the school finally became untenable in the autumn of 1936, ostensibly as a result of a bizarre incident. I arrived in my classroom one morning to find that someone had chalked on the blackboard: 'Alle Christen sind Lügner und Betrüger' (all Christians are liars and swindlers). I was accused of having perpetrated this, and my denials were dismissed as yet another sign of my perverse Jewish nature. I was required to stand in front of the class and listen to an anti-Semitic diatribe by my Nazi form teacher. Thereafter the persecution by fellow pupils intensified and when, a few days later, I was hauled before the headmaster for having opened the heavy door of the school with my foot (I was carrying things in my hands), he and my parents agreed that I should leave the school. My sister was, strangely, able to continue her education for some time longer. Many years later I discovered that other Jewish children all over Germany had been subjected to very similar contrived incidents.

My parents were now in a most invidious position: what to do with their precious son? How was he to be safeguarded and his education to be continued? I have no idea what alternatives they considered, if indeed there were any. But my father knew of the director of a Jewish boys' orphanage in Berlin, Dr Kurt Crohn, who had been born in Köslin, and he agreed to take me in even though I was no orphan. This was true also for other boys accepted into the orphanage at that time, when life became too difficult for them in their home environments. I implicitly accepted my parents' decision as having been taken in my best interest and so, one day in the winter of 1936, I found myself, accompanied by my parents, on a fast train to Berlin. I was eleven. It proved to be a fateful move.

Chapter Four: Life in the Orphanage

A safe haven

The orphanage in Berlinerstrasse was in a Berlin suburb called Pankow. It was a rather grand but gaunt, dark grey stone-faced building set back a little from the road, with a playground and small gymnasium at the rear. Apart from the main entrance there was an entrance to the courtyard in a side street, safeguarded by a high two-door iron gate. I mention this because it has some relevance to an incident I shall describe presently.

The history of the Second Orphanage of the Jewish Community of Berlin was researched in the early 1990s by Matthias Frühauf and a group of his senior school students and published by them, albeit in German (*Jüdisches Leben in Pankow: Eine Zeitgeschichtliche Dokumentation*). The orphanage was founded in 1882 as a response to the arrival in Germany of large numbers of Russian Jews who had fled to the West because of widespread pogroms in their own country. Initially forty boys were chosen, to be cared for and taught in an existing building in Berlinerstrasse and to be trained as skilled artisans. As some of them emigrated to the United States or left to take up jobs their places were gradually taken up by German Jewish orphans, and by 1892 the institution formally became an orphanage. Evidently life there was pretty severe under its first director, Isidor Grunwald, though a softer approach was encouraged by the director's second wife, Rosa, who became a mother figure to many of the boys. Following an extensive fire in 1911 the building was demolished and a purpose-built three-storey replacement was constructed, with classrooms, five dormitories, dining hall, assembly hall with decorated murals, library, workroom, a

22

small synagogue with ornate ceiling panels, staff rooms and a small flat for the director and his family.

Another director took over after Grunwald's death in 1925, but although the institutional uniform had become more appealing when the boys began to wear sailor suits, life remained somewhat harsh by all accounts. Dr Kurt Crohn became director in 1936, by which time the number of boys had grown to about 100, with another twenty older boys who were apprentices in a variety of manual trades in nearby workshops. According to Solomon Muller, who arrived in the orphanage as a five year old in 1930 and is quoted in Frühauf's book, the Crohn regime was 'strict but fair'. There was some emphasis on music in the form of a choir and an orchestra consisting largely of mandolins, recorders, mouth organs and small percussion instruments. There were dramatic performances, too, and of course football, table tennis and athletics. The boys were thus exposed to a variety of cultural influences, and among the teachers and housefathers were some young, idealistic men who were deeply concerned for the welfare of their charges and were greatly admired and loved.

It is this community that I entered late in 1936. The director was clearly well disposed towards me and this showed itself in several ways. At an open day I was chosen to recite large chunks of Schiller's 'Die Glocke' ('The Bell'), a vast allegorical poem in which the bell and its creation epitomises and is compared with human life, and I remember the opening lines perfectly. Although I was quite unable to read music I was allowed to join the orchestra in a performance of Haydn's *Toy Symphony* by being entrusted with the triangle, which I suspect I played with unerring inaccuracy. Dr Crohn usually made the rounds of the dormitories after 'lights out' and on one occasion, thinking I was asleep, he paused by my bed and stroked my head. He may have thought of me as the son he never had, his only child having been a girl, Reni, who lived with her parents on the second floor. After some months in the orphanage school he arranged for me to attend a Jewish grammar school on a daily basis, on the grounds that I would make more rapid progress there. And, finally, he invited me in March 1938 to a performance of Mendelssohn's *Elijah*, my first ever concert. Although rather a long work for a twelve year old it was very exciting, and it influenced the development of my musical interests. It seems astonishing that a performance of this intensely Jewish work by a Jewish composer was still possible at that time, but it was performed by a Jewish choir and orchestra in the Oranienburgerstrasse Synagogue, under the auspices of the Kulturbund.

Kurt Crohn was a small, dapper man who usually wore a bow tie. He was born in Köslin in 1896, had lost his mother early in life and had been sent to the very same orphanage that he was later destined to lead. After leaving school he trained as a teacher in Berlin, but his career was interrupted when he volunteered for an infantry regiment during the First World War and was, in due course, wounded on the French front. After his release and convalescence he continued his studies, the title of his thesis having been 'The internal completion and consolidation of the Empire since Joseph Chamberlain' (my translation). When he became director of the orphanage his wife Susanne, who was likewise a teacher by training, was appointed as housemother and put in charge of all domestic arrangements. Between them they ran the orphanage humanely and with a genuine interest in the welfare of the boys.

Kurt Crohn's humanity and passionate interest in the development and fate of 'his' boys shines through in several letters that he sent to the teacher and housefather Heinz Nadel, after he had emigrated to England in the spring of 1939. In them he referred anxiously to several boys who had gone abroad and to others who had stayed behind. In response to a letter by Heinz Nadel , in which Heinz had described visiting me in Bunce Court School, Kent, he wrote, 'What you have written about Lothar gave me great joy. I am so glad that my opinion of him has been fully justified. He will surely remain the charming, valuable person I have always found him to be. A few days ago I received a delightful letter from him; it contained several genuine, refined [*vornehme*] "Lothar expressions" . . . He belongs to those boys whom I miss very much.'

Nonetheless I found the atmosphere in the orphanage rather intimidating, having spent my childhood up to that point in a close family setting. Communal life, with a bed in a large dormitory, came as something of a shock. Not a few boys were deeply disturbed by their previous experiences, which for most included the loss of their parents, and some meals were disturbed by boys throwing noisy tantrums. Some were regular bed-wetters. I made friends, however, and enjoyed playing football and table tennis. My closest friend was Fred Gerstl, a half-Jewish boy whose father had committed suicide in 1933 when he was no longer allowed to work on the Berlin Stock Exchange. I was privileged in that I was able to spend some holidays with my family in Köslin, until they too were forced to move to Berlin in very straitened circumstances.

The Jewish school Kurt Crohn later sent me to was certainly more challenging than the orphanage school, but I attended it for a relatively short time and I seem to have an almost complete memory block about it. I became attached to two young housefathers, Rudi Herzko and the above-mentioned Heinz Nadel, especially the latter, who later in England adopted the name Harry Harrison and became a close friend.

One of the highlights of my stay in the orphanage was a week in Agnetendorf, a village in the Riesengebirge near the Czech border where the Jewish community had a chalet used for short holidays during the summer. I was sent there with a number of other boys, and Dr Crohn, his wife and another teacher accompanied us. There I was exposed to mountains for the first time, and it began my love affair with mountains and climbing. Although I was totally ill-equipped to go on a long mountain walk – I was wearing ordinary shoes – I joined a large group of children who went up the Schneekoppe, the highest mountain in the area (1602m). It was a memorable experience, not only because I developed a huge and painful blister on my heel on the way up (I refused to turn back) but because the views from the top, into Czechoslovakia, were breathtaking. That holiday was also notable in that I sort of fell in love with a very pretty girl in a neighbouring chalet; a classic case of calf love.

Kristallnacht and its 'dress rehearsal'

In the late summer of 1938 a dramatic incident occurred. Presumably as a rehearsal for Kristallnacht (the night of the broken glass), which was to happen several months later, the orphanage was stormed by a mob that had suddenly and mysteriously gathered outside. The heavy front doors having been hastily locked, the rabble attempted to gain entrance through the gate leading into the courtyard at the back. A group of older boys tried desperately to stem the surging tide of bodies by leaning against the gates from the inside, but they were no match for the raging mob, which burst through and then into the rear of the building. The boys melted into the crowd and no-one came to any harm.

Having seen what was happening, my friend Fred suggested to me that we should race up the stairs and hide in a dark corner under the rafters of the roof, a route with which he seemed to be familiar, and there we stayed with beating hearts until everything became eerily quiet. When we emerged we found that the basement and ground floor had been ransacked but that the rest of the building had been left untouched, thanks to the heroic intervention of Heinz Nadel. The worst mess was quickly cleared up and, extraordinary as it may seem (and I sometimes wonder whether my memory is playing tricks with me), we all sat down at the wooden tables in the yard and celebrated our survival with strawberries and cream that had evidently escaped the notice of the invaders.

If the political implications of this incident were discussed, as they must have been, they seem to have passed over my head.

Kristallnacht followed on 9 November. Strangely, the orphanage was not targeted on this occasion, but just about all other Jewish institutions, synagogues, shops and even many private homes were attacked throughout Germany, and many individuals were assaulted in the streets or in their homes. Without doubt these attacks were meticulously planned and coordinated and undertaken by the SA, the SS (Schutz Staffel, an élite Nazi paramilitary organisation whose members wore black uniforms with a distinctive emblem who thought of themselves a cut above the SA but were even more pernicious) and private citizens who had by then been thoroughly imbued with rabid anti-Semitism. The date was that on which Ernst von Rath, the German ambassador in Paris, died of wounds inflicted on him a few days earlier when a desperate young Polish Jew, Herschel Grynszpan, attacked the ambassador (who was not a Nazi), because he had been unsuccessful in securing a visa for his parents. They had been expelled to Germany by the Polish government, together with thousands of other Polish Jews, and forcibly returned into a sort of no-man's land between the Polish and German borders. It is this heartrending story on which Michael Tippett based his poignant oratorio *A Child of Our Time*. My choir, the Crouch End Festival Chorus, performed it in 1994 at the fiftieth anniversary of its first performance and in the presence of the aged composer; for me it was an indescribably poignant experience.

Kristallnacht also coincided with the commemoration in Munich of the abortive Hitler Putsch (uprising) on 9 November 1923, and of those early Nazis who died in it. Hitler himself attended this, and there can be little doubt that Goebbels and Hitler between them had authorised the pogrom, which extended also to Vienna, where, to quote Michael Burleigh, 'the local edition of the *Völkischer Beobachter* published the location of the city's synagogues and prayer houses a few days before they were destroyed'. The *Völkischer Beobachter* was a newspaper acquired by the National Socialist German Workers' party (NSDAP) as early as 1920, and a vehicle of Nazi propaganda.

The events surrounding Kristallnacht have been well described by Michael Burleigh. Suffice it to say that throughout Germany roughly 7,500 Jewish business premises were destroyed, damaged or looted and some 150 synagogues were burnt to the ground, including the noble edifice in Köslin. One or two synagogues in Berlin escaped because they were closely surrounded by blocks of flats, and the Nazis were afraid of setting fire to the homes of 'Aryan' citizens; but they were desecrated, vandalised and looted. Fire brigades and the police were conspicuous by their absence, with the one notable exception of the Neue Synagoge in Oranienburgerstrasse, which was saved though the brave intervention of a senior police officer. Ninety-one Jews were killed and many more were assaulted and wounded. Some 20–30,000, mainly men, were incarcerated in concentration camps such as Dachau and Sachsenhausen, where they were treated with the utmost callousness and brutality; many were subsequently released but were scarred for life. Grotesquely, Goebbels introduced a law that compelled Jews to pay for the replacement of the vast amount of shattered glass, half of Belgium's glass production having been purchased in order to make good the damage. Needless to say the repaired business premises were forcibly taken over by 'Aryans'.

Kristallnacht was a watershed for German and Austrian Jews. Those who had believed up to then that things must surely get better had their illusions rudely and dramatically shattered. The frantic scramble to emigrate began but by this time that had become extremely difficult. Not only were the German authorities unhelpful and required emigration payments, but most western countries had strict limitations on the issue of visas. Having a relative or sponsor abroad and access to funds was undoubtedly a great help, but my parents, who like many others were by then totally impoverished, were left stranded. They had moved to Berlin in early 1938 because life in Köslin had become untenable and it was easier to merge into the general population in a large city. My father was reduced to earning a pittance by working in a timber factory. I saw my parents at weekends and they tried hard to behave normally. Looking back at those fleeting moments of contact, I can only marvel at their bravery and fortitude.

Life in the orphanage, which had been untouched by the mayhem of 9 November, continued, though for me not for very long. Together with seven or eight other boys I had the great good fortune to be nominated by Dr Crohn to travel to England in the first of the many Kindertransports, and this left Berlin on 1 December. My life was saved.

Chapter Five: Kindertransport: Flight to England

A brief history of the Kindertransports

The complicated and touching story of how some ten thousand children from Germany, Austria and Czechoslovakia were rescued has been described vividly by Barry Turner in his excellent book *And the Policeman Smiled* and more recently and in great detail by Amy Zahl Gottlieb in *Men of Vision.* Jewish refugees had arrived individually in Britain during the 1930s and special provision was made for academics, who were offered places in universities or research institutes, a dispensation that has recently been well documented by Jean Medawar and David Pyke in *Hitler's Gift – Scientists who Fled Nazi Germany.* The headmistress of a Jewish boarding school in Ulm, Anna Essinger, had the astonishing foresight to transfer as many of her pupils as possible, together with some of the teachers, to a country house in Kent as early as 1933 (see below). But the mass exodus of the Kindertransport children was triggered by Kristallnacht, and commenced within a few weeks of that calamitous event.

Following the declaration of the Nuremberg Decrees and the beginning of the systematic persecution of German Jewry in 1933, the British press tended to play down what was happening, preferring to think of Hitler as a man of peace. The *Manchester Guardian* (now the *Guardian*) was a notable exception. Nonetheless there were stirrings in the Anglo-Jewish community, and in 1933 Otto Schiff, a city stockbroker and philanthropist of German extraction, set up the Jewish Refugee Committee, with the objective of aiding refugees and pressurising the Home Office to allow greater numbers to enter the country. He proposed that if the entry conditions were relaxed his committee would provide financial guarantees, thus making sure that the refugees would not become a burden on the state. However, it soon became apparent that the numbers involved could completely overwhelm the committee's resources. To boost fundraising the British Central Fund was therefore created by the banker Lionel de Rothschild and the head of Marks and Spencer, Simon Marks, and in under a year £250,000 was raised (well in excess of £10m in present terms). Britain was looked upon primarily as providing a temporary residence, and it was hoped that many refugees would travel on to Palestine and elsewhere. This proved to be illusory, for the British government was determined to limit the entry of Jews into Palestine because of fears that large numbers might destabilise the Middle East. Even in the Anglo-Jewish community there were misgivings, because of fears that the entry of large numbers of European Jews would lead to anti-Jewish agitation – a point that did not escape the Home Secretary, Sir Samuel Hoare.

An important initiative was taken by the Dutch Refugee Committee, which sent a delegation to the Prime Minister two days after Kristallnacht with a request that residential permits should be given to an unlimited number of German and Austrian children. This was accepted in principle on condition that 10,000 guilders would be deposited in support of the proposal. This money was provided on 15 November, the very same day on which a Jewish delegation, led by Viscount Samuel, approached the Chamberlain government with a similar proposal. After some shilly-shallying and discussions with yet another deputation, this time led by Sir Wyndham Deedes, the proposal was accepted and yet another organisation, the Movement for the Care of Children from Germany, was established by Norman Bentwich and his wife Mami. Although it is generally assumed that a limit of 10,000 was set, this does not appear to have been the case. The actual number of children who arrived in England was close to that figure, but the limit was ultimately set by the outbreak of war, which put an end to the Kindertransports.

One of the lucky ones

Together with a small group of boys I was nominated by Dr Kurt Crohn to join the first transport, together with some 200 other children, many from another orphanage that had been razed to the ground and others of Polish nationality (and therefore liable to be deported to Poland). My friend Fred Gerstl should have been with me, for the director was well aware of our friendship, and his name had indeed been on the list. However, at the last moment it turned out that Dr Crohn had exceeded his allocation and Fred's name was removed, presumably because, being half-Jewish, he was considered to be less at risk. As it happens, Fred left some months later on a train destined for Holland, where he was well taken care of in a Quaker school until, halfway through the war, he was rounded up by the Germans. He survived the war in rather extraordinary circumstances and finished up in Berlin, to find his non-Jewish mother alive and well. As I heard nothing more about him after our separation in Berlin I assumed that he had died, as I indicated in an article written for the book *I Came Alone - The Story of the Kindertransports* in 1990. It was a few years later that we found each other again, when Fred, who lived in Berlin, happened to switch on his television set only to see me standing in front of the orphanage building recounting our joint experience when the orphanage was stormed! A German TV company had made a film about the Kindertransports when their fiftieth anniversary was commemorated in 1989, and the film was being shown again on the evening when Fred chanced upon it.

Whilst some other boys from the orphanage left on Kindertransports or by other means, many others had to stay behind, as did Dr Crohn and most of the teachers. The orphanage was closed by the Nazis and amalgamated with another, the Auerbachsche, where they remained until 1942, when the deportations to the eastern concentration camps began. Most of the boys perished. Dr Crohn and his family at first moved to West Berlin, where he was engaged in forced labour and his wife worked first in a factory and later as cleaner in a tram station, before the whole family was deported to Theresienstadt in the middle of 1943. There he was separated from his wife and daughter and, having survived until September 1944, was sent to his death in Auschwitz. His war service in the First World War had not saved him. His wife Susanne and his daughter Renate survived the war and then moved to Israel, where Renate still lives.

The evening before my departure there was a family gathering in my parents' minuscule flat - an opportunity for saying farewell and at the same time an induction session in which, to my huge impatience, I was given all kinds of no doubt excellent advice. I was excited, of course, but I couldn't see the point of being told to be a good boy and not to be too trusting of strange men. Sexually I was a complete innocent - somehow sex education seemed to have fallen by the wayside thanks to the turbulence of my early adolescence - and the notion of homosexuality hadn't occurred to me. My dear mother had prepared a small suitcase containing essential clothes, each item carefully marked with labels bearing my initials, as well as a few other items such as my prayer shawl, which I had been given at my Bar Mitzvah a few months before. I was to take with me a violin that a favourite cousin of my mother's, who had been a professional player, had given her, as well as the rather splendid stamp collection that my father and I had put together over a number of years.

Everyone present at this last evening in Berlin tried to be very calm and not to show any emotion; this must have been unbearably difficult for my parents, who were about to lose their precious son. I was told that this would almost certainly be a temporary separation and that they would do their best to follow me to England, together with Eva. It never occurred to me to ask why Eva was not travelling with me, but long after the war I was told by a family friend that Eva had refused to join a Kindertransport because she had fallen in love with a doctor in the Jewish hospital in which she worked as a trainee nurse.

Flight to England

So it was that on the morning of 1 December 1938 I found myself on the platform of one of Berlin's railway stations – it might have been Anhalter Bahnhof – to board a train together with some two hundred other children, boys and girls, destined for the Hook of Holland. I cannot remember too many details, except that it was a chaotic scene, with parents clutching their children and saying tearful farewells. My own parents did their best to hide their emotions. I finished up in a compartment with a number of other children, at least some from the orphanage. I had with me a packed lunch of sandwiches and fruit.

The children in my compartment were, not surprisingly, subdued and the atmosphere was tense. The train was patrolled by German police and we had been warned to be on our best behaviour and not to make any noise. And so we rattled through the German countryside, stopping occasionally. Whenever the train stopped there was a marked rise in tension, for fear that we would be ordered to leave. However, we encountered none of the unpleasantness to which some children were evidently subjected by the police or accompanying SA men. On crossing the Dutch frontier there was a dramatic change in our behaviour; suddenly we joked and laughed and felt free. Even so, my facial expression in the photograph taken of the children in my compartment by a Dutch journalist *(see frontispiece)* is distinctly wistful: the face of a child who had no inkling of what the future held. I first encountered this photograph in the *Guardian* in 1989, when the fiftieth anniversary of the Kindertransports was commemorated, and it has since appeared in many newspapers and books. In it one of the boys from the orphanage is Solomon (Moni) Muller, who still lives in the UK; another is Erich Goldstein, who later became a professional violinist, I believe, but who seems to have disappeared.

The sudden change in atmosphere was greatly enhanced by the appearance of friendly Dutch women on the station platform, offering us not only smiles but sandwiches, fruit, biscuits, chocolate and drinks. What a difference when compared with the sullen, antagonistic attitude of the Germans! At last we seemed to have been relieved of our role as scapegoats, villains and victims.

We arrived in the Hook of Holland in the evening and embarked almost at once on the Dutch ferry *De Praag* on our way to Harwich. This overnight trip has been described by many others, not least in Barry Turner's book *And the Policeman Smiled*. It was a foul and stormy night and most children were violently seasick, which meant that even those who, like me, were fairly resistant to this condition were hard-pressed not to vomit. I was so preoccupied with all this that thoughts of homesickness or fears of the future didn't really surface. Our arrival in Harwich at the crack of dawn came as a huge relief. Apparently each child had been given a label on a string bearing his or her name, but I cannot remember that I had one; in fact, I seem to have almost complete amnesia about many of the details of our arrival, except that many of us were loaded on to double-decker buses (an exciting new experience) that trundled through the English countryside, with its quaint hedgerows and cottages, to take us to Dovercourt Reception Camp, not far from Harwich.

Thus life in England had begun, however uncertainly.

Chapter Six: Quiet Hero of Berlin

I shall now digress from my own story to recount that of Heinz Nadel, later Harry Harrison, to whom I have already referred in my chapter on life in the Berlin orphanage.

A well-loved teacher

There was on the face of it nothing very extraordinary about Heinz, although he was an empathetic pedagogue and, in his youth, a talented middle-distance runner. When he died in 1989, after several years of rapidly advancing Parkinson's disease, I was moved to write an obituary that, to my great surprise and delight, the *Guardian* published under the title 'Quiet Hero of Berlin'.

As Heinz Harri Nadel he had been the son of a Jewish Berlin businessman Marcus and a Jewish mother Rosa, and Heinz first followed in his father's footsteps by working in the office of a company dealing in building materials. The firm must have been Jewish, for Heinz left in the autumn of 1936 with a testimonial in which it was explained that he had to leave because the firm was taken over by a 'fully Aryan management'. It was then that he decided to take up teaching and to build on what was clearly a natural talent for working with children.

In 1937 Heinz accepted a post in the Jewish orphanage for boys in Berlin-Pankow, his appointment being as Erzieherpraktikant (teaching probationer). This is where I first met him. He was a friendly, approachable and quietly charismatic young man who was liked and admired by many boys. It was Heinz who gave us sports lessons. When at last he managed to get a visa for emigration to England – he arrived in May 1939, having been preceded by his

33

brother Theo – the orphanage director Kurt Crohn gave him a glowing reference.

Dr Crohn wrote to Heinz during the course of 1939, after he had made his escape to England. His letters abound with expressions of admiration for him. In the letter dated 16 May he wrote, after expressing his deep regret that Heinz's farewell party had to be aborted ('it is so typical of our times'), 'You know, after all, what I had intended, and I was very pleased that you wrote so touchingly about your activities. I am convinced that that you will make your way whatever happens in your life.' The letter ends, poignantly, 'Keep well, dear Mr Nadel. Do sometimes think of us. I am sure that you realise that a letter sent from distant lands by a dear friend means a great deal for those of us left behind.' (My translation.)

Heinz had to report weekly to the English local police to have his residential permit extended. His entry visa was granted on condition that 'the holder proceeds forthwith to Richborough Refugee Camp, registers at once with the police and remains at the camp until he emigrates'.

Heinz joins the army

This camp, situated in Kent, became the main army recruiting ground for Jewish refugees, still classified as enemy aliens, to the Pioneer Corps, a non-combatant unit of the British Army. Heinz enlisted in January 1940, and soon afterwards was obliged to adopt an English name. Having struck up a friendship with Ted Harrison – a friendship that was to last a lifetime – he decided to call himself Harrison, and Heinz Harri Nadel became Harry Hugh Harrison. They met again in 1944 whilst serving in France near Bayeux, as they waited in a long queue for the NAAFI canteen. They subsequently lived together for four decades, parting company only when Ted, himself a sick man, could no longer look after his friend; and it fell on me to move Harry into a nursing home.

On 22 November 1945 Harry wrote a nineteen-page letter to his brother Theo, who lived by that time in Australia. It is an extraordinarily vivid account of his last fifteen months in the Army, including the invasion of France and ending with his demobilisation in November 1945. His unit, 220 Company, in which he had become a lance-corporal, followed the invasion force within a few days and served in France, Holland and Belgium before entering Germany.

Harry's role in the liberation of Bergen-Belsen concentration camp

I shall focus on the episode in Harry's military life that made such a devastating impact on him and that left him with never-ending nightmares in his old age: the liberation of Bergen-Belsen concentration camp. His descriptions of how he came to be involved there and his impressions of the camp are very detailed, and I shall be highly selective.

Two days after British troops had entered, Harry was asked by his commanding officer to travel to the camp and to offer his services there, and so he did, accompanied by his driver. He was aghast at the sight of the vast mounds of corpses and the thousands of starved, emaciated and sick inmates. 'Picture a graveyard suddenly peopled with the dead,' he wrote. The camp was in chaos, with little food and virtually no water. Although it was realised that the German army rations that had been left behind, with their high fat content, were quite unsuitable for starving people, they were nonetheless used. Many died. Furthermore, there was an outbreak of typhus to add to the problems faced by the British liberators. Harry acted as interpreter, went round the camp with a loudhailer making urgent announcements, listened to people's stories, smoothed things out for some, and generally helped in organisational matters. For one whose own parents might well have been among the victims it was a special ordeal, though he hardly had the time to reflect on this. Quite accidentally he ran into an old friend from Berlin, Lotte Grunow, who had survived by virtue of her membership of the camp orchestra; and he also met Margo Aufrecht, the sister of one of his former pupils.

Harry was inexplicably asked to return to his unit. Having survived some hairy moments he was sent on leave, the first in sixteen months. Victory in Europe (VE) Day was declared whilst he was on leave in Holland: 'I went for a quiet walk – I thought of lots of things but of none as deeply as one might have expected.'

On returning to Lüneburg Harry found that his unit had gone back to Belsen, and he swiftly followed. 'It was a different place. The actual concentration camp had been burnt and all people lived in new surroundings.' Most of the relatively few German-Jewish men had gone, and he made it his business to look after the remnants as well as a group of girls, whom he gave additional food and rides in his car, also helping them to find work.

Now came Harry's most significant contribution – the opening of a school for the surviving children. He also acted as compère for stage shows that an educational sergeant had 'so cleverly produced' in order to entertain and raise morale. The school was the most gratifying of all his commitments, but he still found the time to assist in the repatriation of a group of Swedes to their country. He was soon asked to be the school's headmaster, and 'had fun with a class in English for adults in which I prepared two young lads for an ambitious interpreter's job'. Then, in the middle of all this, his unit was ordered to return to Hannover, much to Harry's dismay.

In Hannover Harry was asked to supervise the German chief editor of the local paper, to ensure that nothing detrimental to the Allied cause was printed. Then his demob papers came through. But first he obtained compassionate leave to travel to Berlin in an attempt to uncover the fate of his parents; not surprisingly this proved to be unsuccessful.

Harry was given a glowing testimonial by the British commander of the camp in Belsen, but his bravery and devotion were never recognised by an appropriate honour – even though his commanding officer described his conduct as 'excellent, exemplary and of the highest order'. Harry had certainly earned the epitaph given him by the *Guardian*: the 'Quiet Hero of Berlin'. In my address at his funeral in Golders Green Crematorium in 1989 I concluded: 'We will remember Harry for his courage, his modesty and, despite the bitter and horrific memories that burdened him so greatly, for his sense of fun and his dry wit; and perhaps above all for his integrity and humanity.'

Chapter Seven: Dovercourt

An uncertain future

overcourt Reception Camp had been designed as a Butlin's summer holiday camp near the Essex village of Dovercourt, a few miles outside the port of Harwich. It was a collection of small wooden chalets pleasantly situated on a wooded slope leading down to a North Sea beach, with some large buildings housing recreational and dining halls and washing facilities. It was clearly intended for family use in summertime: the chalets had no heating and the heating facilities in the halls were confined to a few old-fashioned iron stoves.

This camp was put at the disposal of the Refugee Children's Movement in 1938 when it became clear that there would be a major influx of children; its history and functions have been well described elsewhere (see Barry Turner's *And the Policeman Smiled*). The choice of this camp – quite apart from its availability – seemed appropriate in that it was close to Harwich, where most of the children arrived, and not too distant from London, thus facilitating the children's dispersal. The one thing that the organisers could not have foreseen is that the winter of 1938/9 was to be one of the coldest and snowiest English winters on record. It is therefore hardly surprising that the intense cold dominates the personal recollections of many who passed through the camp.

Anna Essinger had been asked to help with the organisation of the reception camp and the provision of an educational programme. She was the redoubtable headmistress of Bunce Court School, located in a manor house on the North Downs of Kent, to which she had evacuated her progressive, coeducational boarding school (Herrlingen) from Ulm in Southern Germany as early as 1933. I shall have a great deal more to say about her in my next chapter, but her choice was not fortuitous in that she was an experienced pedagogue, a good organiser, a determined woman who would not let any obstacle stand in her way, and the head of an established school for refugee children. It was Anna Essinger who saw to the temporary appointment of some teaching staff and brought with her, from Bunce Court, several teachers and older boys and girls to help with the running of the camp. One of the teachers was Hanna Bergas, one of the school's educational pillars, who taught English and French and had great organisational ability. It was through the Bunce Court presence in the camp that a number of children, possibly as many as fifty to sixty, were chosen to join the school. For many, including myself, this proved to be extremely fortunate in that it provided us with a home, a good education and a sound basis on which to build our lives (see next chapter).

On arrival at Dovercourt Camp we were allocated to small chalets – I shared mine with two other boys of roughly my age – and introduced to the camp's routine. Meals were provided in the huge dining hall and I had my first encounter with delicacies such as tea and kippers, and a second introduction to porridge, all of which I have continued to enjoy. During the day we were divided into groups according to the standard of our English, and given English lessons in the large recreational hall called the Palm Court. Other activities such as table tennis were also conducted here, and the noise, as the camp filled up with new arrivals, was pretty deafening. It soon became very cold and we tended to huddle around the few rather smelly stoves in order to keep warm. We were taught traditional songs such as 'The Lambeth Walk' and 'Daisy, Daisy' and a small choir, which I joined, was formed. Although we were reasonably well supplied with blankets, our survival at night was ensured by the issue of rubber hot water bottles (courtesy of Dunlop), which we filled up from a tap near our chalet.

My Kindertransport, which had arrived on 2 December 1938 from Berlin and Hamburg, was one of the first (probably *the* first) and so we had time to adjust before the camp became impossibly crowded. Soon Viennese children joined us, and I found it disturbing when the odd knife fight broke out between older boys from Berlin and Vienna. Here were Jewish boys, who had escaped from the Nazis, aping ancient enmities that apparently existed between the two cities; how completely incomprehensible! They evidently allowed national rivalries to override their Jewish bonds and their shared experience of persecution. One hopes that they soon grew out of that nonsense. Harry Schwartz recalled in *And the Policeman Smiled* that 'The Germans still thought of themselves as Germans and the Austrians thought of themselves as Austrians; they didn't think of themselves as Jews primarily. When you think back on it there was no justification.'

The BBC radio broadcast: my message to the nation!

The reaction of the British media to the arrival of so many refugee children is well recounted by Barry Turner. Whilst some of the tabloids were hostile ('charity begins at home'), others like *Picture Post* took a far more positive view and felt that the children would, in due course, make a positive contribution to British life. The camp organisers were anxious to enlist the support of British couples by encouraging them to accept children into their homes, an issue that became critical as more and more children arrived and the resources of the camp became overstretched. The BBC sent a producer with a small recording team and they interviewed some of the organisers and a few children. The result was a half-hour programme entitled *Children in Flight*, highlighting the plight of the children and the need for couples to come forward. I was one of those who took part, and I am grateful to Barry Turner for having tracked down the recording in the BBC archives half a century after the event. My own contribution was preceded by a small mixed choir, which included me, singing 'Dona nobis pacem'. Introduced as Lothar and speaking in my rather excited unbroken thirteen-year-old voice, not surprisingly with a strong German accent, I gave a brief account of how we spent a typical day in the camp. The transcript is as follows:

A bell rings at eight o'clock and we have to get up. Some boys get up earlier to make a run to the sea, which is near the camp. At 8.30 we have a good English breakfast, which we enjoy. First we did not eat porridge but now we like it. When we finish the breakfast we get the letters or cards from our parents, and we are all very happy. After that we clear and tidy our rooms, then we have two hours lessons in English. When the lessons are over we take our lunch and then we can make what we like. After tea we can go to the sea, which is wonderful, or we play English games of football. In the evening we learn a lot of English songs till we go to bed. I sleep in a nice little house with two other boys. Now it is very cold and we cannot stay in our house. We like to sit around the stove in a very large hall, and we read or write to our parents. The people are very kind to us. A gentleman invited me to go with him in a car; then we drove to his house and there we had tea. Oh, it was very nice. Sometimes we go to a picture house in Dovercourt. We have seen the good film *Snow White and the Seven Dwarfs*. We were all delighted. Now I will go to school, then I can speak English good and then I would like to become a cook. We are all very happy to be in England.

We had been told to be positive in what we wrote down, and that certainly comes through in this broadcast. My surname was not mentioned for fear of jeopardising my family in Germany. How I wish they could have heard it, but by that time German Jews were prohibited from owning radios. The 'English gentleman' I mentioned lived in the country some miles away, and there I was exposed for the first time to an attractive and opulently furnished old country house with an open fire and toasted crumpets for tea. My selection of cooking as a future profession was probably because I couldn't think of anything else and because I had enjoyed helping my mother in the kitchen.

The broadcast had its desired effects: parcels of food and clothes came flooding in, and many couples visited the camp with a view to adopting a child. The selection sessions became something of an ordeal for the children, who had to present themselves to be 'viewed' in the best possible light at certain times of the day. Children were often chosen for quite the wrong reasons, and the whole procedure became something of a cattle market. Many couples were genuine in offering a child a loving home, but others saw it as an opportunity of acquiring a home help who was there to be exploited. The older children, and those who were perhaps physically less attractive, were more difficult to place. Whilst it would be easy to criticise the organisers it must be remembered that there was an urgent need to find homes for children in order to make room for the constant flow of new arrivals, and it is understandable that some awful mistakes were made. As my little speech indicated, by the time of the broadcast (3 January 1939) my fate had already been determined: I was to join Anna Essinger's school, and did so soon after.

A stroke of luck: Bunce Court School beckons

How this came about is quite amusing. One of the older Bunce Court boys, Gabi Adler (later Alden), worked in the camp, and he and I played ping-pong together occasionally, a game at which he excelled and I played with passion. One day he told me about the school and asked me whether I might like to go there if invited to do so. I had no difficulty in saying that I would, and that seemed to be the end of the matter. A week or so later I ran through a door and bumped into the soft and by no means negligible belly of a lady who, her stoutness apart, seemed to be so short-sighted as to be almost blind. She stooped down, lifted up my head by my shock of black hair and said, 'And whooo are you?' I gave her my name and she immediately replied, 'Well, would you like to come to my school, Bunce Court School?' I stammered, 'yyyes please', and that was it. A week or two later I was on my way to Bunce Court, together with a small group of other children and accompanied by Gabi and one of the older BC girls, Thilde Weil (now Fraenkel).

This was the third fortunate happening in my life that affected my survival, development and career very profoundly. I spent only about four weeks in the camp and escaped the 'cattle market' – and the trauma it caused many children who were passed over by prospective foster parents or placed in less than favourable environments. Ein Sonntagskind, as my dear father reminded me in a Red Cross message in 1942? Yes indeed!

I can't say that I was exactly unhappy in Dovercourt, but I was certainly bewildered by the uncertainty concerning my future and the separation from my family. In the BBC film *No Time to Say Goodbye*, made in 1989 to commemorate the Kindertransports, there is a shot of me taken in Dovercourt in which I do not look exactly self-assured. I lost touch with the other boys from the Pankow orphanage, and none of them followed me to Bunce Court. It was many years later that I met some of them again.

By March 1939 only about a hundred children, mostly older boys, remained in the camp. They were sent to two other institutions, and Dovercourt once again became a holiday camp until it was requisitioned in 1942 as a prisoner-of-war camp. It served in this capacity until well after the war.

Chapter Eight: Bunce Court School

Arrival

The journey to Bunce Court, which lies on the North Downs, roughly in the middle of the quadrangle described by Faversham, Maidstone, Lenham and Ashford, was exciting and magical. We were glad to get away from Liverpool Street station, which was noisy, steamy and smoky, and totally bewildering with its many platforms, trains, porters and scurrying commuters, and to make our way on to a short, meandering steam train. This left Victoria station and headed for Dover via Lenham in Kent. For someone who was used to travelling on hard wooden benches in German trains, the padded seats of the small third-class compartments seemed the height of luxury. And soon we found ourselves in a landscape deeply covered in snow, with orchards that looked like armies of ghostly warriors.

We were taken from Lenham station to Bunce Court by taxi. The 3-mile ride along narrow lanes, with their hedgerows groaning with heavy snowdrifts, was fairyland stuff. The pull up to the top of the Downs was slow and hazardous but arrive we did, to be greeted with a warm welcome from the headmistress, staff and pupils. The main house itself was an imposing mansion, its grounds extensive and comprising lawns, an ornamental pool, a vegetable garden, an open air amphitheatre and a large playing field – quite apart from workshops, additional classrooms in wooden bungalows, a long wooden hut for the older boys, an isolation hut for sick children and, across another field, an old cottage that housed the youngest children. The cottage was at that time run by Hannah Goldschmidt and Hans Meyer, and the isolation hut by Anna Essinger's youngest sister, Paula. She was known as

Tante Paula or TP; Anna Essinger, the headmistress, was universally called Tante Anna or TA.

I was allocated to a room on the third floor of the main house, where I stayed for the first year with five or six other boys until I was old enough to graduate to the 'boys' house', where I inherited a small cubicle room that was much in demand because my predecessor had worked wonders polishing the wooden floor to an enviably shiny finish with a so-called 'blocker'. One of the boys who shared my small dormitory in the main house was Gerd Nathan, an only child from Hamburg who arrived in Dovercourt Camp in the same Kindertransport; I have maintained a friendship with him ever since. He was one of a small number of children who were distinctly unhappy in Bunce Court and unable to adjust to the communal life of a boarding school.

Having spent the last two years of my life in Germany in the Berlin orphanage, Bunce Court was paradise for me. Had it not been for my separation from my parents and sister, whose fate was unimaginable at that time but nonetheless burdensome to me, I could have been blissfully happy in my new environment. Even so, I *was* happy: it was a life away from the formal constraints of the German school system, and I felt liberated from the persecution and hate I had encountered in Germany. Here I lived in beautiful rural surroundings and in the company of boys and girls with whom it was possible to strike up friendships that lasted a lifetime. Perhaps most important of all were the teachers, all deeply committed to the ideals of Anna Essinger in the running of a liberal and humane establishment, and genuinely caring for their children.

Anna Essinger: Tante Anna (TA)

TA had moved her avant-garde Landschulheim (country boarding school) from Ulm to Kent in 1933 with about seventy children and some of the teachers. The story of that move is quite dramatic, as the emigration of so many children en masse had to be hidden from the Nazi authorities, and it is graphically described by Paula Essinger in the film *Anna's Kinder* and by her niece, Dorle Potten, in *A Chronicle of Childhood*. Briefly, groups of children, led by one or two adults, left Germany from different towns and were then reunited in Dover, to be taken to Bunce Court in three East Kent buses. There they joined a smaller group of older pupils and a few teachers who had arrived earlier to prepare the house. This mass emigration thus escaped the notice of the Nazi authorities, who might otherwise have created difficulties and possibly imposed financial sanctions. The farsightedness of TA in realising so soon after Hitler's rise to power that it had become impossible to bring up and educate Jewish children in Germany was quite extraordinary, and indicative of her

43

intelligence, perceptiveness and humanist educational ideals. It is right and proper that her achievements have been recognised by an entry in the 2004 *New Dictionary of English Biography* – a signal honour for one who became British late in life.

TA was born in Ulm, Germany, in 1879 and was one of nine children; she was almost certainly the most outstanding of these. At the age of twenty she was invited by a maiden aunt to join her in Nashville, Tennessee, and before long she embarked on a course of study at Wisconsin University, where she continued to work until after the First World War. Having meanwhile become interested in the Society of Friends (the Quakers), she was sent by them to South Germany in order to act as liaison officer between Quaker famine relief teams and local government officials, work that had a profound influence on her future development. She remained an agnostic Quaker for the rest of her life and she stayed on in Germany, initially employed by a trade union to establish further education institutes for working women in and around Stuttgart and later to pursue her objective of creating a co-educational boarding school. This was to be based on progressive and, for the 1920s, revolutionary ideas (Reform-pädagogik) that were intended to break with the formal and disciplinarian German educational tradition. In England this had already been attempted in Dartington school and in A.S. Neill's Summerhill school in Suffolk. TA maintained a close interest in and contact with Neill's school, and with Neill himself, after her arrival in the UK; and there was at least one exchange of small groups of pupils.

Her sister Klara Weimersheimer had established a Kinderheim (children's home) in Herrlingen, near Ulm, in 1919 and by 1924 the older children had reached school age. Because the local village school was not in sympathy with her own educational vision she decided to establish her own school, and with this in mind she acquired, with the financial help of some members of her family, a large meadow in nearby Oberherrlingen on which to build according to her own specifications. Anna soon became involved, for here was the opportunity of carrying her educational ideas into practice. Two other women played an important role: Paula, TA's younger sister, who had become a trained children's nurse in Berlin and who was experienced in taking care of children from birth; and Käthe Hamburg, who had abandoned her career as a mathematician to adopt a group of needy illegitimate children who bore her name. Paula became a pivotal figure in the Landschulheim and later in Bunce Court as housemother for small children and as a nurse; and Käthe was so excited on hearing about this educational venture from TA herself that she moved her whole 'family', all seven of them, into the Landschulheim as soon as its doors opened. She too became a much loved housemother who later, after the closure of Bunce Court School in 1948, ran a hostel for boys in

Manchester. TA's Landschulheim in Herrlingen was not exclusively a Jewish school; it only became that in 1933, when the remarkable Hugo Rosenthal took over from TA and decided to make it a boarding school in which Jewish children could be given refuge from what became an increasingly hostile environment. The histories of the Landschulheim and the Jewish Landschulheim (especially the latter) are well told in Lucie Schachne's book, *Education Towards Spiritual Resistance: the Jewish Landschulheim 1933–1939* and in the carefully researched but so far as I know as yet unpublished diploma thesis of Doris Beatrix, *Heimat oder Zuflucht - die Landschulheime Herrlingen und Bunce Court School/ Kent*, the latter also covering the Bunce Court period.

This, then, gives the background to the establishment of Bunce Court (or New Herrlingen) School near Otterden in Kent. Not all the children liked TA. Her physical presence was somewhat off-putting – she was corpulent and disconcertingly short-sighted – and despite her love for the children she came over to many as somewhat cold and remote. Some children were distinctly frightened of her. TA's most serious fault as a pedagogue was, I realise in retrospect, that she could judge children (and sometimes members of her staff) rather harshly and that, whilst favouring some, she could be prejudiced against others who didn't quite fit into her scheme of things. I happened to be one of her favourites – indeed she had many – and I got to know her extremely well after having left the school, to which I returned as my home whenever I had a holiday, army leave or university vacation. She felt at ease with me, and was glad to discuss with me some of her problems and her fears for the future of the school after the war, when she had returned the school from Wem, Shropshire, its place of enforced evacuation.

The removal of the school from the North Downs of Kent, which became a protected military zone in 1940, to Shropshire was a masterpiece of organisation, especially as the country house acquired by TA (Trench Hall) was rather smaller than she would have liked. The move had to be executed in a tearing hurry, the authorities having given her only a week or two in which to vacate Bunce Court, and in the event Trench Hall proved to be just about adequate even if it meant the conversion of a group of stables into dormitories for the older boys. After the war she summoned up enough energy to restore the Kent school buildings, which had been occupied and somewhat vandalised by the army, and to return the whole school to Kent – a remarkable feat, for by that time her eyesight had greatly deteriorated. Apart from her educational vision and ideals, her chief contribution to school life was as organiser and fund-raiser, and perhaps a certain detachment from the more mundane aspects of school life was a pre-requisite for this. The school was desperately short of funds once war had been declared and parents could no longer pay school fees, and her niece Dorle Potten, who as a fourteen-year-old was made to help in the office, tells me that on one occasion there was no money in the bank and the school's only asset was a sack of cocoa! TA earned money by giving lectures, and it is as a result of these that she established a close relationship with Norman Bentwich, who had been a diplomat in Palestine, and Iris Origo, the American wife of an Italian count, of whom I shall have more to say in another chapter. Bentwich was extraordinarily helpful in finding benefactors and Iris gave the school a substantial donation.

One aspect of school life for which some have criticised TA is that she did not encourage children to stay in touch with their Jewish roots, thus depriving them of their Jewish heritage. Unlike Hugo Rosenthal she was neither a practising Jew nor especially interested in Judaism, and presumably her Quaker experience was in part responsible for this. Children who had come from religious homes were given the opportunity of improvising Friday evening services with the help of one of the teachers (Dr Walter Isaacsohn, generally known as Saxo), but they did not receive much encouragement. This group soon proved to be small and, to me, somewhat forlorn, and my own interest in it gradually waned. In this I was not atypical. Although conscious of my Jewish roots, and with vivid memories of the religious services in which I had participated in my earlier childhood, I gradually grew away from formalised religion and later I became agnostic. This process was probably facilitated by my overwhelming sense of the impotence of the Jewish God – any God – once the horrors of the Holocaust had dawned on me, and by becoming a scientist who found it impossible to reconcile religious ideas with a scientific view of the world. This criticism of TA may have had some justification but it was simply not in her nature to do otherwise; and I doubt that it would have made a huge amount of difference had she been more positive in her attitude, for these children were immensely preoccupied with learning a new language and building a new life for themselves, and this for many took precedence.

TA died on 2 June 1960, and I was asked to give a commemorative address at her funeral (as well as, later, at those of her two sisters). TA's took place at Charing Cross Crematorium. Here is what I said:

> The death of Anna Essinger will be deeply mourned by her many relatives and friends all over the world, not least by those of us whose fragmented lives she helped to rebuild in Bunce Court. She was a remarkable woman who will be remembered with affection, gratitude and admiration.
>
> TA devoted herself single-mindedly to the cause of education and the saving of young lives from the persecution of Nazi

Germany, and in this she was sustained by an unshakeable faith in the idea of human progress. Her part in Quaker relief work in war-torn Germany after the First World War was characteristic of her whole life: she was quite incapable of hating. I should be tempted to describe her as a perfect example of scientific humanism, in its highest sense, were it not for the fact that although TA was always anxious to keep in touch with modern scientific developments, she steadfastly remained an endearingly unscientific person!

Above all she had the courage of her convictions, as instanced by this simple ceremony. Although TA was by no means an atheist, and although she was forever conscious of her Jewish roots, she found herself unable to accept the dogma of any one religion, either in life or in death.

Those of us who have watched her struggle against blindness and failing health have had cause to admire her tremendous courage. Without the unceasingly loving care of Tante Paula and Mrs Kahn the last years would have been infinitely harder for her to bear. Our grief at her passing may be tempered by the knowledge that Anna Essinger has truly had the satisfaction of realising the fulfilment of her life's work.

Gretel Heidt

In TA's educational philosophy intellectual and physical development went hand in hand, and emphasis was placed on the responsibility of each child for the common good of the school. Thus, following an hour's 'rest period', during which we were supposed to lie on our beds, there was an hour's practical work. A list of practical activities went up each week – from gardening to work in the kitchen or the wood workshop, or washing up after meals – and we were able to express a preference. I tended to sign up for the kitchen or the workshop. The kitchen was ruled – literally – by the motherly but temperamental Gretel Heidt (known as Heidtsche), a non-Jewish German woman who had joined the school as a cook in the mid-thirties and had elected not to return to Germany when war threatened to break out. By that time she had become emotionally so bound up with the school that she couldn't bear the thought of leaving, even though her own mother and sister lived near Frankfurt-am-Main. She was an excellent cook who made the most of the wartime rations once these were imposed. Indeed, when she was interned in 1940 as an 'enemy alien' and temporarily banished to the Isle of Man, the standard of food, both in quality and quantity, dropped precipitously and only recovered after her return. When Heidtsche's assistants worked below the standard she expected of them, or when something went wrong in the preparations for a meal, she could throw a spectacular tantrum that could be heard a mile away. Nonetheless virtually all staff and pupils liked and admired her. She was not at all intellectual but she radiated an uncomplicated motherliness and warmth that was extended to a great many of us, myself happily included. Indeed, Heidtsche became a sort of mother figure to me who always welcomed me with open arms when returning to the school and who sent me food parcels once I had joined the army. We remained very close until she died.

After the closure of the school Heidtsche became the *Daily Telegraph*'s music critic's cook. She had a room in Gerd Nathan's flat in Kilburn and once a week a bunch of OBCs used to meet there, among them occasionally Gerard Hoffnung, who held forth in his inimitable style and had us in stitches when he recited his famous story of the bricklayer, and other anecdotes. I heard it again quite recently, as recorded at a meeting of the Oxford University Union in the 1950s; not a particularly amusing story in itself but uproariously funny as told by Gerard. Eventually she had to return to Germany to help her sister look after her ageing mother in Griesheim. It was not a happy experience: she and her sister did not get on well and I don't think that she was ever forgiven for being 'on the other side' during the war. Whenever she returned for extended holidays (Gerd Nathan had arranged a room for her in his house in Mill Hill) Old Bunce Courtians gathered to sit at her feet, to eat her delectable cheesecake and to talk about old times. On those evenings we also used to sharpen our intellectual faculties by arguing endlessly about the state of the world and, naturally, solving all problems to our satisfaction, only to find that we hadn't the next time we met. Karl Grossfeld (Grossfield), Vera Rose, Thilde Weil (Fraenkel) and Rainer Schuelein were among the regulars, and of course Gerd Nathan and myself.

Hans Meyer

The workshop, which likewise attracted me for practical work, was ruled by Hans Meyer (Meyerlein), who by that time was married to Hannah Goldschmidt (Hago), a greatly loved, motherly and at the same time intellectually lively woman who taught geography. Hans was born in Mainz in 1913 and had come to England in 1934, having been unable to continue his medical studies. He came over without any qualifications except that whilst still at school he had passed an examination as a sports instructor. When I spoke to him in 2000 he told me that he had heard about Bunce Court from a distant relative and sent TA a letter applying for work, accompanied by a photograph on which he acrobatically balanced his young nephew on his hands. On the strength of this TA exclaimed, 'We must have him!' His arrival in Bunce Court was, however, something of a disaster: he was dead tired and had a sty with a bandage, and to TA the heroic figure of the photograph turned out to be something of a disappointment. According to Hans, his reception was correspondingly frosty and it inaugurated their subsequent uneasy relationship: he was sent to help in the office where he typed with two fingers. Subsequently he was asked to assist the incumbent sports teacher and the carpenter (Mr Mortensen), a Dane and a skilled carpenter, repairing furniture in the workshop. There he developed great carpentry skills, which he did his best to pass on to those boys (and the odd girl) who elected to do their practical work with him. I enjoyed carpentry very much and under Meyerlein's expert guidance fashioned a few rather nice objects, such as a wooden calendar that I gave to TA on one of her birthdays; it graced her desk until she died. He was a very caring and understanding housefather who was particularly good with some of the more difficult boys. Like a vintage wine he has mellowed wondrously over the years and, happily, he and I have remained very close to each other.

Meyerlein was not liked by *every* child because he presided over the early morning gymnastics in the open air, which were much hated by some. What's more, he had the unenviable task of ensuring that we got out of our beds in time. He fell in love with Hago and they married in 1936. Their first son, Joseph, was born in 1938 and I well remember him in his pram, which was parked outside the kitchen window so that Heidtsche could come to the rescue when the need arose. (Joseph became a consultant in paediatrics and has recently retired.) The Meyers lived in a small cottage (Greet Cottage) a mile or two from Bunce Court, and Hago and Norman Wormleighton, our much admired English teacher, arranged play readings there from time to time, in some of which I took part. It was a special pleasure to walk over the fields and along the wooded lanes to Greet Cottage (where Hans still lives) or to cycle there with the wind rushing through my hair. How did I come to have a bicycle? One of the older boys, who later became one of the world's greatest copper barons, took a shine to me and managed, miraculously, to construct a bike out of some wrecks lying behind the gym hut. (In this hut we were able to buy chocolate such as Milky Ways and Mars bars with our monthly pocket money, which amounted to one shilling and sixpence). The bike was extremely basic but it worked, and its brakes were just about adequate to prevent disasters at the bottom of one or two steep hills.

Hans had the misfortune to be interned in 1941, together with some of the older boys. The local police sergeant, who served him his notice of internment, was 'most apologetic'. After a stay in Huyton, Liverpool, he chose to accompany several boys from the school to Australia in HMS *Dunera*, on which German Nazis and Jewish refugees were carelessly mixed and treated equally badly by some members of the crew. He finished up in an internment camp in New South Wales and was returned in 1944, in the company of one of his former pupils. He rejoined his family and the school in Shropshire, and after the war went back to Bunce Court as part of an advance party that laid the foundations for the school's return. Whereas some of the male Jewish refugees who were interned never forgave the British authorities for what had been a badly conceived panic measure, Hans is sanguine about that episode in his life, doesn't feel badly about it and discerns in it some positive features. He later qualified as a schoolteacher and worked with special needs children in Maidstone until his retirement.

Although Hans Meyer had an uneasy relationship with TA and is still somewhat critical of some aspects of her leadership, he was in complete agreement with the school's ethos. It was the kind of school in which he himself would like to have been a pupil. He feels that TA was too authoritarian, allowing herself to be advised by a small coterie of trusted colleagues rather than by majority vote at staff meetings; but he recognises that at a time of severe financial constraints and exceptionally difficult circumstances it may have been the only way forward. It was a matter of preserving what TA had created from her 1933 vision, and she undoubtedly succeeded. He believes that Bunce Court exerted a powerful influence on his development as a person, teacher and pedagogue. Now, at the age of ninety-six, he feels strongly that it was TA and the school that allowed him to mature and to carve out for himself a productive and enjoyable professional life.

Hannah Meyer

I recently rediscovered the address I gave at Hago's funeral in 1977, when she was buried close to her beloved youngest son Tyll, who had died at a tender age in a tragic road accident in the USA. Like many others I had been deeply fond of her. She radiated tranquillity, warmth and good humour and acted as a surrogate mother to many pupils. She was also greatly liked as a teacher. After the school's closure she did some stalwart work in the local (Doddington) Reception Centre. Hago had the generosity of spirit to rebuild bridges, after the war, with friends she had left behind in her beloved Hamburg. She was a wonderful and dear woman.

Other teachers

Lessons were given in small groups; my own comprised about twelve of us, and that made learning both easy and a pleasure. The standard of teaching was generally excellent and it covered the arts very broadly, though science was a very much neglected area. The school did not have the resources for laboratories, nor access to science teachers (other than in biology), and chemistry and physics were not taught. It is therefore extraordinary that many pupils later took up science or medicine and excelled in their chosen subject, making their mark in their chosen fields.

I was unlucky to have had Mr Herbert, who was an English conscientious objector, as my maths teacher. Teaching was clearly not his forte – though he was a very engaging man – and I have remained mathematically challenged for the rest of my life. Indeed, whilst I had extremely good results in my matriculation exam (taken in Trench Hall in 1942) I failed maths and had to take it again. Perhaps I was simply too dim, for one or two mathematically gifted boys thrived under his guidance. There were one or two other teachers who evidently taught maths brilliantly, especially the formidable Adolf Prag ('Praha'), who was also in charge of the scholastic timetable during Hanna Bergas's absence in Italy. Praha was one of TA's most trusted colleagues, but he left the school in the early 1940s to become a master at a public school, Winchester College.

Biology was taught by Dennis Brind, who had studied agriculture and economics at Reading University and arrived in Bunce Court in 1934 soon after graduating with two degrees. He stayed until 1941, when he joined the navy as an intelligence officer on a destroyer. Jobs were few and far between in the mid-thirties and he was keen to help refugees. For reasons unknown to any of us, least of all to him, he was universally known as 'Maggy'. He was a gentle, unassuming man who was very much respected by both staff and pupils and exercised a natural authority. Our unwillingness to take liberties with him may have been partly down to his Englishness. He had a profound influence on me for two reasons.

First, his biology lessons fired my interest in the subject, which led me in 1947 to study zoology. Although his lessons were conventional they were lucid and sufficiently interesting to make me feel that I wanted to delve more deeply into the subject should I ever have the opportunity. Thus, very indirectly, Maggy helped to propel me towards immunology. And second, it was Maggy who started up field hockey in the school and who made me wildly enthusiastic about it. We had a large and fairly rough sports field on which we played soccer in the winter and hockey in the summer, umpired by Maggy – who also helped us to develop our skills. I was one of the better players and usually took the centre-half position. Thus began my love affair with this game, which continued during my army service and later at Birmingham University. During my time in Birmingham I played for Staffordshire, for British Universities and, after leaving university, for Beckenham – a South London club that was at that time one of the best in the country.

Other teachers who influenced me strongly were Norman Wormleighton, Lotte Kalischer and Hanna Bergas. Norman ('Wormy') taught me English and to him I largely owe the fact that my English is barely distinguishable from that of a native. He was an Englishman par excellence: tall and handsome, with an aquiline nose, usually wearing sandals, and with a natural calmness and gentleness – an admirable role model. I don't think I ever saw him rattled, even by the worst behaviour of some of his pupils. His lessons were always engrossing, something I looked forward to, and I developed a great love and affinity for the language from them. Hearing him read poetry was a revelation. It was Wormy who taught us many idioms that have stayed with me, and he encouraged us to write essays that he invariably annotated with helpful and encouraging remarks.

Lotte Kalischer, strangely always known by her surname, was the music teacher and also a talented violinist. She was a highly strung woman who was given to tantrums when things went wrong, but she was also charming and an inspiration to us when she played the violin, which she did frequently, accompanied by Helmut Schneider, a gifted amateur pianist who I am told also taught maths very eloquently but who was officially employed as a gardener. The grand piano was to be found in the hall at the bottom of the stairs leading up to the first floor of the main building, and whenever they gave a recital the staircase and the hall itself would be crammed with listeners. At these recitals I was introduced to Mozart and Beethoven sonatas, and listening now to the *Spring* sonata invariably transports me back to those days. I began to take violin lessons with Kalischer, but alas they didn't last long – for she found me to be a less than brilliant student, and I did not have the patience to persist.

There were other teachers who aroused in me a love for their subject. Mr Horowitz, an English Jew from London's East End, was an excellent teacher of history who brought the nineteenth and early twentieth century vividly to life. We used to snigger about him behind his back because, apart from teaching with a cigarette in his mouth, he usually had both his hands in his trouser pockets, and we boys speculated that he was playing pocket billiards as a way of passing the time. Another outstanding teacher was Walter Isaacsohn ('Saxo'), who taught scripture. Our syllabus was exclusively devoted to parts of the Old Testament, but such was his ability to talk about biblical times, as if it was news hot off the press, that I was spellbound. I was taught French by Hilde Oppenheimer (later Todd) who was known as 'Hutschnur' because she once exclaimed in severe irritation at some misdemeanour by a pupil, 'das geht mir aber über die Hutschnur', an expression I find rather hard to translate (literally 'that goes well over my hat-string', meaning 'that's really going too far'). She was a somewhat stern woman but with a twinkle in her eyes and she had a very precise, distinctive voice; she spoke English fluently and was a good teacher. I liked sitting at 'her' table during meals because conversation often rose above the mundane, and she did not discourage the acquisition of 'second helpings' on behalf of her table!

One other person who contributed to my happiness was Mr Peckover, a small, unassuming man with a limp who was not a teacher but worked in the wood workshop. He was a conscientious objector, lived in a tiny hut in the grounds of the school, and as his hobby looked after several bee hives. Having expressed an interest in his bees, I felt privileged to be asked to observe and assist him with their feeding in winter and expressing honey from the combs in late summer. Catching a swarm that had settled in a field some distance away was exciting, and the bees probably encouraged my developing interest in biology.

Gwynne Badsworth (now Angell) was a delightful and popular young woman who came to Bunce Court in 1935 immediately after completing her Montessori training. Offered the opportunity of helping to look after the smaller children for a period of six months, she stayed for six years and remains in close touch with some of her former charges. She recalled when I spoke to her in 2001 that when interviewed by TA, who was 'spread out on a settee', she was commanded to 'tell me about yourself'. She liked the atmosphere of the school and got on well with TA, whom she admired and found to be astute in the appointment of staff. She found TP very helpful, 'a gentle soul' who was loved by the children. Bunce Court was clearly an important part of Gwynne's life. She left in 1941 to train as a nurse and a midwife, and after the war spent four or five years in Bangladesh as a field worker, teaching young girls to be health workers and midwives.

Another young woman who helped with the smaller children was Lucie Schachne, whose book is mentioned above (p. 45). Born in 1918, and having experienced great difficulties in her non-Jewish school in Berlin once the Nazis came to power, she became one of the first pupils in Rosenthal's school. Saxo was one of the teachers there; they soon married and then went to join Anna Essinger in Bunce Court. She became the housemother for children in the cottage and taught biblical history to the youngest. To her, TA was a somewhat distant, even lonely figure. Although the staff meetings were democratically run they were, in a sense, going through the motions and dealt mainly with practical issues rather than educational policy, Lucie thought. Because TA did not teach she did not get to know the children particularly well, and there was usually a less restrained atmosphere when TA was not present.

Lucie felt, when I spoke to her in 2001, that Bunce Court was very much 'the sum of a devoted staff' (who, incidentally, were paid a mere pittance as funds were in very short supply), with TA bearing the ultimate responsibility, both financial and educational; she had 'made it all possible'. TA also helped to get many people out of Germany, for example Helmut Schneider. (He had had a nervous breakdown, was without a work permit and recovered in Bunce Court whilst working in the garden.) Although there was an ethos of tolerance and the children were required to engage in work for the community, Lucie's main criticism was directed at the lack of traditional (Jewish) community ethics and values. In other words, she was concerned that children were not encouraged to identify with Judaism. Assimilation was the main objective, and this did not encourage the development of a Jewish identity.

TA's other sister, Bertl (Bertha) Kahn (Frau Kahn – no nickname for her!), was in charge of domestic matters – the linen cupboard, for example, and numerous domestic matters which, though far from glamorous, were essential to the life of the school. Among her chores was doling out our daily ration of cod liver oil, an activity hardly likely to have endeared her to the children. She had two children of her own in the school and was a very well-meaning woman who served the school loyally.

Hanna Bergas (HB)

Hanna was universally known as HB (pronounced in the German way, 'hah-bay'), a thin and angular woman with a dark bun, very serious and without an obvious sense of humour: definitely not someone to trifle with. Her manner was somewhat severe and not all children liked her. However, she took a deep interest in the children in her care and remained in close contact with a number of us long after she had left the school. Once the war had ended she and her cousin, Helmut Schneider, moved to Mountain View, California. HB expected a lot of the children to whom she taught English and French – she was without doubt a strict teacher – but she was highly respected and her history of art lessons, which were optional, were well attended and hugely appreciated. That is where my love of art began, and I feel I owe her a great debt of gratitude for having kindled it. She and I maintained a steady and lively correspondence after her departure from this country, and whenever I was in California for professional reasons I made a special point of visiting her and Helmut. Her letters and Helmut's wry postscripts were warm and affectionate and we spent much time discussing the world's problems. My last long letter arrived a day or two after her death, a fact that haunted me at the time.

In 1979 HB wrote a monograph, *Fifteen Years – Lived Among, With and For Refugee Children*, largely for the benefit of her Californian friends and the staff and students at the Peninsula School in Palo Alto in which she then taught. In it she vividly recounts her involvement with Bunce Court School, starting with her summary dismissal in April 1933 from the school in which she taught in Berlin, joining TA's school in Ulm just in time for its evacuation to England in September of the same year, early life in Bunce Court, an interlude when she joined Helmut Schneider's similar but much smaller school, Schulheim Vigiljoch, in the Italian Alps, her temporary work as an organiser and teacher in Dovercourt Camp, and the war years in Bunce Court and Trench Hall. If Heidtsche was my emotional mother, HB was undoubtedly my intellectual mother. She loved literature, music and art and in all these she had a distinct influence on me.

HB died on 11 January 1987, having been preceded by Helmut by a year. A memorial gathering was organised for her a month later by the Peninsula School, where she had taught for many years. I was very touched to be asked to give one of the addresses, as was my old friend Ernst Weinberg.

Memorable activities

TA was acutely aware of the inability of many children to spend their holidays with their parents or relatives, and with this in mind she arranged for at least some of them, if not all, to visit English couples or families who had come forward. They were known as our 'English families'. I was introduced to Mr and Mrs Baulch from Basingstoke, with whom I spent a couple of holidays; they were most kind to me. When visiting me at Bunce Court on one occasion they took a photograph of me lying on the lawn, with a happy face that was completely at odds with the photograph taken in the German train. In the summer of 1939 they offered to adopt me, a proposal I found difficult to deal with as I didn't want to hurt their feelings by rejecting it. On the other hand I was aware that they came from a very different social milieu and cultural background – Mr Baulch was a railway worker – and I did not feel that I had a great deal in common with them. Furthermore, I did not regard myself as an orphan at that time, and nor was I; to have agreed would have been profoundly disloyal to my parents. So the offer was turned down by me, with the approval of TA, who had been careful to leave the decision to me. My last holiday with Mr and Mrs Baulch was in the late summer of 1939. They had taken me to Bournemouth, and whilst there they heard that war had been declared. As members of the Territorial Army they had to report immediately to their local base, and the journey in their little Austin 7 back to Basingstoke on 3 September was quite surreal. Knowing that Germany and England were now at war, I had visions of bombs raining down on us, and there was the dreadful thought that my family and I were now separated in a wholly unpredictable way.

There were certain cultural highlights in Bunce Court and Trench Hall. First, there was the performance of part of *The Magic Flute*. The director had selected the Papageno/Papagena plot, and the principal roles were very engagingly sung by Wormy and Lotte Kalischer and the Queen of the Night dramatically by Hutschnur. Among the Moorish slaves/followers were my friend Ernst Weinberg, Heinz Rotholz (Redwood) and me. Our skin was darkened with a mixture of butter and cocoa so that we exuded an overwhelming aroma; I have photographs of the triumphant performance in the open air amphitheatre, which had been built very expertly some years before by the older children and some of the teachers and had a fine natural backcloth of densely planted and mature yews. The school was invited by the 'Red Dean' of Canterbury, the Rev. Dr Johnson, to give a charitable repeat performance in the chapter house of Canterbury Cathedral, and this was the occasion of a well-remembered episode. During the interval my friend Ernst and I decided to explore the cathedral vaults, and whilst we were cavorting through them in our butter and cocoa make-up the gates were suddenly locked behind us with a great clang. It took several minutes of increasingly desperate shouting to draw the attention of the verger to our predicament, and we managed to return in the nick of time for the second half of the performance.

Other cultural events included Prokofiev's *Peter and the Wolf*, in which the principal role of Peter was danced by the girl with whom I had (sort of) fallen in love, Lotte Deak. She was petite and a natural dancer, and I suffered many pangs when my feelings for her (which were never made very explicit) were not returned. I was involved in a performance of part of *Twelfth Night*, in which I was Sir Toby Belch to the Sir Andrew Aguecheek of Heinz Rotholz and the Malvolio of Ilya Sonnenschein (now Ian Spenser). I have recently exchanged letters with Ian and he writes that 'the performance made me realize that I would never be an actor', an appraisal that is less than fair to himself. Had he become an actor the loss would certainly have been to organic chemistry. My adored Lotte was Maria. The play was a great success and it later encouraged me to take part in one or two other dramatic ventures. Thus, in Birmingham, after leaving school, I was Tony Lumpkin in Goldsmith's *She Stoops to Conquer*, performed by the dramatic group of the International Centre. An operatic performance that proved to be controversial was that of Gilbert and Sullivan's *Trial by Jury*, which two temporary visiting teachers organised despite the rather sniffy objections by TA and the musical establishment, who regarded G&S operas with some contempt as too lightweight. Heinz Redwood organised a round robin letter to TA stating the case for such a performance; it evidently had its intended effect even though he, as ringleader, received a good dressing down by her. There was undoubtedly an element of cultural snobbery in the school, but the performance was nonetheless enjoyed by the pupils.

In Trench Hall I joined a group of older boys whose dormitories were in some outbuildings, a group of converted stables at the far end of a courtyard well away from the main house. We had bunkbeds and my friend Ernst and I shared, with me on the top one. That is where our friendship became firmly cemented, and happily it has lasted a lifetime. He emigrated to the United States after the war to join his parents, who had miraculously survived in hiding in Belgium, and later married my early childhood friend Inge – my only achievement as a marriage broker! In the stables we had a somewhat greater degree of independence. Whenever the news came, after we were supposed to be in bed, that TA was on her way for an inspection, lights went out in a trice and everyone was silently tucked in, regardless of what horseplay might have preceded her visitation.

TA always insisted that only English should be spoken, and it would be a brave pupil who continued to talk German in her presence. This was very far-sighted of her for it undoubtedly helped us to improve our English very quickly. At meals TA always sat at the top table, which was carefully avoided by many children as they felt rather intimidated by her and by her rather formal conversation. Whenever the hubbub in the dining hall reached a certain number of decibels she would call out 'silence, pleeeaaase'. On one of her birthdays the staff presented her with a small silver bell to use on such occasions, and on it was inscribed 'Pleeeaaase!!!' This bell was given to me by TA's sister Paula (TP) after TA's death, and it sits proudly on our mantelpiece.

TP played an important role in the school. As a trained children's nurse she was in charge of the isolation hut, the school hospital, where she ran a very tight and some would think authoritarian ship. She insisted on absolute quiet and obedience and seemed to be remarkably successful in her treatment of sick children. TP was not an intellectual by any stretch of the imagination, but she had a warm heart and felt most at ease with small children. She never fully mastered the English language and occasionally came out with some wonderful howlers. For example, 'who eats up his plate will become a tart' (meaning, one presumes, whoever finishes his food will get a tart for pudding). (I am indebted to Hans Meyer for reminding me of this priceless example.)

Considering that the school was coeducational the sex life there was curiously innocent, or so it seemed, and as far as I know no pregnancy ever occurred. Not surprisingly there were liaisons and secretive nocturnal walks. The only even vaguely sexual 'happening' in which I was indirectly involved was a rather strange and carefully arranged wrestling match between a boy and a girl who happened to be rather well developed and sexually somewhat provocative. I don't know the reason for this fight, except perhaps that she wanted to prove herself. A small band of pupils were told that this fight was going to take place one evening on the tennis court behind the yews of the amphitheatre, a 'referee' was appointed, and a few of us trooped along to witness the bizarre event. It proved to be quite innocuous (I think), and I have no recollection as to who 'won', though the 'boy' told me recently that he did, by a whisker.

Sex education did not seem to exist in Bunce Court, except perhaps for some of the older girls. Some of us boys were told by our doughty headmistress that if we ever had sexual urges come upon us we should take a cold shower. Excellent advice, indeed!

One other incident is worth recalling. During Heidtsche's absence in Trench Hall a delightful girl called Recha Moch and I were helping the substitute cook to bottle damsons in large metal containers with screwed-on metal lids. Immediately before sealing the lids with wingnuts the contents had to be brought to the boil again to ensure sterilisation. Evidently I had tightened the screws too much, for the lid of one of the containers began to bulge. In a panic I started to loosen the nuts, whereupon the container exploded, with the damson jam badly burning Recha's and my face, throat and upper arms, and her chest. I was so shocked that I did not become aware of a gash on one of my knees from a metal splinter until quite some time later. It was HB who instantly took command, sat us down on chairs in the open air (it was a warm summer's day) and arranged for an ambulance to be called. We spent the best part of five weeks in Shrewsbury Infirmary, where we were known as 'the damson children' because our hair could not be washed for two or three weeks and the sickly damson smell clung to us. We were lucky to get away without serious facial scars, though both of us acquired lifelong scars elsewhere on our bodies. I was consigned to an adult male ward and was astonished to find that the adults were given a daily pint of Guinness as part of their treatment. After leaving the hospital our scars received lengthy radiation treatment. I felt guilty at having been the cause of dear Recha's injury, and can only hope that the mammary carcinoma from which she died eventually had no causal connection with the accident.

Whilst at Trench Hall I learnt two agricultural skills that have not proved to be of much use to me in later life. To earn a little extra pocket money a few of the older boys helped the local farmer at weekends, an activity that was encouraged by TA because she was keen to maintain a friendly relationship with the local population. I spent some hours laboriously cutting down thistles in his field, using a scythe, which is not as easy as it sounds. The other skill was the 'stripping' of cows. Once the farmer had milked his cows I was allowed to continue, in order to ensure that all milk had been removed, an exercise that yielded disappointingly small amounts of milk but was vital in encouraging further milk secretion. It is a technique that requires a certain manual dexterity, and I felt flattered to be let loose on the farmer's precious animals.

Was Bunce Court the perfect school?

For me it undoubtedly was and I thank my lucky stars that I was selected to go there. The teachers gave me the loving care that my parents were prevented from giving themselves, and the standard of education was generally exceptionally high. I made lifelong friends: for example, I am in close touch with Ernst Weinberg although he has lived in California since the end of the war, and I frequently see Gerd Nathan, Karl Grossfield, Eric Bourne ('Ulli') and others, while Hans Meyer and his second wife Susanne have continued to be very dear friends and wonderful hosts in Greet Cottage. By encouraging me to develop not only academically but also in other spheres, the school made me into an all-rounder, as Maggy Brind described me in one of his reports. I passed my school certificate within three years of my arrival in Britain, with distinction in most subjects (with the exception of maths), and whilst at the time the possibility of a university degree did not even enter my consciousness it undoubtedly provided the springboard for that when, after the war, I unexpectedly obtained a government grant to enable me to study. The school shielded me to some extent from the pain of separation from my family, for the teachers made it a point not to speculate about the dire fate that might have overtaken them and to be as reassuring as possible. At the same time we were encouraged by TA to take an interest in the progress of the war, and extracts from the *Manchester Guardian* and the *New Statesman* were posted regularly on a wall. In short, Bunce Court allowed me to develop my identity and it nurtured my self-esteem.

But of course there is no such thing as the perfect school. I have already referred to one or two of its weaknesses. The school found it difficult to cope with some children who did not fit in naturally and for whom the separation from their parents was so calamitous that they were deeply unhappy. In a sense I was fortunate in that I had already spent two years in an orphanage and away from my family, so that I was able to cope more readily with the institutional aspects of school life. Some children were unable to make that adjustment and had a very unhappy time, but I suspect that they would have been distraught in almost any environment that England was able to offer at the time.

A few, like my friend Peter Stoll, who professed to be a Trotskyite and was something of a rebel and an outsider, likewise failed to find contentment. His particular personality did not go down well with some of the teachers, who not only liked children to be intelligent but also to conform to their idea of cultured and attractive human beings. But, with the kind of background that most of us had in Nazi-controlled Central Europe, it would have been astonishing if we had all settled down to school life in a foreign country without any problems.

To TA's great credit she took in, after the end of war, a number of boys who had either survived concentration camps or who had been hidden in Poland. They were not easy to integrate – in those days one didn't even consider counselling or psychotherapy – but nonetheless they all benefited from a relatively short stay in the school. I befriended some of them whilst on army leave. At least two of them have done very well indeed: Ervin Buncel, who is Professor of Chemistry at Queen's University, Kingston, Ontario, and Samuel Oliner, Director of the Altruistic Personality and Prosocial Behavior Institute at Humboldt State University, Arcata. Sam's remarkable story of survival among Polish peasants was highlighted in a television documentary a good many years ago. In a recently published book, *Sevek and the Holocaust – the Boy Who Refused to Die*, another of these 'boys', Sidney Finkel, wrote most touchingly of what Bunce Court had meant to someone who had survived the war years in ghettos and concentration camps.

Each Old Bunce Courtian will have his or her own memories, although there is bound to be much common ground. In fact, the reunions that have taken place in recent years – the last very large one in 2003 in the home of one of the former teachers, Hans Meyer – show that there is a powerful and lifelong bond between Old Bunce Courtians. Professor Michael Trede, who returned to Germany after the war, has published an interesting autobiography in which a major chapter is devoted to the few years he spent in the school, for him too a very formative period of his life and one remembered with affection and gratitude. He kept a diary and sent frequent letters to his mother, who was in England too, so he was able to recount his life in great detail, including a blow-by-blow account of an exciting early morning relay race in which Lothar was just pipped to the post in the final lap by Gabi (Adler)!

If the school is to be judged in terms of the careers of its pupils it was clearly immensely successful. I cannot think of any former pupil who has not made an honourable and productive life for him or herself, and many have excelled. Professors and doctors abound, including a number of women, but I will mention only a few who have achieved great public acclaim. The first of these was mentioned earlier: Gerard (Gerd) Hoffnung, the artist, cartoonist, musician and humorist who died in 1959 at the age of thirty-four, but not before he had established his reputation. He was in Bunce Court for a relatively short time before the war. The school found it difficult to cope with this highly eccentric young man who liked to sit on second-floor window sills with his legs dangling on the outside, playing jazz on his saxophone at all hours of the day. This and other unusual behaviour did not endear him to some of the staff. He is still well remembered in Great Britain for his musical cartoons and for the 'Hoffnung Concerts', the first of which was held in the Royal Festival Hall in 1956.

Frank Auerbach is almost certainly Bunce Court's most widely acclaimed ex-pupil. He was sent to England by his parents in 1939 at the age of eight and stayed in the school for eight years. There he played a major part in several theatrical productions, orchestrated by Wilhelm Marckwald (a theatre director in Germany but officially employed by the school as a boiler man!). However, it was in art classes that he began to show his unusual talent. He left at the age of sixteen, having decided to become an artist, and he studied at St Martin's School of Art. He is now considered to be one of Britain's finest painters, with a worldwide reputation, and in 2001 he had a major retrospective at the Royal Academy of Arts (in competition with 'Rembrandt's Women'!). He is a self-declared workaholic who paints obsessively almost every day, all day. Carol and I invited him several years ago to dinner in order to meet an old Bunce Courtian friend of his, Professor Michael Trede (who lives in Germany and is a gifted amateur painter), together with a few others. With this bait I managed to persuade this recluse to put in an appearance, though it proved to be only for drinks after the meal. Nonetheless, he stayed for several hours and we had a most congenial and interesting evening.

Another OBC who made his reputation was Frank Marcus, who drew attention to himself in the 1960s by the publication of a play, *The Killing of Sister George*, which was a national and international success; he was also theatre critic of the *Sunday Telegraph*. Unfortunately he died prematurely.

The end of the Bunce Court story

The school closed in July 1948, having in a sense run out of both pupils and teachers. It had served its main function, which had been to give succour to refugee children, and its isolation on the North Downs made teacher recruitment exceedingly difficult. What is more, its teachers had given their services on minuscule salaries (£9 per month, regardless of status or experience): for them it had been a labour of love as well as, for many, a refuge. Many left to find better paid jobs or, like HB, emigrated to the United States. An attempt was made by TA to allow it to continue under a new head, Fridolin Friedman, but this proved to be a disaster partly because he was not strong enough and largely, I suspect, because

TA's presence in what used to be the isolation hut made it hard for him to develop an independent approach. Friedman was an engaging man with a distinguished career. Before the war he had been headmaster of a Jewish coeducational school in Caputh, near Potsdam, and from 1945 to 1947 he had worked with Polish boys who had survived concentration camps and had been flown over to this country for rehabilitation. (Their story is told in Martin Gilbert's *The Boys: Triumph Over Adversity.*) Friedman arrived in Bunce Court in 1947, accompanied by several of 'his' boys, and it is a tragedy that his trial period there ended in failure. TA was desolated by the impending closure, and in the year in which I commenced my undergraduate studies she felt desperate enough to ask Ulli and me whether we could not take on the running of the school. We had both only just left the army, admittedly with a fair amount of administrative experience, and though feeling greatly flattered we decided that it would be wrong for us to embark on such a vast enterprise before completing our education.

My move to Birmingham

Because I had failed maths in the school certificate examination (and had therefore not 'matriculated'), I stayed on for some months to retake the subject. I took this opportunity to receive some instruction in Mendelian genetics from Maria Dehn, our gardener and biology teacher following Maggy Brind's departure, and this proved to be very useful later on. Maria was small and stocky and immensely cheerful. I had several lengthy debates with her, whilst digging the garden, about the ethical dilemma one faces when accidentally slicing an earthworm in two with a spade; and her field trip demonstrations of carnivorous plants were quite riveting.

Financial support for me had run out (my fees had been paid by the Central Jewish Fund for German Refugees), and I was therefore unable to join a small group that included Heinz and Georgie studying for the higher school certificate, the equivalent of A levels and serving at that time as an entrance qualification for university. So what was to happen to me? The ever resourceful TA got in touch with Ruth Simmons, who had been appointed as secretary of the Refugee Children's Movement in the Midlands, and she suggested that a job might be found for me in Birmingham as a laboratory assistant. Although hardly qualified for such a post I agreed, and before long I was given an interview in the chemistry department of Birmingham Central Technical College. With this fateful decision I began, at a very lowly level, life as a scientist, at the princely annual salary of £59 (including war bonus, whatever that may have meant). It was January 1942 and I was sixteen years old.

This was not the end of my relationship with Bunce Court, for I visited it whenever I could and it continued to provide me with a fixed point of reference in a rapidly changing world both during and after the war. It also gave me the opportunity of falling seriously in love for the first time!

Chapter Nine: Wartime Birmingham

Ruth Simmons turned out to be a delightful young Jewish Englishwoman - vivacious, full of energy and with a great enthusiasm for the work she had elected to do. According to *Survivors: Jewish Refugees in Birmingham,* her father's family had been settled in England for several generations; her great-grandfather had served at Trafalgar and had subsequently been a rabbi in Penzance. Ruth's mother had emigrated from Germany early in the twentieth century, having met her husband when he was on a walking tour on the Continent in 1907. One of the first things Ruth did for me was to take me to Burtons the Tailor, where she allowed me to choose my first suit in time for my interview. It was pale blue and with a fine pattern, and I thought it incredibly and almost embarrassingly smart. She invited me to her family home on one or two occasions on a Friday evening; it was the first time since leaving my family that I had been in a Jewish home and I found it correspondingly nostalgic and at the same time slightly overwhelming.

Judging from some personal records I was able to obtain from Bloomsbury House not so many years ago, Ruth wrote regular reports about me to the Jewish Refugee Committee. Her view of me was interesting and somewhat surprising. Here are some extracts.

September 1941: Rather a timid boy, and it was felt unwise to bring him into B'ham for the winter. It was agreed he stayed on in Bunce Court, studying in the morning and taking the younger boys in the afternoon. The [Children's] Movement agreed to pay 10 shillings per week for him.
January 1942: Came to B'ham to live with Mrs Widdowson, 1 Barnsley Road.

February 1942: Employed by Central Technical College. Wages: £1.2s.9d. Time allowed for study for Intermediate BSc and he is also taking weekend classes.

April 1942: Rise in wages to £1.4s.8d. Subvention reduced to 3 shillings.

September 1942: Informed Lothar that subvention will be stopped. He will come to the Office for repairs and clothing when necessary . . . Forwarded £1 towards a pair of flannels sanctioned by Mrs Michealis . . . Lothar was most loathe [*sic*] to accept assistance.

Later the same month: British Council in favour of giving free membership card to the International Club to Lothar if he helps with the film projector.

October 1942: Received £3 from Regional Committee to purchase books for his study. Also arranged for Mrs Lindenstein to go through his clothes and do his mending. *This boy needs careful watching as he will not come and ask for help.*

Early 1944: This boy has been in close touch with our office and I feel sure he will continue to write to us. We have arranged for him to spend his army leaves in B'ham. He has made many friends here and has always received an invitation for Friday nights and Jewish Festivals. His ambition is to become a teacher. He tried for his Inter. BSc in Nov. 1943 but unfortunately failed – we feel sure that this was only due to working so hard as well as studying. The Director of the B'ham Tech. College speaks most highly of him and he has left with excellent references. His parents and sister have been deported to Poland. [I was not informed of this at the time, and how could she possibly have found out? And they *weren't* deported to Poland.] We feel most strongly that it is important to keep in touch with this boy – although he has a fine character we feel he will have a difficult time in the army in spite of the fact that he felt bound to join up.

The last entry in July 1947: Lothar called at the office. He has been promoted to Captain. Is still in Germany on 'operation woodpecker'. Spent 19 days leave in B'ham, Bunce Court and Devon or Cornwall. Will be demobbed in two months time. Sat for entrance examination for B'ham University, where he hopes to study for BSc . . . Continues to keep in touch with friends in B'ham and family Widdowson where he lived for several years and where all his luggage is stored. He has applied for naturalisation.

These notes give the bare bones of my life in Birmingham, and I will fill in a few of the more interesting gaps, if only to thank one or two people who were very helpful to me at that time. So far as Ruth Simmons was concerned, she was an important anchor even though I did not get to know her particularly well. She worked tirelessly for the British Central Fund for Jewish Refugees on behalf of several other waves of refugees from Hungary, Egypt, Czechoslovakia and Iran, and in 1978 was honoured with an MBE. Sadly I lost touch with her, and before I was able to repair that omission she had died.

Ruth Simmons had pointed me in the direction of Mr and Mrs Widdowson, who had a house in Edgbaston just off Hagley Road. One Bunce Courtian had already stayed there (Gabi Adler) and I shared a room with Peter Stoll. The Widdowsons were kind and well-meaning Christian Scientists, and I was asked to pay them an absurdly small sum, 10*s* per week, for board and lodging. This represented about half my wages. Mrs Widdowson's brother was badly crippled and bent double; he was a photographer and had a dark-room at the top of the house. He very kindly made enlargements of the only small passport photographs I had of my parents, and I am enormously grateful to him for that. Here I had my first extended exposure to English cooking: not marvellous but perfectly acceptable. The Widdowsons' son was in the army in India, where he died following an infection that could have been prevented by vaccination and/or treatment with antibiotics but which, as a Christian Scientist, he did not accept.

1 Barnsley Road

The Widdowsons allowed me to use their son's sports bicycle, and I frequently cycled to work on this. On several weekends I also cycled to Trench Hall, some 50-odd miles away, leaving immediately after tea on a Friday and returning late on the Sunday. It was not a particularly hilly journey but there were a few very long climbs the other side of Wolverhampton, and as lorries travelled at a fairly slow speed I usually managed to hang on to the backs of them to haul me up the inclines. The drivers did not approve and it was quite a hazardous trick; however, it did get me to Trench Hall a little more quickly. Even so, it took about five hours and I usually arrived just before the teachers and Heidtsche had turned in for the night.

On these visits to Trench Hall I got to know a not so very young teacher from New Zealand, Miss Clifford, or Cliffie as she was generally known. She was a delightful, intellectual and politically somewhat left-leaning woman about whom I know very little, except that she died prematurely after her return to her own country. She lived in a small caravan parked to one side of the main house – and when I arrived after my lengthy cycle ride her lights were usually still on, and so there was time for a chat. I was always welcomed with open arms: I was home! I enjoyed sparring with Cliffie intellectually and she and I decided one weekend to go on a 100 mile cycling trip to Lake Bala in North Wales, spending the night in a small hotel somewhere near the lake. Ours was a purely platonic and affectionate relationship, but TA evidently didn't think so and made her disapproval known. It was my first experience of Wales and I loved the landscape, to which I returned frequently later in life. (My second wife Carol is Welsh, though she comes from a less romantic part of the country.)

Laboratory work

My lab work at Central Technical College, in the middle of town, went reasonably well, though I had to pick up chemistry at a rate of knots. The head of the chemistry department was Dr J. Cooper Duff, DSc, FIC, a distinguished and fair-minded man who provided me with a good reference when I left in December 1943.

One of the lecturers for whom I worked was Mr Vallance, a kind and courteous man whom I liked very much. Major Dr Friend DSc, who was a reader or senior lecturer, was a very different kettle of fish: a man of the old school who had served in the First World War and made his reputation with research on mustard gas. He treated me with some disdain, which at the time I interpreted as anti-Semitism. Retrospectively I believe it possible that he saw me more as a German than as a Jewish refugee, and that his anti-German stance influenced his attitude towards me. If it was indeed anti-Semitism it was the only time in my life in the UK that I have been exposed to it.

The person in the department who was most helpful was Dennis Wood, the senior laboratory assistant under whose immediate supervision I worked. He was at that time studying for his BSc in chemistry as an external student of the university and he helped me very greatly, both in carrying out my duties in the department and in my studies. I ran into him again after the war, when I began my undergraduate studies at Birmingham University and he was completing his PhD, but I subsequently lost touch with him. Thanks to the ingenuity of Ruth Durrant, the wife of Major Durrant, who had worked in a citizens' advice bureau and with whom I re-established contact half a century after leaving the army, I was able to contact him and we exchanged a few letters.

Dennis played the piano rather well. He and I shared fire-watching duties a number of times; in other words, we had to prowl around the large, dark building at night, armed with a stirrup pump and a bucket of sand, to extinguish any fires that might have been started in the event of an air raid. As there weren't any raids on our tours of duty we spent quite a lot of time in the large assembly hall, which was graced by a grand piano, and Dennis helped to while away the time by playing Elgar, Walton and Chopin. Those were eerie nights and it was a relief to hear music. Although our skills as firefighters were never put to the test, there were plenty of air raids at other times: I well remember the sickly smell of chocolate carried over by the wind to my bedroom when Cadbury's factory in Bournville, a few miles away, was heavily bombed.

It was Dennis who introduced me to the free organ recitals given in Birmingham Town Hall every Wednesday at lunchtime. G.D. Cunningham was at that time the city organist and he introduced me to a wide range of organ music, from Bach to Widor and César Frank. I became a regular listener: the acoustics of this large Victorian hall with its great side columns were well suited to the organ, and when Cunningham let fly in, say, a Bach toccata and fugue, the whole edifice seemed to tremble.

Social life

My social life – insofar as I had time for one because of my intensive studies – centred largely on three refugee hostels, one for boys and girls in Wheeley's Road, one for boys only in Gough Road and a girls' hostel in St Mary's Vicarage in Selly Oak. On one of my visits to Wheeley's Road I became acquainted with a girl called Hanna Hirsch, the daughter of the rather formidable Dr Hirsch who was warden of Elpis Lodge in Gough Road. She became very fond of me but although we saw each other a number of times the relationship petered out as I felt that she was far more mature than I was, both intellectually and emotionally. My attempts to get in touch with her in recent years have unfortunately failed.

Because Thilde Weil resided in St Mary's Vicarage I tended to gravitate there. The hostel was run by Sophie Friedländer and Hilde Jarecki who, being keen Zionists, attempted unsuccessfully to draw me into that fold. I was persuaded to take part in a performance of *Tobias and the Angel* in which I took the part of the angel. A white sheet was sacrificed for my costume. The play was reasonably successful, though I am not sure that I felt entirely comfortable in my role!

As I had a full-time job and took evening and weekend classes at the Central Tech I was extremely busy, but this did not prevent me from joining the Home Guard when that became possible in the spring of 1942. I trained with the 21ˢᵗ Warwickshire Battalion in Harborne and became a good shot, which served me well when I joined the army proper some eight months later. I was allowed to keep my Lee Enfield rifle in my bedroom and was mighty proud of that, especially in view of my official status as enemy alien! The Home Guard I knew had little resemblance to 'Dad's Army' in the BBC comedy series, and I have little doubt that it would have been a reasonable fighting force had the Germans invaded.

My occasional weekend trips to Trench Hall, tiring as they were because of the long cycle ride, were always delightful and a shot in the arm. They allowed me to develop closer ties with members of staff and I got to know a new generation of children. I became a sort of housefather to some of the smaller children and helped in any way possible, for example by organising football and hockey matches.

Contact with my family in Germany

Until war was declared I exchanged letters with my parents and sister, but these soon dried up. Alas, only one or two have survived. On the day of my departure for England my father gave me a note saying, 'Glückauf in der neuen Heimat, bleibe immer brav, mein lieber Junge. Vatsch' (Good luck in your new homeland, always remain upright, my dear boy. Dad). On 1 May 1939 he sent me a picture postcard illustrating the incorporation of Austria into the Reich, with the banner heading 'Wir danken unserm Führer' (we thank our Leader). On the back he had written, in German of course, 'Only a brief May greeting today, May has after all arrived [a quotation from a Schubert song]. Keep this card safely, **don't** return it to me!' In a letter written by my father just after his birthday in May 1939 he wrote among other things (and I translate), 'Yesterday we at last received from the consulate the American registration number. We had already applied in January and were given the number 68,000. With such a high number one can wait for years to receive permission to emigrate, as at present they are dealing with numbers around 40,000! And, on top of everything, we still need an affidavit from the USA, which the Lewins wanted to send us. So, you see, it is not as simple as it was with you, little boy, and with Eva too it doesn't seem to work out; yesterday I wrote again on her behalf to England. Could you perhaps ask Miss Essinger whether she knows of any possibility of getting Eva into England? From your Mr Berger [*sic*] we have heard no more for several months. Should he be with you again could you ask him calmly whether he has forgotten the exchange of letters with us and with Eva?' I wonder whether there was confusion with Hanna Bergas? I marked his question with a red cross but cannot remember what representations I made to TA or HB. There is a PS in which he enquires about my friend Ulli and asks whether I have heard anything from Dr Crohn, the director of the orphanage in Berlin; evidently my parents had lost touch with him.

On the back of this letter was a typed poem by my sister Eva, written in honour of our father's birthday on 14 May. It consists of four ingeniously rhymed and very jolly stanzas, clearly intended to be sung to the tune of a German folk song 'Jumheidi, jumheida'. She can't possibly have felt jolly. My father commented in his letter, 'Didn't she compose the poem well? She seems to have a hereditary disposition in this respect!'

I still have a letter written by my sister a week after her seventeenth birthday in January 1940, in which she thanked me profusely for two handkerchiefs I had sent her, one of which she had given to our grandmother. She implored me to save my 'pence' and not to send any more presents. If only we could all be together again, she wrote. The temperature in their suburb of Berlin had apparently dropped to 23F. Her friend Stella (who survived several concentration camps and with whom I kept in touch in Berlin) and several other friends had joined her to celebrate her birthday. She added, 'Von den Eltern habe ich u.a. einen Koffer bekommen, den ich hoffentlich bald benützen kann' (From the parents I received, among other things, a suitcase which I hope to be able to use soon).

The International Red Cross facilitated the monthly exchange of twenty-five word messages on special forms that I was able to collect from their message bureau in the town hall. The messages could be initiated in this country or in Germany and a reply form was printed on the other side. It was fiendishly difficult to know what to write, as it was essential to avoid anything that might have been offensive to the German censors. My messages were therefore anodyne and dealt with my work and studies, my trips to Bunce Court, my prowess at athletics and so on. I will translate most of the messages I sent and received.

14 September 1940 (from Bunce Court): Am well and cheerful. Do not worry. Holidays over. Am in class V. Write immediately! New address! Kisses for all. Lothar.

24 December 1940: Beloved boy, we are happy about your message. We are well. Write immediately and in detail to Tante Margot. [My mother's best friend, in New York since 1938.] Take note of our new address. Mu, Vatsch, Eva.

21 January 1941 (from Trench Hall): Received your message. Am well and healthy. Aptitude test excellent. Exams in July. Wolfgang [my cousin] and Heinz Nadel both well. Am playing the violin. Love to all. Lothar.

14 February 1941: Beloved boy, received your December message, were overjoyed. All four of us are healthy. Eva is already trainee nurse in hospital. Write to aunt Margot! Stay healthy, many frantic kisses. Mu, Vatsch.

10 March 1941: Beloved boy. We are well. Glad to have your letter. Practise the violin. What exam in July? Note our new address. Loving kisses, Vati, Mu. [By this time my father was called Arthur Israel, an enforced change of name.]

7 June 1941: Beloved boy! We are well. Margot wrote about your school plans, agreed. Write to Ewald [my uncle] in New York. Loving birthday and examination wishes. Kisses. Vatsch, Mu.

18 November 1941: Dear boy! We four are well, hopefully you too. Write to us more frequently. Have you grown a lot? How is school? A colleague sends greetings. Lovingly, Vati, Mu. [This reference to a colleague is rather mysterious.]

24 January 1941 (from Birmingham): Dearest parents, Eva. Change of address: 1 Barnsley Road, Edgbaston, Birmingham 17. Greetings to colleagues, Münzers, granny, Kronheims. Do not worry! Regards from Tante Anna. Kisses, Lothar. [The Kronheims were my paternal cousin Ruth and her family, also deported.]

2 February 1942 (from Birmingham): Am well. Hospital job didn't come off. Will probably work in a laboratory of the University, study at the same time. I have been exceptionally fortunate with my lodgings. Kisses, Lothar.

24 February 1942: Beloved parents. Hope you are well. Have passed my Easter exam in Chemistry very well. Warmest good birthday wishes. Fresh courage in the New Year. See you soon. Kisses, Lothar. [This is the most daringly optimistic message I could have sent them, suggesting that the war was by no means lost.]

13 April 1942: Beloved boy! Your last letters gave us much joy. Would like more details of job and lodgings, also your new address. What is your weight? With love, Vati, Mu, Eva.

14 April 1942: Beloved parents, Münzers! Wolfgang and I recently spent some enjoyable hours together. He spent his holidays here with old friends. Thought a lot about you. Lothar.

5 May 1942: Beloved parents, grandmother, Eva. Hope you are well. I am well taken care of here. Work is great fun. Am learning a great deal. Will soon visit Tante Anna. Regards to Käthe. Kisses. Lothar.

19 May 1942: Dearest parents, grandmother, Eva! Hope you have received messages and that you are well. Work is tremendous fun and am learning a lot. Have written a very good chemistry homework. Kisses, Lothar.

2 June 1942: Beloved parents, grandmother, Eva. Have heard from Lewins. They are well. Have you heard from Fred, my friend? Greetings to his mother. Will have holidays soon. Kisses, Lothar.

10 June 1942: Beloved boy, hope you are well, as we are. How do you like your new job? Laboratory work must be interesting. Do your clothes still fit? Tante Anna? Foster parents? Remain well, lovingly, Vati, Mu.

17 June 1942: Dear boy, very pleased with your letter. Hope that your wishes and plans will be fulfilled. Congratulations on the chemistry exam. Note new address. Loving kisses, Vati, Mu.

30 June 1942: Beloved parents, granny, Eva. Will spend holidays with Tante Anna, am very happy about that, Have broken the school high jump record! Don't worry about me. Lothar.

13 July 1942: Beloved boy. Very happy to have your messages. You'll make your way all right, you are after all Sunday's Child [ein Sonntagkind]! We three are healthy. Greetings to Tante Anna, foster parents. Loving kisses, Vati, Mu.

17 July 1942: Beloved boy, your letters arrive regularly, ours too? Where are you spending your holidays? Mu taking four days off! Eva, me not! Stay well, loving kisses, Vati, Mu.

21 July 1942: Beloved parents, much happiness about your messages! Spent my birthday very enjoyably, thought a lot about you. Spent lovely holiday in the school. Essinger sends regards. Lothar.

23 July 1942: Beloved boy! Your messages are arriving regularly, what about ours? We three are healthy, note our new address. Granny, Münzers on a journey ['verreist' was code for deported, though I did not understand the full significance of this at the time]. Did you visit Tante Anna? Stay healthy. All our love, Vati, Mu.

1 August 1942: Beloved boy. Write to Lewins again. Heard nothing from Fred. Are you well? Playing the violin? We are all OK, speak daily about you. Have trust in God. Lovingly, Vati, Mu.

18 August 1942: Beloved boy, your messages arrive regularly, ours too? Your enthusiasm for work pleases us, carry on! Have you become bigger? We three are well. Many loving kisses, Vati, Mu.

25 August 1942 (from Birmingham): Beloved parents, Eva. Received your congratulations. Spent birthday very enjoyably in the school. Many lovely presents: especially your message. Am wearing my Bar Mitzvah watch again! Hope to see you soon. Lothar.

16 September 1942: Beloved boy, your letter arrived on New Year's morning, many good wishes for the New Year! We are all well, constantly think about you. Greetings to Anna. Foster parents well? May your luck continue. Warm kisses. Vati, Mu.

5 October 1942: Beloved boy, your message pleased us greatly. Have thanked Tante Anna. We three are well. Carry on with gymnastics. How are your studies? Violin? Stay God-fearing. Loving kisses, Vati, Mu.

9 October 1942. Received letter end of July, we are glad for you. We three are well, very busy. Write to aunt Margot! Playing the violin? Clothes? Our thoughts are always with you! Stay well, lovingly, Mu, Vati.

23 October 1942: Beloved boy! Letters received, great joy! We 3 well. We are glad for you! Tante Käthe (my aunt, author): Charlottenbug Dahlmannstr. 5, Gartenhaus, c/o Landsberger.
Write to her. May God protect you! Vati, Mu, Eva. [My father's handwriting was very agitated, with the first word 'geliebter' in wild capital letters; it was written three days before their deportation.]

Only one more message was received by me, written not long after this last one and immediately before my parents and sister were sent to their deaths on 26 October 1942. Unfortunately it was lost in 1989 as a result of the filming by the BBC of *No Time to Say Goodbye*, but I remember the all-important and ominous phrase 'We are going on a journey ['wir verreisen']. Go on writing to uncle Waldemar Wild.'

I had no idea who this uncle might have been but I exchanged several messages with him. As he too bore the name 'Israel' he must have been

Jewish himself. The burden of his messages was essentially that, as expected, he had no news of my parents. In June 1943 he wrote: 'All our relations have gone on a journey' and in the last message from him in August 1943 he confirms that there has been no further news. The messages then ceased.

These were very anxious times for me. It all sounded thoroughly ominous but what exactly did it mean? I didn't understand why Father's name had been altered to Arthur Israel Baruch. The frequent changes of address were puzzling. Presumably they were driven to seek shelter in smaller and smaller flats and with other Jews. My father's profession on the forms was usually given as 'Krankenpfleger' (male nurse) and I assume that he must have been working in the Jewish hospital (where my sister worked) – a throwback to his time in the German Medical Corps in the First World War, when he had acted as a stretcher bearer. I repeatedly had strange dreams involving a long convoy of grey trucks making their way slowly forward through a gloomy landscape with glowering, red-tinted skies, accompanied by soldiers in grey uniforms. At the same time I developed an intermittent sharp and localised pain in my chest. I was a so-called panel patient entitled to free but second-rate medical treatment, and when I saw a doctor he didn't even bother to examine me. Instead, sitting behind an impressive mahogany desk, he wrote out a prescription for a tonic and that was that. The pain eventually subsided, so perhaps the treatment had worked. In retrospect, it was clearly a typical anxiety symptom. It is rather extraordinary that I was able to function normally and participate in so many activities.

The International Red Cross and its role in wartime

I have wondered over the years how the International Red Cross managed to keep the exchange of messages going during the war. My enquiries with them have yielded ambivalent results, but what became clear is that Jewish refugees benefited from a system set up primarily to allow prisoners of war to communicate with their relatives. Nonetheless it is remarkable that the Nazi authorities should have sanctioned the exchange of messages between their much hated and relentlessly persecuted Jewish population and relatives who had managed to escape.

The reason for this became clear to me a few years ago with the publication of a book by Caroline Moorhead, *Dunant's Dream: War, Switzerland and the History of the Red Cross*. In this she gave an extremely well-researched account of the history of the Red Cross movement, based on Red Cross archives. At a meeting of the International Committee of the Red Cross in October 1942 it was decided to remain silent about the mass deportations that were already in progress and that the committee certainly knew about. All twenty-three members were Swiss, including Carl-Jacob Burckhardt, who had visited two German concentration camps in 1935–36; at that time they were not extermination camps. One member, the Swiss President Philippe Etter, had signed a decree two months previously banning Jewish refugees from seeking shelter in Switzerland. It is clear that the committee wanted to humour the German government, which provided a large slice of the ICRC's budget, and there seems to have been sympathy on the part of some members with the Nazi government. The arguments in favour of silence were that it was more important to safeguard the humanitarian role of the committee, and that by remaining strictly neutral they would not endanger their work with military prisoners. It was even suggested that, were they to draw attention to the plight of European Jews, an angry Hitler might invade their country. There were misgivings on the part of some committee members but Burckhardt and the chairman, a diplomat (Edouard Chapuisat), succeeded in overcoming the moral objections raised by arguing that it would be better to work behind the scenes. Their reasoning seems mendacious and morally bankrupt; it was even argued that by publicising the fate of the Jews it might make matters worse for the victims! If the Red Cross as well as Pope Pius XII (who had been told about the mass slaughter) had alerted the world about what they knew to be happening to Jews in Poland in 1942, it is just possible that Hitler might have been persuaded to moderate his policy of extermination. It is a sobering thought, though Moorhead believes that no protest would have slowed down the destruction of European Jewry. I disagree, for in view of the large number of Catholics in Germany and Austria, public representations by Pius XII supported by the ICRC might conceivably have had some effect.

The failure of the Vatican to intercede on behalf of European Jewry

So far as Pius XII is concerned, his sympathies with Nazi Germany have been well described by John Cornwell in his massive book *Hitler's Pope: the Secret History of Pius XII,* having been given full access to Vatican archives. He set out to exonerate the Pope but found that his accusers had been right all along. The pro-German stance of Pius XII (when he was Eugenio Pacelli) was developed during his sojourn in pre-war Germany as the Vatican's ambassador, and had its origin in his great fear that Soviet communism would overrun Europe. Because he saw Hitler's Germany as a bulwark, he signed a concordat with Hitler in 1933 on behalf of the Vatican. At the same time he fatally undermined the Centre party supported by German Catholics before the war and agreed to its disbandment, despite protests from many bishops. Shortly before his death Pius XI realised that the Vatican's policy was flawed and wrote a statement condemning the Nazis, but this document was suppressed by Pacelli who, a year later (in 1939), was elected to be the new Pope. In 1942 he was fully briefed on what was happening in the Warsaw ghetto and the fate of European Jewry must have been known to him; yet he failed to condemn Hitler's slaughter and didn't even speak out against the deportation of Italian Jews by Mussolini. No wonder Cornwell has described him as 'Hitler's Pope', and that the belated statement on the Holocaust in 1998 by John Paul II was received less than enthusiastically by the Jewish community, especially as plans were already afoot for the sanctification of Pius XII.

All this does not, of course, imply that some individual Catholics and monasteries and convents, both in Germany and in Italy, did not help to save and hide Jews.

Hardly any nation emerges with credit – not even the French. There is no controversy as to the unfortunate results of Switzerland's so-called neutrality during the war, especially the closing of its borders to German and Austrian Jews desperate to find refuge. Thus an international panel of historians concluded in 1999 that the Swiss policy had led to the exclusion or deportation of some twenty thousand people and that this had contributed significantly to the Nazi extermination programme. Nonetheless some thirty thousand had been given sanctuary before the barriers went up. A previous report had already drawn attention to the fact that the Nazis were permitted to transfer large amounts of gold to Swiss banks – much of it stolen from their Jewish victims – and that after the war the accounts of German Jews were frozen, together with the accounts held by non-Jewish German individuals or organisations. There seems to be some controversy as to whether the Swiss government allowed sealed German trains carrying Italian Jews to the death camps to cross Swiss territory, but I have read at least one eyewitness report of such trains stopping off in Zurich. So much for the much-vaunted Swiss neutrality during the war. It pains me to write this, for I adore the Swiss mountains, in which I have made my most exciting alpine climbs and, to use that well-worn cliché, one of my best friends is Swiss!

It was impossible for me at the time to comprehend what life for my family must have been like. In their terse messages my parents could not of course give the slightest hint of how their lives had changed and in what desperate circumstances they lived in Berlin until their deportation. The full horror of it dawned on me only on reading, some years ago, the diaries of Viktor Klemperer (published in Germany as *Ich Will Nicht Zeugnis Ablegen Bis Zum Letzten*). This academic German Jew had been baptised earlier in his life and was married to a non-Jewish woman; this gave him some measure of protection. However, his diaries, kept meticulously on an almost daily basis from 1933 to 1945, show how he was gradually forced to identify with the Jewish community, which in general he despised, and how the screw applied by the Nazi authorities was inexorably tightened day by day from the early 1930s onward. Klemperer's diaries made me realise what deprivations, humiliations and brutalities my family must have experienced. I want to weep every time I think about it, and I do so often. My father's army service in the First World War and his Iron Cross evidently counted for nought. Even Viktor Klemperer, the baptised and academically eminent Jew, was about to be deported and had already been herded into the main railway station when, together with his wife and a small group of Jews who had survived until then in Dresden, he was miraculously saved by the fire bombing of the city late in the war.

I decide to volunteer for the army

Early in the war enemy aliens were not permitted to join the armed forces and I had no particular wish to offer myself for the Pioneer Corps, a non-combatant unit that attracted many male refugees and which, unknown to me at the time, my former teacher Heinz Nadel had joined immediately after arrival in this country in 1939. (So had my cousin Warren Munroe.) However, towards the end of 1943 it was announced that 'friendly enemy aliens' were to be permitted to join the regular army. I saw this as the best possible way of helping my family in Germany – I wasn't to know that by that time they had been murdered – and to help the country that had given me refuge. So in December 1943, at the tender age of eighteen, I volunteered to serve in the Royal Warwickshire Regiment. Although my formal studies for the intermediate examination were due to be completed in the following summer, I offered myself for it six months early and was required to sit the exam in zoology, botany, chemistry and physics in the large hall of the Natural History Museum in London, in the company of hundreds of others. It was an extremely eerie feeling to be in London at a time when it was subjected to bombing raids, and hardly offered the most propitious circumstances. Even now I can hardly look at the museum without recalling this experience. I subsequently learnt that I had passed the first three subjects but failed physics, which came as no surprise in view of my mathematical shortcomings. Unfortunately this meant that I had failed the whole examination.

Chapter Ten: From Refugee to British Army Officer

I have some patchy recollections of my three and a half years of service in the infantry, from January 1944 to the autumn of 1947, for once I had 'done my stuff' I got on with my life and didn't give my military service much further thought. Nonetheless, I have no doubt that my time in the army was highly formative. Not only did I have to become 'British' in double-quick time but I became confident, self-reliant and with a sense of belief in myself. And, whilst I may be a little hazy about precise dates and locations, certain episodes stand out clearly. As it turned out I had a 'good' war, in that I did not have to kill anyone, and my war service provided me with some interesting educational and sporting opportunities.

A painful induction in Glasgow

Having sworn the oath of allegiance to His Majesty King George VI, I was sent for general training to Mary Hill Barracks, Glasgow, where I received a basic grounding in the use of fire-arms and grenades. We were subjected to a rigorous fitness routine, with forced route marches and assault courses, and practised bayonet fighting. 'Square-bashing' and drill were high on the agenda. Some of the drill sergeants were survivors of the First World War and had a tendency to be sadistic to the raw recruits, the vast majority being conscripts and therefore not willing or unable to satisfy their superiors, for whom they had a healthy contempt. Mary Hill (generally known as Merry Hell) Barracks was an eye-opener. Sited in a depressed and neglected part of the city and having been condemned to demolition many years previously, it provided a glum and miserable setting for young recruits. The violence outside was such that we were allowed out at night in pairs only, for fear of being set upon by gangs of ruffians wielding bicycle chains and razors. All the same, the 'normal' Glaswegians were an extraordinarily friendly and hospitable lot: you could hardly walk down Sauchiehall Street without being offered an invitation to a party or a meal.

I was astounded at the obscene language used by my fellow recruits, who were mostly from a working-class background and had a rich vocabulary of swear words that had become part of their everyday language. Having been brought up in the more genteel ambience of Bunce Court I found this quite hard to cope with. Most soldiers smoked, and when we 'fell out for a smoke', as the five-minute break between training sessions was called, I usually found a solitary place where I could continue to read *War and Peace*, which Hanna Bergas had given me as a farewell present. The four volumes were very small and one of them just about fitted into the back pocket of my battle dress. It helped to preserve my sanity, and earned me the reputation of being a bit of an oddball. In fact, had it not been for the fact that I was fit, athletic and easily able to cope with the physical demands placed upon me I might have had a rough time, especially as my accent still marked me out as a foreigner.

At the interview in which it was decided which branch of the army I was to join I expressed a wish to enter the Royal Army Medical Corps, possibly as a stretcher bearer. As this is what my father had been in the First World War (of course on the other side; naturally I didn't say that!), I felt that there was some sort of appealing symmetry to this suggestion. However, I was told that I was too intelligent and fit for that, and it was suggested that I should undertake officer training in the Royal Warwickshire Regiment as an infantryman. I agreed to this and felt flattered to have been offered the opportunity. It is distinctly possible that the decision saved my life, as the training period was lengthy and therefore precluded my being sent to the front when France was invaded in 1944. Having spent a short time, by now a lance-corporal, at the regimental barracks in Warwick, I was sent to pre-OCTU (officer cadet training unit) to commence preliminary training to be an officer.

A change of name

Before I went on one of my leaves I was told that I had better return with an English name, as my German/Jewish name could be fatal for me if I were ever captured by the Germans. As a German national I could conceivably be shot as a traitor – and as a Jew I would be especially at risk. For this reason Jewish refugees serving in the armed forces were required to change their names. I had spent the leave at Trench Hall, as usual, and on my way back via London I suddenly remembered that I hadn't given this any further thought. I wanted to keep my initials, and there weren't many first names starting with L that appealed to me. As the actor Leslie Howard was all the rage at the time I settled for that. But what about a surname? I frantically searched through the London telephone directory and came up with Brent; and thus Leslie Brent was born. When I left the army in 1947 I could have returned to my old name, but rightly or wrongly decided to stick with my English name. There were several reasons for this. First, many people had now known me as Leslie Brent and it seemed cumbersome to change back; even TA seemed to think so. Second, I felt that I wanted to assimilate into British life rather than to be marked as a refugee for the rest of my days. And third, the name Baruch is virtually unpronounceable for English people and I did not like the idea of being called Baroosch or Baruk. I had some misgivings about this decision, as it seemed to signify a turning away from the past and smacked of disloyalty to my family. Half a century later I decided that it was important for me to reconnect with the past and I inserted the name Baruch as my middle name, thus causing least confusion because, as a scientist, I was internationally known by my English name.

The pre-OCTU course that was designed to weed out any misfits was located on top of the Wrotham escarpment in Kent, not many miles from Bunce Court. Apart from the standard military training, which included wild bayonet charges up the steep embankment and instruction in map and compass reading, I was taught to drive and service Jeeps, 15 cwt trucks and motorbikes. Driving through the Kentish roads and lanes at a time when there was virtually no traffic was an eerie experience, and I passed my driving test in the space of a fortnight. I had to take part in an officers selection board, a weekend of hectic group activity in which we were set military problems and given intelligence tests, and I came through that all right. One of the excitements was that the camp was directly under the flight path of the V1 rockets on their way to London, and when an engine cut out one tended to dive under the nearest table. It was an uncomfortable feeling that one of them might, within minutes, demolish houses in London.

Having been selected for training as an officer, I was sent to Morecambe, Lancashire. Here the cadets were given a rigorous two-month course in leadership and other skills, at the end of which I graduated with one pip on my shoulder. I acquired a smart second-hand Sam Browne that I kept in a highly polished state, and a brand new made-to-measure dress uniform. There are only two episodes I want to mention about my stay in Morecambe. I very nearly drowned in a bog one dark night when we had been dropped off individually on the moors in the middle of nowhere, having been given a compass bearing and a map with which to find our way back to barracks. Following my compass reading I suddenly found myself in a deep bog, sinking in deeper with every desperate attempt to extricate myself. This I eventually managed to do, and I arrived back at base very wet and bedraggled. The other was rather more agreeable. I occasionally went to the Saturday evening dances in the local ballroom and there met a charming young woman, Rae Shepherd, with whom I developed a friendly relationship that never went beyond a demure kiss at the end of the evening. I tried to look her up when the war had ended, but was told by her mother that she had since married.

Service in Northern Ireland

Having been commissioned in February 1945 I was posted to Northern Ireland to train soldiers in a camp near Ballykinlar in County Down, close to the Irish Sea and not many miles east of the Mountains of Mourne. This is where I first learnt about the Orange Order and the enmity between Protestants and Catholics, and we were warned not to get involved. Some officers went to Dublin for an occasional weekend; this was permitted provided one went in civilian clothes, as the Irish government evidently felt that British uniforms would be prejudicial to their so-called neutrality. This neutrality was a sham as German agents were said to operate quite freely in the city, and the Irish saw the war as an opportunity for settling old scores with Britain. I preferred an occasional outing to nearby Newcastle, to have a meal and perhaps go to a dance.

Sometimes it fell upon me to travel with a Jeep driver to Downpatrick to collect the cash for the soldiers' weekly pay packets from the bank, and for the first time in my life I found myself handling hundreds of pounds. The soldiers liked me because I treated them with respect, and the fact that I still had a slight German accent didn't seem to bother them. I was one of the few officers who took his task of checking the quality of meals served to the soldiers seriously when going round the mess with the question 'any complaints?' and felt compelled, on occasion, to agree with the complainants that the food was unspeakably bad. Occasionally I was asked by a soldier who had been guilty of some misdemeanour - usually absence without leave or 'dumb insolence' to a non-commissioned officer - to speak on his behalf during the court martial. On the whole this was a thankless task as they were invariably guilty, and all I could do was to plead for leniency.

One of the soldiers at Ballykinlar turned out to be Karl Grossfeld (now Grossfield) from Bunce Court. As officers and soldiers were not allowed to mix socially and we were both keen chess players, we sometimes met in the sand dunes near the camp to have a chat and a game of chess. It relieved the tedium and we both took delight in this clandestine activity. We discussed politics - I was further to the left than Karl so our discussions were quite lively - and the possible post-war scenario in Britain.

Crossing the Irish Sea, when going on leave, could be very
disagreeable as it was usually stormy and the ferries were tossed about. I
enjoyed the train journeys to and from Stranraer, though, especially the
wide-open spaces of Dumfriesshire and Galloway. As an officer I was
expected to travel first class, and at first this caused me some
embarrassment. On my return to Northern Ireland in the autumn of 1945
the scenery seemed to be particularly stunning and the expanse of sky at
dusk extraordinarily beautiful, and I was moved to write some poetry on
the train. I felt melancholic and some of my poems reflected that. The
poem that I re-discovered in my files quite recently, and which strikes me
as still highly topical more than half a century later, was called 'Peace
1945'. Here it is.

> 'We don't want war', say Russians, French and British.
> 'We pray for peace', Americans maintain.
> 'Why, war is truly out of fashion
>   now the atomic bomb has been our gain.'
>
> And so the people crave for peace – or is it an illusion?
> Whilst statesmen sit in conference and quarrel in confusion.
>
> 'We pray for peace,' Americans say
> and take worldwide lend-lease away.
> 'We don't want war,' Russians insist,
> and thump the table with their fist.
>
> 'Our love for peace is France's fame,
> but Western Germany we must claim.'
> 'We British really *are* sincere;
> but leftish views we will not hear.'
>
> And so, whilst statesmen have their say
> humanity slowly dies away.

Plus ça change! I showed the poem to HB at the time. She thought it
was 'nice' but did not encourage me to send it to the *New Statesman*, as I
had proposed to do.

When travelling through London I listened to one or two wonderful
piano recitals by Myra Hess, herself a refugee, given very courageously
weekly in the National Gallery whilst the bombs were still falling, and that
is where I first heard the talented Dennis Matthews, then still in RAF
uniform. I usually stayed overnight with Ulli's ageing mother in Maida
Vale and, on one occasion, in Thilde Weill's flat. On other occasions I

had an army pass for the Strand Palace Hotel, which was comfortable but then much frequented by prostitutes.

Victory in Europe

On VE Day, 13 May 1945, I happened to be passing through London and I joined the celebrating throng in Trafalgar Square. Whilst I wanted to participate I felt horrendously oppressed. I wanted to be joyful but was filled with forebodings about the fate of my family, having previously seen a Pathé News bulletin in a cinema showing the liberation of Bergen-Belsen concentration camp the month before. Those devastating pictures had, for the first time, opened my eyes to the horror of the Holocaust, and I had a terrible and aching premonition that my family had suffered a similar fate. Whilst I felt great relief that the European war was at last over, I could not share the wild elation of those milling around me in Trafalgar Square.

I had been placed on standby for the Far East but was saved from having to fight the Japanese by the two atom bombs, the first dropped on Hiroshima on 6 August and the second three days later on Nagasaki. These devastating bombs may well have saved my life, and at the time I accepted them as an unfortunate if cruel necessity. By ending the war in the Far East abruptly they undoubtedly saved many Allied as well as Japanese military lives, but at the cost of tens of thousands of civilians. I do not, however, believe there was any possible justification for the second bomb, the point having already been made dramatically by the first. Would these bombs have been used on German cities had they been ready in time? I doubt it.

Soon after the end of the war I applied for compassionate leave to visit Berlin, in an attempt to find out what had happened to my family. This was declined. I can only imagine that the army authorities did not let anyone who did not have official duties in Berlin visit this war-ravaged city, which was still in a state of shock and chaos. My second application a year later was successful.

With the British Army on the Rhine

Instead of going to the Far East I was posted to join Montgomery's Eighth Army in Germany in the spring of 1946, and I was seconded to the 1st Battalion of the Worcestershire Regiment. After fighting in North Africa and Italy this unit had been sent to Germany and was stationed at Bad Gandersheim, a pleasant little town east of Celle and Hannover and north-west of the very attractive Harz mountains. To return to Germany as an army officer less than seven years after escaping in a Kindertransport was quite extraordinary: I was now one of the victorious army, and the same people who had persecuted Jews until a year ago were now obsequious and eager to please. Contact with the Germans was at that time still minimal and I had no great wish to deal with them. Our main *raison d'être* in that part of Germany, west of the river Elbe, was to act as a barrier to the Russians who were present in force on the other side of the river, as well as to keep order. Unless it proved to be critically important I did not reveal my knowledge of German, which by that time was somewhat rudimentary, or my German origins.

I seemed to be accepted by my fellow officers, among them some much-decorated professional soldiers who came in the main from a public school background. As might be expected they included both arrogant and condescending men as well as those, like Major A.H. Nott, who were of a gentlemanly disposition. I was ignorant of the military history of most of them. Thus, I only learnt in March 2001, when the obituary of Colonel Bill Bowen MC was published in *The Times,* what a brave and colourful life he had led.

I was allocated a pleasant young private soldier to be my batman. His name was Jack Straw, and the idle thought has crossed my mind that he might have been the recent foreign secretary's father! It's most unlikely. He looked after me well and we developed a good relationship. Every morning he would wake me up with a cup of tea and a biscuit. As I hated drinking tea first thing in the morning and I did not want to give offence I usually poured the tea into the washbasin . . .

Once demobilised I lost touch with my fellow officers, with the exception of Gerry Browton, whom I met again at the University of Birmingham in 1947 and who has remained a lifelong friend. One other, Bob Durrant and his wife Ruth, got in touch with me in 2001 after reading an article about me in the *Mail on Sunday,* and it has been very pleasant to meet them again and to reminisce. (Ruth was an army wife who had joined her husband in Germany, and it was she who had immediately recognised me in my army photograph.) Another officer with whom I became friendly was 'Tug' Wilson, mainly because we had sporting interests in common such as horse riding, dirt track racing and rock climbing. More correctly, it was he who introduced me to all these sports. We were as different as chalk from cheese: he was small, stocky, a bundle of energy, extrovert, given to showing off and positively reckless (he took me rock climbing without the appropriate equipment), and he tried to persuade me to stay on as a professional soldier. It was Tug who nicknamed me 'Cappy' because of my shock of black hair, a name that followed me via Gerry to the Birmingham University hockey team.

Camp for Displaced Persons (DPs) at Delligsen

One of the battalion's duties was to maintain law and order in and around Delligsen camp, which housed people who had been taken by the Germans from Poland and possibly some other eastern countries and used as slave labour. Housing conditions in Nissen huts were primitive and, as might have been expected, relations between the DPs and the local populations were fraught to say the least. I served in A Company and my platoon was given a tour of duty in Delligsen, lasting several weeks. I had my headquarters in a requisitioned house not far from the camp, and it was my responsibility to inspect the camp daily by walking through the Nissen huts, accompanied by my sergeant, to ensure that all was peaceful. I invariably did this with a heavy heart, not merely because the conditions were so pitiful – there was a disagreeably distinctive musty smell compounded of unwashed clothes, wood smoke, stale cooking and cheap tobacco – but also because I couldn't help wondering whether my parents might conceivably be among these people.

I was approached by one or two young Poles, who asked whether they could challenge my platoon to a game of football. Several matches were arranged and I captained my team; these games undoubtedly helped to raise morale in the camp. One less than agreeable incident that I witnessed was the interrogation of a Pole by a major in the Military Police. The Pole had been accused by some local Germans of stealing, and the interrogating officer used physical violence in an attempt to extract a confession from the alleged culprit – a fist blow to the jaw, which drew some blood. As a junior officer I felt unable to intervene on the spot, but I reported the incident to Battalion HQ; I suspect that was the end of it. I was deeply shocked that a British officer should be capable of such behaviour, though I dare say that it was not unique.

A very curious episode

I had become a keen horseman as the regiment had a string of fine horses captured from the German army, which in turn had taken them from the Polish cavalry. One of our officers had brought his pack of foxhounds from England to our barracks and, in the absence of foxes in that part of Germany, drag hunts were organised regularly. I thoroughly enjoyed these: the ritual of the stirrup cup on a frosty morning, the red hunting jacket worn by the major and the blowing of the horn as the hunt moved off, the excited yelping of the hounds, the unpredictability of the hunt as only the person who had laid the trail knew where it was to lead, my sense of joy at staying in the saddle as my horse jumped fences and hedgerows, and my amusement when spotting a Brigadier's hat rolling on the ground.

I have never taken part in a real fox hunt and nor would I wish to; and I have never understood the fuss made by those who feel that the abolition of fox-hunting would be the end of the world. What's wrong with drag hunts? Admittedly, laying an aniseed trail might be tricky in territory inhabited by foxes . . .

Whilst stationed in Delligsen I frequently went for a ride on my favourite chestnut along nearby lanes, and among the houses I passed was one from which a youngish woman had observed me on several occasions. Indeed, I once spotted her leaning out of her window and I gave her a chivalrous wave of the hand. One day I was astounded to be told that a German woman had called at my HQ house, wishing to speak to me personally. I suggested that she should be shown up to my bedroom/office, and a strange and faintly unsettling interview took place. She became tearful and told me about her father, who had been arrested because of alleged Nazi sympathies, and she protested his innocence. Could I possibly intervene on his behalf? The woman was buxom and attractive, probably in her late twenties, and was poised to embrace me had I given her the slightest encouragement. Though there was something distinctly erotic in this encounter I decided to be totally correct in my response. I explained that as I did not know anything about her father's past there was nothing I could do. I was sure, I said, that justice would be done and that, if innocent, he would be released before long. After the woman composed herself and had left there was a certain amount of smirking among the men who had escorted her to my room, as the interview, which was conducted in German, lasted quite a while, and no doubt they had drawn what were to them the obvious (but wrong) conclusions.

Naturally we had our share of parade ground drill, with or without a band (I have become rather 'allergic' to military bands), firearms drill and spit and polish, and I remember a visit by General Montgomery for which irritatingly meticulous preparations had to be made. For example all white lines or posts, and there were plenty of them, had to be repainted. The great man addressed the multitude out in the open with a mixture of ingratiating chumminess and lordly hauteur and I had the feeling that at least some of the men, who cheered him enthusiastically at the end of his speech (weren't they expected to?) saw through the façade of a man who, whilst having achieved some famous victories, has recently been judged (at least by some) to have had a flawed personality (see, for instance, Nigel Hamilton's *The Full Monty*).

On the whole I had a pretty good time in Gandersheim. I was permitted to play hockey for the battalion and to compete in its team in cross-country running races (I have a silver medal to show for it). My only injury sustained in the army, apart from a boxing injury I'll mention again a little later, arose from a game of 'mess hockey', played indoors and almost certainly instigated by Tug Wilson after a mess dinner involving a few glasses of wine. I fell off a chair on which I was standing (heaven knows why) and sustained a gash over my left eye – the second time in my life that I injured myself by falling off a chair. An embarrassing photograph on horseback, with a large plaster over the eye, will forever remind me of that foolish evening. One or two of us also made a weekend trip to Goslar, which was an army rest centre, and the beautiful Harz mountains.

Compassionate leave in Berlin

Before my unit was transferred to Trieste I applied once again for compassionate leave to visit Berlin, which was due east of us and not all that many miles away. This time I was successful, and my unit provided me with a jeep and a driver to take me there. We had to cross the Soviet Zone and the long drive along roads with deep ruts and potholes flanked by ruined houses filled me with awful forebodings.

Although I had of course heard about the destruction of Berlin through Allied bombing and German house-to-house fighting against the Russians in the last weeks of the war, nothing could have prepared me for what I encountered. I could barely believe my eyes, such was the scale of the destruction, and it was hard to credit that hundreds of thousands of people continued to live in this ruined urban landscape. I would be dishonest to claim that I did not experience some *schadenfreude*: weren't these the people who had supported that madman Adolf Hitler right to the very end and who were, however indirectly, responsible for the fate of the Jewish population, and had blighted my childhood? At the same time it was impossible not to feel pangs of compassion when watching poorly dressed and clearly hungry and wan-looking women picking through the ruins in the hope of finding something of use. Whilst I had heard of the pillaging, raping and brutality of the Soviet soldiers when they first entered the city I was unaware of the horrendous scale of all this until I came across Anthony Beevor's book, *Berlin: the Downfall*.

I had been given three days' leave, and did not have time to dwell on any of this. My first thought was to visit the last address my parents had given me in a Red Cross message, and with beating heart I knocked on the door of what was a so-called garden flat on the third floor of a block, which was approached from the inner courtyard. Miraculously the building had remained intact. A pinched and cagey woman opened the door. Had she known a Jewish family named Baruch who had lived in this flat until October 1942? She professed to know nothing at all. My next port of call was to the town hall authorities, housed in temporary accommodation somewhere near the city centre. There they looked up some dossiers and eventually found my parents' and my sister's names, listed as 'sent east'. This was the first sickening confirmation I had of their deportation from Berlin, and the rest was left to my feverish imagination. I could not take the search any further, and from then on assumed that they had been murdered in a concentration camp, probably in Auschwitz. It was only decades later that I discovered what had really happened.

My Berlin visit left me devastated, although it provided me with no proof of my family's death. I didn't know the precise details of their deportation – 'sent east' could have meant anything - but I put the worst construction on this information and assumed that they were no longer alive. Because of the element of uncertainty and my ignorance of where they had died, and the absence of a grave, I could not properly grieve at the time and found it very difficult to do so in the following years. It was not until I visited Auschwitz concentration camp many years later, in 1976, where I erroneously thought they must have perished, that I broke down for the first time and wept uncontrollably. Similar information later came to light concerning my uncle and aunt, my grandmother and my cousin Ruth and her very young family. Apart from a maternal uncle and cousin, who had managed to find their way to England and the United States respectively, no-one was left. My way of coping with this tragic state of affairs was to display a stiff upper lip, to sweep some of this emotional baggage under the carpet and to immerse myself to the full in everyday living. Even so, whenever I saw a film taken in the Theresienstadt ghetto or elsewhere I anxiously looked for the faces of my parents and my sister. Had they miraculously survived they would surely have tried to get in touch with me at the Bunce Court address.

A pleasant interlude in Trieste

My battalion was moved south to Trieste in September 1946 as Brigade Mobile Reserve. Trieste is a major port in the north-eastern bay (the Gulf of Venice) of the Adriatic Sea, and although it had once been part of the Austro-Hungarian Empire it had been ceded to Italy after the First World War. In 1945 its nationality was disputed again and it became the centre of a power struggle between the Russians and the Yugoslavs on the one hand and the Western Allies on the other. The port is located at the northern apex of the Istrian peninsula, with the port of Pola near the southern end, and there was severe tension between the Italians and the Yugoslavs. Soon after the war the peninsula became part of Yugoslavia and whilst we were billeted in Trieste the town of Pola was handed over to the Yugoslavs under the army's supervision. There was a mass exodus of Italians from the town and for several days, before Yugoslavs moved in, it was a ghost town.

My platoon was given the task of patrolling the border between the Yugoslav peninsula and the karst, a rocky and desolate limestone plateau surrounding the eastern part of Trieste. We were quartered in rather primitive accommodation but enjoyed the feeling of independence and of doing something useful. The intention was to ensure that there was no overt friction between the Italians and Yugoslavs. We were there for several weeks but nothing untoward happened.

I liked Trieste and one evening went to a trotting race meeting near our barracks. This was a delightful and for me unique experience, and it was interesting to mingle with an excitable Italian crowd. A visit to the opera house to hear *Lohengrin* was rather less successful. This was my first Wagner opera – indeed my first opera - and I cannot say that I greatly enjoyed the evening; it was sweltering, and the opera began very late and finished well after midnight. The Italian cast, for whom acting was evidently not a natural talent, made it seem rather ludicrous; the swan juddering across the stage, getting stuck a few times on the way, added to the unintended comedy. Not quite what Wagner had in mind.

I continued playing hockey, being captain of the battalion's team, and thanks to a new influx of Austrian horses I was able to indulge my new passion for riding. An inter-company novices boxing competition was organised with a view to establishing a battalion team. 'Lieut. F.B. Wilson is still with us, but unfortunately he cannot be classed as a novice this time', the *Regimental Gazette* stated. It was this very same Tug Wilson who persuaded me to fill a vacancy in the middleweight division, on the dubious grounds that I was a fit young man. I had never worn boxing gloves in my life, and after a few minutes of practice in the ring I was left to fend for myself. With the help of a walkover in the first round and wins on points in the second round and in the semi-final, I was duly knocked out in the final by a professional soldier with extensive boxing experience. To add insult to injury our medical officer did not have the wit to diagnose a broken nose, and I suffered the consequence of not having it reset until I underwent an operation some fifteen years later. Curiously I have maintained an interest in boxing ever since, and a few years ago took the trouble to wake up in the dead of night to listen to the radio broadcast of Lennox Lewis's epic fight against the odious Mike Tyson, which established Lewis as the undisputed heavyweight champion of the world. Crazy? Probably.

Gerry Browton and I, and one or two of the other junior officers, occasionally went swimming off Miramare beach to cool off. Although fraternising with the 'enemy' was still frowned upon I struck up a friendly relationship – purely platonic – with a very young woman who tended to swim from the same part of the beach, and I learnt a few Italian phrases from her that have stood me in good stead later in life. These minor forays apart I didn't really get to know Trieste and, according to the delightful book, *Trieste and the Meaning of Nowhere*, by Jan Morris, who was there as a young (male) officer at roughly the same time, I missed a great opportunity – though admittedly I spent only six months there. Clearly both the history and the cultural background of this port are remarkable. James Joyce wrote some of his novels there and it once had a thriving and influential Jewish community. A large synagogue was built in Byzantine style in 1912 and, having been used by the Germans as a bullion depot, it survived the war relatively undamaged. Some of the city's Jews fled in 1942 when the Germans took over the city following the signing of the armistice between Italy and the Allies, but more than 700 were killed or deported from the local concentration camp of San Sabba, previously a rice treatment plant. This has since become a national memorial.

I had the good fortune to be sent not only on a sports instructors' course, from which I graduated with the qualification (never used!) of a professional soccer referee (third division), but also to Cortina d'Ampezzo, which had been taken over as a British Army rest centre. There I learnt to ski, a sport which I came to love.

Back to Germany: the Lüneburger Heide

In the early spring of 1947 the battalion was moved back to Germany, this time to barracks on the Lüneburger Heide, east of Hannover. The train journey north, through the Alps, was incredibly beautiful but also very slow and tedious. We arrived in Hannover and were escorted to a basement restaurant, where we were greeted by a string quartet playing sentimental tunes such as 'Back to Sorrento' and bits of Mozart's *Eine Kleine Nachtmusik*. All this struck the wrong chord with me: the victors being greeted by the subservient vanquished. We were soon routed to the Lüneburger Heide, a vast expanse of heath and woodland, where the whole brigade became involved with Operation Woodpecker. Its objective was the extraction of thousands of tons of timber, to be sent to Britain to help with the rebuilding of our bombed cities. The felling was carried out with military precision but with the reluctant cooperation of the German foresters, who encouraged us to spare 'seed trees' to help with the regeneration of the forests. Each company vied with the others in a daily competition to extract the heaviest load of timber, which was taken to Hannover in 30-ton trucks. A genuine camaraderie developed between officers (well, some!) and men, and barrack square drill was kept to the minimum. Whilst, in a sense, we were plundering the German forests I saw some poetic justice in all this, and felt that this period of my army life, which continued until my demobilisation in the summer of 1947, at least achieved something tangibly useful. Meanwhile I had been promoted to acting captain, and as I was still barely twenty-two years old I felt rather proud of this.

On falling in love

Needless to say, Bunce Court School was indirectly responsible for my falling in love. I was on leave in the late autumn of 1946 and naturally gravitated to Bunce Court, the school having returned to Kent from Shropshire. As I arrived dinner was being served, and as I came down the stairs I spotted a young woman unknown to me sitting at TA's table. She stood out because she was wearing a Dutch folk costume with a lace cap, and she struck me as remarkably beautiful. I immediately fell in love with her. It turned out that Karin Jonker had come from the Netherlands to be a housemother, having read about the school in a Quaker magazine. Her family lived in Utrecht, and as she had received some training as a hospital nurse TA offered her a post for a year. We soon developed a friendship, and my feelings for her were reciprocated. Karin was, not surprisingly, popular with the older boys, and it is perhaps fair to describe her as the Zuleika Dobson of Bunce Court. (Max Beerbohm's witty novel was based on Oxford University.) Our relationship developed during another visit the following year, when she had returned for another six months' stay until the school's closure. As it was summertime I slept in a small tent near the tennis court area, and on several mornings I was woken up by the delectable scent of honeysuckle, held under my nose by Karin. I have been rather partial to honeysuckle ever since. We had one nocturnal tryst in her tiny bedroom cubicle in the isolation hut. It was passionate and joyous and wonderful – the first time that either of us had slept with anyone – but the need for absolute silence (TP was not far down the corridor and the walls were flimsy) and the narrowness and shortness of the child-size bed were unwelcome constraints. It was nonetheless one of those beautiful moments in one's life that stays in the memory. I had always assumed that we had managed to preserve secrecy,, but Karin recently told me that TP, HB and Heidtsche knew about it . . .

I visited Karin in her parents' house in Utrecht on two occasions. The first time I got off a troop train she was waiting for me on the otherwise empty platform, to be greeted by a storm of wolf whistles. Her parents were very pleasant people and her father took us out in his sailing boat on one of the inland seas. This gave me a wonderful introduction to sailing and encouraged me later, when in Southampton, to accept an invitation to 'crew' whenever it came my way. My second visit was in 1948, at the end of a strenuous but absolutely entrancing hitchhiking tour across France and into Italy as far as Rome, made in the company of Ulli. By now things had moved on for Karin, and she had come to the conclusion that although she was very fond of me this rather serious, older man with his experiences of Nazi Germany and of the British army, and destined to go to university, was not really for her, much as she loved me. It was probably one of those exceedingly sensible decisions, though it left me bereft. And so we parted, but not before some very pleasant days spent together with other former pupils in Bunce Court after it had closed down, talking endlessly in a rather melancholy manner – conscious of the end of an era – and listening to a hoard of 78rpm gramophone records that someone had unearthed. These included a wide range of classical music, such as the Beethoven and Mendelssohn violin concerti. This is when I first heard the Brahms clarinet quintet, and it has remained one of my great favourites. Karin became one of Holland's first TV presenters, married a Dutch businessman and had two children. We have remained good friends.

Although I was due to be demobbed in October 1947 I was permitted to go on final leave as early as July, so that I could make preparations for entry to Birmingham University, including an entrance examination. I received my demob suit, a pleasant letter from the War Office thanking me for my services to King and Country and informing me that I was about to be gazetted as hon. lieutenant and that I could use that title henceforth. Unlike the infamous Captain Robert Maxwell I was never tempted to do so. So far as I was concerned I had done my duty, and my army life rapidly faded from my memory. However, I was recently persuaded to join the Association of Jewish ex-Servicemen and Women (AJEX), and in 2007 I attended the annual Remembrance Parade in Whitehall, as well as the separate AJEX parade on the following Sunday. I found both to be surprisingly moving.

That same summer my friend Ernst Weinberg and I decided to take a camping holiday in the Lake District before his departure to the United States. We spent a week in his small tent pitched in a low-lying field near Derwentwater and we had hopes of walking up several mountains. In the event it rained cats and dogs that week and we spent quite a lot of time huddled in our tent, reading, with the field getting soggier and soggier. Eventually we took refuge in a farmer's barn. Ernst has reminded me that I was wearing my officer's demob shoes rather than boots and that I insisted on continuing our limited walks even after one heel had come off. Our friendship has survived that experience.

A postscript

I had spent three and a half years, between the age of eighteen and twenty-two, in the army. I do not regard it in the least as having been a waste of time, for four reasons. First, although I did not have to fight I felt that I had done everything in my power to help in the defeat of Nazi Germany. Second, I learnt a great deal that was to stand me in good stead later on and that enriched my subsequent life. Third, it was a powerful spur to the forging of a British identity, with which I have felt entirely happy ever since. And fourth, it enabled me to claim an ex-serviceman's grant from the Ministry of Education that enabled me to embark on the next important step – study at university.

Chapter Eleven: Study Years: Birmingham University

J wanted to become a schoolteacher, but if it had not been for my friend Peter Stoll the idea of finding a grant enabling me to study for a degree would almost certainly not have occurred to me. We met when on leave early in 1947 – he was in the Royal Engineers and had served in Burma – and he mentioned that he had applied to the Ministry of Education for an ex-servicemen's grant to study chemistry at Birmingham University. Why don't you apply, too? he asked. Thus it was that in July 1947 I received notification that, under the Further Education and Training Scheme, I had been allocated a grant of £236 per annum to study zoology at Birmingham University for a period of four years. The decisive factor had been my part-time studies in Birmingham and the fact that they were interrupted by my war service. All that toil and sweat at the Central Technical College had not been wasted.

My choice of Birmingham was influenced by several factors: my previous knowledge of the city, my service in the Royal Warwickshire Regiment, and the fact that both Peter and my army friend Gerry Browton had already been accepted by the university. In the event it proved to be an extremely good decision, and I spent four very happy and productive years there that shaped my future life professionally as well as personally.

321 Hagley Road: a cosmopolitan and bohemian boarding house

Having led a communal life for many years I was disinclined to apply for a place in one of the halls of residence. I cannot remember who pointed me in the direction of Doris Coleman, who ran a boarding house in Edgbaston, within a couple of miles of the university campus. The house was a large, shambling, Victorian building that had clearly seen better days.

Doris was a most unusual landlady and ran, not surprisingly, an unusual establishment. All manner of people found a home there, from a very elderly and charming Viennese lady (Mrs Helene Reif) and a younger, rather fastidious German refugee (Liesel Sternberg) of uncertain age, who was very keen on music but seemed sad and lonely, to a bunch of university students, a would-be actress, and visitors from abroad, including a couple of supercilious young men from Paris (Paul and Pierre) who had come over to improve their already pretty good English. I was allocated a room on the first floor, which I could enter only by walking through the room of a young Czech working for his PhD in chemistry, Paul Cucka. My room was soon filled with books and documents that spilled on to the floor, especially at exam time, so that one had to tread carefully between them. I decided that I was not a tidy person by nature and that there was no point in trying to fight against this defect in my character. (It remains a bone of contention with my wife Carol.) An important piece of furniture was my newly acquired wireless, and listening to the Third Programme (the precursor to Radio 3) late at night was not only immensely enjoyable but enabled me to get to know and love a wide repertoire of music. Those were the years of the BBC's satirical comedies *ITMA* ('It's that man again') and *Take it From Here*, and we sometimes listened to those deliriously funny radio shows over dinner.

One of the residents had been Heinz Redwood (Sir Andrew Aguecheek) from Bunce Court, but we did not overlap as he left Birmingham after completing his PhD in chemistry just before my arrival. In writing about Doris Coleman I am greatly indebted to him for some of the details.

'Doris's origins are certainly lost in the mists of time,' he wrote to me. She had been a ballet teacher but had given up her career largely because she had to look after her aged and very demanding mother. There was something distinctly bohemian about her and the way she ran her establishment which, apart from lodgers of various hues, also housed a cat, Blackie. This much mollycoddled and cooed-over creature spent a fair amount of its life in the kitchen, and feline as well as human hairs could occasionally be detected in one's food as Blackie had not learnt that squatting on a joint of meat was not the done thing. Doris did all the cooking and, having a heart of gold, often kept a meal warm for someone arriving late for dinner. She was a small, bright-eyed, cheerful woman with a twinkle in her eyes and a high-pitched voice, extremely kind but not averse to making the odd sardonic, if not catty, remark about someone she thought pompous or who had fallen foul of her. Among her boarders were a Hungarian couple who had been displaced persons. They quarrelled endlessly and noisily in their top floor garret – so much so that once or twice I was sent up to the top floor to prevent the violent husband from assaulting his placid, shy and rather pleasant wife. There were also one or two Poles, with one of whom Doris developed a close friendship and who gave her much practical and moral support as she grew older. According to Heinz, the most colourful boarders were theatre people, but that was before my time. Paul Scofield, then a rising star, his wife Joy Parker and their baby apparently stayed there, as well as other actors from the Birmingham Rep. A group of us from no. 321, including Doris, saw Paul Scofield as Hamlet in Stratford-on-Avon. He was already a fine actor but I didn't care for his nasal twang, which struck me as affected and which he never quite shed. Another Old Bunce Courtian was Peter Morland (formerly Meyerstein), who was studying music at the university's Barber Institute and whose violin practice scales weren't always easy to live with.

Doris was a kindly soul, and no. 321 became a well-known refuge for many people who had cause to be grateful to her. I cannot remember what she charged me, but Heinz paid £1 15s per week, reduced from £2 because his total income was £3. Heinz met her again in the late 1970s because she had bought a holiday cottage in Essex not far from his own home. She died in 1989 at the age of ninety.

Sunday afternoons were enlivened by concerts given in the town hall by the City of Birmingham Symphony Orchestra, at that time conducted by George Weldon. He was an energetic, showy conductor who had a large female fan club, always sitting behind the orchestra so that the object of their adoration was seen head on. He took the orchestra through the classical repertoire and I got to know, and love, the Beethoven and Brahms symphonies and much else. He was not the greatest of conductors but he pulled in the crowds and kept Birmingham's orchestral tradition alive; it came to a glorious flowering in the '90s under the magical baton of Simon Rattle.

Having left the army as Captain Brent with a 'Discharge of Aliens: Identity Certificate' dated 27 September 1947, I received my Certificate of Naturalisation on 14 October, a rapid transition from loyal alien to loyal citizen. Thus began my British citizenship, with which I have since felt entirely happy.

The university

I entered the university rather starry-eyed, thinking that it would prove to be that great cauldron of intellectual cut and thrust that one reads about in novels. Despite the fact that the majority of my intake were ex-servicemen and women and therefore much older than those who had come straight from school, it wasn't quite like that – and I was a trifle disappointed. However, in every other way the university lived up to expectations. It had a fine campus with an impressive clocktower, affectionately known as 'Big Joe' after Joseph Chamberlain, the university's founder and first president. The tower was modelled on the Mangia campanile in Siena but was defiantly built in red brick, like the rest of the university. An important and unusual feature of the university was that the playing fields were right on site.

Among the outstanding scientists working in the university whilst I was there was (later Sir) Rudolf Peierls, a refugee atomic physicist who had constructed the first British nuclear accelerator. He triggered the British government into action by calculating that the Germans had the capacity to develop an atomic bomb, and later worked on the Manhattan Project at Los Alamos.

In my preliminary year, egged on by Ken Tomlinson, the captain of the university hockey team, I tried unsuccessfully to transfer my registration to the medical school ('you've got a place in a good science department,' said the gruff Dean in my two-minute interview, 'so you stick to it'). So I settled into the first year of the three-year honours zoology degree course. The Dean, well known for his lack of empathy with students, unwittingly took the right decision for me as it turned out, for had I gone on to become a doctor I would certainly not have met the charismatic Professor Peter Medawar and become an immunologist. Medawar later told me that the 1948 intake had been by far the brightest he had ever had. It included Desmond Morris, later of *Naked Ape* fame. Desmond was an interesting artist whose paintings were inspired by biological forms, probably influenced by Dali, Klee and Miró, and my class commissioned him one year to paint a caricature of me. It was presented to me on my birthday and still hangs in our house.

I took my studies seriously and enjoyed them. The lecturers were very approachable, and among the demonstrators in practical classes, though not on the academic staff, was Rupert Billingham, a research fellow working with Medawar. The lectures were good, and Medawar's lectures on embryology and immunology were especially stimulating. I shall have much more to say about him in my next chapter, but he was an outstanding lecturer who managed to convey the basics of statistics even to the least numerate student, and was inspirational so far as embryology and immunology were concerned. Nonetheless, I soon became embroiled in other activities in my spare time.

Immediately after my enrolment I signed up to become a member of the hockey club and was selected for the first team. As it had a very good centre-half I was converted into a left-back, and that remained my position for the remainder of my playing years. As home games alternated with away games at other universities or clubs much travelling by coach was involved, and most Wednesday and Saturday afternoons were fully engaged, often into the evenings. I continued playing into my penultimate year, a rather daft thing to have done as it competed with my studies. However, the team was a very good one and did consistently well in the inter-university championships, and I loved playing. During the Easter vacation we usually took a team called The Mermaids to the Weston-super-Mare Hockey Festival, a most enjoyable, strenuous and usually highly successful event that introduced me to the joys of drinking bitter ale. (A mermaid is one of the symbols on the university crest.)

My other major commitment was to the Guild of Undergraduates (the students' union), to which all students belonged and which ran, semi-autonomously, a large building with a debating hall, common rooms, bars, billiards room, restaurant and other facilities. At that time students numbered about 3,500 – minuscule compared with today's numbers. Nevertheless, the guild supported a large number of sporting, social, political and religious clubs, including the Communist Society and the Jewish Society, all of which had rules that had to conform to the guild's constitution. I joined neither but in my final year, when I was President of the guild, their existence proved to be of considerable significance.

I began to take an interest in the guild's affairs in my second year, especially in external matters relating to our membership of the National Union of Students (NUS) and the International Union of Students (IUS). The NUS tends to oscillate politically from left to right and back again; at that time it was distinctly leftish, too much so for many members of our middle-of-the-road student body. IUS was very left wing and was busy forging links with student bodies in Eastern Europe and the Soviet Union, so that many student unions up and down the country favoured disaffiliation from the NUS. In Birmingham it was decided to support continued membership in the hope that it would be possible to influence policy from within.

It was in this spirit that the guild decided to send a team of observers to the International Festival of Youth and Students held in Budapest in 1949. They were to observe objectively what transpired there and to report back. The delegation consisted of Peter Goode, an arch-Tory who was possessed of a mordant wit, one staunch trades unionist named John Clewes, my friend Gerry Browton and myself. With the financial help of the guild we travelled to Budapest by train, spending a few days in Czechoslovakia (where Clewes had two charming female friends!), all of us wearing the same distinctive knitted woollen hats for the entire lengthy journey. The train's benches were hard, and great demands were made on our bottoms, patience, stamina and tolerance of each other's foibles. (My friendship with Gerry survived all this; in the 1950s we were each other's 'best man'.) I had told Anna Essinger of my plan and she disapproved strongly, as this was at the height of the Cold War and she felt that I might be prejudicing my future by attending what was thought to be essentially a Communist beano.

That is exactly what it turned out to be, and I suspect we may have been the only foreign non-Communists in a city that thronged with tens of thousands of young party members from all over the world, wearing blue shirts with badges and enthusiastically carrying small national flags. Budapest was beautiful, though still carrying the scars of war; one of the main bridges had been rebuilt and restoration of palaces and public buildings was in progress. On entering a post office to send a card I was embraced by an elderly woman with tears in her eyes when she realised that I came from England. For her, this contact with someone from the west was an overwhelmingly joyous and significant occasion, and I felt I had justified my presence in Budapest.

Gerry Browton has reminded me that at the opening ceremony a doctor, who was sitting behind us with his family and had listened to us speaking English, invited us, very much sotto voce, to supper. We had an agreeable and strictly clandestine evening with his family that gave our visit a deliciously subversive twist. The festival entertainments were on a vast and lavish scale; I remember best a performance of *A Midsummer Night's Dream* in a huge open-air theatre in one of the parks, which included horses on stage. There were rallies and concerts and processions – all in the highly organised Soviet tradition, and we were urged to sign a petition supporting one of the Communist liberation movements in some far-flung country. I sidestepped that request by signing with a nonsensical signature, thus remaining courteous to our hosts but true to my conscience. Gerry Browton recalls that the politically decadent Birmingham delegation chose to visit the celebrated and historic Turkish baths instead of going on a group expedition to watch the Young Pioneers at work – a visit of which I have no recollection at all. The whole trip was extraordinary and instructive, and our joint report was well received by the council of the Guild of Undergraduates.

Parts of my vacations were nearly always spent in Bunce Court, the school having returned to its Kentish premises. TA and TP, and of course Heidtsche, always welcomed me with open arms, and as TA was virtually blind by then I spent many hours reading to her. One of the books was Stephen Spender's autobiography, and I recall being struck by the fact that, although the Jewishness of one of his grandparents had been kept from him until he was in his twenties he had, nonetheless, always felt a special empathy with Jewish people. It is on one of these visits that I met Annemarie Meyer, secretary to the Warburg Institute, who had preceded me at Bunce Court and was also spending some days in the school. We became very close and spent one delightful holiday in France, where we visited some friends of hers in the south. We were hitchhiking, and I have a hazy memory of walking up the Col du Galibier, between Chambéry and Briançon, one of our car lifts having terminated near the bottom of the mountain pass. As I was wearing shorts it seemed pretty cold up there. It was Annemarie who introduced me to such delicacies as moules marinière, which has remained a great favourite of mine and which I cook occasionally, and the deliciously foul Gauloise bleu, one of which I smoke symbolically every summer in our house in the Dordogne. Of greater importance was my introduction, through her, to Benjamin Britten's music when we went to hear his *Serenade for Horn, Tenor and Strings* – with Peter Pears and Dennis Brain, of course. I cannot think of any other modern chamber work that so engages the ear and the emotions as well as the intellect, based as it is on some of the finest poems in the English language. Only a genius could have embellished such beautiful poetry. Annemarie was several years older than me, and at the time that seemed to me like an unbridgeable gap. We parted ways once Joanne burst on to the scene but remained good friends. She died a few years ago.

Iris Origo

One other summer vacation, in 1948, is well worth recalling. Ulli and I were planning to go on a hitchhiking trip through France and into Italy, hoping to get as far as Rome. I mentioned this to TA and she encouraged us to visit Iris Origo, the Englishwoman who had married an Italian count and had been a good friend to Bunce Court School. She lived in Florence but had a villa in the hills south of that city. TA told me that she would write to her to find out whether she would welcome a visit from us. The answer soon came back: yes, she would be delighted to see us, but as she would be spending the summer in her country villa could we make our way there?

Our trip went wonderfully well as hitchhiking was still comparatively easy then, especially wearing our khaki shorts and with a small Union Jack stuck on the back of our army rucksacks, while army issue water bottles and one or two pots and pans dangled from them. Motorists were remarkably kind to us. We walked whenever we were without a lift and either camped or stayed in youth hostels. The night's camping in the municipal park on the seafront at Cannes was memorable because we woke up early in the morning to find an army of ants marching through the tent, and because a policeman – fortunately reasonably well disposed – popped his head into the tent wondering why we were camping on a municipal lawn. We made our way to Florence and towards the end of our trip to Venice, where we stayed in a youth hostel on the Lido. Both cities excited us hugely by their beauty and their cultural wealth, and we walked ourselves off our feet trying to see as much as possible in our three-day stays.

The bus journey from Florence to the village near Iris Origo's villa was a fascinating experience, rivalled only by the 'Bantry Flyer' from Cork to the Bay of Bantry. It was a very hot day and the bus was packed with people and luggage and hens in baskets, much of the luggage having been stored precariously on the roof. The bus stopped in every village, in each of which it was met by a crowd of friends and relatives who greeted the arrivals noisily and with great excitement, kissing and embracing endlessly. The stops seemed to be interminable, especially as the driver, to our alarm, tended to disappear into the local bars. Eventually we arrived at our destination, extremely tired and overheated and wondering what kind of reception awaited us.

It seemed like a very long walk from the village to the villa, through olive groves and vineyards and up a long hill along a dusty track. The afternoon sun was beating down mercilessly and we must have looked a pretty sight, wearing our khaki shorts and carrying our huge rucksacks. On arrival at the imposing-looking villa at the top of the hill we rang the bell and a butler wearing white gloves opened the door. We explained who we were, and the butler seemed remarkably unfazed by our appearance. Iris soon appeared. She proved to be a delightful and highly intelligent and well-informed woman. Alas, TA had told me very little about her background – I didn't even know that she was born in Gloucestershire of an aristocratic mother (Lady Cybil Cuffe) and a wealthy American father – and we were fascinated to hear a little about her wartime experiences in Italy over dinner. Only much later did I read her book *War in Val d'Orcia*, published in 1947, in which she vividly describes her life in Tuscany before and during the war, where she and her husband, the Marchese Antonio Origo, had a large farm. She was a close friend of prominent anti-Fascists and looked after orphaned children in a home she established close to the farm. She also risked her life assisting escaped British prisoners of war. It is therefore not surprising that she was awarded the gold medal of the Italian Red Cross and created a DBE. She will be best remembered for her books, which included an autobiography (*Images and Shadows*) and a scholarly and well-researched book on the life of an Italian merchant (*The Merchant of Prado*). She died in June 1988 at the age of eighty-five.

This, then, was the woman who sat facing us over an exquisitely laid dining table and who acted as a most gracious hostess. We must have seemed remarkably ignorant to her, and I cringe when I think about it now. (A socially even more embarrassing situation arose in recent years when Carol and I were invited to dinner by a German film director and his wife. If names had been mentioned they had passed me by, and I realised only when it was too late that two of the other guests had been the well-known playwright Michael Frayn and his equally famous wife, the writer Claire Tomalin.) Iris was extremely well informed about international political affairs and was keen to hear our views on the situation in Britain, as well as how we felt about the Labour government. We stayed two nights under her roof – it was heavenly to sleep between clean and immaculately ironed sheets – and made our way to Rome, where we spent three days sightseeing. Although I corresponded with Iris briefly I unfortunately lost touch with her.

Climbing in the Hohe Tauern mountains; and a note on global warming

In the summer of 1949 I joined a small climbing party organised by the NUS – a five-day tour in the Hohe Tauern mountains, including Grossglockner, the highest peak in Austria (12,461m). There were three of us from the UK, though one came along mainly because of his interest in photography and he turned out to be something of a liability, having to be coaxed along delicate ridges, roped up in the middle. Our guide was a highly competent Austrian medical student. We began by climbing Ankogel and stayed in several high huts. The whole trip was hugely exciting and enjoyable, and for me, who had never before climbed a major peak, Grossgockner was an eye-opener. This experience encouraged me to undertake later climbs in Switzerland.

What struck me forcibly was the size of the Pasterze glacier, which we had to ascend before reaching the mountain itself. The Austrian authorities had taken the trouble to erect posts every ten years or so indicating the end of the glacier, beginning on or before the beginning of the nineteenth century. By 1949 the glacier had retreated by several hundred metres: clearly warming had begun long before global industrialisation and the pollution that followed after the Second World War. Indeed, it is clear from recent geological observations that this retreat was already underway when records began in 1850, and that between 1950 and 2000 the annual rate of shrinkage had doubled or even trebled. It is therefore reasonable to conclude that, although global warming was already in evidence in 1950, the man-made contribution significantly increased the rate of shrinkage.

At the end of the tour our guide invited me to join him in climbing the Grosse Wiesbachhorn, a well-defined and delicately pointed snow- and ice-covered peak. This gave me a huge thrill.

My last hectic year at university

Towards the end of my penultimate year I was approached by Reg Galer, the president of the Guild of Undergraduates, asking me whether I would consider the possibility of standing in the elections as a presidential candidate. As Reg was politically a Conservative and I was anything but, I found this suggestion both intriguing and flattering. To cut a long story short, Gerry Browton offered to nominate me and he wrote a short profile of me for the student paper, which was published with profiles of the other nominees and showed me smoking a pipe. I was elected. The vice-president, who had to be a member of the opposite sex, was Joanne Elizabeth Manley, who was just completing her degree in English and was to stay on for another year studying for a diploma in education. I did not know her, but she had cut something of a figure as a member of the entertainments committee.

1950–51 was the last academic year in which the president of the guild was expected to carry out his duties without taking a sabbatical; this was changed in the following year. I therefore had to balance my crucial final year studies with the heavy and time-consuming responsibilities of my office. Before taking the plunge I discussed this with the head of my department, Professor Medawar. To my surprise he was tremendously supportive, and it was his encouragement that led me to proceed. He made it easier for me to reach my decision by saying that my becoming president would be to the department's credit.

The guild was semi-autonomous of the university but there were close links, and every now and again representations were made by the university about such things as the unruly behaviour of students on, say, carnival day or the risqué, not to say vulgar, nature of the carnival magazine. To ensure that good relations were maintained between the university and the guild, the vice-chancellor – Sir Raymond Priestley – met the president and the vice-president over coffee once a week, and this gave us the opportunity of getting to know this modest and pleasant man. These meetings enabled us to consult him on problems we encountered and this proved to be very helpful on one or two occasions. Sometimes he would seek our opinion on problems facing the university.

One of my presidential duties was to attend the annual student dinner and dance at other universities, to which the president and the vice-president were often invited. Some were more enticing than others and I frequently managed to pass on my invitation to a member of my executive committee. It is on these social forays that I got to know Joanne Manley and an intimate relationship developed between us, rocked briefly when she supported some rebellious members of my executive at a turbulent discussion on some pressing problem or other. It was then that I discovered how highly I value loyalty, and not to be supported by her seemed (stupidly of course) like a stab in the back. As president I had to chair the executive and council meetings, and it is here that I honed my skills as a chairman; this stood me in good stead later in my professional and political life. The president was rarely out of the news, whether dressed in Edwardian clothes during Carnival Week or being the first student blood donor in a mass donation organised on union premises. It was also my responsibility to invite outside speakers for lectures in the debating hall, and quite the most memorable of these was a talk by the elderly and squeaky-voiced Bertrand Russell to a packed hall. He was a staunch pacifist and his lecture was controversial, as might have been expected. In my vote of thanks I had the audacity to say that on at least one issue he and I saw eye to eye, but I cannot remember now what that issue was.

By far the most tumultuous event arising during my presidential tenure was the proposal that a European Society should receive the approval of the guild. Careful perusal of their proposed constitution showed that they were very close to being Fascist, two of the key planks being 'England for the English' and the use of large chunks of Africa as a European colony. Although membership of the society would be 'open to all' its constitution would have been enough to keep socialists, Communists and Jews at arm's length. A furious debate raged in the student body as to whether the proposed activities should receive the guild's recognition. Those who championed the cause of the European Society pointed to the existence of a Communist Society as a precedent. The executive, after lengthy discussions, decided to recommend rejection, but enough guild members signed a petition for an extraordinary general meeting of the whole student body to be called to discuss the matter further.

The debating hall was so crowded that students were virtually hanging from the rafters. I chaired the meeting as objectively as possible, giving the proponents ample opportunity to make their case. (I had discussed the problem with Sir Raymond Priestley and had been happy to find that he thought the executive had taken the right decision.) The debate was of high quality though heated, and most students evidently did not find it too difficult to distinguish between Communist and Fascist societies, a distinction that might have been more fraught if the debate had taken place a few years later when the iniquities of Soviet Communism became widely known. One of the speakers opposing the new society was Gabriel Horne, the Jewish chairman of the Debating Society, who later became Professor of Zoology at Cambridge. In the end there was a massive majority against the formation of the European Society, and I felt mightily relieved and vindicated.

The cultural jewel in the university's crown was the Barber Institute, a modern building that housed an art gallery and a small concert hall designed for chamber music. The Professor of Fine Art, Thomas Bodkin, was the gallery's curator and he had managed to accumulate an exceptionally fine collection of medieval and impressionist paintings, among them Bellini's *Portrait of a Young Man*. I was particularly fond of this painting and was later given a copy of it, at my request, as a wedding present. It was a Ganymede print and a superb reproduction, which continues to grace our sitting room. The chamber music concerts were invariably highly prized occasions, and I remember especially vividly the performance, by Clifford Curzon and the Amadeus Quartet, of Schumann's *Piano Quintet*. It made a deep impression on me, possibly influenced by the fact that Curzon's face reminded me vividly of my father's. When I went up to him after the concert to tell him how very much I had enjoyed the performance I was sorely tempted to mention this resemblance, but fortunately had the good sense not to do so.

The guild was very fortunate to have a medical student, John Reckless, who had a great love for Gilbert and Sullivan operas and a talent for staging them. We were therefore treated to an opera once a year, from *The Gondoliers* to *The Mikado*. These performances were of a high calibre, tremendous fun and have left me with a weak spot for G&S.

A fateful diversion from teaching to immunology

In the summer of 1951 I was asked by Professor Medawar whether I would care to join him as a postgraduate student. Apparently Rupert Billingham had spoken to him about me. I was so delighted to be asked that I didn't even enquire whether research with him would lead to a higher degree – it was of no great consequence to me – and I had no difficulty in deciding to cancel my application to Cambridge University for a postgraduate diploma in education. So it was that my ambition to become a schoolteacher was subverted, and I cannot say that I have had the slightest regrets about that. Medawar had just been appointed to the Jodrell Chair of Zoology at University College London (UCL), and Billingham and I were to follow him there at the end of the year. The subject of my research was to be immunological tolerance, a phenomenon for which there was only circumstantial evidence at the time. We were to show experimentally that it really existed. Having been exposed to extreme racial *in*tolerance in my boyhood the idea of working on immunological tolerance appealed to me greatly. Here was yet another instance of fortune smiling upon me; ein Sonntagskind once again.

Despite the enormous distractions of my presidential duties in the final year I managed to obtain a decent honours degree – only just missing a First, Medawar told me. I was pleasantly surprised when told that I had been awarded the vice-chancellor's prize 'For the Most Outstanding Undergraduate Student of the Year, 1950-51'. It was awarded at the degree ceremony presided over by Anthony Eden, the chancellor, and was worth £50. With this I bought a suitably engraved silver cigarette box, the done thing at the time though I didn't smoke cigarettes, and three books, among them Bertrand Russell's *A History of Western Philosophy*. It was Eden who took a fancy to my vice-president, Joanne, and famously chased her down one of the corridors of the main university building clad in his academic robe. It did not come as a surprise to me that Eden, some years later, came to a sticky end both politically and personally.

Sir Raymond Priestley

To both Joanne and me, Raymond Priestley (1886–1974) came over as a courteous and modest man who showed a genuine interest in the student body and who saw it as his responsibility to ensure that relations between the university and the students were amicable. When he talked to us it was very much on equal terms – there was nothing condescending about him. His academic life had been a far cry from the usual academic ladder in that he had first made his mark as the geologist who had accompanied Ernest Shackleton and Robert Falcon Scott on two expeditions to the Antarctic before he had even taken a university degree. He later founded the Scott Polar Research Institute in Cambridge. His selection as vice-chancellor in the 1930s had been a wise move, for he was a man with great humanity, an understanding of academic life and of young people, and someone who commanded respect. That was before the days when vice-chancellors were required to have experience in high finance as money raisers.

An affectionate and informal appreciation of Sir Raymond was published, soon after his death, by his friend and brother-in-law Sir Charles Wright. I regret that I was so preoccupied with student affairs at the time when I came into contact with Priestley that I failed to quiz him about his extraordinary experiences. It is only in recent years that they have aroused the interest of playwrights and the general public, having long been overshadowed by Scott's ill-fated attempt to be the first to reach the South Pole. I have therefore become fully aware of Priestley's heroic role in Scott's expedition only quite recently. This epic story can be pieced together from his obituary, Priestley's own account and David Young's play (see his article 'When Hell Froze Over' in the *Guardian* (October 2001).

Despite the title of this chapter I have in fact written very little about my studies! That would, I think, be rather boring. Suffice it to say that I enjoyed them, worked very hard when I managed to find the time for it, and achieved a reasonable result by dint of frequently burning the midnight oil.

I was awarded a hockey 'blue' in three consecutive years, entitling me to wear the appropriate tie, which I still do from time to time for auld lang syne. Before leaving I was made an honorary life member of the Guild of Undergraduates. Like all presidents I had my name inscribed on an oak board on the wall of the council chamber. University life had given me four happy and fulfilling years.

Chapter Twelve: From Intolerance (Racial) to Tolerance (Immunological)

Jwas awarded a research fellowship of the Agricultural Research Council (ARC), which at that time took a liberal view of the research it was willing to support. Billingham and Medawar had already done some immunological/ transplantation research with an agricultural twist to it. My interviewer was Professor Roger Brambell, who had also been the external examiner for my BSc examination. Three years later he was to be the external examiner for my PhD thesis, too.

Professor F.W.R. Brambell

A few words about Professor Brambell are called for, as he impinged on my life on several occasions. He was Professor of Zoology at Bangor University College and a member of the ARC Standing Committee on Animals as well as a council member. His research interests were in invertebrate biology, but relatively late in life he became interested in developmental biology, in particular in the passage of proteins across the placental membranes from mammalian mother to foetus. To study this problem he used antibodies as his marker molecules, with which he was able to trace their progress across the membranes by virtue of their specific binding sites. This was groundbreaking work that earned him the Fellowship of the Royal Society in 1949, and made him a suitable examiner of my PhD thesis.

Brambell chaired a Ministry of Agriculture working party in the 1960s to enquire into 'the welfare of animals kept under intensive livestock husbandry system'. The Brambell Report was published in 1965, with numerous recommendations. Had that report been implemented it would have saved the country widespread and highly damaging salmonella epidemics among chickens as well as in hen eggs, and in other livestock kept under intensive conditions.

On vivisection

Rupert Billingham (Bill) and I stayed on in Birmingham until after Christmas, whilst our laboratories and the animal house at UCL were being constructed. We knew that our studies there would involve working with small mammals such as mice and rabbits, and that one of our principal techniques would be the transplantation of small skin grafts under anaesthesia. The idea of vivisection was not especially appealing to me but I decided that if I was to take part in what seemed a very exciting project I would just have to buckle down to it. Medawar had previously, when in Oxford, carried out studies in rabbits as well as in a patient suffering from severe burns that had unequivocally established the immunological basis of foreign skin graft rejection, and it seemed to me that this field of research could be of great medical significance.

Vivisection was even then carefully controlled by the Home Office, which issued licences and instructions on how animals were to be kept and what experiments were permissible, but the regulations were not nearly as stifling as they are now. Nor was there any militant opposition to vivisection. As late as 1968, when I held the Chair of Zoology at the University of Southampton, I had no qualms in engaging in a public debate with the secretary of the local anti-vivisection society. My opponent began by showing some horrendously gory slides that on closer inspection turned out to be of a whale being dismembered, and therefore had nothing at all to do with vivisection! I stated my case in favour of vivisection by quoting several important medical discoveries that could not have been made by any other means, such as the discovery of insulin and advances in organ transplantation. The debate was conducted in a perfectly civilised way, but I doubt that there are many scientists who would now be willing to take the risk of exposing themselves in public: there have been too many acts of mindless and criminal violence against prominent scientists known to work experimentally with animals. Having said that, I do not believe that vivisection is justified if it is merely intended to further the cause of the cosmetic industry.

It is frequently said that experiments with animals could be done away with by the development of *in vitro* (test tube) methods, an argument that was effectively if misguidedly used in the early 1980s to justify a gross reduction in the size of St Mary's Hospital Medical School animal facilities. I was chairman of the animal house at the time and my opposing arguments fell on deaf ears. A decade on it turned out that the facilities were barely able to cope. Whilst all scientists would prefer *in vitro* methods because they are simpler to use and to control, there invariably comes a stage in most fields of biomedical research when the significance of *in vitro* data has to be tested in animals. Not to do so would inevitably lead to the application of methods and procedures and new drugs directly to patients as guinea pigs, hardly a desirable development.

The transplantation of small skin grafts and the injection of cells into animals are relatively innocuous procedures. My conscience would not have allowed me to conduct more drastic operations of the kind used, for example, by neurophysiologists in the study of brain function and dysfunction.

The move to University College London

Peter Medawar established himself in London three months before Rupert Billingham and I joined him, and in that period he created some modern laboratories for us and a small animal house suitable for small rodents at the top of the building in Malet Street, off Gower Street.

Towards the end of 1951 I installed myself in a bedsitting room in Hampstead, not far from the southern tip of Hampstead Heath. There I shared a kitchen with several other residents, including a fluttery elderly Welsh lady, Miss Jones ('You are such a gentleman, Mr Brent,' she frequently exclaimed), a talented commercial artist, Pembroke (Pem) Duttson and a Nigerian postgraduate student who used to cook a somewhat off-putting mixture of pilchards and stewed beef for breakfast. Before I left this establishment Pem made a rather fine life mask of me, painted bronze.

The department of zoology

The department of zoology was intellectually an extraordinary place and brimming with talented and unconventional people. Peter Medawar, its head, presided over it with a natural and easy-going authority. Its members were scientifically and politically a motley group. Most were already there when Medawar took over. His predecessor, Professor D.M.S. Watson, had been allocated a room at the back of the building, where he and his elderly research assistant Miss Townsend continued their research in vertebrate palaeontology. Watson was a small, avuncular though quite shy man who had been elected FRS in 1922, and he caused considerable amusement when, quite out of character, he became somewhat intoxicated one Christmas at a departmental party. It fell to me to drive him home in

Medawar's car, and in the confusion he went off with someone else's hat adorned by a colourful feather, which I had to collect the following day from his house. Both he and his wife seemed totally bemused by all this.

Another eccentric member was George Philip ('Gyp') Wells, the son of H.G. Wells, the well-known writer of science fiction (*The Invisible Man, War of the Worlds, The Wheel of Chance*). Gyp had a laboratory on the ground floor, near the aquarium, and had studied the anatomy and physiology of the lugworm (*Arenicola marina L*). In 1954 he became a professor and a year later he was elected FRS. He viewed the developments in the department following Medawar's appointment with an amused tolerance and perhaps some disbelief, for the immunology that became the driving force in the department's research programme was hardly zoology as he knew it.

Among the lecturers was John Maynard Smith, a geneticist working with the fruit fly *Drosophila*. He had a degree in engineering, had been an aircraft stressman in the 1940s and later became a leading light in the field of evolution. He became Professor of Biology at the University of Sussex, where he was also Dean of Biological Sciences for some years. He too was elected FRS. He had a very sharp mind and often shone in discussions around the tea table, where the departmental staff met for coffee and tea.

David Newth was the department's embryologist. He was a serious, courteous and charming man who, though very bright and knowledgeable, never achieved great things in his research on the development of *Xenopus*, the South African clawed toad. One of his research students, Tony Blackler, was an enthusiastic music lover who was the first to introduce me to the music of Gustav Mahler. Another of Newth's PhD student was Frank Billett, whom I appointed to a readership in my Southampton department in the mid-sixties. David became a good friend and I enjoyed sharing in his family life occasionally, with his wife Jean and their three young children. Like some others in the department he had joined the Communist party before or during the war. He was devastated when the horrors of Stalin's regime became public knowledge following Krushchev's denunciation at the party's twentieth congress in 1956 and he immediately resigned from the party. He felt hugely let down and it took him a long time to recover from this blow.

Other lecturers included Mary Whitear, who was one of the many women to fall under Peter Medawar's spell. Kenneth Kermack was a palaeontologist and spent most of his time in his office poring over fossil remains. He was politically on the right, as was Richard Freeman, reader in entomology. Richard was a good teacher, with a razor-sharp mind and an acerbic wit; he later married the charming Mary. He was a Conservative who relished taking on the left-wingers in discussion round the tea table. When Professor Joseph Needham, the distinguished Cambridge biochemist and Chinese scholar, was invited to the department to give a talk on what he claimed to have been the use of biological weapons by the Americans during the Korean War in the early 1950s, it was Richard who asked the most critical questions. I was pretty much convinced by Needham's detailed documentation.

Alex Comfort was at that time a research fellow working on senescence (ageing), using the goldfish as his experimental subject. He was a clever man whose pacifism had led him to become an anarchist. He had written several pamphlets on anarchism and had published three novels (including *The Power House*, 1944) and some poetry by the time he joined the department of zoology. It was his medical background that encouraged him to take up research into ageing in the hope that it might have some human application, and he published several books on gerontology in the 1960s. Comfort was a most unusual man, fast-talking and eager to apply his mind to any problem that took his fancy. In his younger days he had blown a finger off one hand in a chemical experiment but had developed remarkable manual dexterity to make up for the loss. It was the publication in 1972 of his book *The Joy of Sex: a Gourmet Guide to Lovemaking* that made him a household name in a world that was only just on the threshold of sexual liberation. Not only did he become famous but very rich, as well as a guru to the flower people of California. Having met his first wife, a pleasant and demure woman, in their suburban home I found it hard to understand the circumstances in which the sex manual came to be written, until I learnt many years later that it was the result of a liaison with a woman who later became his second wife. He died in 2000 aged eighty.

To complete the picture I should mention two other research fellows. Anne McLaren was a delightful, friendly young woman already interested in mammalian developmental biology; she later became Director of the Medical Research Council's Mammalian Development Unit, Vice-President of the Royal Society, and a Dame of the British Empire. She and her husband Donald Michie, who later became Professor of Machine Intelligence at Edinburgh University, were staunch Communists. They invited me to dinner one evening and tried to interest me in joining the party. When I raised the treatment of Russian Jews under Stalin I was told that this was western propaganda, and that Soviet society was tolerant and civilised. I found it incredible – and still do – how two such intelligent people could have had the wool pulled over their eyes so easily, but of course they were not the only ones in Britain, as the recent controversy generated by Martin Amis's book *Koba the Dread* shows only too clearly. It is understandable that politically conscious and anti-Fascist people should have been drawn to Communism before and during the war; the Soviet Union, after all, became our ally during the war and without it the war might never have been won. I find it more difficult to comprehend that anyone should have retained their links with the Communist party after the twentieth congress in 1956 and the invasion of Hungary.

Professor J.B.S. Haldane, the geneticist, statistician and biometrist (FRS 1932), had been offered an office by Medawar in which to continue his theoretical studies: here was yet another highly eccentric member of the department. (His sister was Naomi Mitchison, the writer, who had a clutch of very bright children – including three professors.) Haldane sat in a deckchair, with the floor around him littered with books and papers, thinking deep thoughts. He emerged only to traipse to the toilet at frequent intervals and to join the department round the tea table. His opinions, expressed with a slight stutter, were invariably fascinating as he had a brilliant and wide-ranging mind. Soon after the discoveries of the Dead Sea Scrolls he gave a college lecture in a large hall packed with students, who were riveted and excited by his description of the momentous discovery and the conclusions that he drew from the findings. Whilst generally absent-minded and courteous to his colleagues he could be quite rude to people in no position to defend themselves. This once happened to Medawar's secretary, Rosemary Birbeck, and a very angry Medawar confronted him and made him apologise. (Rosemary, a delightful and unpretentious young woman, had been a fellow student of mine in Birmingham and, when offered the post with Medawar, had taken a crash course in secretarial skills after completing her degree.) Medawar was invariably highly protective of junior members of his department.

Haldane was yet another academic in the department who had joined the Communist party before the outbreak of the Second World War, but he became disillusioned in the 1950s when T.D. Lysenko's half-baked ideas were adopted in the Soviet Union. Lysenko rejected the theories of western geneticists (Mendel, Morgan, Weissman) in favour of a notion placing the environment, and not the genes, at the centre of the evolutionary process, a notion that fitted well into Soviet ideology. Haldane was married to Dr Helen Spurway, who was carrying out genetic experiments using the fruit fly *Drosophila*. She was an excitable and highly-strung woman who seemed very intelligent. Her shrill voice could often be heard from one end of the corridor to the other. Her discourses were often barely intelligible to me. Helen Spurway's most decisive and at the same time most foolish act was to tread deliberately on a police dog's tail when the police had been called for some reason, a fit of temper that earned her an appearance at the local police station. With Haldane, who had by then been diagnosed as suffering from colonic (or rectal) cancer, she emigrated to India in 1957, where they were welcomed with open arms, Haldane having been appointed to a post in the Biometry Research Unit at the Indian Statistics Institute in Calcutta. With typical detachment

Haldane wrote a long and witty poem about his cancer. Avrion Mitchison, the distinguished immunologist who had been a PhD student of Medawar's at Oxford University, is his nephew.

There were a few others, such as Brian Boycott, a former student of Professor J.Z. Young's (in the department of anatomy), who studied the nervous system of the cuttlefish; and Graham Hoyle, who tried to induct me into what was then the latest dance fashion, rock and roll, but without much success. And, of course, there was Medawar's own small research team – Billingham and several research students, including myself – who fitted somewhat uneasily into this strictly zoological ménage.

Peter Medawar's standing was so high and his social graces so disarming that he presided over his diverse department effortlessly and to great effect. He made a point of spending some time in his own small laboratory, where he did some test tube work and took charge of experiments involving his (and our) latest toy, an American high speed centrifuge. He dropped by frequently whilst Bill and I were carrying out experiments in Bill's laboratory, and enjoyed paring his fingernails with some ancient surgical scissors whilst discussing with us the progress of the work and the design of future experiments. He kept his political opinions strictly to himself and was more often than not an amused bystander when political issues were discussed around the tea table. I remember well when the young Queen passed down Gower Street, and the excitement with which he called on us all to run out and cheer her progress, possibly with premonitions of royal favours to come?

Medawar's international reputation soared, and attracted a succession of young and gifted post-doctoral research fellows from abroad, mainly from the United States. These included Paul Russell, a gentle and cultured Bostonian who later became Professor of Surgery at Harvard University; Paul Terasaki, a Japanese American who chose his own, not wholly 'approved' research programme (he opted to study antibodies at a time when our group believed that it was cells – lymphocytes – that were primarily responsible for graft rejection) and subsequently became the world's leading specialist in tissue typing; and Bill Hildemann, who came from Ray Owen's department at the California Institute of Technology. Bill was a veteran of the Korean War whose political views were ultra-conservative; he felt he had entered a nest of vipers on arrival in the department. By the time of his return to the States he had mellowed quite a bit and he later, surprisingly, embraced the philosophy of the 'flower people'. He died at a relatively young age.

This, then, was the department in which I was destined to spend the first eleven years of my academic life – a time that shaped the whole of my scientific career.

Immunological tolerance: setting the scene

The team setting out to study tolerance consisted of Medawar, Billingham (by then a senior research fellow) and myself. Medawar had obtained breeding pairs from several highly inbred strains of mice and this made our approach vastly easier. Prolonged inbreeding had turned the members of each strain into identical twins carrying the same histocompatibility antigens – molecules that in other strains elicit immune responses. It was therefore possible to transplant small pieces of skin between members of an inbred strain (isografts) without raising the spectre of rejection, and to use their tissues interchangeably. The very first thing we did was to establish with great precision the rejection times of skin allografts transplanted from one strain to another. They varied between eight and eleven days, depending on the strain combination. As Medawar had previously established in rabbits, there was a latent period of several days whilst the immune response gathered force, and this varied slightly from one strain combination to another. It permitted the grafts to heal in and to have, initially, an entirely healthy appearance before they were destroyed and became necrotic.

The cattle twin story – a paradox?

Whilst still in Birmingham, Medawar and Billingham had carried out a research project that involved the exchange of small skin grafts between cattle twin calves. They did this because they had hoped to provide a relatively simple test that would distinguish, at an age when anatomical criteria could not be used, between identical (one-egg) and fraternal (two-egg) twins. The former would be expected to accept each other's skin and the latter to reject them. The potential agricultural importance of such a test was that the female member of a fraternal twin pair is almost invariably infertile in cattle (the 'freemartin'), and it was therefore in the interests of farmers to be aware of this at an early age. To their utter astonishment the results turned their premise upside down in that *all* grafts were accepted more or less permanently.

They had considerable difficulty in interpreting what was going on here, until someone drew their attention to a monograph published in 1949 by two Australians, F.M. Burnet (later Sir Macfarlane) and F. Fenner, *The Production of Antibodies*. In a brilliant review of the immunological literature they highlighted a very brief paper published four years earlier by Ray D. Owen, which drew attention to the fact that cattle fraternal twins have two kinds of red blood cells: those genetically their own, and cells that could only have been derived from their twin partner. Owen had established this by using a battery of antibodies recognising cattle blood groups and, knowing that cattle twin foetuses usually develop a fusion of their blood streams quite early in foetal life, he proposed that not only red cells but also cells that give rise to mature red cells - so-called precursor cells - had been exchanged and accepted by the opposite twin. Burnet and Fenner concluded that the precursor cells must have been accepted because of the immunological immaturity of the foetuses at the time of the foetal cell exchange, and they assumed that the cells owed their ultimate survival in the foreign hosts by the development of some sort of tolerance.

(Those who wish to look at original papers referring to this scientific work can do so by consulting my book *A History of Transplantation Immunology*, though the reader is warned that this is an academic history not written for the layman.)

The experimental evidence

Experimental proof was needed that the phenomenon of tolerance really did exist. To this end we decided to mimic in mice, so far as we were able, the situation found to be a normal component of development in cattle foetuses. The mid- to late-term foetuses of mice of one strain were therefore injected with living nucleated cells, i.e. cells capable of dividing, taken from the tissues of donors of a genetically different strain. Foetuses that went on to term and survived into adulthood received a small skin graft taken from donor strain animals, on the assumption that animals that had developed tolerance would accept their skin grafts.

All manner of technical difficulties were encountered and it took nine months before we encountered mice that tolerated their skin grafts significantly longer than normal control animals. (The mice received their skin grafts as young adults, at a time when they should have been capable of rejecting them.) Although graft survival was not necessarily permanent this told us that we were on the right track and encouraged us to continue the experiments. We had one extraordinary result: all members of one litter proved to be permanently tolerant, and whilst we at first rejoiced this seemed too good to be true. Could a mistake have been made in the animal house? Perhaps we had been given a litter born to a cross between the donor and recipient strains? Such first generation hybrids (F_1) would be expected to accept grafts from either strain because they had inherited the histocompatibility antigens of both strains. The placement of skin grafts from the litter to either of the parental strains soon showed that this had indeed been the case, for they were rejected - as would be expected when F_1 hybrid skin is transplanted to members of the parental strains. The euphoria was therefore short-lived.

Eureka: tolerance!

We persisted nonetheless, and in due course we had a number of mice carrying healthy skin from the donor strain. For example, a white recipient would have a patch of brown fur on its chest, grown by the transplanted skin. It was an astounding sight, and it made us feel that we had achieved our prime objective. However, we now had to establish whether this 'acquired immunological tolerance', as we called it, was specific to the donor strain and what immunological mechanism was responsible for the survival of the allografts.

Tolerance proved to be very highly specific to the donor strain, for a B strain mouse tolerant to skin from the cell donor strain A rejected grafts from strains C or D quite normally. Remarkably, it had been achieved without recourse to irradiation or other agents such as drugs that suppress the immune response non-specifically. By early 1953 we felt in a position to send a paper with our preliminary results to the journal *Nature,* and at the spring meeting of the British Society for Experimental Biology we presented our findings for the first time.

It says much for both Medawar and Billingham that they gave the youngest member of the team – me – the responsibility of giving this talk. The hall in the building of the Royal Society of Medicine was packed, for it had been rumoured that something very unusual was afoot and the audience included senior members of the biological and immunological communities. The slides of a white mouse carrying a brown skin graft created a sensation and I was bombarded with questions, some of which I was unable to answer because they anticipated experiments in progress. The phenomenon of immunological tolerance has continued to be of interest to this day – attempts are now being made to create tolerance in transplant patients – and the British Transplantation Society decided to ask me to give the same paper, insofar as that was possible, at its spring meeting in 2003, which celebrated the paper's fiftieth anniversary. Fortunately I still had some of the old slides. In referring to the *Nature* paper, the society's website stated: 'This is probably the most important paper in the history of transplantation.' It is a big claim, and I hope it hasn't made the organisers, led by Professor J.W. Fabre, too many enemies on either side of the Atlantic! It is too bad that neither Medawar nor Billingham could be present: the former died in 1987 and the latter died soon after the meeting.

Once the *Nature* paper had been published it triggered an avalanche of research throughout the world, and it soon became clear that our findings were equally valid for all kinds of other antigens, including soluble proteins and bacterial organisms, as well as for tissues other than skin. Our own studies were pursued at a fast and furious pace. Not only were similar findings made in chickens, following the injection of allogeneic cells into the bloodstream of chicken embryos, but in this species we were able to repeat faithfully the 'experiment of nature' described by Owen in cattle twins. This became possible when a Czech biologist, Dr Milan Hašek, published the technique of parabiosis in chicken eggs. This involved the removal of a small piece of shell and shell membrane from fertile eggs that had been incubated for ten or eleven days, the apposition of the two exposed chorioallantoic membranes (the embryonic 'lung' of chick embryos) and, after sealing the area with wax, continued incubation until hatching. Having come into close contact, blood vessels from the two membranes fused and allowed the free circulation of blood from one embryo into the other. When both partners survived after hatching, small skin grafts were exchanged between them two weeks later, by which time the recipients' immune system would be sufficiently well developed for control (normal) chicks to reject their grafts. The experimental chicks, which had shared each other's circulation, did nothing of the kind. When we examined their red blood cells for their blood groups, using some antisera (antibodies) Ray Owen had kindly made available to us, it became clear that each parabiont had genetically its own red cells but also cells that had patently been derived from its partner. Again, precursor red cells must have been exchanged with the embryonic blood, establishing in each twin a pool of cells genetically programmed to produce their own red cells. We had thus succeeded in re-creating in our experimental system the naturally occurring tolerance Ray Owen had described in cattle.

Studies in Prague: an error of interpretation

Interestingly, somewhat similar experiments were carried out by Hašek in Prague but, thanks to the fact that he had allowed himself to be carried away by the wayward genetic theories of Lysenko and Michurin, he completely misinterpreted his data. According to him the embryonic contact between chick embryos from distinct breeds brought about a phenomenon that he called 'vegetative hybridisation', a kind of coming together of characteristics of the two breeds. This seemed to fit beautifully into the genetic theory devised by Lysenko and it was therefore greatly celebrated in the Soviet Union and in Eastern Europe. It was only after Hašek met Medawar and me at an embryology congress in Helsinki several years later that he began to understand the full significance of his work and thereafter we became good friends. All reference to Lysenko and Michurin (and 'our great leader Stalin') were dropped from the introductions of future publications from his laboratory, and he reinterpreted his data as having been brought about by immunological tolerance as defined by us.

In the 1960s Hašek organised several symposia on tolerance in Liblice castle near Prague and these were always conducted in a friendly and convivial fashion, with much drinking and toasts to international friendship, despite the cold war. He was a tall and strongly built man, and to see him arm-wrestle with Medawar, who matched him for size and strength, was a sight for the Gods. Hašek had become the director of the Institute of Biology but paid the price for signing the Dubček Declaration in 1968 after the Russian invasion of Czechoslovakia, when he was summarily removed from the directorship. He was eventually rehabilitated, but died prematurely in not fully explained circumstances.

The ultimate demonstration that tolerance can be an entirely natural process, as in cattle twins, came when we examined the immunological reactivity of chicks that had hatched from fertile double-yolked hen eggs. They were not easy to come by, so Medawar had asked one of the tabloid newspapers to publicise our search for such eggs and to encourage any farmer who had access to them to come forward. One day a farmer and his very attractive wife appeared in our laboratory with a clutch of eggs that they swore to be the answer to our prayers, and Medawar paid a handsome price for them. Billingham and I thought that he had been unduly influenced by the farmer's wife and paid far too much. As it turned out, following ten days' incubation, some of them did indeed harbour twin embryos, and a very simple experiment with a few eggs - the injection of the vital dye trypan blue into the circulation of a few embryos - revealed that the dye almost immediately appeared in the circulation of the other. Their blood systems were evidently fused together, exactly as in cattle twins. We managed to hatch a few pairs and were able to show that they permanently accepted each other's skin grafts, and that they possessed two kinds of red blood cells, their own and their twin's. The Owen story had turned full circle.

Immunological tolerance - its mechanism

Much of our effort was devoted to unravelling the tolerance mechanism. There were essentially two possibilities. Either contact with foreign material in embryonic life had profoundly altered the ability of the immature immune system to recognise it as foreign, or we had induced a response - such as the production of a certain kind of antibody - that actively suppressed any potential response to the skin grafts. Either way any interpretation would have to take into account the specificity of tolerance. To distinguish between these two possibilities we carried out experiments that were based on the transfer into tolerant mice of normal spleen or lymph node cells from animals of the host strain. Such cells, being genetically identical with those of the tolerant mice, would be accepted and expected to function normally in their new environment. (This had previously been established by us in a skin graft model and, previously, by Avrion Mitchison in a tumour transplantation model.) If some active suppressive mechanism was operative in the tolerant mice the transferred cells would be expected to come under its influence and tolerance should persist. If the tolerance depended on a *failure* of the immune system then the freshly transferred cells should 're-equip' it and cause the rejection of the tolerated grafts by the non-tolerant transferred cells. In the event the grafts were rejected within three weeks and even more quickly, within ten to twelve days, when the cells were taken from mice that had already been immunised against the donor strain. Here was a very clear-cut answer to our question: tolerance was due to what we called a central failure of the immune system.

Although this was an entirely valid conclusion we were, in a sense, lucky – or unlucky as the case may be. It fitted snugly into Burnet's clonal selection hypothesis, according to which there is a clone (group) of cells (lymphocytes) genetically programmed to respond to one particular antigen, and it was later assumed that tolerance must have been caused by the elimination of such a specific clone or clones. However, in other combinations of mouse strains it was subsequently shown that suppressive mechanisms, through the action of lymphocytes with the ability to suppress immune responses (again very specifically), can occur. Such 'suppressor T lymphocytes' were first identified in the early 1970s by an American group.

By the end of 1955 we had accumulated a mass of data and in 1956 we published these, together with our speculations on their biological significance, in an extensive monograph of the *Philosophical Transactions of the Royal* Society. The paper was not only long and comprehensive, with a full review of the literature, but it was illustrated by several plates with photographic evidence in glorious Technicolor. We believed that our experiments had shown beyond doubt that, whilst there are exceptions, the body of any one individual does not normally react against its own cells and tissues because the immune system acquires tolerance to self-molecules during the course of normal development. By introducing foreign molecules in foetal life the immune system is hoodwinked into regarding them as 'self' and therefore fails to react. In those diseases brought about by an aberrant immunological response against some self component, for example in autoimmune thyroiditis, self-tolerance has been eroded by one means or another or had never developed.

We published a number of other papers on tolerance as well as on several related lines of research and led the field, and by the end of the 1950s the three of us had become known in the United States as 'The Holy Trinity'. I *think* this was intended to be a compliment! Whilst

Medawar would clearly have been the Father and I the Son, it was hard to imagine the iconoclastic Rupert Billingham as the Holy Ghost. The tolerance story formed part of my PhD thesis in 1954, and Professor Brambell, my external examiner, gave me a pretty easy ride in what can be a gruelling oral examination.

It was not long before Billingham and I worked out a far more reliable method of inducing tolerance. Instead of injecting cells rather randomly into foetuses, a procedure that was technically difficult and had a high mortality rate, we found that injection directly into one of the veins of newborn mice produced far more reliable results, and all laboratories around the world quickly adopted this technique. The analysis of tolerance in all its complexity was therefore greatly speeded up.

An unfortunate theft

There is one incident that caused me severe anguish at the time and that could have prejudiced the publication of our 1956 monograph. On Christmas Eve 1953 my girlfriend Joanne and I were on our way to her parents in Todmorden, Lancashire. Joanne's brother David had offered us a lift in his elderly MG sports car and, as we travelled through Lichfield, we decided to park the car in the square and look at the interior of the very beautiful cathedral. Unfortunately I had not realised that the lock on one of the car doors was defective, and when we returned after a short while we found that one suitcase - mine - had been stolen. It contained not only my dinner jacket, my only decent suit and all my Christmas presents, but also the experimental notebooks for some of our joint research. As I was writing my PhD thesis at the time I had taken them with me to examine some of our data over the Christmas holiday.

I was devastated. Our visit to the local police station was not in the least reassuring; it was Christmas Eve, after all, and the police had other things on their mind. Yes, of course they would contact me if the notebooks turned up, they said, but I felt that I had not succeeded in convincing them of their huge importance. Needless to say the notebooks were never found and I spent the Christmas period in a state of doom and gloom. When phoning Peter Medawar he seemed astonishingly relaxed about the loss and reminded me that most of the data were already either in print or in manuscript form and largely embedded in my thesis. He was right and I don't think that we lost anything significant.

Peter Medawar's Nobel Prize

The importance of the discovery of tolerance, for which Peter Medawar shared the 1960 Nobel Prize with MacFarlane Burnet, was fourfold. First, it provided an explanation for the fact that animals do not normally react against their own tissues. Second, it showed for the first time that it is possible to create unresponsiveness to normal allografts by a strictly biological mechanism that did not depend on drastic treatments such as X-irradiation or immunosuppressive drugs. Third, it encouraged the hope that it might one day be possible to apply it clinically, and it spawned a great deal of research designed to extend these results to adult animals. Finally, indirectly, it provided a new insight into a related phenomenon, Graft-versus-host disease (GVHD).

Shortly after the award to Peter Medawar and Macfarlane Burnet, my wife Joanne received the following letter, in which was enclosed a sizeable cheque. I have corrected a number of typing errors.

My dear Joanne

This comes to you and Leslie with love and gratitude from Jean and me but I wish to make it absolutely clear that it is in no way a present but comes to Leslie as of *right*. You will have to overlook my typing this letter but I have already written 200 by hand, so dear friends just have to put up with typing, and anyway my typing is so beautiful it must be a pleasure to read. I find it much easier to say to you than to Leslie what an incomparable source of strength it is to have a close and devoted colleague who is also a dear personal friend, and how delighted I am that our work is to continue at Mill Hill. I should not have accepted the job unless Leslie had agreed to come too and I took jolly good care to find out whether he would before I signed the fateful contract. And anyway it was his PhD thesis, not mine, that won the Prize – as I told my ARC friends to their absolute delight, and I do so wish that he could have shared the titular award. I ought to add that I have already deducted something from his share so that the acceptable gifts to Trevor and Rosemary should come from the three of us, so it is entirely unnecessary and would be embarrassing if he did anything further on that score.

And finally, as I warm up to the subject and my typing improves let me add that I have a clear understanding of how much Leslie owes to you, because it is exactly the same with me and Jean. So whoopee, as the saying is, and our fond love to you both.

Peter

Graft-versus-host disease (GVHD)

We almost invariably used living spleen and lymph node cells for tolerance induction. The reason for this was that such cells could easily be prepared as single cell suspensions, suitable for injection into small foetuses and capable of passing through a very fine syringe needle, and that they possessed on their cell surface the antigenic molecules (histocompatibility antigens) required for tolerance induction. Other tissue cells, provided that they were nucleated, might have done equally well, but the choice of lymphoid cells was especially felicitous because these cells tend to make their way into the developing lymphoid tissues of the foetus, where they would be in the best possible position to influence the development of the foetal immune system.

The cells came from animals of a genetically different strain and we were perturbed to find that many of the injected foetuses died in utero or soon after birth. The tendency was to ascribe the foetal deaths to technical problems associated with our technique. It was only after Bill and I had devised a way of injecting the cells directly into the bloodstream of newborn mice – a totally reliable and highly appropriate way of administering the cells into animals that are still immunologically immature – that we came to realise why quite a few of the cell recipients died within two weeks of birth. Death, it appeared from post-mortem examinations, must have been due to an immunological reaction of the foreign cells against the histocompatibility antigens of the recipients. The lymph nodes of the recipients were largely involuted, often almost non-existent, and the spleens could be greatly enlarged. These were the very tissues to which the allogeneic cells tended to gravitate; and, having been accepted by the newborn recipients and being mature donor lymphocytes, they were activated by the host antigens present in their new environment and reacted against them. Because this process interfered with normal development the animals looked runted (backward in weight and development, like the runt of a pig litter). We called this syndrome 'runt disease', our hypothesis being that it was brought about by a graft-versus host reaction. It subsequently became known as GVHD, the inverse of the 'host-versus-graft' reaction that ensues when allogeneic grafts are transplanted to adult recipients.

Bill and I published our preliminary results, together with a description of the technique of intravenous injection into neonates, in a brief paper in the *Transplantation Bulletin* (1957) in which we drew attention to the clinical implications of our hypothesis. In particular, we advised against the treatment of patients who were for one reason or another incapable of immunological responses with foreign cells such as bone marrow cells in the hope of reconstituting their immune system.

Morten Simonsen, a Dane, published somewhat similar data in the same year, obtained by the injection of mature lymphoid cells into chick embryos. Graft-versus-host reactivity remains a formidable obstacle to bone marrow transplantation to this day. Our formal proof of the immunological cause of the runting phenomenon, together with many other data, wasn't published until two years later in another massive monograph. Its publication was delayed by my departure to Caltech as a Rockefeller research fellow in the autumn of 1956, and by Bill's emigration to the United States in the following year before my return.

My principal collaborators

These two discoveries – tolerance and GVHD – were the most important with which the three of us were ever involved. The 1950s were certainly extraordinarily productive. Medawar, in his witty and amusing autobiographical book *Memoirs of a Thinking Radish*, written years after having suffered a massive cerebral haemorrhage, refers to it as 'the most fruitful period of my academic life'. It was indeed an exciting period – hardly a week passed without something new and interesting turning up in the laboratory. I tended to get home late in the day, and I now realise more than I did then that this put a considerable burden on my wife Joanne, who thought that I had fallen into the clutches of a driven guru whom she did not admire nearly as much as I did (or if she did wasn't willing to admit it). It is true that I admired and liked Peter Medawar enormously and that he imbued me with the urge to get to the bottom of things, and to think nothing of turning up in the lab on Saturday mornings to inspect skin grafts, feed mice or do some other essential work. He himself led by example, and he was an inspiring PhD supervisor and colleague. Before my marriage Peter often invited me to a meal at his house and to play chess on a Sunday morning. Through this I got to know Jean and their four children well. Jean spoke German (and French) pretty fluently, and it was she – never Peter – who asked me about my earlier life in Germany. For Peter this seemed to be a taboo topic; although quite emotional, especially when it came to opera, he preferred to keep other people's emotional problems at arms length. I think that he felt it was too painful a subject for him to touch on.

I had a very good working relationship with Bill, who was a fine experimentalist, and we spent many happy hours together in his laboratory. He was a down-to-earth man with an impish sense of humour; practical jokes were not beyond him. In fact, he was the opposite of Peter in most respects – not particularly interested in things cultural, though he enjoyed reading biographies and military (preferably naval) histories. He followed the more juicy court cases reported in the papers avidly, arguing that one learnt a great deal about human nature and its vagaries from them. Bill tended to leave the department at a sensible hour, leaving Peter and me to complete the day's work; he struck me as a good family man. However, his wife Jean told me after his death that his evenings were largely occupied by professional matters. Jean's strong and loyal personality stood her in good stead in helping Bill in the fight against his steadily encroaching Parkinson's disease, and in this she has been sustained by her Roman Catholic faith. Bill died on 16 November 2002, and I published an obituary in the *Independent* newspaper, and later memoirs in the *Oxford Dictionary of National Biography* and, most extensively, for the Royal Society.

Peter and I had very similar tastes and hobbies, from chess, squash and cricket to music and opera. Not infrequently he would say, near the end of a day, 'Hey, [this or that] is on at the Royal Opera House – why don't we hop over there, I have a couple of tickets.' That is how I became acquainted with a composer whom I have come to like enormously, Janáček, his *Jenůfa* being one of the operas we heard. The same was true for cricket. In those days one was able to gain free entrance to Lords on the last afternoon of a test match, and Peter sometimes suggested a foray there to watch the West Indians or the Australians play England, usually with England fighting a desperate rearguard action to save a match.

Peter was a good cricketer – a medium fast bowler and a dashing batsman – and it was his enthusiasm that led me, a complete novice, to form a departmental cricket team. UCL had an extensive and well-kept sports ground north of London, and we played other departments such as botany and occasionally teams from research establishments as far away as Harwell in Berkshire in time-limited matches lasting three to four hours. Never having learnt the art of bowling, which needs to be acquired at a young age, I turned myself into a wicket keeper. This demands a good eye and considerable agility. My untutored batting bore the hallmark of a hockey player, with the sweep my favourite shot. These matches were enjoyed enormously by one and all, not least the convivial tea and sandwiches in the interval, and Peter played whenever he was available. My claim to fame as a batsman came in a match against the botanists. I had reached eighty-six runs against some pretty loose bowling, close to the much-coveted century, when someone shouted from the touchline, 'Only fourteen to go, Leslie!'. I was out next ball and I never managed to reach the same delirious batting heights again. (I had developed an interest in cricket, as well as in fox-hunting, when I was at school, having read Siegfried Sassoon's evocative *Memoirs of a Foxhunting Man*, in which the joys of village cricket featured prominently.)

Other major discoveries

I continued my collaboration with Peter Medawar long after Bill's departure in 1957 for the United States, both in the department of zoology and at the National Institute for Medical Research (NIMR), when Medawar was appointed as its director in 1962. Peter very much wanted me to go with him; indeed, he told me that he would accept the post only if I accompanied him there; and so I gave up my lectureship at UCL and was duly appointed 'Scientist' at NIMR, but stayed there for only three years. There came a time when I felt the need to get away from Peter, and when I was offered the Chair of the department of zoology at Southampton University in 1965 I decided to accept it.

In deciding on the order in which authors' names appeared on the papers we published, Peter followed alphabetical order quite rigidly. Bill's name therefore always appeared first and Peter's last, with me sandwiched in the middle. This was very democratic; most senior workers liked to have their name at the front, or else the name of the colleague who had contributed most to the research project. But it also had its disadvantage. Because everyone knew that Peter was the senior member of the team it was generally assumed that it was he who had initiated the experiments outlined in any joint publication, although this wasn't necessarily the case. For example, our comparison, in guinea pigs, of the allograft reaction with another reaction known to immunologists as delayed-type hypersensitivity, derived from some speculations of mine in a lengthy review paper published in 1958, and it was I who initiated the appropriate studies with the help of Jean Brown, a PhD student of Peter's. I was well pleased with this work, for it showed that the two reactions have much in common and it helped to place allograft rejection in the main framework of immunology, i.e. as a lymphocyte-driven response in which antibodies play a subsidiary role. Nonetheless, Medawar's method avoided potentially invidious discussions as to whose name should come first, as happens not infrequently in other laboratories, and I have always followed his example.

I don't wish to burden these memoirs with lengthy descriptions of the many other studies in which I was involved, right up to my retirement in 1990. My bibliography consists of well over 200 research publications, quite a modest number compared with that of many other senior immunologists who insist on having their name on papers with which they have had precious little to do and who run large research teams. Peter was absolutely adamant that his name was not to appear on any paper to which he had not made a significant contribution, and I took my cue from him once I ran my own research programme. Bill and I offered to include his name on our graft-versus-host papers, as this discovery had arisen directly from the tolerance work, but he declined quite firmly. This kind of selflessness is rare among scientists.

Tolerance induction in adult animals

Two other areas to which I have made major contributions are the induction of tolerance in adult animals and the function of a subpopulation of lymphocytes known as suppressor T lymphocytes in tolerance. My work with G. Gowland made it very clear that tolerance cannot be induced easily once the graft recipients' immune system has matured: even the injection of very large numbers of cells into mice fourteen days after birth, the equivalent per weight of the number injected into newborn mice, failed. However, when we gave such intravenous cell doses repeatedly, twice weekly, tolerance eventually developed. In fully adult mice the presentation of foreign cells was generally found to be inadequate. Here the immune system of the cell and graft recipients had to be compromised and reduced to the level of the neonate, with the aid of drugs or other immunosuppressive agents, before tolerance could be induced. The tolerance was again specific and seemed to have possible clinical implications.

T lymphocyte suppressor cells

In mice made tolerant in adulthood the mechanism was quite different from that described by us in the 1950s. Here tolerance was mediated by suppressor T lymphocytes. With P.J. Kilshaw and others we established this at St Mary's Hospital Medical School by transferring spleen cells from tolerant mice to non-tolerant mice of the same strain: without ever having been exposed to the donor strain antigens, such mice became tolerant and accepted donor strain skin grafts. This important finding was studied by us over a number of years. Unfortunately we did not then have the technology to identify the precise nature of the T lymphocytes responsible by showing that they carried unique cell surface markers. Conventional immunologists, especially the molecular immunologists, were therefore extremely sceptical of their existence. Despite the fact that my group, as well as others, had shown that there *are* T suppressor cell populations in tolerant animals, immunologists working with more conventional antigens such as soluble proteins did not like to acknowledge their existence, and T suppressor cells became a dirty word – so much so that my last grant application to the Medical Research Council in the early 1980s was declined. We have since been proved right: these cells are greatly in vogue now and crop up in many experimental and clinical situations, and things have been taken further by the identification of a distinct subpopulation of lymphocytes with suppressive powers, now called 'regulatory T cells'.

A heroic failure

Of course I have regrets and some failures – regret at never having mastered molecular biology techniques, for example, and at having perhaps spent too much time and energy on local community and political activities in my spare time, thus diluting the impact of my research. My most spectacular if noble research failure was my attempt to induce tolerance in the foetuses of cynomolgus monkeys in the 1980s.

Having secured a special MRC research grant, I was given permission by the Royal College of Surgeons to make use of their closed colony of cynomolgus monkeys at Buxton Brown Farm, Downe, close to Charles Darwin's house. I wanted to study the possibility that one might alleviate the condition known as beta-thalassemia by the implantation of normal paternal bone marrow cells into affected foetuses. The assumption was that such cells would establish themselves in their foetal hosts, induce tolerance and – being normal red blood cell-producing cells – prevent the symptoms of beta-thalassemia. (Using a technique called foetoscopy experts could withdraw from human foetuses small amounts of blood for diagnostic purposes.) One critically important precondition was that, by first depleting the bone marrow of mature T lymphocytes, GVHD could be avoided. Beta-thalassemia is largely confined to Mediterranean countries but because of the presence of a sizeable Greek population in Britain it has become far from uncommon here. The treatment available – drugs and frequent blood transfusions – is far from satisfactory and the lifespan of affected individuals is deplorably short.

A sub-human primate model was therefore essential and the Buxton Brown Farm seemed to be ideal. Despite the consummate skills of two obstetric surgeons – Charles Rodeck and Kipros Nicolaides, both highly highly experiences in foetoscopy – and David Lynch, an expert haematologist, and the skilful collaboration of my postdoctoral fellow, Lee Rayfield, the study ultimately failed because the antibody we had to use was not directed against *monkey* T lymphocytes (no such reagent was available at the time) but against *human* cells. Although this eliminated 95+ per cent of T lymphocytes, the small residue surviving led to the development of lethal GVHD. This regrettable fact told us, of course, that the paternal cells had survived in their foetal environment, but we were unable to demonstrate the development of ongoing tolerance.

After our project ended the college decided to reassess the future of the monkey colony, which was expensive to maintain and at that time underused. Sir Stanley Peart, the Professor of Medicine from St Mary's

Hospital, was called in for advice. He recommended that the facility should be closed, and so it was in 1996. I raised objections because it seemed to me to be perverse to close down a valuable research facility that was unique in Britain, but to no avail. And so workers in the field of AIDS and vaccine development and testing were denied an important aid to clinical research.

On the ethics of vivisection

I did not enjoy working with monkeys, and I was fortunate to escape the attention of anti-vivisectionists. I don't think that I would want to undertake that kind of research again. I am convinced, though, that it can be justified. The ethics of animal experimentation have since come under close scrutiny of moral philosophers and the public at large, and rightly so. I had a discussion with a philosopher not so long ago, over a conference breakfast, and it ended somewhat unresolved by the arrival of her taxi; it was, maybe, an honourable draw. Whilst the cold logic of philosophers is hard to counter – that animals as well as humans should be accorded rights – she couldn't offer an alternative, and it seemed impossible to avoid the dilemma posed by the question of whether animals rather than human beings should be used in the introduction of new drugs and treatments. The Nazis found no difficulty in using 'inferior' human beings for medical experiments: the use of patients as guinea pigs could soon lead us down that slippery slope.

To take an example closer to home: in the mid-1960s I was sent a scientific paper to referee for an American journal. To my dismay it concerned the implantation of cancer cells under the skin of 'volunteer' prisoners in a penitentiary, in order to establish the fate of these cells and the body's response to them. Such an experiment struck me not only as unethical but also as pointless – unethical because the 'volunteers' had been given incentives and could not possibly have been aware of the risks entailed (such as the possible transfer of a pathogenic virus), and pointless because experiments like it had been conducted in animals and the answer should have been well known. I wrote a very negative report, and so far as I know the paper was never published. A complaint to the New York Academy, of which I was a member, did not elicit a reply and I promptly cancelled my membership of that august body.

I am not implying that unethical procedures have never been carried out in the UK. One only has to think of the appalling events in the Chemical Weapons Establishment at Porton Down, Wiltshire, which came to light a few years ago. Towards the end of the Second World War soldiers were used as guinea pigs in experiments exploring the biological effects of the lethal nerve gas sarin. These 'volunteers' evidently believed that they were taking part in relatively innocuous attempts to find a cure for the common cold. Many hundreds were in fact used to establish the toxic dose of the nerve gas, and at least one died in horrendous circumstances whilst others suffered from a variety of long-term ill effects. All this might never have come to light if it had not been for the recollections, half a century later, of an ambulance driver who had witnessed the dire state of one of these human guinea pigs. This soldier was haunted by his memories and driven by his conscience to divulge them. The original Ministry of Defence inquest in 1953 had recorded a verdict of 'death by misadventure', but at the insistence of Lord Chief Justice Woolf the inquest was reopened in 2006; this time a verdict of 'unlawful killing' was established. The Ministry of Defence admitted to gross negligence and the family received some compensation, but it remains a wholly lamentable episode.

A case of Lamarkian inheritance?

One other research project deserves to be mentioned – not because it greatly advanced the sum of human knowledge but because it embroiled me and my colleagues, Liz Simpson, Lee Rayfield and one or two others in a major and very public controversy, and because it serves as a warning to young (or not so young) scientists not to become too wedded to their pet theories. Liz was at that time working in Peter Medawar's MRC research unit at Northwick Park Hospital. She has since had a distinguished career and has recently retired as head of the Transplantation Biology Group at the MRC Clinical Sciences Centre. She has been a dear and steadfast friend, and has so far been yet another casualty of the quixotic and male-orientated selection process for fellows of the Royal Society. Lee had been one of my bright PhD students, but later left my department to become a lecturer at another London medical school. He eventually left science to become a vicar, and a few years ago Carol and I were invited to his consecration ceremony as the Bishop of Swindon in St Paul's Cathedral!

To continue the narrative: a young Australian immunologist, Ted Steele, had published a book in the late 1970s in which he put forward the hypothesis that it should be possible to prove the existence of Lamarkian inheritance using an immunological model, followed shortly by an experimental paper in which he claimed that he and his colleague Reg Gorczynski had shown just that. Lamark was a nineteenth-century biologist, a contemporary of Charles Darwin's, who had put forward the hypothesis that physical characteristics could be acquired during the lifetime of an organism and passed on to the next generation. The experimental system used by Steele and Gorczynski was based on our neonatal tolerance work. They took the offspring of a tolerant male mated with a non-tolerant (i.e. normal) female and claimed that their lymphocytes showed a loss of specific reactivity to the donor strain's antigen; that tolerance had been passed on by a genetic mechanism. They showed this by *in vitro* experiments in which the cells from tolerant or non-tolerant animals were incubated with cells of the donor strain, and they claimed that the cells from mice that had a tolerant father were less responsive than those that came from normal animals.

Their paper was greeted with much scepticism, especially from Medawar and his former colleagues as we had performed a very similar experiment, but with skin grafts, in the mid-fifties. The offspring of tolerant males mated with tolerant females had rejected skin grafts from the donor strain entirely normally. Nevertheless, when Steele applied to Medawar for a place as a visiting research fellow in his Transplantation Biology Unit in order to continue these studies, Medawar, who some years before had suffered from a grievous cerebral haemorrhage, offered to accommodate him. His offer was all the more remarkable because Medawar had published, many years earlier, a damning critique of studies that claimed to have demonstrated Lamarkian inheritance.

Meanwhile Liz, working in Medawar's unit, and Lee and I at St Mary's Hospital Medical School, had already decided that, setting aside our scepticism, Steele's claims were too important to be ignored. We therefore set out to repeat his observations, using both the *in vitro* (Liz) and the skin grafting (Lee and myself) approaches in tandem. By the time Steele arrived on the scene our study was well under way. I will ignore the dreadful tensions that built up in Medawar's unit, arising partly from the fact that Steele was spending much of his time courting the media instead of pushing on with his own experiments, and partly from Liz Simpson's conviction that it would be detrimental to reveal to Steele the results of our study until the data were complete. We were totally unable to repeat his observations but, having been (rightly) accused of not following the design of his experiments with *complete* precision, felt it necessary to repeat the experiments following his protocol to the letter. Our negative findings were published in the journal *Nature* and Steele wrote a rebuttal. There followed several articles, by Steele and by us, in the popular science journal *New Scientist*, each repudiating and criticising the claims of the other. Eventually we published a second paper in *Nature*, again giving the entirely negative results of our latest study in which we had rigorously adhered to Steele's protocol.

Both the scientific and popular press took a great interest in all this, the latter because here was a young man pitting himself against the stuffy establishment; it was all grist to the mill of the then editor of *New Scientist*. The *Sunday Times* published a major article about the controversy, with pictures of Darwin, Steele and Lamark, and other newspapers took up the story. The editor of *Nature* ran one or two leading articles, siding on the whole with the Simpson/Brent camp. Now we come to the most dramatic episode of this sorry saga. The editor of *Nature*, John Maddox, decided that it might be a good idea to have a discussion between me and Steele on BBC radio, and he invited the two of us, together with an 'independent' immunologist/geneticist, Jonathan Howard, who had just published a book on Darwin. Maddox was in the chair. Having hinted to Maddox before the recording began that he might have a bombshell up his sleeve, Steele said in the middle of the debate that he had 'reworked the statistical analysis of Brent's data', and far from showing that they were negative they actually proved his own hypothesis.

Pandemonium broke out and Maddox stopped the recording. He questioned whether Steele had the right to introduce entirely new material into the debate, and asked me whether I might be willing to examine Steele's statistical 'reworking' of our data. I felt trapped but agreed. Very fortunately, a few minutes spent poring over the statistical calculations revealed a flaw in Steele's argument. He had lumped male and female mice together without realising that their reactivity to skin allografts is subtly different; and that a comparison of 'experimental' males had to be made with 'control' males, and likewise with females. I was therefore quite happy to continue the discussion, and I explained why I felt Steele's data were flawed. Steele nonetheless published his 'reworking' in *New Scientist* under the heading 'The tables turned', which we countered with an article entitled 'The tables unturned' – all somewhat childish and time-consuming, but we felt it necessary to vindicate our data. Ted Steele soon returned to Australia, where he is evidently still 'news' in that a film about him, for which I was interviewed, was made a few years ago. I felt then, and still do, that here was a classic case of a scientist being so committed to his hypothesis as to be impervious to convincing experimental evidence against it. However, I understand that Steele believes that he has more recently proved his point in a totally different experimental system.

Teaching

Ever since my appointment to an assistant lectureship at UCL my researches have, of course, been accompanied by teaching commitments. I have always enjoyed teaching, but throughout my academic life I have been fortunate in having a fairly light teaching burden. At UCL it was largely confined to giving some lectures on embryology and immunology, and the supervision of practical classes in which animal dissections and small biological experiments were carried out. A few years ago I ran into an old friend of Carol's, who had studied medicine at University College and had been one of the students I supervised when they were required to dissect the dogfish, an old-fashioned practice that has long been abandoned. The creatures had been preserved in formalin and had a rank smell. This lady remembered one particular episode. She hated the fine dissection of the nervous system and asked me whether it was *really* necessary for her to see it through to the end. Apparently my answer impressed her sufficiently to have stuck in her memory. 'It's like this,' I had said. 'There are two ways of getting to the top of Mount Everest: one is to be dropped by helicopter on to its icy peak and the other is to climb it. Which do you think is more satisfying and instructive?' She completed her dissection . . .

Evidently I was not always *wholly* successful in putting over complex ideas. When my daughter Sue was due to be born at University College Hospital in 1958 I had to rush Joanne there in the dead of night. At that time husbands were not allowed to be present at a birth and so I waited anxiously in the corridor. A young doctor arrived, looking very dishevelled, and I said to him, 'My wife and I are rhesus incompatible – she is negative and I am positive – and we failed to ascertain the rhesus group of our son, who was born in the States a couple of years ago. So I am just a little concerned that the baby might have symptoms of haemolytic disease of the newborn.' The embarrassed houseman looked at me sheepishly and replied, 'I remember you teaching us about haemolytic disease of the newborn, Dr Brent, but I never quite managed to get the hang of it.' My confidence in what was about to happen declined rapidly. In the event baby Susanna was born quite normally, without any complications.

At UCL and at the University of Southampton I taught science students in the main, whereas at St Mary's Hospital Medical School the students were all destined to become doctors. The contrast between them struck me powerfully when I first began to lecture at St Mary's. Science students were, on the whole, 'seekers after truth' and didn't mind being told that we didn't know the precise mechanism for a particular observation; it could be a, b or c. Medical students hated this approach. They wanted things to be cut and dried; they were interested mainly in facts that could be useful to them as doctors; and they were far less willing to venture into the more theoretical aspects of immunology. Well, immunology was still a fledgling science then, and many phenomena did *not* have clear-cut explanations. I therefore learnt to adapt my teaching method without making immunology sound wholly factual and/or boring. The intellectually lively students used to quiz me after a lecture, and it was always a delight to find that some of the excitement inherent in immunology had rubbed off on them.

Simplifying the department of immunology's teaching methods was especially important because my predecessor, Professor Rodney Porter, had been pretty incomprehensible to many students. He had a slight stutter but, most importantly, had not made sufficient allowance for the limited capacity of medical students to take in complex ideas. He was a brilliant research worker who was awarded the Nobel Prize a few years after his departure from St Mary's for his role in the elucidation of the structure of antibodies, and I felt very privileged to follow him as head of department.

Lecturing to an audience of students more than 100-strong is akin to giving a theatrical performance if one is to hold their attention. In my introductory immunology lecture to first-year students I used to give a brief survey of the history of the subject, dwelling on topics that were relevant to medicine. To liven things up, when I considered the role of antibodies and cells in immunological conditions I quoted from George Bernard Shaw's *The Doctor's Dilemma*, in which the good doctor praised the curative powers of 'the phagocyte' to the skies. 'Stimulate the phagocytes', he cried. When discussing vaccination I quoted an eighteenth-century account by the intrepid Lady Wortley Montagu, who was so convinced of the preventative powers of exposing people to material taken from the pustules of smallpox patients who had the condition relatively benignly, that she exposed her own children to it. And I quoted a passage written by Voltaire in which he described how the Turkish sultan used to do just that for the most beautiful and voluptuous members of his harem. If read in the right way this was a potentially salacious quotation, and it always raised a welcome laugh that told me the students were still awake.

Sir Peter Medawar

Medawar died on 2 October 1987, and the *Independent* asked me to write his obituary immediately after his death – a rather daunting task as I was, of course, deeply affected by it. Below are two paragraphs from it. This obituary is less formal than the anonymous obituary of *The Times*, which I had been asked to rewrite quite some time before his death.

> Peter Medawar was an experimental scientist *par excellence*: he loved nothing better than to work at the bench, doing experiments on his own or in collaboration. Although an imposingly tall man, with large hands, he carried out precise and delicate manipulations with impressive deftness. Doing experiments, as opposed to watching others perform them, was a vital part of his creativity. Coupled with this was an outstandingly incisive and untrammelled mind that rejected the trivial and pedantic and that was forever open to new ideas and hypotheses.

He had an enviable talent as a communicator, whether on the written page or through the spoken word; his lectures, including those to undergraduates, were never less than riveting. Few young immunologists regard scientific papers written more than ten years ago as worth reading; but many of Medawar's early papers are classics and impress the reader not only with the importance of their findings but equally with the elegance and lucidity of their prose.

Peter's handsome looks and great height were arresting enough for people to turn towards him when he entered a crowded room. When I first met him I thought that he might have had Jewish ancestry, but his faintly semitic features stemmed from a Lebanese father. Although he seemed to be supremely self-confident, Jean told me after his death that below the surface there had always been some anxiety, probably brought about by the fact that he felt himself to be something of an outsider as a result of his experiences at Marlborough College as a young lad. This is both unexpected and ironic, for Peter was later embraced by the loftiest realms of the English establishment, was knighted and made a Companion of Honour, and seemed to embody the very best qualities of English academe. Anxiety is a trait that one would not have easily detected in him, although it could explain that up to the late 1950s he had been a heavy cigarette smoker, a habit he discarded once the connection between smoking and lung cancer had been demonstrated.

I have heard Peter described as a genius and have tended to resist this description. A genius is, to me, someone like Bach, Mozart, Shakespeare, Newton, Darwin or Einstein, all of whom changed the world dramatically. However, he does qualify for this accolade according to the definition of the *Oxford English Dictionary*, which includes 'special mental endowments, exalted intellectual power, instinctive and extraordinary imaginative, creative or inventive capacity'. These he had in good measure. Add to this an enviable gift for writing as well as lecturing and we have the picture of a very extraordinary man. He was a superb and meticulous experimentalist, whilst at the same time always seeing the big picture and the wider significance of whatever data he uncovered, and he was careful to select problems that he knew, instinctively, to be soluble. He insisted on washing up his own glassware used for tissue culture, claiming that he needed that time to think, though I suspect he didn't really trust anyone to do the job with sufficient care; and at the end of the day one could hear him clattering away at his typewriter, always with two fingers – meticulously typing up his experimental notes on sheets that went into Twinlock binders, a habit he passed on to both Bill and me – or preparing his notes (typed in black and red) for a forthcoming lecture.

Being of a mathematical bent and with a great interest in statistics, Peter was the team's undisputed statistician.

Peter's charm was legendary and many women fell for him; it would have been surprising if he had not fallen for some women. He was a witty raconteur and lived life to the full. He profoundly influenced my development as a scientist, though I readily admit that my adoption of his long working hours was not beneficial for my family life. Nor, it turned out later, was life in the Medawar family quite as idyllic as I had imagined it to be from my Sunday morning visits to their Hampstead home.

Postscript

Before I leave the topic of immunological tolerance, I would like to recall that some years ago I was asked to attend a dinner given by World Jewish Relief, the successor of the Central British Fund that had been so generous to me when I came to the UK as a child. It was a fundraising event and I had been asked to donate an object to the auction that was to take place after the meal. After much cogitation I offered them reprints, signed by me, of our 1953 *Nature* paper and 1956 monograph on tolerance, hoping that they might raise a few pounds. To my astonishment the two reprints went under the hammer for £230!

The author's father, Arthur Baruch, *c.* 1938.

The author's mother, Charlotte Baruch, née Rosenthal, *c.* 1938.

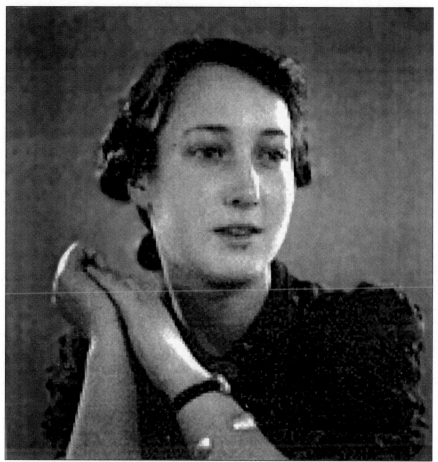

The author's sister, Eva Susanne, *c.* 1938.

The Baruch (and Brent) 'family whistle' - see p. 8.

The author aged six on his first school day – with Schultüte.

The author aged six with his sister Eva.

The Jewish Boys Orphanage, Berlin-Pankow, pre-war.

The synagogue in Köslin, *c.* 1935.

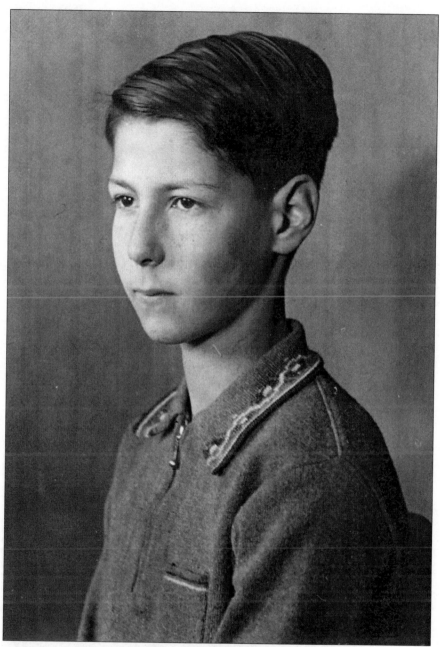
The author's passport photograph, 1938.

(left) Harry Harrison (Heinz Nadel), *c.* 1950.

(below) Bunce Court School, Kent, main building, pre-war.

The author at Bunce Court School, 1940.

Anna Essinger, 1930s. *(courtesy M. Lubowski)*

Hanna Bergas, late in life. *(courtesy E. Weinberg)*

Gretel Heidt, mid-1930s. *(courtesy M. Lubowski)*

Hans and Hanna (née Goldschmidt) Meyer, mid-1930s.

The author with R.E. Billingham at a conference, mid-1960s. N.A. Mitchison is in the background.

Hans Meyer, aged ninety-six.

The author serving as an infantry officer in northern Italy, 1946.

UNIVERSITY COLLEGE LONDON
DEPARTMENT OF ZOOLOGY

Telephone: EUSton 7050
Professor P. B. Medawar

GOWER STREET WC1

Friday

My dear Joanne,

This comes to you and Leslie with love and gratitude from Jean & me but I wish to make it bab absolutely clear that this is in no sense a present but comes to Leslie <u>as of right</u>. You will have to overlook my tiping this letter but I have already written 200 by hand so dear friends just have to put up with typing and anyway my typing is so beautiful it must be a pleasure to read. I find it much easier to say to you than to Leslie what an incomparable source of strength it is to me to have a close and devoted colleague who is also a dear personal friend and how delighted I am that our work is to continue together up at Mill Hill. I should not have accepted that job unless Leslie had agreed to come to & I took jolly good care to find out he would before I signed the fateful contract. ANd anyway it was his PhD thesis, not

mine that won the Prize -- as I told my A.R.C. friends to their absolute delight , and I do so wish that he could have shared the titular award. I ought to add that I have already deducted something from his share so that the Acceptable Giftie for Trevor and Rosemary should come from the three of us, so it is entirely unnecessary and would be embarassing if he did anything further on that score. And finally, as I warm up to the

subject and my typing improves let me add that I have a very clear undderstanding of hw much Leslie owes to you because it is exactly the same with me & Jean. So xxppxx woopee, as the saying is, and our fond love to you both.

Peter.

Peter Medawar's letter to Joanne, 1960.

Sir Peter Medawar, 1960.

A 'tolerant' mouse, bearing a healthy foreign skin graft after *in utero* treatment, 1954.

Ernst and Ingelore Weinberg, 2008.

Dr Ray Owen and his wife June, 1986.

The author with his first wife, Joanne, and Professor W. Brendel and his wife Jutta, at a 'ski-conference', *c.* 1975.

Fun on Brighton Racecourse: the author with Lady Medawar, and Robert Sells in the background, 1982.

The author with his children, Simon, Jenny and Sue, celebrating his eightieth birthday, 2005.

The author with his wife Carol, 2006.

Zdzislaw (Zibi) Pacholski, his wife Janina and Father Henryk Romanik by the memorial sculpture on the site of the 'new' Jewish cemetery, Koszalin, 2008.

The author and his wife Carol after the re-dedication of the 'old' Jewish cemetery, Koszalin, with a group of local Jews, 2006.

The author with the gravestone of his great-uncle, David Baruch, in the courtyard of Koszalin Museum, 2005.

The *Stolpersteine* embedded in a Berlin pavement to commemorate the author's parents.

The *Stolperstein* embedded in a Berlin pavement to commemorate the author's sister.

Chapter Thirteen: Marriage, and 1s and 2d

The second part of this heading derives from Peter Medawar's autobiography, in which one section was called '2s and 2ds' (d for daughters and s for sons, of course). In fact, much of the section was devoted to other matters. However, the take-home message, given in Medawar's witty and self-deprecating style, was that he was extremely contrite at having seen so little of his children in their youth, though he concluded that 'I am happy to say that my many and grievous shortcomings as a parent apparently did no lasting damage to my children. There can be no "control" for such a statement but at least I avoided being parental to a fault, that is, altogether too intrusive and bossy and too anxious to create my children in my own image.' Although I saw very much more of my children than Peter did of his, I feel that I too should have spent more time with them when they were young. Nonetheless, I have a loving relationship with Simon, Sue and Jenny, and I am delighted at the way they have developed and at the lives and livelihoods – however precarious, at least for the girls – they have fashioned for themselves. Like Peter's children none of mine have, wisely, followed in their father's footsteps, and only one has been to university.

Courtship

My relationship with Joanne developed in my last year in Birmingham, where we were thrown together by our work in the Guild of Undergraduates. Rather like opposite poles of a magnet we were soon attracted to each other. I liked her for her high-spirited *joie de vivre* and for her rather 'English' beauty. We fell in love and I visited her several times, strictly against the rules, in her room in Chamberlain Hall, the university's hall of residence for women. The warden (Miss Teverson), a former academic who was both tolerant and well disposed towards both of us, turned a blind eye to these late visits, although she must have been aware of me tip-toeing out of the building well after visiting hours. In our capacity as officers of the guild we attended several balls at other universities, and we danced together at student 'hops' on Saturday nights. It was all rather romantic.

After completing her degree in English Joanne had taken the diploma in education, since she wanted to become a teacher. We both moved to London at roughly the same time, she to become a teacher in a grammar school outside London and I to pursue my postgraduate studies. Joanne shared a house in Hampstead with several other young women, and as my own bed-sit was quite near we saw a lot of each other. That is when we met Morton Norton Cohen, then a Fulbright scholar who had specialised in Rider Haggard and who has since become the world's leading authority on Lewis Carroll. He and his long-time partner Dick Swift (who died recently) have remained dear friends.

The Festival of Britain took place in the summer of 1951. It included the opening of the Royal Festival Hall, much lauded for its modern architecture and its brilliant acoustics, which were later much criticised in the light of modern developments and have now been totally overhauled. (Over the years I have attended numerous concerts in the RFH and, as a member of the Crouch End Festival Chorus, have sung in it on a number of occasions. Like many Londoners I still have a deep affection for it.) The festival was on the South Bank and in Battersea Park, which had been turned into an exciting area featuring the Dome of Discovery, an open-air sculpture and mobiles' exhibition, marquees offering a variety of activities, a funfair, treewalks and a highly amusing miniature railway, designed by the cartoonist Roland Emett. At a time when Britain was still steeped in austerity the festival lifted people's spirits for the first time since the end of the war; it was money well spent. Joanne had obtained a summer vacation job selling Emett postcards, and that is how we gravitated one afternoon to Wing Commander Campbell's lecture-demonstration on hypnosis.

On hypnosis

We listened with interest to the lecture, which seemed to be scientifically quite well based. The wing commander explained that people under hypnosis could not be made to undertake actions that went against their moral scruples, and that the best subjects were, on the whole, those who were both intelligent and athletic. Hey, that's me, I thought! He then called for volunteers to join him on stage for demonstrations, and I watched with fascination and in disbelief as, for example, he made a man go through the ritual of early morning ablutions and shaving. When he offered to hypnotise members of the audience sitting in their seats – only those who really wanted to undergo this experience would fall under his spell, he explained – I thought: well, this is my opportunity to put it to the test. So I clasped my hands behind my head and concentrated on what he was telling us. I immediately fell into a trance. I was aware of my surroundings and of Joanne's presence next to me, but my brain seemed to be curiously disconnected from the rest of my body. I believe the whole episode lasted only a minute or two before the wing commander asked the few people who had been hypnotised to wake up. Most did, but a sailor and I did not. This is where matters became interesting and somewhat distressing. I could hear his voice but felt unable to react to it; I simply could *not* lower my arms and felt totally transfixed. I heard Joanne's voice becoming more and more anxious, entreating me to wake up, and her anxiety was transmitted to me. 'Supposing I never wake up' I could feel myself thinking. I desperately wanted to wake, but could not. Eventually the wing commander came closer and addressed the sailor and me individually. I was the last to wake up, feeling distinctly queasy and perspiring freely, presumably because of the anxiety I had experienced. I was at last convinced of the power of hypnosis, whatever its scientific explanation might be.

Many years later, in the mid-1960s, I was working at the National Institute for Medical Research in Mill Hill. Peter Medawar and I had laboratories in the division of biology, headed by Avrion Mitchison, and the head of the division of immunology was John Humphrey, one of the most highly respected immunologists in the UK. He knew a general practitioner called Black who had developed an interest in the medical application of hypnosis, and together they devised an experiment to test its powers using an immunological model. This was based on the delayed inflammatory skin reaction (Mantoux) that ensues when people who have either been exposed to tuberculosis, or been vaccinated against it, have a tiny amount of tuberculin injected into the skin. (Tuberculin is a soluble and non-infectious extract of the tuberculosis bacillus.) Volunteers who had previously given a very strong skin reaction were put into a moderately deep hypnotic state and told that, on waking up, they would no longer test positive with tuberculin, a procedure that was repeated several times. To Humphrey's astonishment the reactions failed to materialise. However, when small biopsies were taken from the injection site two or three days after inoculation of the tuberculin, when the reaction would be expected to be at its height, histological examination revealed that though the vascular changes one would have expected had indeed been suppressed, the area was nonetheless infiltrated with numerous lymphocytes and other white blood cells, as in the controls who had not been hypnotised. Evidently hypnosis can have a powerful effect on the vasculature but not on the lymphocytes. They duly published their data, which again left a lasting impression on me. Although a few dentists use hypnosis in place of local anaesthesia it would seem that it is hugely undervalued by the medical profession.

Hypnosis has, of course, a long history and Sigmund Freud was deeply interested in it as a therapeutic modality in the treatment of certain conditions. In his review of August Forel's book *Der Hypnotismus, seine Bedeutung und seine Handhabung* (*Hypnotism, its Significance and its Management*), published in 1889, he quotes Forel, a Swiss Professor of Psychiatry: 'the discovery of the psychological importance of suggestion by Braid and by Liebeault is in my opinion so magnificent that it can be compared with the greatest discoveries, or rather revelations, of the human spirit'. Freud clearly approved of the use of hypnosis, for he states, 'Any physician who is accessible to consideration of fact will be led to take a less unfavourable attitude when he notices that the supposed victims of hypnotic therapy suffer less after their treatment and can perform their duties better than they did before – as I can assert in the case of my own patients.' Among the conditions that have a favourable outcome following hypnosis are, according to Forel, Meniere's disease, the cough in tuberculosis, psychical and hysterical disorders, bed-wetting, insomnia, fatigue and migraine.

In his 1891 essay on hypnosis Freud stated, 'In general, we shall avoid applying hypnotic treatment to symptoms which have an organic basis and shall apply this method only for purely functional, nervous disorders, for ailments of psychical origin and for toxic as well as other addictions. We shall, however, become convinced that quite a number of symptoms of organic diseases are accessible to hypnosis and that organic change can exist without the functional disturbance which proceeds from it. In view of the dislike of hypnotic treatment prevailing at present, it seldom comes about that we can employ hypnosis except after all other kinds of treatment have been tried without success.' Freud clearly took a favourable and optimistic view of hypnosis, and the fact that, 100 years later, there are a great many hypnotherapists would seem to bear him out to a degree. Yet it seems doubtful that its application to organic disease has been adequately explored.

Marriage

Joanne's parents lived in Todmorden, a cotton town that is somewhat schizophrenic about its county allegiance. Its address is Lancashire, as befits a town with cotton mills, but much of the town, lying in a long narrow valley (Calderdale) between Hebden Bridge and Rochdale, is within the Yorkshire boundary. Such confusion of identity can be calamitous when it comes to cricket, for Lancashire and Yorkshire are traditionally bitter rivals and fight it out annually in the Match of the Roses. The Manley house was high up on the southern slopes of the town, and only a farm separated it from the moors, which you could cross in two or three hours via Wuthering Heights to reach Howarth, the home of the Brontë family. I came to love these wild moors and we spent much time roaming over them.

We visited Joanne's parents several times before we married, including the ill-fated 1953 Christmas holiday I have already described. The very first time, when we were still in Birmingham, my friend Peter Stoll had lent me his motorbike because we wanted to do some walking in Scotland, and as many streets in northern towns were then still cobbled Joanne finished up with a rather sore bottom. Having spent a few days in Todmorden we continued north and climbed several mountains in the Western Highlands, including Ben Lomond and Ben Nevis, staying in youth hostels. The famous high level walk through the Cairngorms from Aviemore to Braemar proved to be something of a disaster: it was hot and humid and the little black flies that are peculiar to that area were out in force, making our lives a misery.

Joanne's father Oates was the manager of a small bank. He had been wounded during the First World War and still had a piece of shrapnel embedded in his chest. On the face of it he was a jolly sort of man, with a broad Lancashire accent, but he seemed to be faintly depressed much of the time, as evidenced by a phrase that he hummed frequently and compulsively. If there was unhappiness I believe that it stemmed from his excruciating wartime experiences in the trenches as a very young man, but I also think his marriage was not a happy one. Jane was the dominant personality in the partnership and appeared to find his unassuming personality and lack of ambition difficult to cope with. Oates was indeed very easy-going, a quality that made him popular both with his colleagues and with the local businessmen, cotton manufacturers and farmers who were his bank clients. In his younger days he had been treasurer to the local Boy Scouts Association, and his expertise as a magician had enlivened his children's parties and later enthralled his grandchildren too. He was an indifferent though very devoted golf player – the golf course lay conveniently high above his house, adjacent to the moors – and I think he enjoyed the bonhomie of the clubhouse as much as the golf itself. I had never played golf, but one day he insisted on taking me with him to teach me the rudiments. Having shown me how to tee up the ball, and having demonstrated the swing of the club, I took one mighty heave and sent the ball soaring an astonishingly long way. Oates shook his head in disbelief, but not surprisingly I failed to maintain this form for the remainder of our outing. I haven't played golf since.

Oates also dabbled with inventions; for example, a golf bag carrier on a ball-shaped wheel that had come from the ball cock of a lavatory cistern, using an old golf club as a handle, to trundle golf clubs over rough ground. This was at a time before more sophisticated bags on conventional wheels were on the market. Although he patented it and had a prototype made this ingenious idea never came to anything.

Jane was very different. Hers was a highly strung personality, and she had long discarded much of her Lancashire accent. She too had worked in a bank in her younger days and I believe that she found the role of housewife frustrating. Intelligent, and with considerable talent as a painter of watercolours, Jane was also a good cook, producing simple but tasty English dishes, and the Lancashire hotpot that usually awaited our arrival was a great favourite of mine. I once rashly offered to make some Yorkshire pudding to go with her beef, but it proved to be a disaster as I misread the amount of flour to be used; it was virtually inedible.

When Joanne and I visited her parents in 1954 to announce our engagement, after the completion of my PhD thesis and after I had been appointed an assistant lecturer at University College at the princely salary of £450 a year, we had an icy reception that made us both feel exceedingly uncomfortable – absolutely no sign of gladness, let alone joy, but a deathly silence. Perhaps I should have handled it differently by formally asking Oates for permission to marry his daughter, as was the custom in Victorian times. The negative reaction emanated mainly from Jane, who had probably harboured hopes that her daughter would have the good sense to marry the son of a local mill owner. Joanne was so aghast that she suggested we should pack our bags and leave, but I didn't want to be the cause of a rift between her and her parents and dissuaded her from an abrupt departure. (She has recently told me that she much regrets not standing firm.) Eventually we did receive parental blessing, but my relationship with Jane never quite recovered; it was always fragile, and we never managed to establish genuine affection, let alone love. This was particularly sad for me, as I had entertained the probably quite unrealistic hope that my in-laws would in some measure make up for the loss of my own parents. I had the impression that Jane didn't really approve of me as her daughter's partner: foreign, Jewish, without a family and with an unfathomable childhood, and with intellectual pretensions to boot. (Our engagement announcement is somewhat reminiscent, though not nearly as calamitous, as the attempt by Herr Klesmer to win Catherine Arrowpoint in George Eliot's *Daniel Deronda*. At least in my case there was no talk of horse-whipping the unfortunate foreign and Jewish suitor!)

My reserved attitude did not extend to Oates and I became very fond of him. He and I went for walks on the moors and he visited us not infrequently after Jane's death in 1969, the year we moved back to London from Southampton. He accompanied us on several summer holidays, one delightful one in Brittany and another in Eire. He was much loved by our children. Unfortunately he became manic-depressive in his old age, and when staying with us in Muswell Hill I had to search for him on more then one occasion on Euston station late in the evening, as he had taken to haunting the station, where he found warmth, toilets, tea shops and, occasionally, company. In his manic state he was not averse to insulting passers-by, his inhibitions having been eroded, and we were afraid that he would be assaulted one day. Oates was a thoroughly decent man who would not have hurt a fly.

I would on no account blame the ultimate failure of our marriage (after thirty-four years) on the ambivalent attitude of Joanne's mother, but it certainly did not help. The real causes were, I think, linked to our very different personalities and aspirations and our different backgrounds, together with the fact that I took my professional responsibilities too seriously to be able to devote enough time to Joanne and the children. What is more, I allowed myself to be sucked into various community and political activities that, again, took me away from home in the evenings when I should have been there to support my wife. I have felt a deep need throughout my adult life to give something of myself to the local community as well as to the academic institutions in which I have worked, over and above teaching and doing research. I dare say that this was triggered by my childhood experiences, and I am sure that I am not the only former refugee who has reacted in this way. Joanne gave me unstinting support whilst I was coming to terms with the fate of my family, despite the fact that she found it emotionally difficult to cope with. Her presence, together with Simon, on my first visit to my birthplace a year before we finally separated, was invaluable, and I shall be forever thankful to her for that.

Following some pressure from Joanne, who was keener at that time than I was to splice the knot, we were married in Hampstead in the spring of 1955. Whilst I would have preferred a secular marriage, I bowed to Joanne's wish – and that of her parents – to get married in a Congregational church. On my way to church I was wearing brand new black shoes, and I remember scuffing them on a street kerb because they looked so disgustingly new. The reception was in Burgh House, in Hampstead, and among those present were Anna and Paula Essinger and the Medawars. Gerry Browton was my best man. Paul Russell, an American surgeon who was working in Medawar's department at the time, very kindly lent us his car, so that we were able to have a touring honeymoon in Cornwall, where we stayed in a small cottage on the sea front at Polperro, a pleasant and picturesque fishing village.

Buying or even renting a flat, let alone a house, was out of the question in London for an assistant lecturer, even when my salary was supplemented by Joanne's income as a fledgling teacher. We first stayed in a bed-sitting room belonging to Mary Davies, a friend of Jean Medawar's, who kindly put us up at an affordable rent in her semi-basement in Hampstead, only a stone's throw away from the Medawars' house. Our stay came to an abrupt end after we complained at having been kept awake by Mary playing her harpsichord late at night immediately above our room. Bach's *Italian Concerto* is a wonderful work but not after midnight, when we were both desperate for sleep.

My first trip to the United States

One episode that occurred in our bed-sit is worth recording. Peter Medawar had nominated me to attend a Gordon conference in New England in the summer of 1955. The Gordon conferences were and still are small and select and I was to talk about immunological tolerance, only about a year after completion of my PhD thesis. About two weeks before I was due to fly (for the first time) to the United States I woke up in the dead of night, sweating profusely, with shallow breath and a faint pulse beat, thinking that I was about to die. What were we to do, as we had not registered with a local GP? I came up with the somewhat demented idea of alerting the Medawars, and Joanne duly ran along the street to do just that. Jean was, heroically, with us in a few minutes and somehow managed to calm me down, suggesting a cold compress and a visit to the University College GP in the morning. In retrospect it became clear to me that this was an anxiety attack brought on by the fact that on my return from New England I had arranged to spend a couple of nights in New York with Margot Lewin, my mother's best friend before the war and the mother of my childhood friend Inge, and I was also going to visit my maternal uncle, Ewald Rosenthal and my cousin Warren. This, then, was to be my first direct confrontation with my German past, and the prospect was emotionally overwhelming.

The twelve-hour flight – this was before the age of the jet – was memorable because the pilot invited me into his cockpit for a while. Unaccustomed as I was to flying, I tended to lean to one side or the other whenever the plane tilted. The conference went well – a senior American immunologist, Merrill Chase, took me under his wing and was very kind to me – and meeting Margot, Ewald and Warren proved to be emotionally taxing but ultimately calming. Staying with Margot were Inge and her small daughter Leah, and Inge and I shared both tears and laughter in what was a highly charged reunion. (My old friend Ernst, who had married Inge, had to remain behind in Syracuse.) I had often wondered why it was that the Lewins had been unable to facilitate my family's emigration before war broke out, and Margot explained that they had been too impoverished to bring it about. Meanwhile she and her husband Kurt, a businessman, had separated. This was beyond my comprehension, considering all that they had endured together both in Germany and in their adopted country.

My uncle, who had remarried following the death of his much-loved first wife, was eking out a rather miserable existence repairing handbags in upper New York, and I subsequently visited him whenever I found myself in that remarkable city. He had started life as a very successful departmental store window dresser in Germany and in Paris, but had been unable to continue this work in America. It was my uncle who later persuaded me, very much against my will, to claim 'compensation' from the German government that was being offered to Jewish refugees at the time. I didn't like the idea at all – how could one be compensated for the loss of one's family and a disrupted and traumatic childhood? After much heated discussion I eventually agreed, on condition that he would accept whatever sum came to me. It turned out to be a few thousand pounds and I was glad to be able to help him in this way. My uncle's second wife was Edith, a much younger German refugee, who looked after him lovingly - though they seemed ill-matched in education and temperament. My uncle was a practising Jew and on one of his rare visits to England I took him to a service in a synagogue in St John's Wood – only my second visit to an English synagogue, though I have since been to one or two services in Berlin. He was inordinately proud of my scientific achievements and entirely supportive when I decided to marry a non-Jewish woman, as was Anna Essinger.

My uncle had been working in Paris when war broke out, and managed to escape to Cuba. There he survived as a kitchen-hand in hotels and restaurants before making his escape to New York soon after the war ended. My cousin Warren Munroe was on a farm in Denmark at the outbreak of war, in preparation for emigration to Palestine, and managed to make his way to England where he joined the Pioneer Corps. He was invalided out of the army because of a severe back problem and emigrated to New York soon after the war, where he made a living as a sales assistant and later as a manager of one or two shops selling men's clothes. Having been held up at knife point more than once he decided to call it a day and moved to a retirement home in Florida, where happily he is still alive at the age of ninety-five.

Sabbatical leave at the California Institute of Technology

In 1956 Peter Medawar arranged for me to spend a sabbatical year with Ray D. Owen at the California Institute of Technology in Pasadena. Ray was the man who, with his study on cattle dizygotic twins, had provided an absolutely vital pointer to the phenomenon of immunological tolerance, the main topic of my PhD thesis, and he had given us some valuable antisera that we used to study cellular chimerism in chickens. I was awarded a Rockefeller research fellowship for one year, and in the late summer of 1956 Joanne and I boarded the French liner *Liberté* in Southampton to take us to New York. We were to fly from there to Los Angeles.

Joanne happened to be in the sixth month of her first pregnancy, and all went well until the liner ran into a formidable storm and she threatened to miscarry. I approached the ship's doctor, but he seemed terrified at the prospect of a miscarriage on board and wasn't much help. Fortunately I had met a very pleasant American paediatrician on the boat and he came to the rescue, giving Joanne a tranquillising drug that carried her over the crisis. Thus Simon escaped a very uncertain future as well as French dual nationality – though he qualified for an American passport.

Ray and June Owen met us at the airport – the evening flight into Los Angeles was magical, with millions of flickering lights. They had found accommodation for us in a bungalow inhabited by a little old lady, Mrs Higgs, not far from the institute. Our stay was made very agreeable by our hosts, who were extremely kind and thoughtful and who made life as easy as possible for us. Ray and June have remained dear friends. With Ray's expert advice we acquired a large green Buick saloon with 90,000 miles on the clock, and I passed my driving test without difficulty. It was unfortunate that Joanne was at that time not able to drive, as this isolated her rather more than need have been the case, though her steadily increasing girth would have made driving difficult. Naturally I had to immerse myself in my chosen research topics and was much preoccupied during the day, though Joanne was able to join us at times for lunch in the staff club, the Athenaeum, and I occasionally went home for a quick lunch. Life in California, with its dry but smoggy climate and tropical trees and plants, was novel and enjoyable. Ray and June showed us some of the sights, including the Mojave desert (absolutely gorgeous in the spring, when the flowers bloom exuberantly for a short time) and Death Valley, said to be the hottest place in the United States in midsummer, where we camped on George Washington's birthday. The valley and its side valleys are extraordinarily beautiful, the many mineral deposits giving the rocks all the colours of the rainbow. Ray caused a slight frisson by remarking that campers had been drowned by flash floods in what was otherwise a dry season . . .

The most significant event was of course Simon's birth, on Guy

Fawkes Day 1956. Joanne had felt labour pains in the middle of the night and Ray kindly drove us to the local hospital, where Simon was born swiftly and without mishap, though the use of forceps caused his head to be slightly misshapen for a few days. Circumcision was all the rage in America at that time and was more or less taken for granted, and we went along with that. Although it was done purely for hygienic reasons I, as a Jew who had been circumcised by a rabbi, was not at all displeased at the thought, but I now feel more ambivalent about routine circumcision. Life *à trois* in Mrs Higgs's little house undoubtedly became rather more trying, especially when Simon developed the notorious 'three months colic' and for a few weeks cried and cried in the evenings, only to be pacified by being driven round the streets of Pasadena in our 'green dragon'.

When Simon was five or six months old June kindly offered to look after him for a week whilst Joanne and I went on a backpacking trip in the Upper Sierras, together with Ernst and Inge Weinberg, who lived in northern California by then. We went with considerable trepidation, but June had established a good rapport with Simon and apparently he only cried seriously on our return. The week was tiring but exhilarating, for we had never been in a forest wilderness that had been left to fend for itself without human intervention of any kind. A Mexican burro (donkey) was hired in Yosemite Valley to carry some of our belongings up the steep path and we had a struggle to make it leave the fleshpots of Yosemite. It was a very different story on our return, when the creature was in such haste to get back that we were able to retrieve it on one occasion only because its path was blocked by a stile a quarter of a mile down the track. We had a very happy time, although Joanne and I frequently wondered how baby Simon was getting along – no mobile telephones in those days, and in retrospect I wonder at our courage or foolhardiness in leaving him. On our descent into Yosemite Valley we decided to have dinner there before returning, and to our mutual amazement we found that Hanna Bergas and Helmut Schneider were in the restaurant, entirely by coincidence. It was a very joyful reunion for all of us.

In a recent letter June Owen gave me some of her own reminiscences of the week she spent with Simon: 'I wanted to take care of Simon whilst you saw the Sierras for two reasons: so you would love California so much that you would want to come back again, and so that [sons] Dave and Griff could observe what it was like to have a baby in the house. My clearest memory is that they spent much time every day trying to teach him to creep . . . They demonstrated creeping tirelessly but he never did it. They were amazed when he did it a few weeks later, and once having done it acted as if he had always known how!'

So far as the laboratory work is concerned, I settled on a project that set out to prove that lymphoid cells (from spleen or lymph nodes) from mice immunised by cells from another strain had receptors on their cell surface (we called them cell-bound antibodies then) that could specifically bind antigens extracted from animals of the cell donor strain. I was joined in this enterprise by Jim Berrian, an American postgraduate student in Ray's department. In brief, we prepared semi-soluble extracts that we knew to be antigenic and tried to ascertain whether their ability to immunise mice against skin grafts was compromised by prior incubation with pre-sensitised lymphoid cells. In other words, would the extracts lose their antigenicity by absorption of the antigens onto the cell surface of the lymphocytes, which were removed before the extracts were tested? A positive result would indicate that the antigenic molecules had been removed by the cells, and this – coupled with appropriate controls – would be evidence in favour of the existence of specific cell receptors. It was rather arduous work but we did obtain positive results that we published in 1957 in the *Annals of the New York Academy of Sciences*. Unfortunately we failed to publish the data in a mainstream journal: on my return to England I immediately became embroiled with other projects, including the preparation of our massive monograph on GVHD, and Peter Medawar had always led me to think that it was reprehensible to publish the same data twice. Therefore the data did not become generally known. I would like to think that our work anticipated the much later discovery, using far more sophisticated tools, of specific lymphocyte receptors.

At this time Ray himself was not engaged in major laboratory studies, but he had several very bright graduate students and much of his considerable intellectual influence was exerted through them. When not teaching or working on behalf of the institute in one way or another he sat in his office, surrounded by piles of journals and papers, refereeing scientific papers submitted to him by journals, reviewing research grant applications or just keeping up with the literature. He usually smoked his beloved pipe and had excellent facilities for brewing tea, and he never stinted with his advice to others. 'Gee, that is *very* interesting, Leslie,' he would say, and then proceed to give me the benefits of his thoughts. Joining him had been a wonderful idea, from a purely personal perspective, though it is true that the experiments I carried out in his laboratory I could have been done equally well at University College. I should probably have spent the sabbatical learning molecular biology techniques, but the year was nonetheless a highlight in my life, and in Joanne's too, and I would not like to have missed the opportunity of getting to know Ray and June and their two boys David and Griffie. (Griffie died, tragically, in a car crash when still a young man.)

Our return to London was via New York, where we were to catch the *Queen Elizabeth* back to Southampton. We decided to travel to New

York in our ancient car; we turned the rear seat of the Buick into a
playpen-cum-bed for Simon and he was pretty comfortable and happy
there. The itinerary was complex but fascinating. We drove across the
Sierras to Las Vegas, and via Yellowstone National Park to Great Falls,
Montana, where we were to visit Ernst Eichwald ('Eich'), a senior
researcher in immunogenetics. We spent one night sleeping in the open
in Navajo territory, having had the excitement of watching a rain-making
ceremony the previous evening. The whole village had gathered together,
many drinking cold Coca-Cola, to admire the exotic dances, which were
accompanied by intriguing music that had repetitive but subtly changing
rhythms. It was definitely not intended for tourists, for we were the only
white people present. Amusingly enough, dark clouds gathered on the
horizon later that evening, but we couldn't delay our departure in the
morning to find out whether the ceremony had been successful. From
there we travelled, via Ray's brother's farm in Wisconsin (where we
were given sweetcorn straight from the field – corn on the cob has
never tasted quite right since then), to Boston to visit the Russells and,
finally, to New York.

Probably the most astonishing happening, the nature of which was
revealed only when we had reached Las Vegas, occurred in the forests of
the High Sierras, coming over the top beyond Tioga Pass. Ray had
sensibly advised us to travel across the desert to Las Vegas in the night
because of the unbearably high daytime temperatures, and even so we had
to keep our windows closed because of the heat. Our car unfortunately
had no air-conditioning. Suddenly and quite silently the darkness was lit
up as if by a gigantic, brilliantly white light. The incident cannot have
lasted more than a few seconds, but we were mystified and troubled by
it. On reaching Las Vegas, with a boiling engine, we learnt that an
atom bomb had been exploded on the Las Vegas test site not many
miles away . . .

One of the highlights for us was a fleeting visit to the rims of Grand
Canyon and Bryce Canyon; it was the latter that really captivated us, its
ochre limestone turrets and towers leaving an indelible impression. (I have
since walked through the canyon in Carol's company and it was magical.)
In Yellowstone National Park we decided to spend the night in the open
on a romantic little campsite, leaving Simon in the car very nearby.
Unfortunately he seemed to have developed German measles since
leaving Pasadena and began to cry in the night. Going to comfort him was
complicated by the fact that a brown bear was stalking around the site,
almost walking over our sleeping bags, and we had to wait for a few
minutes until the potential menace had disappeared. Simon's measles
presented us with a dilemma, as Joanne was not aware of ever having
contracted the disease, and she was about three months pregnant. We

therefore drove, with some trepidation, to Great Falls, where Eich very kindly arranged an inoculation of gammaglobulin in order to protect her baby, even though it was probably just past the stage at which it would have been most susceptible to the measles virus. The baby, Susanna, was happily unaffected as it turned out.

On arriving in New York we couldn't find anywhere to park, but I was fortunate to run into a slightly inebriated man who offered to buy the old Buick, now with another 12,000 miles on the clock, there and then for $100. This was half of what I had paid for it in Pasadena, but I jumped at the offer and quickly unloaded our luggage into the Pickwick Arms Hotel, where we stayed at a ridiculously low price. We almost arrived too late to board the *Queen Elizabeth* the next morning, for the crew had already begun to raise the gangplank. Morton Cohen and Dick saw us off; and so ended a memorable year. Jane and Oates were on the quay in Southampton to welcome us back, and to see their little grandson for the first time.

Family life

We returned to our flat in Hamilton Terrace, St John's Wood, where we occupied the top floor – formerly the servants' quarters – of an elegant Regency house that had been leased by the Duke of Atholl and his mother, Mrs Campbell-Preston. Once again this had come about thanks to Jean Medawar, who had recommended us. Mrs C-P was willing to sublet the top flat at an affordable rent in order to have someone in the house when, during the summer months, she and the Duke resided in Castle Atholl in the Highlands. Alas, they *were* burgled one weekend, when we had gone away, and some jewellery and a painting were stolen. The Duke, a languid young man who was said to be the most eligible bachelor in Britain, took it all very much in his stride. Our other obligation we were able to fulfil more successfully, for we were required to look after the very large garden, which comprised a large lawn and herbaceous borders, at the back of the house. Whilst I enjoyed gardening and it was a wonderful haven for the children, its maintenance was something of a burden to me; even so, I made several improvements and the lawn was in splendid condition by the time we left in 1965 for Southampton.

We had a succession of au pair girls – one or two indifferent or even dismal failures but two so likeable and reliable that they became close friends of the family and remain so to this day. Brigitte Krautwurst had been introduced to us by my old friend Gretel Heidt, and at first it was unsettling for me to have a German living with us as a member of the family. Happily, her presence helped me to overcome my prejudice against Germans. The other highly successful au pair was Christa Sonderegger from Switzerland, who arrived shortly before we moved to Southampton and stayed for two years. The whole family visited her family home near Zurich on more than one occasion, and we had one or two delightful holidays in a chalet in the Bernese Alps belonging to a friend of Christa's family. Christa and I climbed several mountains together, most notably the Blümlisalp traverse (three peaks linked by a narrow snow and ice ridge) and the Breithorn.

The Blümlisalp venture was my first major climb in Switzerland and I remember every minute of it most vividly. It began at the Blümlisalphütte, at about 3000m, and entailed a walk over a glacier on the approach to the peaks. We had hired a young guide from Bern who had been recommended to us, and in the early evening before our climb he was flown in by a friend in a two-seater plane that landed on the lower reaches of the glacier, quite close to the hut, having first looped the loop several times. This dramatic arrival caused quite a stir among the people who were staying in the hut and great excitement to us. Our guide turned out to be very pleasant and extremely competent, and it gave me a great thrill at four o'clock in the morning to be fastened to the rope that held the three of us together, with the snow crunchy and sparkling underfoot. An early departure was necessary because we had to return before midday, after which the snow bridges over the many small crevasses of the glacier became softer and less reliable. The guide led, I was in the middle and Christa brought up the rear. The climb proved to be a most wonderful experience for both of us, especially as we were lucky with the weather: we had a perfectly clear day once the sun rose. Parts of the climb were quite delicate, especially the connecting ridges, which were narrow and exposed. The views were ravishing. On returning we were shown how to 'ski' down a steep snow slope on our boots, using the ice axe as a rudder, and that too was exhilarating. We returned to the hut tired but with the feeling that we had lived through an unforgettable experience. Some years later I made the same climb in the company of Simon; on that occasion we had a different guide but it was a delight to undertake this wonderful climb accompanied by my son.

I was the self-appointed guide for the Breithorn climb, and Christa and I roped ourselves together and reached the top without mishap. It is technically an easy mountain but it involves crossing a glacier. We had left rather too late in the morning and almost got lost on our way down, near the bottom, in semi-darkness.

On another occasion Joanne, Christa and I walked up the Schildhorn, a popular mountain that sports a large café on its peak. It was a summer walk but there had been an inordinate amount of snow in the spring, and soon we were walking in very deep virgin snow. As we arrived at the top there was some embarrassing applause from a small crowd who had reached the top by cable car and had watched our progress from the edge of the platform. Joanne decided to take the cable car back to the middle station whilst Christa and I trudged back through the snow. Joanne told us that someone in the cable car said excitedly, 'Look, there are *footsteps* down there!' Joanne happily explained that they were hers . . . they couldn't believe it. I climbed the Breithorn again more recently, in the company of Carol, and on the narrow ridge on the approach to the top I had the satisfaction of saving a young girl's life. She had run ahead of her parents, passed us at speed and was about to slip on the icy snow down a precipice when I grabbed her by her anorak and pulled her back.

Although there were tensions in our marriage there was also much happiness, not least when we were on holiday in Greet Cottage, the home of Hannah and Hans Meyer, and by the seaside in Westgate, Kent. The Meyers very kindly allowed us to stay in their charming cottage not far from Bunce Court whenever they went abroad in the summer, and from there it was less than a two hour drive to the sea. We also stayed in Bunce Court several times. TA and TP still lived in what used to be the isolation hut, and they had converted one or two of the former classrooms into bedrooms. It was all rather primitive but the children thought it was fun and it enabled the Essingers to get to know our children. When we could afford it we stayed in a little hotel on the seafront of Westgate – the first time thanks to a generous gift from TA. Westgate was at that time an unspoilt little town with a sandy beach, and much time was spent swimming and building sandcastles, reminiscent of my own childhood holidays.

Although it became more difficult to partake of the rich cultural fare offered by London once we had children, there were a number of highlights. Outstanding among them was a performance of Benjamin Britten's *War Requiem* in Westminster Abbey, with an international cast of soloists – Peter Pears, Dietrich Fischer-Dieskau and Galina Vishnevskaya – who had been involved in its first performance in Coventry Cathedral in the previous year. It was, I think, early in December of 1962 and London was suffering from one of the worst smogs in its history, from which a large number of elderly people died. Joanne and I emerged from Westminster underground station and could barely see our hands in front of our faces. We began to walk, we thought, towards the abbey, and realised only when we were halfway across Westminster Bridge that we had taken a wrong turning. The interior of the abbey was foggy, too, though it was just about possible to see the orchestra and the soloists from way back. Even so, it was an inspiring performance of this magnificent and moving work, which I have more recently sung with the Crouch End Festival Chorus. I find it hard to credit that the *War Requiem*, which I find deeply moving, now has its detractors.

Inevitably we were invited out to dinner by friends and colleagues, and had to entertain them in our flat. As the chore of preparing the meals fell largely on Joanne's shoulders this caused some friction between us, and this would continue to be a problem all the way along.

1s and 2d

The birth of Susanna (or Sue as she prefers to be known) in 1958 I have already described. Jennifer (or Jenny, as *she* likes to be called) came five years later, not long before we moved to Southampton. The chosen careers of the two girls became evident quite early on. When my uncle and his wife visited us in Hamilton Terrace in the year of our move to Southampton they were enchanted when the two-year-old Jenny ran around the garden crying 'watch me, watch me'; naturally she became an actor, and a jolly good one at that. Her dramatic talent had been heralded by successes in several regional drama competitions when still at school. Having obtained a good degree in drama at Hull University and having decided against the commercial theatre, she has worked with a number of highly creative fringe companies, the latest being Horse and Bamboo, a group specialising in mime, masks, puppets and music. She has also directed plays at Salford University with great success. It is extraordinary for me that, as I write, my youngest child is celebrating her forty-fifth birthday. She now has a son, Oscar, with her partner Andy Kenny, a talented street performer/entertainer.

Sue's interest in horses became apparent soon after we moved to Southampton and it continued on our return to London. She showed considerable musical talent, but unfortunately abandoned the piano because she felt too pressurised by her piano teacher. She left school with few qualifications – she had decided to opt out without letting us into the secret – and Joanne and I enabled her to take a year's training as a riding instructor at a good residential school in Leicestershire. She worked with horses for the best part of nine years – grooming, training and teaching. Having decided that there was no future in this – she was still paid a pittance despite her qualifications and experience – we agreed that she should take a course as a Montessori nursery teacher. She became a much-loved teacher in the oldest Montessori school in London's East End, but gave that up after a few years because she was convinced that she had not yet found her true vocation. Sue once said to me, 'Dad, I am going to surprise you one of these days' and I was duly mystified. Well, she did surprise me when she decided to join a circus school as a trapeze and cloud-swing artist. She became much sought-after and, despite starting this career at an age (thirty) when others tend to retire from the fray, worked with the well-known French circus Archaos, among others. She also wrote and directed a show with her partner (later her husband) Dan's big band Spannerman, which toured internationally to great acclaim. (Dan has since become a music teacher, but continues to lead a big band.) Now that her two sons Milo and Louis are older she is building up a professional life as a teacher of the trapeze in her local community, and she has recently become, arguably, one of the first trapeze therapists in an English state primary school.

Simon too decided to leave school at the age of sixteen, never having shown much great academic interest. The careers teacher at Highgate School, where he had been a day boy, felt that Simon was best suited to an out-of-doors profession. Of this Joanne and I were already well aware, for he had greatly enjoyed the kind of activities that eventually led him to qualify for the Duke of Edinburgh Gold Award and he was a great companion when fell walking and camping. After considering with him a number of options that included farming, horticulture and forestry, he opted for the latter. Through my friendship with Dr Sue Isaacs Elmhirst we became aware of the forestry course offered by the Dartington Trust in south Devon. He applied and was interviewed in my presence. The head of the forestry department tried his level best to put Simon off by stressing more than once that forestry was a pretty messy and muddy business, but Simon was not to be discouraged. He was paid the minimum agricultural wage right through the two-year course and completed it very successfully, so much so that he was taken on when the course was discontinued and two additional workers were needed to help the instructors look after the beautiful woods (including a grove of redwoods) on the Dartington estate. He has worked in forestry ever since, eventually joining the management team of the large company that took over Dartington Forestry, and still lives in Devon with his partner Debbie, a nursery school teacher, and his children Luke and Emily.

All three of my children had to cope with unusual medical problems, which were surmounted. Simon was belatedly, when already at school, found to have a 'lazy eye', and despite wearing a patch over his good eye for quite a long time no significant improvement came about. He therefore has had to rely largely on vision in one eye, but this has not prevented him from playing cricket and squash. Jenny developed an excruciatingly painful back at the age of twelve or thereabouts and the doctors, even the specialist at Great Ormond Street Hospital, were mystified as to the cause. It was decided that the problem was probably 'developmental' and she had to cope with wearing a plaster corset for the best part of a year. This was very distressing for a young adolescent and hard on her parents too. In order to divert her – she was the only child at home at the time – we bought a beagle puppy to keep her company; Beth was much loved and was with us for twelve years before she died. She was ceremoniously buried in our garden. When the plaster was removed Jenny's back had spontaneously improved. It was Jenny to whom I read, at bedtime, not only Tolkien's *The Hobbit* but also all three volumes of *The Lord of the Rings*, attempting to maintain a distinct voice for each of the characters.

Sue went through two severe medical crises, and one of them probably accounts for her failure to make more of her opportunities at school. The first occurred at the age of six, when she developed Henoch-Schoenlein's Purpura. This is an autoimmune condition that sometimes follows a streptococcal infection, and it shows up dramatically with rounded red spots over much of the body. It is usually a self-limiting disease but in severe cases it can lead to kidney damage. Sue was treated at St Mary's Hospital by Professor Stanley Peart, an exceptionally good physician, and we felt that she was in excellent hands. Unfortunately she was in the Children's Hospital for two months and felt abandoned and frightened by the experience. At that time it was not possible for parents to stay with their sick children – and in any case Joanne was busy looking after baby Jennifer and Simon, while I was professionally very committed and contemplating my move to a Chair in Southampton. Poor Sue did not therefore see as much of either of us as she should have done. At about the time that Professor Peart was thinking of giving Sue a course of steroids – not a desirable therapy but possibly the only way to avoid kidney damage – Sue's condition improved spontaneously.

Sue's other encounter with hospitals was when she broke her coccyx: an insecurely fastened hammock fell down during a holiday in Switzerland, when she was nine years old. It was extremely painful but the senior orthopaedic surgeon at St Mary's did not think that it was broken and he was unwilling to undertake surgery. As a result we did not take the problem as seriously as we should have done, misled by the fact that Sue continued to go on horseriding. However, I eventually enlisted the help of an American orthopaedic surgeon friend, Gene Lance, who was working in Peter Medawar's laboratory at Northwick Park Hospital. He discovered, with the help of further X-rays, that the coccyx *was* broken and undertook the necessary surgery. It was a tricky operation that could easily have gone wrong, but it worked brilliantly and Sue was at last relieved of her pain.

I am immensely proud of my three children, not only because they have been true to themselves but because they are civilised, articulate and warmly affectionate, and care for the underdog and about the important issues of the day. All three have become exemplary parents.

Life in Southampton

It turned out to be a short stay in Southampton, a mere four years, and this account will be correspondingly brief, although my first years as a professor and head of department were very important to me. The university had invited me for interview in 1965 without an application on my part and I was able to insist on certain provisions, such as the appointment of three or four new members of staff and a 'temporary' Terrapin building (which needless to say exists to this day). It was conveniently located immediately outside the old-fashioned zoology building and it provided research laboratories for my own group and some of the new staff representing modern disciplines such as cell and developmental biology. The former head of department, having left quite some time before my arrival, had bequeathed me a couple of traditional zoologists, who by this time seemed somewhat demoralised and were more than a little fearful of how they would fit into a revamped department. They included Arthur Hockley, a marine zoologist who has just died at the age of ninety, and Estlin Hall, an entomologist, who likewise died recently – both without higher degrees but highly competent in their fields of interest and most pleasant colleagues. They need not have had any fears, for I was happy to integrate them fully as I was keen to have a broad curriculum that would not ignore whole animal zoology and ecology. The marriage between the old and the new proved to be very happy and productive from a teaching point of view.

Joanne had not been keen for me to become head of a department, mainly because she did not fancy becoming a professorial wife and possibly because she felt in her bones that this appointment would make me even busier. In this she was right, though life in provincial Southampton was in many ways much easier. I went through a severe crisis before accepting the post, but after fourteen years I felt the time had come to leave Peter Medawar's orbit and to establish myself independently. Peter evidently thought so too, for it was he who had recommended me to the university.

Reorganising the department proved to be hard work, and before taking up my appointment formally I commuted weekly between London and Southampton to sort things out at the Southampton end, which was hard on both of us. I was able to help with the design of the 'temporary' building and to make several crucial appointments – Tony Bell as reader, Norman Maclean as lecturer in cell biology, Frank Billett as senior lecturer in developmental biology, and Arthur Wild, who straddled both disciplines, as lecturer. All proved to be good appointments and all took their teaching as well as research very seriously. Several have remained good friends, especially Arthur and his Welsh wife Bronwen, a piano teacher. They all stayed on until retirement, and I recently attended Arthur's leaving party after thirty-seven years in post. Arthur Hockley was a keen sailor, and from time to time I was invited to crew for him in the Solent, which was always hugely enjoyable. Alan Cock, a geneticist, was already there, and the appointment of Philip Howe, whose interests lay in insect physiology, came a little later. The department became very popular with potential student applicants, partly because we had incorporated a major research project into the final year and partly because we taught both traditional and modern biology. Student selection involving a large number of interviews came to take up a great deal of time.

It was Arthur Hockley who had to adjudicate when a large and very dead three-legged cat was brought into the department, allegedly the 'wild beast' that had been spotted on a number of occasions roaming around in that part of Hampshire, attacking lambs and creating fear and excitement. Stories of such beasts, usually thought to be pumas or leopards, surface in the press from time to time, as happened quite recently in one of the Home Counties. They usually turn out to be false alarms, and on this occasion, too, Arthur Hockley decided that the wild creature was nothing more than a large domestic cat that had become feral.

Student unrest developed in British universities in the 1960s, having spread from the continent, and culminated in the occupations of university buildings in 1968. I was eager to avoid confrontation between students and staff in Southampton and allowed myself to be sent on a national weekend seminar on staff-student relations, on which I had decided views. As a result I reported back to the university senate and suggested several measures to strengthen staff-student relations. Most of these were adopted, including the representation of students in the senate. As a result the university suffered far less disruption than most.

Life in Southampton was pleasant enough for my family. We were able to buy a large Victorian house with an attractive garden, Sue was able to indulge her horse-riding hobby, there were walks in the New Forest and visits to the sea, and for me and Joanne the university provided a rich cultural as well social life, with chamber music concerts and lectures. Christa was with us for the first two years and so enabled Joanne to take part in some of these events. Even so, there were strains in our relationship, brought about partly by my heavy commitment to my department and the university, and my feeling that I did not have her whole-hearted support.

I tried not to impose my family history on my small children, though they knew that my parents and sister had been German Jews and that they had died in the war. Joanne must have told them rather more, for one day I returned home on my bicycle to be asked by Sue, who was eight, whether she could wash my feet. She had collected rose petals from the garden, which she placed in the footbath. I was taken aback and deeply touched at this demonstration of sympathy and at being comforted in this way by my little daughter. And so I underwent a little 'healing' foot-washing ceremony. Both Sue and Jenny tell me that they knew more about my past than I realised, and that they found my family's fate emotionally hard to cope with.

A few other incidents are worth recalling. In 1967 Peter Medawar (by now Sir Peter) was made an honorary fellow of the university, together with Sir Basil Spence, the architect, and several other distinguished people. After the ceremony Spence expressed his wish to show Peter and Jean and one or two others the very pleasant staff common room he had designed a few years earlier, and I accompanied them to it. One of the features of the bungalow-style building was a long window covering almost the whole of one side, equipped with a single Venetian blind. As the blind was closed Sir Basil gave its cord a mighty tug and the whole blind came crashing down, landing at our feet. I could barely suppress a guffaw as Spence said in an embarrassed voice, 'Oh well, it clearly hasn't been properly fixed,' and moved on. Peter and I exchanged an amused wink.

The second incident was rather less funny. I was cycling home one evening wearing a heavy duffle coat. Into each pocket I had put a box of eggs, which had been purchased from the departmental animal technician who ran a smallholding in his spare time. As I cycled down a steep hill barely out of the university precinct a motorbike that had been stationary in the gutter halfway down the hill made a sudden U-turn right in front of me, leaving me no choice but to squeeze the brakes hard. I shot over my bike's handlebars and landed in the middle of the road, with yellow stuff – yolk – leaking from my body. It must have been a frightening sight. I had a gash on one knee, my trousers were torn and I was slightly shocked, but otherwise uninjured. As I felt that the motorbike rider had been wholly to blame I reported him to the police, who decided to prosecute. He turned out to be a university student. His father was clearly well heeled as he engaged a high-powered London lawyer to defend his son in court. This is where I learnt for the first time that the law can be an ass. The police prosecution was feeble, to say the least, and allowed the defending lawyer to argue successfully that this mad professor careering down a hill at a rate of knots had caused the defendant's downfall. I wasn't even called to give evidence, and the young man was found to be not guilty.

The local weekly paper, the *Southern Evening Echo*, sent a young reporter to interview me when the first heart human transplant, carried out by Dr Christian Barnard, the South African heart surgeon, was reported. Although the reporter did not use shorthand my comments, which were not entirely uncritical, appeared in direct speech. There were as many as seventeen errors in the short article, and I wrote a letter to the editor to complain. He very properly published a correction of the more substantial points. A few weeks later I received a letter from a well-known London firm of libel lawyers stating that I had impugned the professional integrity of the reporter, threatening to take me to court unless I published an apology. I wasn't willing to do anything of the sort but felt I needed to get advice from the Professor of Law on how to respond. He suggested that I should consult a local solicitor, who turned out to be so overawed by the reputation of the London law firm that he advised me to compose a carefully worded letter of apology. This went totally against the grain but, having consulted a solicitor, I felt obliged to accept his advice. I squeezed out a very guarded apology and thought that would be the end of the matter. However, the editor replied that he would on no account publish my letter because he felt the reporter had been entirely at fault, and had indeed left his employment. No more was heard from the law firm. I have ever since been wary of consulting solicitors on anything other than house purchase or making a will.

The critical comments I had made referred in the main to the fact that a Californian team, led by Dr Norman Shumway, had in fact done the spadework on heart transplantation by careful research in dogs, and Barnard, who had great surgical skills, had taken a great risk in jumping the gun. Barnard was a flamboyant character who enjoyed his sudden status as a mega-celebrity. Though opposed to apartheid, he left South Africa soon after its downfall. Suffering from rheumatoid arthritis, he had to give up surgery at the age of sixty-one and allowed himself to become involved in some dubious commercial rejuvenation protocols.

The British Universities Vietnam Orphans Fund

In the winter of 1966 I had a bad bout of influenza, which forced me to take to my bed for several days. In my fevered state I read in the *Guardian* several articles by Martha Gellhorn, the American journalist, about the desperate plight of the thousands of children who had been orphaned in the Vietnam War. In both South and North Vietnam these children were either abandoned or herded into large and impersonal orphanages, usually in atrocious conditions. Gellhorn was an outstanding and passionate war reporter and the articles struck a chord deep within me. Although I had my hands quite full enough at the time I felt that something needed to be done about these children, and the idea of a British Universities' Vietnam Orphans Fund was conceived. Joanne thought it was a good idea, even though it promised to be yet another diversion from family life, and so I sent a letter to the *Guardian* calling for financial support, and letters to just about every university in the country. My friend Nigel Glendinning, the Professor of Spanish, agreed to act as honorary treasurer and I was the fund's self-appointed secretary and chairman. (Nigel's wife at that time was Victoria, who has since become a much admired biographer.)

The response was extraordinary, both from *Guardian* readers and from the universities. Within days we had several thousand pounds to bank, and a year later the fund had swollen to around £30,000. That was a lot of money in the mid-sixties. Each contribution was formally acknowledged and personal letters were written to major donors. Nigel and I were anxious that children in both the South and the North should benefit, and Martha Gellhorn suggested one particular orphanage in Saigon which, she thought, would almost certainly spend our money sensibly. North Vietnam presented a greater problem, but the International Red Cross promised to transmit our funds to an appropriate organisation in Hanoi. And so it was that around £15,000 was transmitted to both North and South Vietnam for the alleviation of the plight of their war orphans. It was a remarkably successful venture Nigel and I found deeply satisfying. It did, however, make considerable inroads into our personal lives.

Martha Gellhorn, who had set this ball rolling with her impassioned reporting, was an extraordinary woman. To my regret I lost touch with her and discovered only by reading her obituary in 1998 just what a major contribution she had made to war reporting in general; and what a colourful life she had led. It seems sad that a book published about her more recently, *Beautiful Exile: The Life of Martha Gellhorn* by Carl Rollyson, arguably dwelt more on the men with whom she had slept, including Ernest Hemingway, than on her singular courage and the quality of her writing.

Back to London

In 1967 I received an invitation from Professor Brambell to visit his department of zoology in Bangor, north Wales, with a view to taking over from him on his retirement. My loyalty to my department, and my feeling that I had not completed the task of modernising it, led me to turn that offer down, even though I visited Bangor for a day or two, and had every possible encouragement from Brambell.

However, when two years later I was asked by St Mary's Hospital Medical School in Paddington, London, to be interviewed for the Pfizer Chair of Immunology I accepted gratefully, though after much heart-searching, and not before a hastily arranged meeting with Av Mitchison to seek his advice. I had become frustrated at my inability to spend enough time in the lab whilst building up my department, and I felt that my research was in danger of becoming trivial. My predecessor was Rodney Porter, who had been the first Professor of Immunology in Britain and who was to receive the Nobel Prize for his contribution to the unravelling of the structure of antibodies. St Mary's also had a great reputation through men like Almroth Wright and Alexander Fleming, and it had very good clinical departments. One other attraction was that it had an active programme of kidney transplantation run by Professor Peart's department, and that the Professor of Experimental Pathology had a special interest in the pathology of transplanted organs. Because the Chair had been vacant for a year or two the department was virtually defunct and physically in poor condition. As the school was keen to have me I was able to persuade it to allow me to employ a reasonable group of academic and technical staff, and to purchase equipment that a research-funding body such as the Medical Research Council would not normally provide.

And so, after only four years, the Brent family moved back to London, this time to a pleasant house and garden in leafy Muswell Hill.

Chapter Fourteen: Twenty-One Years at St Mary's Hospital Medical School

*J*oanne and I found a house in Wood Vale, which we took to as soon as we saw it, partly because it answered our needs and had a large garden, and partly because it was very close to Queen's Wood, a delightful natural and hilly wood suitable for walks and sledging when there was snow. We found schools for the three children: Camden School for Girls for Sue, Hornsey Girls' Comprehensive School for Jenny and Highgate School for Simon. The latter was a minor public school (i.e. private) and we chose it because it was very near to us, had small classes and offered Simon a congenial environment in which we hoped he would flourish. Camden School had a very good reputation, both academically and for its music, and we thought we were lucky to have Sue accepted there as we were not in its catchment area. As it turned out, Sue did not respond well to the academic pressure and competitive climate of this school, whereas Jenny was happy in Hornsey School even though it was single-sex, and she did well in her A level examinations. We were able to place Simon at Highgate because Joanne's parents had very kindly offered to pay the fees for the first few years.

Arriving at St Mary's

I had used a bicycle for most of my life (except for the four years at the National Institute for Medical Research, which was too far away) and St Mary's was just within cycling range. Uphill on the way home, though! The first weeks in the department were absolute bedlam: the technicians I appointed – especially Alan Bain as senior technician – and a few members of staff and I had to clear out the laboratories before some of them could be renovated, and there were times when I was wondering what I was doing there. It all settled down, there was plenty of space and more staff moved in gradually. The teaching and research programmes developed and my colleagues and I managed to obtain grants to maintain active research programmes.

My own research group – one or two postdoctoral fellows and two or three postgraduate research students – devoted itself to transplantation immunology, my own interests being in the induction of immunological tolerance in adult mice and the study of the mechanisms that underpinned it once it had been achieved. As in Southampton, I felt that there should be diverse teaching and research skills, and the lecturers I appointed all worked in quite different areas of immunology.

School politics

I was warmly received by the school. Fortunately Rodney Porter had already blazed the trail as a non-medical Professor of Immunology in a medical setting. The part-time dean was Robert Williams, the Professor of Bacteriology, whose department was immediately above mine – and with which we soon established both teaching and research links. He was a jovial man who refused to be bound by red tape and I got on very well with him. The school secretary, Mr Stevenson, was very much of the old school, formal and conservative in his opinions, but extremely helpful when it really mattered. When I raised the low proportion of women students at the time – of the order of 20 per cent – at a meeting of the academic board, as a question that needed to be addressed, he famously intervened by saying: 'But Mr Dean, if we were to take in more women we wouldn't have enough toilet facilities for them'! I think that the main concern was that women students would undermine the high quality of the rugby team, which was carrying all before them. Before I left twenty-one years later the ratio was at least 50:50 and in some years there were more women than men. Toilet facilities were improved, the rugby team's success continued unabated and academic standards were even higher.

When Robert Williams became tired of the administrative chores that the deanship involved he was succeeded by a physician, Harold Edwards. He was a charming man and an excellent doctor, but he seemed to be somewhat out of his depth when it came to decision-making for the academic departments and the complexities of the school-hospital interrelationship. The post of dean had become more and more onerous and when Edwards' period of office came to an end the school decided to appoint a fulltime dean from outside. We were fortunate in appointing Dr Peter Richards, a physician who had considerable administrative experience and aptitude. Indeed, his presence was of great benefit to the school at a time when its small size threatened to spell disaster, for the university was anxious to reduce its expenditure on medical education and threatened to merge medical schools and possibly close some of the smaller ones. Richards proved to be an astute advocate for the school, and he initiated discussions with Imperial College with a view to merging the two institutions.

Whilst some of the professors and many of the physicians saw the merger as a threat to the identity of the school, its small size making for a good relationship between staff and students and favouring an exceptionably active sporting and cultural life, the majority of members of the academic board agreed that it would be a wise move in the political climate that prevailed in the 1980s. The dean believed in strong government, without unduly kowtowing to the niceties of the democratic process, and as a result the academic board became something of a rubberstamping body. Few of its members found the courage to argue against proposals emanating from the dean and his closest advisors, and I did not court popularity with him by expressing dissent on some issues. Whilst I did not oppose the merger I predicted that it would have certain adverse consequences, such as the probable loss of the preclinical departments. That is precisely what has happened: these departments were moved to the site of Imperial College, and the school is now largely clinical and research-orientated. However, I am sure that the merger was in the best interests of the school and its survival, even if the *ésprit de corps* that was its hallmark has been greatly diminished.

As a non-medical scientist I did feel somewhat disadvantaged when engaging in debate with my clinical colleagues. It was therefore a lovely surprise to receive a letter, one day, from Dr Oscar Craig, the head of the radiology department of the hospital, expressing his warm appreciation of the role I was playing on the academic board and urging me to continue to express my views without fear or favour. My main regret at not having been elected to a Royal Society fellowship – Medawar had nominated me unsuccessfully in the late 1970s – was that it would have added to my political clout in the school.

The department of immunology, and other responsibilities

I had an active research group throughout my stay at St Mary's. Following in Medawar's footsteps I kept it small. The PhD students included Colin Brooks, Lee Rayfield and Rosemary Sherwood. I also supervised Vivian Rumjanek, a Brazilian student who is now Professor of Immunology in Rio de Janeiro and who recently re-established contact with me. I succeeded in reclaiming from the USA one very talented post-doctoral fellow, Ian Hutchinson, who spent some productive years with me before moving on to Oxford. It was a privilege to be able to carry out research without being hemmed in by the school in any way, the only limiting factor being the availability of research grants. In the 1970s medical research was still well funded in the UK, principally by the Medical Research Council. It became much harder in the 1980s, when the MRC was forced to turn down highly rated grant applications for lack of funds. Sir James Gowans, FRS, the physiologist who discovered that lymphocytes recirculate from the lymph to the blood and back again, became secretary of the MRC. The story goes that when he attended a reception given by the Prime Minister, Mrs Thatcher, he was greeted coldly with the words, 'Ah, this is the man who allowed the monoclonal technology to go to the United States!' She had evidently done her homework but not quite thoroughly enough, for Gowans had nothing whatever to do with that unfortunate episode; it happened well before he took office.

I have already referred to the research I carried out at St Mary's (pp. 127–32). My teaching duties were light and I was therefore able to spend a fair amount of time in the laboratory. I was also well served by my excellent secretary, Gill Arscott, who saved me from numerous chores and patiently typed my research papers, usually in two or three drafts. When in later years I acquired a word processor for her she was very unwilling to induct me into its secrets: 'you stick to your typewriter and leave me to the computer, Leslie' was her attitude; I loved her dearly.

As in Southampton, I took full responsibility for my department but ran it democratically, with staff meetings attended by all members of the academic staff as well as the chief technician. The problems we had to consider weren't of the same magnitude as in Southampton, where such meetings could take up the best part of a Saturday morning and on one occasion ran into the afternoon, but major decisions were always taken by agreement of the majority. Teaching, especially the running of the intercalated BSc courses that included a significant piece of original research for each student, took up much time, as did the creation of a London University-based MSc course in immunology. I was chairman of the committee that founded and ran this course, and my department contributed two modules, one in transplantation immunology and another in clinical immunology. The intercalated BSc course in immunology became very popular with students from St Mary's as well as one or two other medical schools, and the MSc course is still flourishing.

I served as chairman of the school's BSc committee for a number of years. This was normally a pretty straightforward task – the approval of new courses and the ratification of examination grades – but I had to deal with one very delicate situation. A lecturer in another department had been accused of having given a student taking his intercalated BSc course a higher grading than was justified, and it fell upon me and the committee to look into what was a serious allegation of academic misconduct. Having extensively interviewed all concerned, including the external examiner who was not happy about what had occurred, the lecturer was duly reprimanded and reported to the dean. As a result I was informally threatened with legal action for defamation of character. This time I did *not* bother to consult a solicitor and stood my ground, and the lecturer eventually left the employment of the school. Fortunately this kind of thing happens rarely, and I have not encountered anything else like it in almost four decades of university life.

The library

At the expense of my research activities I allowed other commitments in the school to make inroads into my time and energy, for I believed that as a professor I had a duty to serve the school not merely by being a competent head of department. For example, I was chairman of the library committee for a number of years, during which we undertook the wholesale renovation and improvement of our splendid library. (Nigel Palmer was its valued librarian.) It was oak-panelled and with a shelved balcony extending all the way round it, and until the school built a recreation centre nearby it was used about once a month for chamber concerts and for student operatic and dramatic performances. Its acoustics were good and it provided a very intimate ambience for piano recitals or chamber music. The artists were mainly young and up-and-coming, and sent to us by a dear elderly lady at Ibbs & Tillett, the music publishers. These young performers were glad to have a dress rehearsal for concerts at the Wigmore Hall or elsewhere and they gave their services free. It was here that I first heard the Endellion String Quartet, who have since become so very well known. Some of the established performers had been patients in the hospital, and Segovia gave several recitals following the birth in the hospital of two children to a much younger wife. Although he was then already past his prime those evenings were quite magical. The concerts were highlights in the life of the school, and Joanne came along whenever possible. I was delighted when the Music Society asked me to be their president, following in Sir Stanley Peart's footsteps.

Nonetheless, as chairman of the library committee I saw it as my task to ease student activities out of the library, for they caused some upheaval, especially when a stage had to be erected for operatic and dramatic performances. This could disorientate the library's functions for a week at a stretch. But the new recreation centre had good acoustics, too, and was much better suited for some of the musical and dramatic activities even though it lacked the atmosphere of the library. Queen Elizabeth the Queen Mother was patron of the Operatic Society and she came to a number of performances, particularly when Gilbert and Sullivan operas were performed.

Almroth Wright and the lectures dedicated to him

The intellectual jewel in the crown of the medical school took the form of the four annual Almroth Wright lectures, named after the pathologist/ bacteriologist who had worked in the school in the first half of the twentieth century. He had espoused the cause of anti-typhoid vaccination during the First World War and made a number of discoveries in the field of pathology. The most important of these, so far as immunology is concerned, had been to achieve a compromise between the German school of immunochemists, who believed that antibodies are the body's main line of defence, and the Russian biologist Metchnikoff, who believed equally fervently that certain cells of the body, the phagocytes, fulfilled that role. Wright and his colleague S.R. Douglas achieved a synthesis by showing that phagocytic cells take up foreign material such as bacteria far more avidly when they had become coated with antibodies directed against the bacteria. Thus both antibodies and cells were shown to be important. It was Wright, a great friend of George Bernard Shaw's, who gave Shaw the inspiration for the doctor in the play *A Doctor's Dilemma.*

The annual lectures were set up to commemorate Wright, though I always thought it odd that Alexander Fleming was not associated with them. Fleming worked in Wright's department when he discovered the penicillin mould and the relationship between them was said not to have been very amicable, presumably because Wright saw the discovery of an antibiotic as undermining the need for vaccination, but also because their personalities differed markedly. It was Wright who had accumulated substantial funds from his clinical work and he left these to the school when he retired. The Almroth Wright lecturers were paid from these funds. Like other pathology departments mine benefited from time to time, until the fund was absorbed into the school's general coffers.

I never knew Wright, who died in 1947 long before I arrived, but he was well known to be an extreme misogynist who would not permit women to work in his 'inoculation department' at St Mary's and who wrote virulent pamphlets against the suffragette movement. He instituted mid-afternoon tea for the academic staff in his department. Tea was taken around a splendid Victorian table covered with a white tablecloth. This somewhat bizarre ritual, to which members of my department were invited, persisted well into the 1970s. More can be gleaned about this colourful personality from a recent article by Francis Diggins and from the history of St Mary's Hospital by E.A. Heaman.

I was chairman of the Almroth Wright lectures committee for many years. Suggestions of topics and lecturers came mainly from the pathology departments, and because immunology came to be seen to underpin so many other disciplines, each year one or two were devoted to one aspect or other of immunology. The lecturers were in the main from this country and they were chosen for outstanding research. On one occasion we went well beyond the realm of pathology by inviting Fred Hoyle, the well-known astronomer who, with a colleague, had proposed the theory that primitive molecules had come from outer space and had formed the building blocks of living organisms. Apparently viruses were continuing to rain down on to our planet via certain meteoric streams, causing some of the major influenza epidemics. He put up a faintly plausible case but was politely given a hard time from a packed audience, which included many microbiologists. Hoyle had been a participant in the development of several major astronomical theories – the notion that the universe developed, and is still developing, in a continuous state (1948), as opposed to the big bang theory that had previously been favoured, and a theory (1957) explaining the origin of the elements from the build-up of elements in the hot interior of stars. Although he had been elected to fellowship of the Royal Society and been awarded a knighthood, he was passed over for the Nobel Prize given to some of his collaborators in the formulation of these theories. He died in 2001.

The creation of the Clinical Immunology Laboratory, and the battle for the Allergy Clinic

Within a few years of my appointment I decided that the department ought to have a clinical laboratory providing a diagnostic service to the hospital. I found the hospital departments very responsive but it was hard to persuade the school and the hospital to find the funds for the creation of a lab, in a space that had become available close to my department, and for the appointment of a clinical immunologist and one or two technicians. The senior lectureship for a clinical immunologist was eventually funded jointly between the hospital and the school. In 1974 we were fortunate to secure the services of Dr Helgi Valdimarsson, an Icelander then working at the Hammersmith Hospital, and Jill Boler, who became senior technician in the clinical lab. Helgi was in overall charge of the diagnostic tests offered and their interpretation, and I was the fund-holder. His research interests in immunodeficiency – a cluster of conditions caused by suppression of the immune system through natural causes or drugs – fitted well into the department's research programme, and the range of the diagnostic tests on offer to clinicians was steadily expanded. Helgi proved to be an excellent clinician and he was soon seen to be a great asset to the hospital. He had a succession of PhD students, including Gordon Bridges, who in due course had the good sense to marry Jill Boler.

Our clinical laboratory was one of the first in the UK and other medical schools soon followed suit. As immunological processes are at work in so many medical conditions – from allergy to autoimmune and immunodeficiency diseases to cancer – it is not surprising that there are few major hospitals now without such a laboratory and a clinical immunologist. I also felt that the clinical laboratory benefited greatly from its attachment to the academic department, and vice versa. It is continuing to be an important provider of diagnostic assays though it is no longer located within the department of immunology – thanks to the short-sightedness of my immediate and short-lived successor.

St Mary's Hospital had the largest outpatients allergy clinic in the UK. It had been established in the 1930s by A.W. (Bill) Frankland and J. Freeman and had a very good countrywide reputation, treating allergic conditions right across the spectrum. Frankland was its director for many years until his retirement in 1980. Although a good clinician, he had not taken full advantage of the research opportunities presented by so much clinical material and the hospital authorities decided to discontinue the clinic after his retirement. Here seemed to be a good opportunity to save funds and to make precious space available to other departments. That is why there wasn't much opposition to this move and it was left to me, a non-medical scientist, to argue the cause of the allergy clinic. I was very familiar with the field of allergy as I had given lectures on both its scientific and clinical aspects to pre-clinical and clinical undergraduates: to axe a thriving clinic seemed to me to be absolute madness. As well as arguing the case with the dean I had a lengthy interview with the hospital's chief executive, Barbara (now Baroness) Young, and I was astonished to discover that she thought, and clearly had been led to believe by some of the physicians, that allergic conditions were relatively trivial and did not present significant medical problems. I pointed out that there were not a few that were life-threatening, such as anaphylactic reactions in response to bee stings, drugs and certain foods, and that allergic reactions were on the rise. (Barbara Young left to become secretary of the Royal Society for the Protection of Birds and is now director of the Environmental Agency.)

Eventually my arguments won the day and it was agreed to retain a somewhat slimmed down allergic clinic. But who was to fund the salary of its director? I worked my socks off to persuade the Asthma Research Council to provide a five-year grant covering half the cost of a senior lecturer, and the hospital and school between them provided the other half. So it was that Dr Pamela Ewan was appointed, with her research base in my department. This arrangement was greatly to the benefit of the hospital, the school and my department.

The scourge of AIDS and the emergence of St Mary's as the first treatment centre

In 1982 Helgi Valdimarsson returned to Iceland to become the country's first Professor of Immunology, and I appointed Dr A.J. Pinching as his successor in the clinical laboratory. Like Valdimarsson he came from the Hammersmith Hospital, where he had worked on diseases associated with immune deficiency. Tony proved to be an able clinician, and the laboratory expanded under his leadership, both in the range of tests offered and the number of technicians employed.

Soon after his arrival one of our venereologists, Dr Willy Harris, came to see me about a clinical problem with which he had been confronted. He was studying the incidence of hepatitis B in gay men, and some of their behavioural characteristics struck him as very similar to those reported very recently in American gay patients suffering from AIDS. What is more, one or two of his patients had presented with Karposi's sarcoma, a cutaneous disease that can progress to the lungs and the gastrointestinal tract and is most commonly seen in people infected with HIV (human immunodeficiency virus). Could I put him in touch with an immunologist willing to take an interest in this phenomenon, he asked. I pointed him in the direction of Tony Pinching, thus triggering a productive partnership in the study of AIDS and the treatment of patients. It wasn't long before St Mary's became known as 'the AIDS hospital', rather to the disapproval of many physicians. However, St Mary's became one of very few hospitals in London able and willing to deal with these patients, and it fulfilled a vital role in this respect.

Pinching set out to study the pathology/immunology of AIDS and obtained research grants to enable him to do this. Within a year or two it became clear that AIDS was not confined to homosexuals, and that the threat it posed was one for the wider community, including heterosexual men and women, intravenous drug users, recipients of blood or blood products, and the children of HIV-positive mothers. There was a huge amount of ignorance and prejudice in those early years and some parents refused to send their children to schools in which an HIV-positive child had been identified. Tony did some stalwart and time-consuming work to put the record straight and to counteract the irrational fears held by many people. He did so by writing popular articles and, on a few occasions, by visiting schools in which the problem had arisen. It was only after he had met parents of children at a school in Chandler's Ford, Hampshire, that some of them allowed their children to return, a single haemophilic child having been identified as possessing the virus. This vitally important educational work did not endear him to grant-giving bodies, and he had to struggle to maintain his research base. On one occasion the MRC turned down his proposal for a grant to study cytotoxic T lymphocytes in AIDS patients because, he was told, another worker was about to commence work on similar lines. These cells have since been shown to play an important role in the body's defence against this highly mutable virus, which is particularly vicious in that it infects the very cells involved in the elimination of viruses. (See J.A. Levy's *HIV and the Pathogenesis of AIDS.*)

Tony calculated that by the end of 1990 there could be as many as 100,000 infected people in the UK. Whilst some thought this to be a gross and wilful exaggeration – one pathologist told me that AIDS was just a temporary blip and that Tony was wasting his time – this figure was never reached precisely because of the educational campaigns fought by physicians like Pinching and eventually by the Ministry of Health. The widespread use of condoms has been a major factor in limiting the rate of infection in the UK. The decline in mortality rates is largely owing to the development of anti-retroviral drugs, which are reasonably effective in limiting the HIV infection as well as some of the secondary infections. They do not, however, provide a cure. I attempted (unsuccessfully) to have Tony's readership upped to a personal Chair, and he left St Mary's in 1992, two years after my retirement, to become Professor of Immunology at St Bartholomew's Hospital.

Millions have died worldwide of the disease, and at the time of writing it is estimated that 30–40 million are infected. Death is usually associated with secondary infections because the immune system is compromised by HIV. The worst affected areas are Africa and parts of Asia, and some African countries have an infection rate as high as 30 per cent. Many countries have been slow to acknowledge that there is a problem, including Catholic countries like Poland, where AIDS simply wasn't talked about until it became a serious problem. I remember being the guest of the Polish Society for Immunology, of which I later became an honorary member, in the mid-1980s, to talk about organ transplantation. In my introduction I urged the society to take AIDS seriously before it took a real hold in their country, but I was told that homosexuality was not officially acknowledged and that the subject of AIDS was taboo.

The situation in Africa is well known to be dire. Virtually a whole generation will be wiped out, leaving millions of orphans, many themselves infected from birth. The drugs that could prevent the transmission of the disease from infected mothers to their babies, and which could rein in the disease in adults, are too expensive to be widely available; neither the international community nor the drug companies are willing to shoulder the burden to change this, though there are signs that they are becoming conscious of their responsibility. Unfortunately the situation has been made much worse by the incomprehensible and irrational, not to say perverse, stance taken by the former South African president Thabo Mbeki, who until very recently has consistently denied that AIDS is caused by a virus. Instead, he has proposed that malnourishment is the main cause of the disease. He has based his opposition to the conventional explanation for AIDS on the views of one maverick American virologist, P. Duesberg. Nelson Mandela has done his best to set the record straight, both when he was president and since his retirement, and it looks as if the tide of opinion has at last turned in the face of the horrendous evidence.

Princess Diana became very much involved with AIDS patients and did much to undermine the stigma of the disease. She opened a new AIDS ward at St Mary's Hospital in 1988 and it was said that she sometimes visited AIDS patients in the dead of night, away from prying cameras. Thus it was that when writing my book on the history of transplantation immunology, after my retirement, in the Clarence wing of the hospital I looked out for her whenever I left the hospital in the small hours. This happened not infrequently in the rush to meet the editor's deadline – but I never caught sight of her.

External examining

Academics are expected to agree to act as external examiner when asked by another university department. I performed this role for the zoology department of the University of Wales, Aberystwyth for some years and for the MSc course in immunology at Birmingham University. The BSc theses at Aberystwyth were quite often devoted to an immunological topic but my background as a zoologist enabled me to be a reasonable judge of projects in widely different subjects. The trips to Bangor were invariably pleasant, for they entailed changing on to a single-track railway line in Wolverhampton, the train slowly meandering through an attractive landscape (once we were out of the Black Country) that included the north Wales coastline. Drivers had to exchange batons with oncoming trains at certain passing points to prevent collisions. Ah, those were the days! I don't suppose this line has survived modernisation. I was also glad to be reminded of what life was like in a somewhat isolated provincial university: agreeable, but without the zing of cosmopolitan London.

The MSc theses in Birmingham were all immunological and they involved original research on a wide variety of topics. I enjoyed returning to my Alma Mater and on one occasion I took the opportunity of being in the Midlands on a Friday afternoon to go on to the Lake District, where I stayed in a youth hostel for a couple of nights. Blacksail Hostel is the smallest and most basic hostel in England and it is well positioned for some glorious walks. I was greeted by the friendly warden with a cup of tea and later a delicious meal. I climbed Great Gable the next day. This was at a time, in 1983, when Joanne had left me for the best part of eighteen months and I relished the calming solitude of the mountains. On the way I had stopped off in Blackpool, which I had never visited, thinking that I would spend a night there. A drive round the one-way circuit of the town, which was hosting a Labour party conference, was enough. I was so appalled by the town, which seemed to consist of nothing but amusement arcades and shops selling trinkets and fast food, that I drove out without stopping and made for my beloved Lake District.

It is my favourite spot anywhere in the world, and at one time or another I have stood on many of its peaks and viewed these glorious mountains, with their green valleys and secretive lakes, from a variety of angles. Although the highest of them – Scafell, Scafell Pike and Helvellyn – are only just over 3000ft high they are formidable all the same, mainly because they rise not far from sea level and have stark cliffs and precipices. The simplest routes up are quite easy but, depending on the weather, they can be treacherous to the unwary and ill clad.

Other examining took the form of PhD and MD theses. These always require much time and very great care, for to damn a thesis would be to blight the career of a young person forever. Yet the role of external examiners is to ensure that a high standard is upheld throughout the university sector and I had to refer a few theses back to students for further work and/or revision. Only one thesis was rejected outright by me. This happened to come from Australia and my co-examiner was the eminent virologist/immunologist Macfarlane Burnet, who had played such an important role in the discovery of immunological tolerance. I found it quite abysmal and wrote my report accordingly, offering to give the student an oral examination and to confer with my co-examiner. Back came the uncompromising answer that Burnet had thought it quite as bad as I had, and that he was unwilling to have it given any further consideration.

On reading these theses – some twenty or thirty – I was frequently struck by the intimate knowledge displayed by the candidates of their immediate field, going back in time by perhaps a decade or so. But most seemed to have no idea of where the concepts they were grappling with had come from: there was no sense of the continuity of science and of a historical perspective. I usually asked at least one historical question during the oral examination, and the answers were frequently dismal. It was this deficiency that prompted me to write *A History of Transplantation Immunology* after my retirement.

I was asked by successive deans to serve on small panels that interviewed candidates for admission to the school and later I chaired a number of these. The students had been selected for interview by the secretary and the dean on the strength of their application forms and the A level grades predicted for them by their headteachers, and about half could be expected to make the grade. One tried to assess their intellectual qualities as well as their personalities and to draw them out to talk about their special interests. I am afraid that some of the clinical interviewers seemed to set much store on whether the candidate had doctors in the family, a question that I regarded as irrelevant and inappropriate. I tended to give students from comprehensive schools the benefit of the doubt when comparing them with others who had been educated in grammar or public schools. This whole question has recently become a subject for hot discussion, for the government is trying to persuade universities to make their intakes more inclusive. Whilst I am in sympathy with this I also believe that, ultimately, it is the intellectual potential of young people that must be paramount.

Dean Peter Richards very courageously allowed a BBC team to film a number of interviews and then to follow a small group of students throughout their training and beyond. This series, which has been shown on television several times, hugely increased the popularity of St Mary's and the number of applications soared. However, the last two programmes showed some of the problems young doctors had to face – inhumanely long hours and relatively poor pay – and it was depressing that one or two of the small group dropped out in the end.

Presidency of the (International) Transplantation Society, and a very baffling incident

In 1976 I was elected to be president of the International Transplantation Society, an event that pleased me greatly, both Peter Medawar and Rupert Billingham having preceded me in this highly esteemed office. Medawar had been the society's first elected president in 1968, and the only other British president had been a transplant surgeon, Professor Sir Michael Woodruff. All except me had been fellows of the Royal Society and two were knights of the realm: in both respects I was the odd man out. Other British presidents elected later on were Richard Batchelor (immunologist) and Sir Peter Morris, FRS (surgeon). A recent incumbent was the society's first woman president, Kathryn Wood (immunologist) from Oxford, a felicitous choice.

The congresses of the Transplantation Society are held every two years and the presidency covers the preceding two, leading up to the congress. They alternate between the so-called western and eastern hemispheres, and the congress for which I had some responsibility was to be held in Rome in 1978, with a surgeon, let us call him Dr X, as chairman of the local organising committee.

The preparations for the congress went full steam ahead and I visited Rome on one occasion to help the local committee to draw up the final programme. All was sweetness and light, and Dr X informed me that my family and I would be put up in style in the Hilton Hotel, that we would be installed in the front row at the special audience with His Holiness Pope John Paul so that I could be introduced to him together with some other officers of the society, and that a car would be put at our disposal for the duration of the congress. Dr X was influential in the Vatican and had arranged this special audience for the whole membership of the congress on the Sunday morning of the opening ceremony.

On arrival the day before the congress we were indeed accommodated luxuriously in the Hilton Hotel. Only Simon and Jenny were with me and Joanne as Sue had other commitments. The arrangements were confirmed: Dr X's secretary would pick us up next day and escort us to our seats at the front of the hall. However, on the day itself the atmosphere in the office of the local committee suddenly became very frosty. I was virtually ignored and Dr X barely managed a cursory greeting. I was totally baffled and not a little upset at this inexplicable discourtesy. His secretary failed to turn up at the appointed place and we made our own way into the audience hall, sitting somewhere near the back. Dr Guy Voisin, a senior French transplantation immunologist, and his wife were with us, and they thought it outrageous that I should not be sitting near the front. Thanks to Guy's urgent intervention we were eventually escorted to the front, but I was not among those introduced to the Pope. I was very impressed by his address to the congress and by his sincerity and genuine humility. I harboured some doubts as to appropriateness of a papal address as part of a scientific and medical congress that was made up of men and women from all kinds of religions and none, but it undoubtedly gave the congress worldwide publicity.

The presidential car failed to materialise and I had to fend for myself at all social functions. I, the president of the society, was suddenly and mysteriously *persona non grata*. I found it especially embarrassing for Joanne. This was to be one of the highlights of my professional career and here I was, totally isolated and ignored by the local organiser and left both baffled and angry. Most congress participants but by no means all were happily ignorant of what was happening. I have never received an explanation or apology, but it occurred to me only as the congress proceeded – and a very good congress it was, too – that on the morning of the opening ceremony, before the papal audience, Dr X might have been told that his election for the vice-presidency had been unsuccessful. The only plausible explanation for his extraordinary behaviour was, I felt, that I had failed to ensure that he was elected. If this was indeed the case, it would have shown a lamentable lack of understanding of the democratic process, involving the secret ballot of the whole membership used routinely by professional societies such as ours.

Even more astonishing was the fact that this cold-shouldering was also extended to Sir Peter and his wife. Although he was badly handicapped following his cerebral haemorrhage nine years before he was given little assistance, and I still remember with a shudder the aftermath of a most wonderful chamber concert in a beautiful church. The heavens had opened up and there was no way in which we, the Medawars and others could get back to our hotel without being soaked to the skin. Robert Sells, the transplant surgeon from Liverpool, and his wife Paula helped Peter down the long flight of steps, laboriously lifting his paralysed leg one step at a time. Dr X waited for them at the bottom in his car and took them, soaked to the skin, to their hotel. Joanne and I and other concert-goers were given black rubbish bags by the priest, into which we tore holes for our eyes and which we donned as protective hoods. We then staggered into the flooded street to find a taxi; several wouldn't stop for these sinister hooded figures, but eventually we arrived back at our hotel, drenched.

After my return to London I wrote to Dr X to express my outrage and to ask for an explanation, but I received no reply. A surgical colleague of his expressed his regrets to me; he soon emigrated to the USA and I received a Christmas card from him until his death a few years ago. I sent a copy of my letter to all officers and councillors of the Transplantation Society so that they could form their own judgement, and a number wrote back to express their astonishment and sympathy. Thus ended my two-year period as president, which nonetheless proved to be very successful from the society's point of view.

Chapter Fifteen: Life in London

Life in Muswell Hill was pleasant enough. We made local friends, the children seemed to have settled into their schools, and Joanne and I soon became embroiled in local community affairs. As well as Queen's Wood we got to know Hampstead Heath intimately, and criss-crossed it many times, later accompanied by our beagle Beth. There was an excellent spot from which to fly kites. Kenwood House, with its excellent collection of paintings and furniture, was much frequented and shown off to visitors. St Mary's was just about within cycling distance but it was something of a slog to cycle home after a full day's work – no hanging on to the tailgate of lorries now! Sometimes I took the easy way out and went by Underground, and on a few snowy and icy occasions when there was no public transport I walked all the way to Paddington and back again.

Haringey Community Relations Council (HCRC)

Joanne inaugurated the first English as a second language (ESL) scheme in the borough of Haringey, and it was a great achievement to get it off the ground. As a result many immigrant housewives, most of them Asian, were visited in their homes by volunteer teachers and taught the rudiments of English. She also became embroiled with the education committee of HCRC, which did stalwart work for the ethnic minorities in the borough, mainly Caribbean, Asian, and Greek and Turkish Cypriot. One of its main concerns was the improvement of relations between the white majority and the ethnic minority communities, a never-ending uphill struggle in view of the widespread prejudice that prevailed at the time. On one occasion she and some colleagues were told by some cadets attending

177

the Hendon Police Training College that some of the instructors there had expressed overtly racist views during their course. Joanne reported this to the education committee and, following this, discussions between the HCRC and the college were held, and some improvements were made. The local police force also appointed a liaison officer to the council; he became a member of the police committee and his presence proved to be very helpful.

That was a time when relations between the black community and the police were extremely fraught, and it seemed vitally important to get the police to shed their prejudices and to adopt a non-discriminatory stance to people in the street. The notorious 'stop and search' (SUS – Search Under Suspicion) law, originally a post-Napoleonic War law that was meant to be used against former soldiers who had become vagrants, was being used selectively against young black people, and unfortunately still is. When I later became chairman of HCRC the council developed an energetic campaign against SUS, with thousands of leaflets handed out in the streets and representations made to the local member of parliament (the Tory Sir Hugh Rossi) and the Home Office. It struck me at the time that our campaign on the ground was only half-heartedly supported by black people, most of the hard work having being done by indigenous white, Greek Cypriot and Asian members of the council. There seemed to be a distinct reluctance to get involved.

Having recently read through some of the minutes of HCRC meetings in that period I realise what an immense amount of time and energy I put into the anti-SUS campaign. I chaired two public meetings, with local MPs and leaders of political parties taking part, quite apart from leafleting on street corners and making innumerable written and verbal approaches to the powers that be. Alas, the battle was not won even though it led, for a while, to a reduction in the number of street arrests. SUS is still the order of the day and continues to discriminate against blacks and Muslims. Unfortunately it has become a major weapon in the 'war on terror'.

It is certainly far more common now to see black and white people walking arm in arm and schoolchildren of different ethnic minorities playing happily together. Yet racism continues to be a blot, both among the general public and in the police force. One has only to think of the racist chants at football matches, abusing black players, and the numerous contemporary incidents in the police force. The most dramatic of these was revealed as the result of a BBC investigation by an undercover reporter, who enlisted in the police as a cadet and secretly filmed and taped conversations between cadets. The result, shown on television, gave a horrifying picture of racist cadets who were only too willing to allow their extreme and irrational views to influence their attitude to black people, especially Asians, on the street. The programme created an outcry and a number of cadets were immediately suspended; eight had the good grace to resign before action was taken against them. Will these disclosures make a difference in the long run? The jury is out.

Other signs of racism in the police force are the notoriously botched police enquiry into the death of the young black man Stephen Lawrence, and the hounding of a senior Asian detective by fellow policemen. This man was falsely accused of a number of misdemeanours, one of them the sending of hatemail to himself! It took several years for him to clear his name and to receive an apology, financial compensation and, finally, reinstatement. All this is disheartening and reflects the deep-seated racist attitudes of some sections of the white population.

There is also the dismaying election of members of the British National party to a number of council seats in the north of England, notably in Bradford. Although of little general significance, their presence further inflames the already fraught relations between the white population and the large Asian communities in many of our towns. I was interested to hear the view expressed by the Mayor of London's race relation advisor that ethnic schools should be created, catering for only black pupils. Whilst this advice was based on the observation that many black pupils fall through the educational net, it struck me as misconceived and I wrote to the mayor accordingly. My main objection was that such a move would further separate the white and black communities when integration and mutual acceptance were the preferable option.

I have intervened on two occasions in what I perceived to be racist incidents, both of which left me with egg on my face. The first occurred in the late 1980s. My colleagues David Lynch, Lee Rayfield and I were travelling to Downe, to conduct our experiments there, when we saw a group of adolescent boys at a bus stop in Dulwich. Two of them, one black and the other white and somewhat bigger, were fighting hammer and tongs, with serious punches being thrown. I automatically assumed that the black boy had been assaulted, stopped the car and told them to stop it at once. They did indeed stop fighting, but the black boy told me to 'fuck off'!

The second incident occurred on some waste ground by a road in Paddington. I was on my bicycle and saw what I perceived to be a young black man being assaulted by a rather more powerfully built white man. The latter had the struggling black man in a powerful arm-lock. I shouted at them at the top of my voice, but no notice was taken. Shortly afterwards a police car drew up and the black man was bundled into it. Apparently he had been suspected of stealing some electronic equipment from a nearby house. So much for this white knight in shining armour; more like a Don Quixote!

Back to the HCRC. In 1975 they found themselves short of a treasurer and with Joanne's encouragement the community relations officer asked me whether I would take on this honorary office. Although I had some misgivings – finance isn't exactly my forte and I was very busy – I served in this capacity for four years before I was elected chairman of the council. It was a turbulent body, with all the tensions and problems and sometimes anger experienced by the ethnic minorities played out at executive and council meetings, and it absorbed a great deal of my time. Its financial support came mainly from the borough of Haringey. It was therefore especially galling that some black councillors, such as Bernie Grant (who later became a member of parliament and who, since his death, is much revered), expressed extreme hostility to the HCRC.

On the resignation in 1976 of the community relations officer, who had performed valiantly and with great integrity, HCRC in collaboration with the borough of Haringey appointed Jeff Crawford as senior community relations officer. He had come from Barbados in 1955 and had been active and combative in the field of race relations by, for example, playing a prominent role in the 'Stop the Tour' campaign against the visit of the South African cricket and rugby teams to the UK, and by founding the North London West Indian Association, of which he became the secretary. Crawford was something of a firebrand, never afraid to speak his mind even if it might have been deemed politically expedient not to do so. Appointing him was something of a gamble. In the event, he led the HCRC very ably and developed the activities of the council substantially, especially when it came to defusing the tensions between the local police and the black community. He was not always a comfortable ally but I had a good relationship with him, built on mutual respect. Jeff died in 2004.

Apart from keeping the boat generally steady, fostering social and educational initiatives, supporting the police liaison committee in its very important activities, and running the anti-SUS campaign, perhaps the most important initiative whilst I was chairman was the preparation of a report listing the causes of vitamin D deficiency in the local Asian community and recommending a number of possible solutions to what our research showed to be an acute problem. Although the report, which I wrote together with Helena Sheiham, then working for the local community health council, raised the awareness of the community and its health workers to what was happening, I don't think that any of our recommendations, such as the addition of vitamin D to chapattis, were ever implemented.

My election as chairman came just after my expulsion from the local Labour party (which ran the council), and I wondered whether this might work against the interests of the HCRC. In the event, it turned out to be all right.

I will discuss the question of anti-Semitism in a later chapter. Although I have never been subjected to it personally I vividly recall one episode in the early 1950s, when I was walking along Charing Cross Road in London's West End. In a side street near Foyles bookshop I saw a man standing on a soapbox, raucously haranguing two or three bedraggled listeners. I thought I would find out what it was about, only to discover that the speaker was a rabble-rousing member of the British National Front, railing against Jews and the iniquities they were inflicting on the British public. Jewish capitalists were evidently draining the lifeblood from society and Jewish Communists were intent on destroying it in favour of a Marxist dictatorship – the Fascists always seem to want it both ways. I was outraged and went to the nearest telephone box to alert the police to what was happening. They duly sent a senior officer to investigate. He explained to me that as the Fascist was not causing a public disturbance there was nothing he could do about it. He agreed with me when I exclaimed with some indignation that, logically, the man could be arrested only if I assaulted him. The officer quite understood the weakness in the law, which fortunately has since been changed. Perhaps I *should* have assaulted the speaker – it might have paid dividends – but it would almost certainly have led to my arrest too; and I had the completion of my PhD thesis uppermost in my mind.

During my involvement with HCRC in the early 1980s Joanne and I sent a letter to the *Telegraph* complaining about the harassment of young black people by the police and calling for the abolition of the SUS law. We received several very disagreeable letters from readers, the most bigoted and obscene from someone describing himself as a member of the Shoreditch Brigade British Volunteer Force. It was addressed to Joanne and includes the following, among other even less printable sentiments: 'When conflict with the niggers begins shortly in our country and indiscriminate killing becomes normal as in Lebanon and Ulster we shall see that old slags like you who have collaborated and fornicated with this greasy filth which as [sic] invaded England will be dealt with. We are aware of the real motives behind your involvement with niggers.' It goes on to refer to me as 'the old queer Leslie Brent'. This, alas, was the level to which some people were prepared to sink, and I believe, though without great conviction, that we have moved on from there. I bitterly regretted involving Joanne in my letter writing.

Family life

Whilst the tensions in our marriage continued and were almost certainly exacerbated by my evening activities in the local Labour party, HCRC and the Haringey Council for Social Service, of which I became the founding vice-chairman, there were also many positive aspects to our family life. Indeed, looking back on those years it astonishes me how much I was able to pack in. Family holidays included camping trips to Brittany and youth hostelling in Snowdonia and the Lake District, the children having become keen walkers.

Back in the 1960s we had several very enjoyable stays in the Berner Oberland with our former au pair Christa, and that is were my fascination with climbing began. At an immunological conference in Switzerland I mentioned to a senior American immunologist, Byron Waksman, who was an experienced mountain climber, that I had read Edward Whymper's classic description of the first ascent of the Matterhorn, *Scramble Amongst the Alps*, and that I felt a great urge to climb it myself. He wisely suggested that I should first sharpen my teeth on the Blümlisalphorn and, as already described, I took his advice.

It was following the Transplantation Society's International Congress in The Hague in September 1972 that I took a train to Zermatt, where I had arranged to meet the guide from Bern who had previously led me and Christa along the Blümlisalp traverse. It had snowed heavily and earlier than usual, and when I met my guide at the railway station he took one look at the Matterhorn and immediately suggested that we climbed some other mountain instead. I persuaded him against his better judgement to stick to our plan and so we proceeded up the lower slopes. We spent the night in the Hornlihütte and the extent of the recent snowfall was already evident there. None of the local guides had decided to venture forth and the only other climbers in the hut were a French couple, who likewise planned to make the ascent early in the morning. We left at about 5 a.m. and had to use our crampons from the start because of the deep snow. It proved to be a brilliant day, with not a cloud to be seen, but the going was so heavy that the French couple turned back before long. We seemed to be the only people on the mountain, a quite unprecedented situation as it is normally covered by swarms of climbers, and I found this to be both exhilarating and intimidating. We made our way up laboriously and with much huffing and puffing on my part. On reaching the final shoulder, where the fixed ropes are to be found, my guide had to take a decision on whether to proceed to the top or beat a strategic retreat. As we were in danger of running out of time – my guide had to be back in Bern the same day – we decided on the latter. It proved to be just as well, for on reaching the final vertical rock wall near the hut we found it badly iced up (the temperature had plummeted) and had some difficulty negotiating it. Before we made our descent we were hailed by three German climbers who had attempted the ascent on the previous day, had spent the night in the Solvay refuge below the top and had used the whole day making their way down again. The icy wall was beyond them and my guide helped them to abseil, one of them rather embarrassingly splitting the seat of his trousers whilst doing so.

As we walked quickly down the lower slopes, my guide being in a hurry to catch his train, my right knee began to be very painful. I was glad to reach my hotel - it was dark by then - and to relax in a hot bath. Although I didn't make it to the top it was a most exciting and rewarding experience.

Two holiday trips stand out in my memory. One was a week's walk along a stretch of the Pennine Way, from Derbyshire into Northumberland. Simon was fourteen and we had a French exchange boy, Tège, staying with us. The three of us went on this trip, each carrying a rucksack; mine was rather heavy as we had taken a lightweight tent, a small camping cooker and some provisions with us. The intention was to camp whenever we could and to stay in youth hostels at other times. The first night was spent in a desolate part of the Peak District and all was fine: the three of us *just* about managed to squeeze into the low tent and the night was dry. It was not to stay that way as we got drenched on the following day, but we were able to dry off in a youth hostel without straying too far off our course. The walk took us through some astoundingly beautiful and wild landscape, which would not have been accessible in any other way. Alas, my suspect right knee began to hurt and I hobbled along: to abandon the trip would have been unthinkable. Simon proved to be a hero, for he offered to lighten my burden by carrying the tent and one or two other heavy objects. I can't remember what Tège made of all this, but he was game enough and seemed to enjoy this rather crazy and typically British caper.

The other was a trip to Snowdonia, this time accompanied by Joanne, Jenny and Suzanne, a French girl on an exchange visit. I had arranged for us to spend a couple of nights in the climbing hut of St Mary's Hospital Medical School Mountaineering Society, in which I had stayed before. It was conveniently located near Snowdon, the highest mountain in Wales, which we hoped to climb, and it was very simply furnished, to put it mildly. This is where our problems began. Suzanne was appalled at the hut's shabbiness and threw a Gallic tantrum, so we hastily moved to a nearby youth hostel that she found more acceptable - though only just. It was all excruciatingly embarrassing. Poor Suzanne was then taken up Snowdon, not along the boring zig-zags of the Pyg track but along the much more interesting Cryb Goch knife-edge ridge, which involved a little gentle rock climbing and commands breathtaking views. This was *not* revenge on my part, for it had been planned long before the climbing hut débâcle. It was a glorious day, and it must be said that Suzanne, although still disgruntled, proved to be fleet of foot, negotiating the ridge without undue difficulty, although I kept an eagle eye on her. I climbed Snowdon for the last time, with some difficulty, at the age of eighty-two.

Joanne and I had a busy life, both socially and culturally, and the many dinner parties I felt it necessary to arrange for departmental colleagues, visiting scientists and friends were not always to Joanne's liking; I imagine they added to her feelings of frustration. She was teaching English part-time in a language school in St John's Wood, not far from where we had lived in the 1950s, and she made some good friends there. Fortunately our succession of au pair girls made that easily possible, and they enabled her to undertake both professional and community activities.

However, love and trust in each other were gradually eroded; there had been too much emotional turmoil over the years and both of us seemed to feel that the support we had expected from each other was not forthcoming. I had a transient affair, and she developed an attachment to the Canadian widower of a distant cousin of hers, whom she had met during the war when he was in the UK in the Canadian army. When, one day, I discovered just how deep their relationship was it signalled for me the end of our marriage.

The Ninth International Congress of the Transplantation Society, Brighton

The British Transplantation Society, which I had helped to form in the mid-fifties and of which I had been the founder secretary, won the bid to host the International Society's 1982 congress in Britain. An organising committee had been formed several years earlier and I was its chairman. We hoped to have the congress in London's Barbican Conference Centre, which was being built at the time, and it seemed an exciting choice even though our congress would have been the first in the brand-new building. As more and more delays were announced for the completion date we became extremely anxious that it might not be ready in time, and a year before the congress was to be held the centre's manager advised us to find another venue.

We had precious little time but settled for Brighton, which had a large conference centre. Together with the nearby Metropole Hotel it offered an adequate number of lecture halls and smaller rooms for the parallel sessions we had planned. The main problem was hotel accommodation, but by using some hotels in nearby seaside towns we overcame that problem. In the event, we probably gained from our enforced move to Brighton, for it provided a venue without the many distractions that London would have offered. The congress proved to be extremely successful, for it was the first large transplantation meeting at which the biochemistry, immunology and clinical application of the new immunosuppressive drug cyclosporine was discussed. This very effective drug held sway for the next ten to fifteen years and is still in use, though others even more effective have since been discovered.

One organisational feature of the congress was that three or four of us edited all the written contributions in the few days immediately following the congress, so that the four volumes appeared in *Transplantation Proceedings* within a few months. It was a somewhat hair-raising experience but definitely character-forming, and friendships were forged as a result of the intensive effort involved. Members of the organising committee included Robert Sells (transplant surgeon and secretary), Ross Taylor (another transplant surgeon, who has since died), John Salaman (transplant surgeon and treasurer), and Richard Batchelor, Michael Elves, John Fabre and Arnold Sanderson (immunologists); Sir Peter Medawar was our honorary president. And thereby hangs a tale.

For our gala evening, which included a banquet, a lively and skilful group of young ballet dancers had been engaged, courtesy of Arnold Sanderson's wife who was associated with the East Grinstead Ballet School. We were keen to have a witty after-dinner speaker, and Peter Medawar suggested his friend Lord Bernard Miles, the actor and director of London's Mermaid Theatre. He kindly accepted our invitation. A couple of days before the congress I had a phone call from his secretary, warning me that one or two of his anecdotes were likely to be distinctly 'blue'. I didn't feel that it was my remit to tell the lordly thespian what he could or could not include, and assumed that he was a sufficiently experienced speaker to know where to draw the line on such an occasion. In the event there were some extremely risqué stories (one of them involving a bell), and I sat through his speech feeling uncomfortable on behalf of some of the less open-minded participants and their wives or husbands. It was very amusing, all the same, and our continental colleagues, especially the Dutch, thought it was uproariously funny. Some of our American colleagues were less enthusiastic. Anyway, it was an occasion that was long remembered by those who were present, as were several other events on the social programme.

These had been arranged with the greatest care. They included a visit to Glyndebourne to see Mozart's *Cosi fan Tutte*, the National Youth Jazz Orchestra, the Endellion String Quartet, whom I had heard at St Mary's and were just beginning to make their mark (they played, at my suggestion, Haydn, Britten and Dvorak) and a visit to Chichester Theatre. The most extraordinary social event was, however, reserved for the 'free' Wednesday afternoon, which was unencumbered by scientific presentations. Arnold Sanderson had some influence with the Tote (or some such body), thanks to some research he had undertaken for them on equine histocompatibility antigens to assist with the breeding of racehorses, and he managed to arrange for members of the congress to attend the mid-week races on Brighton racecourse. Not only that: several races were dedicated to the congress, such as The Transplantation Stakes, for which Jean Medawar gave away the winner's cup. Dame Flora Robson, the actress famous for her roles in horror movies, who lived locally, was ensconced in a marquee. This aged but still very charming woman became gently tipsy on the champagne that flowed liberally, and held court, for there were many, especially among the British and Americans, who wanted to pay their respects to her. The other 'Lady' who graced the proceedings was Jean, who enjoyed the event enormously and also had not spared the champagne, like the rest of us. It was a truly memorable event – my first (and last) race meeting since those trotting races in Trieste after the war.

Separation, divorce and remarriage

My relationship with Joanne had taken a turn for the worse just before the congress and she decided that she would not accompany me to Brighton. Soon after the congress she left our home altogether and I assumed this was to be a permanent separation. It was during her absence that I met Carol Martin at a friend's party and we developed a close relationship; I was convinced that my marriage was over. When eighteen months later Joanne asked whether she could return to our house in Wood Vale I had little choice but to agree, and we made an unsuccessful attempt to mend bridges. With Joanne on the one hand and Carol on the other I became positively 'schizophrenic', and this is when I began a course of psychotherapy with an excellent therapist that was to last some six years. This, among the other problems, also helped me to confront my childhood experiences and the loss of my family, and after much dithering it eventually helped me to decide that the best course would be for the two of us to separate, which we did in 1989. A divorce came within a year or so. It was, however, an emotionally taxing period of my life and there were times when I felt in danger of disintegrating.

Insofar as a divorce can ever be 'amicable' ours was, but of course it was exceedingly traumatic all the same. Thirty-four years of living together, with all its ups and downs, came to a deeply unsatisfactory end. I experienced an acute and distressing sense of failure: could or should I have done more to avert all this? All our possessions were split down the middle without acrimony, our assets were divided with a strong bias in favour of Joanne so that she could be financially independent of me, and Joanne continued to live in our house until it was sold. I moved temporarily into a bedsitting room in the large Hampstead house of my friend Karl Grossfield, who made me feel very welcome. I stayed there for a year until I moved into the house in Tufnell Park that Carol had meanwhile acquired. My essential chattels were with me but I felt like a displaced and rootless person, despite Karl's generous hospitality. A divorce is almost by definition deeply unsettling and upsetting, and a second marriage, especially so soon after, poses its own problems. Carol and I had no common history to speak of, and new bonds had to be forged with members of her family, especially with her three children, Nicholas (Nick), David and Siân (all Oxbridge graduates) – a task in which I have been partially successful. I have a very affectionate grandfatherly relationship with Siân's small children, Noah and Colenso; and there is genuine mutual fondness between me and David and his partner Catherine. The same is true for Nick's daughter Caroline Brown, who recently spent an exciting year in China as a teaching assistant before commencing her studies at Leeds University. As for Carol's aged parents, they were both extremely welcoming and affectionate towards me and I got on very well with them – as I do with her brother Clive and his 'Welsh' family, and with her sister Diana and her 'French' family!

My own children were greatly supportive to both Joanne and myself and that was a very great boon. For Joanne some aspects of her subsequent life were unfortunately filled with tragedy. Her father and brother died a few years later, soon followed by the Canadian who had hoped to marry her. Although we did not see each other for quite some time Joanne and I remained in touch, and we have now reached a stage where we can look upon each other with affection.

Carol is a psychotherapist, and she and I are different in many ways. I would not want to pretend that *everything* in our marriage has been rosy; we have had both highs and lows. Yet we have lived together now for sixteen years and we are strongly bound together by the comfortable home we have created in Tufnell Park, by our common interests in the arts, especially music, which we both feel passionate about, and by our nine grandchildren. Carol has been a very great support in my latter-day attempts to come to terms with my past, and she has accompanied me on my visits to Koszalin and Berlin. Her psychotherapeutic training makes her a very sympathetic and understanding listener when I talk to her about my past, and her reactions have been immensely helpful. There are indeed many positive aspects to our marriage (we aren't at all bad at collaborating in concocting rather nice meals for dinner parties), and I am sure that it will happily survive until death do us part.

On friendship

For one who has lost virtually the whole of his family, friends are of special importance. Following my divorce I became acutely aware of what staunchly loyal friends I have. The support of Ernst and Inge Weinberg and their daughters Leah, Toby and Lesley helped me to keep going, as did John and Mary Hawkes, Arthur and Bronwen Wild, Liz Simpson, Karl Grossfield, Gerd Nathan and many others – not to mention Hans and Susanne Meyer. Hans has been something of a father figure to me. He recently celebrated his ninety-fifth birthday, still living happily in the idyllic Greet Cottage, Kent, where he has been since the 1930s, with his devoted and warm second wife Susanne; Hago died many years ago. John and Mary Hawkes were neighbours of mine way back in the 1950s, their son Simon and my Simon having become friends at an early age, thus bringing the two families together. John and Mary acquired a delightful second home in West Cork, Eire, and my family spent several happy holidays there with them. Through Mary's gregariousness and unusual capacity for making friends we got to know some of the local people – a rewarding experience. Carol and I have also valued our friendship with Robert and Paula Sells, who have now retired from transplant surgery and the immunology of infectious diseases respectively. They now live in a family farmhouse in North Wales, where Paula has become an expert horse logger and Robert indulges his passion for music by conducting the talented amateur Crosby Symphony Orchestra, which is based in Liverpool.

It is rare to develop really good friendships late in life, but as a result of the first Kindertransport reunion in 1989 I got to know two women called Ruth! Ruth Albert, married to Douglas, a retired dental surgeon, had been a day pupil in the Berlin orphanage school and we 'found' each other during the reunion. Ruth Wing, too, had come to this country from Berlin in a Kindertransport, but quite late in the day, and she has had a rather more trying life here compared with mine. We met because she had a part-time job with the Paddington Jewellers, opposite St Mary's Hospital, and she and Robert, who is a reader in engineering at Imperial College, have likewise become close friends, as have our neighbours Peter and Anita Rich.

During this second London period I attended many international meetings. In America I visited my uncle and cousin in New York whenever possible, and my dear friends Hanna Bergas, Helmut Schneider and Ernst and Inge Weinberg in California. Although I saw Hanna rarely we maintained a close relationship until she died. As for my friends the Weinbergs, living in far-flung northern California, it really is astonishing how our childhood friendships have not only survived but deepened over the years – a source of great joy and mutual support.

Visits to Auschwitz, South Africa, Australia and Bali

When I was president-elect of the Transplantation Society in 1975 I was invited on a lecture tour in Poland; this took me to Warsaw, Krakow and Wroclaw (formerly Breslau). The tour had been organised by a senior nephrologist, Professor T. Orlowski, who ran a kidney transplant unit in Warsaw – a kindly and courteous man of the old school who had worked with the partisans during the war. It was an interesting trip and my talks were well received. I was very impressed by the rebuilding of Warsaw, though the vast Soviet-style hotel in which I stayed, with poor plumbing and with prostitutes lurking in the reception hall, was less than appealing. Krakow was, of course, a delight, its ancient buildings and castle having survived the war more or less unscathed.

I travelled to Krakow by train and that was an eerie experience, for as we passed through the desolate countryside I could not help thinking about my poor family, who I imagined must have been taken through similar terrain but in cattle trucks in 1942. At the time I still had reason to believe that they had died in Auschwitz. It was therefore a gloomy and dispiriting journey. After a few days in Krakow Professor Orlowski insisted on driving me in his car from Krakow to Wroclaw, where I was to give my last lecture at the Institute of Immunology. On the way he said to me, 'Leslie, we are now very near to Auschwitz, and by making a short detour we could easily visit it. Would you like to go?' I suddenly felt very faint, and my immediate reaction was to decline his suggestion. I don't think that Orlowski knew anything about my German/Jewish background, and I explained why I didn't think that I could cope with the emotional stress of visiting the site. He was very sympathetic and understood perfectly. However, as we drew closer I felt a strong urge to change my mind: I felt drawn, as if by a magnet, to what I conceived to be the nearest to a grave my family will have had, and so we drove to the entrance of the camp, still with its spine-chilling motto 'Arbeit macht frei' above the gate. Many cars and coaches were in the car park, and there was a museum – and a shop in which I managed to buy a bunch of white flowers to leave by the memorial. I was careful not to enter the ghoulish museum with its mementos of the horrors that had been perpetrated.

The barracks that had housed the inmates had long been destroyed, but their chimneys were still standing, row after row. They formed a ghostly and shattering backdrop to the massive memorial that had been erected, with inscriptions in various languages. Orlowski tactfully fell back as I approached the memorial, where I laid down my flowers and uncontrollably burst into tears. This was my first real opportunity to grieve at the finality and horror of the death of my parents and sister, and it took me some time to regain my composure.

We continued the journey in silence. It was only many years later that I discovered my family's true fate.

The other trip was to South Africa, at a time when there was still apartheid – even though it was beginning to weaken by then. The Southern Africa Transplantation Society had invited me to their annual conference in Durban. I had previously rejected an invitation to a medical congress in South Africa because I had not received a satisfactory response to my question of whether there would be black participants. This time I was told that the four foreign speakers invited included Dr John Merrill, the member of the team in Boston that had successfully transplanted the first kidney from an identical twin, Dr Sam Kountz, a prominent black American transplant surgeon, and Dr Ian McKenzie, an Australian transplantation immunologist. I immediately wrote to Sam, who was working at Stanford University Medical Center, to ask what he was going to do about the invitation. He replied that he had discussed it long and hard with his family and with colleagues and had decided to accept. Well, that was good enough for me, and I too agreed to go.

It proved to be a fascinating as well as, for Sam, a fateful trip. The four of us were taken on a safari through a wild game park before the meeting, and almost as soon as I arrived in Johannesburg I was asked by one of the organisers, who was accompanying us, whether I would have any objection to sharing a room with Sam on our travels. It seemed a strange request but naturally I agreed, and Sam and I were perfectly happy with this arrangement. Indeed, being in the company of a black man in South Africa was an interesting experience, as we had many lively discussions about the political situation and the impressions we had formed. I felt that our organisers had carefully squared Sam's presence with the hotel owners well in advance. There was one strange episode when a few of us decided to climb a steep and craggy mountain standing in splendid isolation in one of the native reserves. Legend had it that the higher reaches of the mountain were haunted by the spirits of dead Zulu warriors. I had suggested the climb, which was rocky but which was expected to take no more then two to three hours. One of our South African hosts, Ian McKenzie and I agreed to tackle it. Sam decided at the last moment that he wanted to come along, though he hardly seemed fit enough to get to the top as he was quite tubby and suffered from high blood pressure. Sure enough, long before we reached the summit he turned back, telling us that he would wait for us at the bottom. The local Zulu who had offered to show us the route refused to climb to the higher reaches of the crag, presumably because of the roaming Zulu warrior spirits we had been told about. The three of us went on to the rocky top, from which we had fine views over the flat surrounding countryside, and on our return we found Sam being hospitably entertained by some native labourers in a primitive hut, where he had drunk some home-brewed beer.

John Merrill had, enterprisingly, arranged to visit Janet Suzman, the lone and embattled member of the Liberal party in the South African parliament, and I went with him to her home in Johannesburg. She had done her best to represent the interests of the oppressed black and 'coloured' population, and I admired her for her courage. She proved to be a delightful and down-to-earth politician; I felt greatly privileged to have met her.

In Durban Sam and I found time to go to the beach for a swim. This was intended to be a provocative gesture: I think we both hoped that we might be arrested, for at that time the Durban beaches were still reserved for whites only. Sam was the only black man in the water but no notice was taken, much to our disappointment. Apartheid was already on the wane and the mixing of white and black bodies in the sea was no longer regarded to be a heinous crime.

At the end-of-conference party, as president-elect of the Transplantation Society, I was asked to make a few remarks. Careful not to insult our hosts, I expressed the view that there needed to be some profound changes in South African society. This comment was largely prompted by my horror at seeing a shanty town in Johannesburg and by my visit to Soweto, its hospital (Baragwanath) and a general practice run by a much admired and long-suffering Jewish doctor whose practice had been burgled several times, despite his high standing in the black community. Facilities for blacks were appalling and beds and medication were in short supply, and I was told of black men and women who routinely had to carry their babies and children through the bush for up to a day and a half to seek medical aid. Patients often had to be accommodated on the ward floor. This was in stark contrast with the Verwoerd Hospital in Johannesburg, where (rather piquantly in view of its name) Sam Kountz was the first black doctor to take charge of a 'grand round' – a heartening sight and an omen of things to come.

Shortly after my return to London I was woken in the dead of night by a phone call from South Africa. Apparently Sam had fallen into a deep coma soon after his return to Stanford and I was asked whether I could throw any light on what might have been the cause: the American doctors were completely at a loss. Sam certainly had high blood pressure, but the only possible cause I could advance was the beer he had drunk in the Zulu hut. Could he have picked up a virus? The cause of the coma was never identified. He remained unconscious for several months before he died and, not inappropriately, it fell on me, as president of the 1978 Transplantation Congress in Rome, to read a eulogy for him during the opening ceremony, with Grace, his widow, present.

I remember two other congresses more for their social programmes than for their scientific content. My one and only trip to Australia was to attend the International Congress of Immunology, which was held in Sydney in the mid-eighties. I had asked for modest accommodation and found myself, to my great surprise, in the red light district of King's Cross, one of the city's suburbs. It was an interesting experience! Sydney itself, with the relatively new and dramatic Opera House, was delightful, but the most exciting part was the post-congress tour to Brisbane and the Great Barrier Reef. Brisbane, which hosted the World Fair that year, interested me not nearly as much as the visit to the reef, which was – as it must be for everyone who visits it for the first time – a revelation. There were only a few of us on the tour, plus a guide. Those of us who didn't fancy scuba diving after only twenty minutes of instruction in a pool went snorkelling and, free of the anxiety the scuba divers experienced, probably had a better time of it. The most dramatic moment came when the instructor dived down to an open giant clam and gently touched its mantle. The vast shell closed slowly but inexorably – woe to anyone who allowed his leg to be caught in the vicelike grip of the shells.

A further highlight of this trip was a visit to Dum Island. It has a resort for visitors – the numbers entering the island were tightly controlled – and most of it is covered by rain forest. We were offered a nocturnal walk through the forest and two of us, Eleanor Bradley, a fellow immunologist and the wife of Andrew Bradley, who later became Professor of Surgery at Cambridge University, and I volunteered for this. It was wonderfully exciting and offered some of the most spectacular nature sights I have ever come across. The sights that I best remember are the eye of a far distant nightjar reflecting the light from our powerful torches, and a tree snake stalking a sleeping bird. The snake, lying on a low branch, was to all intents and purposes motionless, the bird sitting about six feet distant. Our guide assured us that both would still be there on our return journey an hour or two later. The snake was but the bird had gone: it had almost certainly made its escape, as there was no sign of it in the snake's body.

Memorable, too, was the first Asian Transplantation Congress in Bali, to which I had been invited to give a plenary session review. Bali itself was extremely pleasant – this was many years before the terror outrage that killed so many people – even though the swimming was not without its hazards thanks to the presence of large numbers of poisonous jellyfish. After the congress I made my way to Java to look at two temples, which impressed me by their great size, beauty, antiquity and their excellent state of preservation. I stayed in a hotel outside the little town and in the evening I decided to eat dinner in a restaurant that had been recommended to me for its local cuisine. Walking the two or three miles to it I was struck by the many open fires burning at the side of the road, outside shops and dwellings, releasing great clouds of black smoke. No smokeless zone here! After an excellent meal I was tired and hailed one of the swarms of bicycle-taxis that are in vogue in Indonesia. It was gently uphill all the way back and my driver, who was somewhat older than I was and certainly less fit, seemed to be struggling. I suggested that I should take over the pedalling and carry him back to the hotel, a suggestion that he found hilarious. The face of the porter outside the hotel who watched me arrive in the saddle, wearing an elegant suit, and pay the driver (for services only partially rendered) is a sight I still treasure!

It was in Bali that I was exposed to gamelan music for the first time. I was fascinated by the subtly changing rhythms of the unusual instruments and the colourful costumes of the performers. A little of it goes a long way, all the same.

The halt and the lame: welcome to the Brent geriatric club

During the 1980s several of my older friends and in-laws fell on hard times and depended on me for support. Sir Peter Medawar had his severe brain haemorrhage in 1969, the year I returned to London, and although I did not work in his department at Northwick Park I kept in close touch with him and Jean. He was paralysed down one side and used an electric wheelchair, but he largely regained his intellectual faculties even if the brilliance and incisiveness were no longer so evident. He subsequently wrote and published a number of books that had a great following among the general public. Peter rather enjoyed 'driving' his electric wheelchair, which he did with great éclat in the corridors of the Clinical Research Centre at Northwick Park, and one of his favourite tricks was to throw his stick down a flight of stairs to one of his colleagues to catch before he himself descended in the lift. From time to time it fell upon me to hold his urine bottle for him, on one occasion in the front of a stalls box at the English National Opera – all carefully hidden under an overcoat.

Others depended rather more heavily on me. Probably because I never had my own parents to care for in their old age I felt the urge to help those elderly people within my orbit who were in need. There was, of course, Joanne's father Oates Manley, whose escapades in London I have already described. Carol's father Sam, a former steelworker, died at a ripe old age; in the last few years of his life he had become very immobile. He was a heavy man and trundling him along in a wheelchair could be backbreaking. He and Lillian (Lil) celebrated their golden wedding anniversary a decade or so ago and I wrote a poem in their honour. I expect that it did less than justice to them, but I thought it not half bad. Lil continued to live in her house after Sam's death until she had a bad fall, as a result of which she not only lost her confidence but also her short-term memory, so that she had to be moved by us into a residential home in Newport. We visited her frequently – our car was almost on auto-pilot on its way down the M4 motorway – and she liked to be taken out to pub lunches; again, getting her in and out of our car and negotiating steps and other obstacles with her wheelchair was taxing. On our last visit in March 2004 she died suddenly, in our presence. This ninety-seven-year-old woman had lived through two world wars and had little formal education, but bags of common sense and insight.

My friend Harry Harrison became very dependent on me in his latter years, when his partner Ted was no longer able to look after him, and I had to find a suitable nursing home for him when his Parkinsonian condition left him highly disabled. He was a dear man and I visited him as often as I was able. He was a subscriber to the *Journal of the Association of Jewish Refugees*, and I often read articles to him from it. Quite a few were of interest, and when he died I decided to take out a subscription to it on my own behalf; I have since published book reviews and articles in it. Harry made me his executor and I had quite a trying task carrying out my duties after his death in 1989 – another major event close to the time of my retirement. It was left to me to arrange Harry's funeral in Golder's Green Crematorium, which included music from one of my choir's audiotapes – Mozart's *Requiem* – to give a short address, and to provide refreshments in our house for the relatively few mourners.

But the most time-consuming 'help programme' was to my next-door neighbours in Muswell Hill, Bill and Gladys Embery. They had bought their house quite a few years before Joanne and I moved there and had led a very secluded life, so that we hardly knew them. Occasionally we saw Gladys, looking somewhat gypsy-like, hanging out the washing in her garden or calling to her cat. Both came from working class backgrounds and Bill had risen to a responsible job checking the quality of lenses in a small factory. They seemed to have virtually no outside interests, although Bill rather surprisingly attended French classes. Their self-imposed anonymity was shattered when Bill had a severe stroke in the late 1970s and I dropped by to ask whether there was anything I could do. Before long I had mobilised some of my local friends, prominent among them John and Lucy Roots, to join me in visiting Bill frequently in order to encourage him to regain his speech. I had read somewhere that intensive stimulation could be therapeutic and it seemed worth trying. In the event, the recovery of his speech was extremely limited, but some of us became close friends of the Emberys and we supported Gladys in all kinds of ways, both before and after Bill's death. As their garden was the apple of their eye I mowed their lawn every time I mowed ours. Unfortunately it meant carrying my heavy petrol-driven mower through our house, into the street, through their house and back again. When Bill died it was left to me to make the funeral arrangements. The funeral was attended, among a few others, by Gladys's brother and sister-in law, with whom contact had been very intermittent. After Bill's death John and Lucy and I and another local couple helped Gladys to continue life on her own, until she joined her brother in Cambridgeshire, where she was eventually settled into a residential home. She died a few years ago.

I did all this gladly, but at times I ground my teeth from sheer frustration at the investment of time that I could ill afford. In retrospect, however, it was peanuts compared with the eighteen days I spent looking after my friend Gerd Nathan, who suffered from terminal cancer of the pancreas. He died in September 2008, and once again it fell to me to arrange his funeral.

Farewell to St Mary's

In 1990 I was given an absolutely splendid departmental retirement party, which was preceded by a departmental cricket match in which I kept wicket for the last time, even though rather less acrobatically than of yore. Jenny appeared in the middle of the game and caused a stoppage by running on to the pitch to embrace me, to the delight of Jean Medawar who was among the spectators. I was presented with several wonderful gifts, not least the word processor without which I could hardly have written my book, a fine Bang & Olufsen music centre, which is continuing to provide me and Carol with much pleasure, and a handsome cricket bat bearing many signatures. My departmental colleagues and friends in and outside the school were incredibly generous, and many former staff and students, and other professional colleagues, attended the party. Some time before my retirement my department had commissioned Humphrey Ocean, a very talented portrait painter, to make a pencil sketch of me, and this hangs in the departmental corridor.

One of the most prized gifts was a hard cover and gold-embossed 'presentation volume' containing 108 letters and poems, some with photographs or illustrations, from present and past colleagues and students, and a wide range of professional people who had got to know me over the years. This was the brainchild of Tony Pinching, the clinical immunologist I had appointed many years before. Heaven knows how he got together such a very eclectic list of people, who included not only postgraduate students who had worked with me but also BSc students, one dating back to my Southampton years, technicians, secretaries (especially dear Gill), the school librarian and administrative officers, Rupert and

Jean Billingham, Jean Medawar, and a number of immunologists and transplant surgeons from far and wide, including Ray Owen. Even the dean, Peter Richards, with whom I had had one or two spats over school policy, wrote a very pleasant letter. 'The School will be a duller place without you. The Dean will have fewer disconcerting questions to field but at the price of a very loyal friend. Others will need to stir the social conscience of St Mary's in your place . . . Your many human and scientific contributions will long be remembered and we thank you most warmly.'

It is invidious to quote from just a few contributions, but a poem written by Madeleine Jinkinson, the personnel officer who was also secretary to the academic board and who died very prematurely a few years later, might be singled out. It was 'to be intoned in the heavily stressed style of *Hiawatha*':

> Leslie's place in academia
> Has been marked by many facets,
> Science is of course a prime one
>
> Others will discourse on this one.
> To the person in the Admin,
> Different talents spring to mind.
> Principles are always foremost
> For the sake of staff and student.
>
> Never one to blench or falter
> In expression of his viewpoint
> Leslie's place at meeting tables
> Will be really hard to follow.

One letter came, unexpectedly, from Dr (now Dame) Margaret Turner-Warwick, who had in the past been intimately involved with the Asthma Research Council and was at that time president of the Royal College of Physicians. Her letter is particularly precious to me because it showed her appreciation of what I had done for the allergy clinic at St Mary's – something that has tended to be overlooked. It included the following:

> Leslie was critically instrumental in re-establishing the Allergy Clinic after Bill Frankland and later Eddie Keal retired from the hospital . . . He appreciated the enormous opportunities for clinical research and that it was essential to have a sound laboratory basis . . . Without his personal sponsorship at this time the scientific work of the Allergy Clinic would not have developed. A part of the

finance for Dr Ewan and her research programme grant came from the Asthma Research Council, and the Council too recognised Leslie Brent's commitment and help. More recently, Leslie contributed much time and effort bringing the Allergy Clinic and the Thoracic Medicine Department together on a single site . . . At this time there was a serious threat that allergy and thoracic medicine might be fragmented and allocated to different parts of the hospital, and it was in no small measure due to Leslie Brent's efforts that a single development was achieved . . . Thus Leslie Brent, while primarily a distinguished academic immunologist, also took a keen interest in developing practical ways for close and important clinical liaisons, so that high class applied clinical research could go forward in the best British tradition. Many of us in allergy and thoracic medicine will continue to be grateful to Leslie for his enthusiastic support and leadership through many hard fought battles.

Thank you, Margaret! She and the Asthma Research Council threw me a lifebelt, of which I was in dire need at the time, for the achievement of my objective; and yes, battles they certainly were against a less than farsighted medical and administrative establishment.

The school gave me the customary book of my choice, inscribed by the Dean. I had identified the largest, most costly and potentially the most useful book – Derrick Mercer's *Chronicle of the 20ᵗʰ Century*. The British Transplantation Society hosted a most agreeable symposium and dinner in my honour. And so ended my professional career – in an entirely satisfactory manner.

A History of Transplantation Immunology *and the Medical School Art Committee and retirement*

Retirement at the age of sixty-five – or at any age for that matter – must always be an unsettling event, but in my case it proved particularly challenging as Joanne and I had just parted ways, the house that had been my home for twenty years had been sold, and I was developing a new relationship with Carol. I had decided to make a clean break with academic life by ending all my research activities; even had I wanted to continue there would not have been space for me in the revamped department, and nor would I have wanted to breathe down the neck of the new head. Having worked in universities for the best part of four decades I was ready for a new life: in so far as I would ever make an impact on my field of study I felt I had already made it, and a few more years toiling away in the laboratory would not have added much to the sum of human knowledge. I had, however, decided to begin my retirement by writing a history of transplantation immunology, and I was immensely fortunate when I was offered a large room in the hospital's transplant laboratory, directed by the nephrologist Dr David Taube. He asked me how long it might take me to write my book and I thought it might be three years. In the event I left my office almost six years later, and I felt deeply indebted to David for having sacrificed so much precious space. Before I left he arranged for the laboratory to be renamed the Brent Laboratory – a very generous gesture that is commemorated by a plaque. Since its move to new premises in the Hammersmith Hospital it has been renamed the Leslie Brent Laboratory.

One of the most difficult aspects of retiring was not only the fact that I was now responsible only for myself, but that I had no secretary. I continued to have an extensive correspondence, which tended to divert me from my main objective – the writing of my book. As a result, progress with the book, *A History of Transplantation Immunology*, was slow and several deadlines were missed. This topic had not been adequately dealt with before, except in chapters concentrating mainly on clinical aspects, and it involved me in a massive manual literature search and evaluating vast numbers of original articles, going back as far as the nineteenth century. Early in 1996 I received a fax from my long-suffering Academic Press editor, Tessa Picknett, demanding the remaining chapters by Easter. As quite a few remained to be written her request put me into overdrive, and I don't think that I have ever worked such long hours, often well into the night. Nigel Palmer, the school librarian, gave me a key to the library so that I could be there after official hours – a strange but productive experience, without distractions of any kind. Poor Carol began to wonder what sort of a man she had married, and I was intensely grateful to her for being so forbearing.

Several years before my retirement I had been invited to serve on a committee which was charged with the task of 'beautifying' the uninspiring medical school corridors and staircases and I became its founder chairman. I did not give this up until 1994, so it was another major hindrance when I was writing my book. We were fortunate in being allowed to borrow, on semi-permanent loan, a number of paintings and reproductions from the Hospitals Art Fund, and before long many interesting – and in some cases challenging – framed pictures went up, mostly of contemporary art. Others were donated by individuals. Kathleen Goff, the secretary of the department of bacteriology, was the committee's indefatigable secretary and even after her retirement she continued to organise the monthly art lectures that have enthralled a small but enthusiastic audience. The greatest achievements of my committee were the creation of two large murals in the entrance hall of the school building and a bas relief commemorating Alexander Fleming on an outside wall. It became largely my responsibility to raise funds for these projects, and as the country was in recession at the time this proved to be both arduous and time-consuming. The first mural was intended to celebrate the achievements of the school's four best-known scientists, and we identified Augustus Waller (the forerunner of the electrocardiogram), Alexander Fleming (the discoverer of penicillin and Nobel Laureate), Almroth Wright (vaccination, opsonisation) and Rodney Porter (structure of antibodies and Nobel Laureate). The design and execution of the mural were entrusted to Faye Carey, and she carried out some diligent research into the activities of these men to enable her to come up with a very original, interesting and informative design. The National Art Collections Fund gave us a major grant and it was unveiled in 1993 with due pomp and circumstance.

The second mural was to hang opposite the Carey mural and it was devoted to the sporting and cultural activities in which St Mary's students had excelled over the years. These included rugby, hockey, swimming, dramatic and operatic performances, athletics and chess. Our choice for this mural was the painter Jacqueline Rizvi, and she produced some fine sketches based on students who had volunteered to pose for her. The mural included a miniature of Roger Bannister, one of our consultants, breaking the tape on his historic one-mile record when he was still a student. Funding was eventually provided by the generosity of the Foundation for Sport and the Arts and the Royal Academy of Art, the then president – Sir Roger de Grey – having taken a very personal interest in the project. The beautifully painted mural did indeed look splendidly decorative. Both Sir Roger Bannister and the Rt Hon. Christopher Chataway, a trustee of the Foundation for Sport and the Arts, were present at the unveiling in 1994. Unfortunately both murals were removed some years ago when the school's entrance hall was refurbished, and so far my attempts to discover their fate have been dismally unsuccessful.

In the same year our third project came to fruition. On the north-west corner of the school building, at first-floor level, was a large block of Portland stone surrounded by a sculpted laurel wreath, but for some reason it had been left blank. It seemed a perfect spot for a bas relief showing Alexander Fleming's profile: it honoured the man and at the same time raised the flag for the hospital and medical school in the face of claims by the Oxford school that penicillin owed rather more to Oxford scientists (Prof. Howard Florey and his team) than it did to Fleming. We commissioned a young architectural sculptor, Tim Metcalfe, to do the carving and to surround the profile with gold leaf-covered lettering that simply reads 'Alexander Fleming discovered penicillin here'. The bas relief looks impressive and especially so at night, when it is illuminated by a spotlight.

I had assumed that this would be by far the easiest of our projects to finance. Surely one of the many drug companies that had made considerable fortunes out of producing penicillin would be only too happy to pay the cost, I foolishly thought. I wrote more than twenty letters to drug companies and some charitable trusts: my reward was a couple of cheques for a desultory £250! All right, times were fairly hard, but I could not believe that prosperous companies could be so niggardly. Tim was already hard at work, and we still had virtually nothing in our coffers. Fortunately the medical school was willing to underwrite the cost, and two charitable trusts came to my rescue in the nick of time. I had read of a foundation set up by Harold Bridges, a Lancastrian who had built up a profitable road haulier business in the north of England. He had published his autobiography, *As I Remember*, and had an OBE and KSTJ after his name, presumably in recognition of his charitable work. The book was a typical 'rags to riches' story, and whilst it was by no means a riveting read, it gave a good glimpse of life in Lancashire early in the twentieth century and how to succeed in business. Having read somewhere that, owing to his own medical experiences, he was sympathetic to applications from the medical establishment, I wrote to him. We corresponded and I visited him after one of my excursions to the Lake District. Quite improbably we hit it off, and the outcome was a cheque for £1500. There was, however, a condition attached to this gift: we were to purchase and sell to members of the school fifty copies of his book. This was disconcerting, to say the least, but my committee decided not to look a gift horse in the mouth and to accept. I fear that few copies were sold, even at the low price of £5; it was decidedly not a bestseller. On the notepaper of this eccentric man was printed, 'I shall pass through this world but once. Any good thing therefore that I can do or any kindness that I can show to any fellow creature let me *do it now*. Let me not neglect, delay or defer it, for I shall not pass this way again.' He was as good as his word, despite the reservations of his trustees.

An even larger donation came from the Kohn Foundation, whose founder had a similar refugee background to mine. And so, with a few smaller donations, we covered our expenses. The unveiling took place on the same day as the Rizvi mural in April in 1994. I handed over the chairmanship of this committee with a sigh of relief, for its work had seriously stood in the way of my book writing.

Since my retirement I have led a very busy life – writing my historical book on immunology and, more recently, these memoirs; maintaining a lively correspondence, keeping in touch with our six offspring and their nine children, writing historical articles and book reviews and, alas, several obituaries, attending scientific meetings from time to time, including of course the 'ski-conferences', spending time with Carol in our house in

France three times a year, going to concerts, plays and art galleries with Carol, serving on the governing body of a local primary school and on the British Scholarship Trust, which awards short-term scholarships to students from the former Yugoslav territories, engaging in political activities, taking courses such as 'The History of Philosophy' (Ralph Blumenau is one of the most articulate lecturers I have come across) with the University of the Third Age, attending and helping to organise school reunions, reconnecting with Koszalin and Berlin, and, last but not least, singing with the Crouch End Festival Chorus.

Chapter Sixteen: 'Ski Conferences' in Austria

In 1969, the year in which I made the move from Southampton to London, I received an invitation to attend the first immunology symposium in Kitzbühel, that glamorous ski resort in Austria. The invitation came from Professor Walter Brendel, who had established the Institute for Surgical Research in Munich and was anxious to develop immunological research, especially in the field of transplantation, in his institute. To that end he had decided to organise an annual conference to be attended by his colleagues and postgraduate students and to which he invited about ten internationally known immunologists to talk about their current research projects. It was a strategy that worked brilliantly, for immunology became firmly established in Munich and the members of his institute later contributed many innovative papers.

Apart from his research and his institute, Brendel had two other passions: skiing and music. Postgraduate students accepted by him had to be not only very bright intellectually but had to share his passions. The foreigners invited excelled in immunology or in clinical matters but were not so hot on skis, and so a symbiotic relationship developed: they taught us very expertly to ski, and we did our best to take them to the cutting edge of research and to become conversant with the intricacies of immunology. Thus everyone benefited greatly. The foreigners were mainly from the UK, the USA, the Netherlands, Italy and a few other European countries, and the symposia were conducted in English. There was a core of 'regulars', which included luminaries such as Sir Peter Medawar (transplantation immunologist), J.J. van Rood (immunogeneticist), F.H. Bach (immunologist), Sir Roy Calne (transplant surgeon), R. Ceppellini (immunogeneticist), J.R. Batchelor (transplantation immunologist) and, later, E. Simpson and R. Pardi (both immunologists), A.P. Monaco (transplant surgeon), Sir Peter Morris (transplant surgeon) and D.H. Sachs (transplantation immunologist) – all experts in their fields. I joined the symposia in 1973 and attended annually until they came to an end in 2002.

I had declined an invitation for the first meeting in 1969 because it was the year in which I took up the chair of immunology at St Mary's and I felt too preoccupied. Furthermore, I thought that the concept of a scientific meeting in a ski resort was somewhat frivolous, and organised by a bunch of Germans at that. Gene Lance, an American colleague of Peter Medawar's with whom I had become friendly, implored me to think again when another invitation came my way a couple of years later, and on his recommendation I accepted that time. How very fortunate, for these meetings, with their mix of science, sport and social activities, were quite the happiest I have attended, and after my first appearance I was invited annually.

The first seven or eight meetings were held in Kitzbühel, in the very elegant Hotel Tennerhof, but when this became too expensive they were moved to Axams in the Tirol (to the very comfortable Hotel Neuwirt run by the charming Monica Bucher and her husband), and many years later still, when the Neuwirt fell on hard times, to Mauls in the Italian Tirol. The format remained essentially the same, for it could hardly have been improved. The mornings were reserved for downhill skiing; while the scientific sessions began at 3 p.m. and went on until 8. They were followed by dinner and social activities, which often included musical offerings of a high standard by students from the institute. (I once had the effrontery to sing a few Schubert songs, accompanied by Gerd Riethmüller, a German immunologist specialising in tumour immunology.) The scientific sessions, attended by about thirty workers from the institute, a few Austrians and the invited speakers, were highly informal so that people felt able to let their hair down and talk freely, even about experiments still in progress. These meetings provided a good insight into new developments in transplantation, and they extended to related fields such as allergy and tumour immunology. Because of Konrad Messmer's interests some papers were devoted to the study of the microcirculation, and after Brendel's death and the appointment of Messmer as director, transplantation and microcirculation were equally represented.

Almost as important as the scientific component of these meetings were the sporting and social activities. Our scientific discussions were often continued when sitting on chair lifts on our way up the mountains, and this led to some collaborative projects. We all got to know each other well and there was a general sense of friendship and bonhomie, and this was much encouraged by the outgoing personalities of the organisers, Walter Brendel and Konrad Messmer.

One unique feature of these meetings was the 'relaxation from immunology' lecture each year. The lecturer was chosen by the director and was kept secret until the day of the lecture. The criterion used to select a speaker was the interest of the topic, which ranged from the discovery of ancient scripts to bird and bee navigation, prions, and the Hippocratic Oath. One of the most memorable concerned the discovery of Oetzi the Iceman, given by an Austrian professor who had been intimately involved in the identification and preservation of this extraordinary body, preserved in the mountains in snow and ice for hundreds of years. Without exception these lectures provided a perfect way of relaxing from the intensive scientific discussions.

Brendel was a man of great energy and considerable, if somewhat authoritarian, charisma. He fostered a research group in the field of tissue and organ transplantation, especially the study of xenografts – grafts transplanted from one species to another. Among his greatest achievements was the ingenious use of ultrasonic shock waves for the disintegration of kidney and gall bladder stones, a technique that was first presented to us at an Axams meeting and has been widely adopted. He had been a member of the Hitler Youth in his teens and had deep regrets about that. It was probably no accident that among the hard core of invited speakers was more than a sprinkling of American and British Jews, for he regarded these meetings as a means of reconciliation and of forging friendships across national borders.

I had the privilege to be asked to contribute a talk to the symposium celebrating Brendel's sixty-fifth birthday. He died of a brain tumour in 1989.

His successor in 1990 was his first co-worker, Konrad Messmer, who had joined him in 1962. He was a very different personality: handsome and suave, with a wicked sense of humour that could create much hilarity in the relaxed atmosphere after a dinner, when he could be delightfully indiscreet. Konrad was a superlative experimental scientist who ran a large and able group pushing back the boundaries of the field of microcirculation, ischemia and haemodynamics. Having always been thought of as a bachelor *par excellence* he married Maria-José, a delightfully vivacious and no-nonsense Argentinian, relatively late in life and they produced two charming daughters. He too asked me to take part in his sixty-fifth birthday symposium, which pleased me no end.

I got to know Walter and Konrad well, and both were kind enough to claim that I was an indispensable component of the meetings, which ended in 2002 with Messmer's retirement.

The institute secretary who ably administered the ski-conferences under both Brendel and Messmer was Frau Mechthild Stein, a dignified and pleasant lady of mature years who took many students under her wing. She and I became good friends, and so it was no accident that we found ourselves on the same sledge at one of the nocturnal toboggan runs on a prepared, banked and winding course lit at intervals with flares. We were all given a glass of Schnapps or two and then let off at intervals that proved far too brief. Our combined weight added speed to our descent, and there came a point when we had to make a quick decision between crashing into the sledge in front of us or throwing ourselves off. We chose the latter and I experienced the most excruciating pain in my left knee. I just managed to hobble back to our hotel and was taken to Innsbruck hospital, which specialises in sports injuries, the following morning. The doctors there decided that I had strained or partly torn my anterior cruciate ligament and encased my leg in plaster. On my return to St Mary's (Liz Simpson nobly pushed me across Munich airport in a wheelchair) the remedy was deemed to be quite the opposite: off with the plaster and intensive physiotherapy. The knee undoubtedly improved but it wasn't until two years later that it was realised that the ligament had been torn, and by this time it was too late to stitch it together. I was able to continue to ski with the help of a knee 'corset' but find it astonishing that two such famous hospitals should have got it so wrong.

Some of the longest 'poems' I have ever written were after-dinner speeches at these meetings, usually for an important anniversary such as the tenth, twentieth and thirtieth conference. As they were always delivered in an alcoholic haze they went down well and, on rereading them long after the event, they do seem apposite and amusing. The last 'speech', given one year prematurely (a horrid mistake, but having written it I wasn't going to let that stand in my way) was written to mourn the end of the conference series. I sang it to the tune of the German folksong 'Ich weiss nicht was soll es bedeuten'. Afterwards this embroiled me in a lengthy discussion with Hansi Ring, a German allergologist and a witty poet, on whether the poetry of Heinrich Heine could be considered to be great. He evidently did not think so. As Heine was one of the few well-known German-Jewish poets, and from my limited knowledge of his poetry (mainly through Schubert lieder), I took the opposite point of view, and found some support around the dining table.

Although unable to take part in winter sports, Sir Peter Medawar and his wife Jean attended many of the meetings and he became a much admired friend and supporter of the Munich Institute. Jean learnt to ski late in life and, hugely to her credit, became quite good at it, having had a junior ski champion as her tutor for several years. By contrast, Carol, who came to a couple of meetings in the early nineties, did not take to it and broke her finger in a tumble, thus sadly ending her interest in the sport.

The ski-conferences had become an important part of my life – an event to which I looked forward annually – and when they ended there appeared a void in my life towards the end of each January.

Chapter Seventeen: My Involvement in Politics

Beginnings

J have always been interested in the world around me and therefore in politics. It began in Germany, with Mussolini's dastardly attack on Abyssinia in 1935, when the Emperor Haile Selassie became my hero; and it extended to my youthful and, naturally highly disagreeable, perception of Hitler and the Nazis, which was more and more forced on my consciousness. I particularly remember the 1936 Olympics in Berlin, if only because I cheered every time the young black American Jesse Owens won one of his four glorious gold medals, to the outrage of Hitler and the German press. In Bunce Court School, where cuttings of the *Manchester Guardian* (now the *Guardian*) and the *New Statesman* were posted on a daily wall newspaper, I naturally took a lively interest in the progress of the war. This, and the attitude of some of the teachers, made me lean quite naturally to the left of centre. Supporting the underdog became one of my guiding principles.

Politics in the army

As an army officer towards the end of the Second World War one of my duties was to give regular ABCA (Army Bureau of Current Affairs) lectures to the soldiers of my company. These lectures were intended to be educational and to widen the cultural horizons of the troops. I was astonished to find that although most came from relatively poor working-class backgrounds the notion that they might vote anything other than Conservative in the 1945 general election had simply not occurred to most of them. Although I was not a member of the Labour party I was in sympathy with its social philosophy, and I made it my business to suggest to my listeners that Labour, under Clement Attlee's leadership, was more likely to represent their interests than the Tories under Winston Churchill. I did so despite my great admiration for Churchill as a wartime leader, and many other non-professional officers in the services must have taken a similar line, for the landslide victory won by Labour in July 1945 on the strength of their manifesto 'Let us face the future' was at least in part thanks to the postal ballot of serving soldiers.

By rejecting their great wartime leader the British people showed extraordinary maturity, for Churchill's domestic peacetime record was far from admirable and the country turned to the untried Labour party to undertake the immense task of rebuilding Britain with its bombed cities, exhausted industry, poverty, food shortages and fuel crises. My antipathy towards the Conservative party did not, however, prevent me from experiencing a genuine sense of loss when Churchill died in January 1965. I was at the time still in London and I felt impelled to join the queue of solemn people from every conceivable walk of life stretching all the way round the Houses of Parliament to pay homage to the great man lying in state in Westminster Hall. It was a moving experience, shuffling slowly round the catafalque, and it brought back vivid memories of the war years. The services chiefs of staff had taken over the watch at the time, and it was touching to see these elderly men standing at each corner, leaning on their swords with their heads bowed.

Like many people in the country I had some affection for Clem Attlee, who had been deputy prime minister in the war cabinet and who now undertook the gigantic task of rebuilding Britain. He seemed a quiet and self-effacing man who nonetheless set about his task with great resolution. He was hardly ever seen without his pipe, and people tended to underestimate his ability. Despite the country's economic weaknesses he tried hard to stick to his socialist principles, which included doing his best for the underdog and nationalising essential industries such as coal mining and the railways. It was under Attlee that Aneuran Bevan, the left-wing firebrand and superb orator, managed to create the National Health Service despite the resistance of most of the medical profession. Bevan eventually resigned as Minister of Health when the government insisted on introducing prescription charges. He would turn in his grave if he knew how far the process of privatisation has advanced.

Attlee addressed an election meeting in the Birmingham Bull Ring in 1951 and I went to hear him speak. It was an inspiring sight. The vast Bull Ring, then a wide-open space, was packed with people, largely men wearing cloth caps, and Attlee in his quiet way gave a rousing speech, with the crowd roaring their approval. To be there was to be made to feel that one was on the side of the angels, even though I did not join the Labour party until many years later. Harold Wilson, who eventually succeeded him, was a different kettle of fish altogether. I never quite trusted his political judgement and his capacity for somewhat sordid compromises made me feel wary of him. His 'white heat of the scientific revolution' concept, in which he postulated that science would provide the solution to just about everything, never saw the light of day, mainly because he either would not or could not invest enough money in our universities and research councils.

One amusing anecdote may be recalled. My fellow immunologist and friend Avrion (Av) Mitchison, the son of the writer Naomi and nephew of G.B.S. Haldane, had asked me to join him in canvassing for a left-wing and socially committed member of parliament, Lena Jeger, in a general election campaign, sometime in the fifties. We called on houses in the Regents Park area, asking the occupants to vote for her and leaving leaflets. The magnificent Nash terraces surrounding Regent's Park were subdivided into offices or flats, and when I rang the bell of one of them a man's voice answered through the entryphone. I said my little piece, and in a drawling upper-class accent he said, 'you're wasting your bloody time as we always vote Fascist here'! Av and I had a good laugh and moved on.

Haringey Labour Parties

Although I was deeply interested in politics and voted Labour until the 1980s, I did not join the Labour party until 1970, after my move back to London. The Conservatives under Ted Heath were back in power and, having lived through the debacle of the Suez Canal adventure in 1956, when Anthony Eden agreed to a madcap scheme with the French and Israeli governments to attack and occupy the Suez Canal Zone, I felt that the time had come to commit myself to the re-election of a Labour government. I therefore joined the Haringey Labour party and was soon embroiled in electioneering and in the formation of a pressure group called the Haringey Labour Parties Research and Action Group on Social Services, of which I became the convener.

The group met regularly and, having discussed at length where social provision in Haringey was lacking, it made wide-ranging proposals. Some of these were directed towards the elderly and families in stress, the establishment of a Council for Social Service, and the provision of pre-school education for all children. A Council for Voluntary Service was indeed established and funded by the Labour borough council. I became its founder vice-chairman. Its responsibilities extended to advising and assisting voluntary organisations in the borough, the provision of links with these organisations and local and central government departments, and reviewing the social needs of Haringey. A professional general secretary was appointed and the council continues to function.

One of our more revolutionary proposals was for universal pre-school education but it was ignored, presumably because of its cost implications. We had argued that children from disadvantaged backgrounds never catch up in their educational attainments at primary and secondary school level compared with children from more affluent homes, and that this disadvantage could only be done away with by free high quality pre-school education. It is extraordinary that it has taken three decades before a Labour government has started to put this seemingly obvious notion into practice.

Hornsey Labour party, which was part of Haringey Labour Parties, was at that time a tolerant organisation, welcoming members from all strata of society; and the monthly ward meetings made for interesting and open-ended discussions on a variety of political, social and economic questions. In the mid-seventies this changed abruptly. New members with militant left-wing views appeared from nowhere and the atmosphere of ward meetings changed abruptly. Middle-class members such as myself were made to feel distinctly uncomfortable. Meanwhile, in 1974, I had become a Labour party-nominated governor of Creighton Comprehensive School, located not very far from my home in Muswell Hill.

The Creighton School governors' scandal

Creighton School was large, and well run by the redoubtable Molly Hattersley, the wife of Roy, who was to become a minister in the next Labour government.. The Labour-nominated governors outnumbered those appointed by the Tories and there were several elected by parents, but party affiliations did not seem to matter very much as all governors were primarily interested in the welfare of the school. With the election of a new chairperson, Jane Chapman, the atmosphere changed and party politics suddenly became paramount. She was extremely left wing and either a member of, or sympathetic to, the 'militant tendency', a shadowy bunch of neo-Communists who were infiltrating the Labour party in the 1970s and doing untold damage to its reputation.

The winter of 1978/9 has been dubbed the 'winter of discontent' because the Labour government under James Callaghan was faced with a damaging series of strikes over pay, which included public employees in schools and hospitals. School caretakers began their strike in January 1979 and most if not all schools were forced to close. Like most other Haringey governing bodies the Creighton governors discussed the problems this posed for their children, and concern was felt for those children preparing for their GCE examinations the following summer. After lengthy discussions a motion endorsing the caretakers' strike was blocked with the help of three Labour-appointed governors – Eva Holmes, an educational psychologist, Harry Rée, a former Professor of Education at the University of York who had opted to return to the classroom, and me. Instead, I proposed a motion calling on the education committee to enter into discussions with the caretakers' union with a view to have the school partly reopened so that children preparing for their exams in the summer could continue to receive some tuition. This motion was passed with the support of Conservative and parent governors, as well as Harry Rée and Eva Holmes. At the time Rée was chairman of the Muswell Hill Labour party ward and I was vice-chairman.

Other governing bodies in the borough passed similar motions without arousing a great deal of ire. However, in May I was astonished to receive a letter from Molly Hattersley expressing deep regret that I was no longer on the governing body and thanking me fulsomely for my services. 'Over the last five years I have greatly valued the support and understanding which you have given to the school and me,' she wrote. 'The school will be the poorer without the benefit of your knowledge and experience, and your concern for the welfare and progress of children of all abilities and backgrounds.' Similar letters were received by Harry Rée and Eva Holmes. This was the first intimation we had of our removal, and we had not had the opportunity of defending ourselves against the charge of breaching the Labour party's guidelines. The three of us were deeply upset and sent a letter of protest to the leader of Haringey Council, Colin Ware. We pointed out that, without just cause, the council had done away with the services of an educational psychologist and two university professors (one of them a former headmaster), all with a long interest in comprehensive education. We asked four questions. Why were we removed? What constitutional procedures had been followed? Why had we been denied the right to be informed of the charge against us, and the opportunity of defending ourselves? And why were we not promptly informed once the decision was taken, apparently more than a week before Molly Hattersley had written to us on a purely personal basis? Support came from the Muswell Hill Branch in the form of an emergency resolution that expressed full confidence in the three 'summarily removed' governors and called for an enquiry into the circumstances.

To cut a long story short, we were not reinstated, although we were given the opportunity of stating our case to the executive committee of Haringey Labour Parties. There were men and women in the local Labour party who were moderates – for example, Nicky Harrison, who was chairperson of the education committee (she died recently, after a successful career in education) and Andrew Macintosh and Toby Harris (both long in the House of Lords) were influential, and Robin Young and

Colin Ware seemed to be reasonable people, but evidently most members were unwilling to put their heads over the parapet and preferred to indulge the left-wingers. To add a touch of farce to the proceedings, at the next meeting of the governing body on 16 July two of the 'dismissed' governors (I was in the USA at the time) turned up, having refused to accept their dismissal, as did their replacements! Councillor Chapman was re-elected as chairperson on a six to five vote but Councillor Chris Hannington, who on the HCRC and the governing body had always represented the more acceptable face of the Tory party, declared that he would be challenging the legality of the dismissal of the three governors and the legality of the vote for a new chairman.

The whole issue soon became a political football. Harry Rée and I wanted to conduct our appeal quietly, but both the local and the national press (the *Guardian*, the *Telegraph*, the *Daily Mail* and the *Evening Standard*) got hold of the story and ran a number of articles about it, all sympathetic to the dismissed governors. A young journalist (Richard Norton-Taylor, later the *Guardian's* security affairs editor and an intrepid investigative journalist) was willing to write a major article about the affair in the general context of malpractice in local government, but my continuing loyalty to the Labour party at that time made me shy away from that. Harry Rée also preferred to keep a low profile. Eva Holmes made a formal complaint to the local ombudsman, who many months later found that Haringey Council had acted illegally because they had removed us without a formal vote, whereas I attempted to seek justice by appealing to the national executive of the Labour party.

Creighton School parents supported us staunchly from the start and drew up a strongly worded statement, which included phrases such as 'These governors have always proved themselves to have had the welfare of the children and the school as their priority,' and 'We think it is a disgrace that Labour should operate such a star chamber tactic as their dismissal.' Opponents of the Labour party had a field day.

My internal appeal in the autumn of 1980 was addressed to James Callaghan, leader of the Labour party, as well as to Shirley Williams and Denis Healey, who were on the party's national executive and already then battling against its more extreme members. In my letter to Callaghan I wrote, 'I hesitate to burden you with a matter that may seem relatively trivial, but do so because I believe that it goes to the roots of what is presently wrong with our party.' Callaghan (Uncle Jim, as he tended to be called for his gentlemanly, kindly but rather ineffectual approach to politics) replied by expressing sympathy but stressing that the appointment of governors rested entirely in the hands of local Labour parties. Shirley Williams took up our cause at a meeting of the national executive, but according to her letter to me in October it was Tony Benn and his left-wing supporters who ensured that the item was not discussed at a meeting in Blackpool. In fact, she attempted to have the matter discussed on three separate occasions. In her letter to me of 23 October she wrote, 'I really feel we must find some way to fight back on this one; the only trouble is that nowadays there are so many things that one has to fight back on! Anyway, may I say that I think your treatment was disgraceful and I think that when you know my part of the story you will realise that it was even more disgraceful than you thought it was.' The national agent of the party, David Hughes, did not bother to reply for several months, and eventually only after numerous follow-up letters to a letter of complaint sent by Eva Holmes on behalf of the three of us. The general secretary of the Labour party was appealed to but to no avail. On 30 October 1980 I thanked Shirley Williams for having taken up our cause and agreeing to give an interview to the press 'if it would help you and your friends in the party'. I concluded, 'It's heartening to know that *someone* in the party believes that we have been hard done by and I am particularly glad that it should be you, as you are the British politician I admire most.'

Denis Healey wrote on 29 October, 'I am deeply distressed to hear the story . . .', and said that he would contact the national agent! He was also sent a letter from Dr Arnold Sanderson, a fellow immunologist and a staunch member of the Labour party in East Grinstead, appealing to him to take up the cudgels on my behalf. It was couched in terms that were somewhat extravagant and modesty prevents me from quoting them at length. However, he concluded, 'The movement we all love cannot afford to discard thinkers, and above all workers, of his capacity and I am deeply saddened by these events. The Labour party can count on few enough friends associated with medical teaching, and his absence will have far-reaching consequences over the next few decades, if only because so many of us were proud to point to him as a professional, intellectual example of what socialism could be all about in this country.' Healey again contacted the national agent, with predictable results.

By early December 1980 I felt that I was left with no option other than to resign from the Labour party, for I could not belong to a party that treated its members so shabbily and unfairly and was so unwilling to admit that a mistake had been made. I was deeply upset and angry, and in a three-page letter to the secretary of the Muswell Hill branch of the Labour party I set out my reasons. 'That my decision has been arrived at with great regret is nevertheless true, for I have always been, and will continue to be, a democratic socialist who values democracy and socialism equally. I could not bear to belong to a party which, though hypocritically professing an interest in democracy, is capable of treating its own members in the way the three us have been treated.' Whilst going through my file on all this I realise how much time and emotional energy I spent in terms of letter writing to all manner of individuals and the press. In May 1979 Callaghan called a general election and Margaret Thatcher won with a sizeable majority, remaining prime minister for the next eighteen years. As for me, I became a founder member of the Social Democratic party two years later, and I was the founder chairman of its Haringey branch.

A few years after my resignation Michael Foot became leader of the Labour party. On Saturday mornings I often took our beagle Beth for a walk on Hampstead Heath, and there I ran across Foot exercising his beloved little terrier Dot. We chatted on one or two occasions and I told him of the treatment that had been meted out to me. He sympathised greatly and asked me to write to him with all the details. However, I felt that it was all water under the bridge by then and had no wish to reopen this chapter of my life. Being a somewhat unworldly intellectual, an unbending socialist *and* a thoroughly decent man he did not stay the course as leader for long.

The formation of the Social Democratic party (SDP)

By this time the rift between the dogmatic left and those of a more moderate bent in the shadow cabinet had widened and, unable to persuade their colleagues to adopt a less partisan approach, four of them (the 'Gang of Four') threatened to break away. They were Roy Jenkins, David Owen, Shirley Williams and Bill Rodgers. When it was reported in the press that Shirley Williams was dithering about leaving the Labour party I sent her an encouraging letter, for I felt that the only factor that could transform the dismal political scene in Britain was a new, centre-left and democratic party. In March 1981 the Gang of Four formally launched the Social Democratic party (SDP), to the disgust of the Labour establishment, which immediately branded them as traitors. A national constitution was drawn up with which I felt very comfortable. It was in a sense a Mark II Labour party, but with the vital difference that it was free of vested interests such as the trades unions, espoused a system of fairer elections, proposed decentralisation, promised to adopt a constructive and committed role in the European Community, and stressed its commitments to democratic and open government and to human rights. Its preamble stated: 'The SDP exists to create and defend an open, classless and more equal society which rejects prejudices based on sex, race, colour or religion.' I could wholeheartedly identify with that.

I became deeply involved in the formation of the Haringey branch. Some like-minded members of the local Labour party joined me in forming a steering committee, and a quite hectic period, which saw the birth of Haringey SDP, began. Looking back I realise that this was fatal to my marriage, for I had of course still major professional commitments to my department, my research and also to the (International) Transplantation Society (the Brighton Congress took place in the autumn of 1982), and the political activities had to be squeezed into what free evenings were at my disposal. I became totally driven: having been forced out of the Labour party by a rank injustice I was determined to help the SDP become a viable political force. What happened next was absolute madness so far as my domestic life was concerned.

An *ad hoc* steering committee was set up to prepare the way by arranging for publicity in the local press, preparing a draft constitution and organising the first meeting of Haringey SDP. It was hoped to appeal not only to former Labour party members but also to those who had supported other parties or none. This meeting took place on 1 June 1981 and it was very well attended. One could sense the feeling of excitement and expectation at the birth of a new party, and the atmosphere was civilised and relaxed and unbureaucratic. A highly flexible subscription was agreed, a steering committee was formally elected with me as its chairman, it was agreed that a dialogue with the local Liberal party should be initiated with a view to cooperation in the imminent elections, the steering committee was asked to give immediate consideration to the appointment of a national party leader, and it was recommended that the leader should be elected by secret ballot of all party members. A public meeting was announced for later in the month, which Bill Rodgers MP had agreed to address.

This meeting, which I chaired, was very well attended by a complete cross-section of the population, with a good sprinkling of people who had never joined a political party before. Bill Rodgers was not the most charismatic of speakers but he gave a good account of the reasons that had led the Gang of Four to form a breakaway party. New members enrolled in droves, and the Haringey SDP was off the ground.

Shirley Williams and David Owen

We had two further public meetings over the next year for which we had succeeded in persuading Shirley Williams MP (now Baroness Williams) and David Owen MP (now Lord Owen) to speak, respectively. Shirley was, and still is, a charismatic and enthusiastic and much-loved speaker but she was not famed for her punctuality. True to form, she arrived about twenty-five minutes late. I did my best to fill in this rather embarrassing waiting period by providing the large audience with bits of information. When she did arrive, somewhat out of breath, she gave a rousing and well-received speech that struck people by its sincerity and its well-argued case for a new party. I remained in correspondence with Shirley thereafter, especially at the time of the SDP-Liberal merger, and I had no difficulty with going along with her on most issues.

David Owen was very different – suave, magisterial and a politician through and through. One could hardly describe him as likeable though I respected him in the 1970s for his intelligence and grasp of issues. I had met him in 1975, when he had been minister of health. The British Transplantation Society had published a closely reasoned article in the *British Medical Journal* about the calamitous shortage of donor organs, and the authors (of which I, as editor, was one) and the society as a whole had plumped for the establishment of an opting-out donor programme, according to which all adult members of the population would be regarded as potential donors unless they had withheld their permission. The BTS therefore sent a delegation, which was led by the transplant surgeon Professor R.Y. Calne, to discuss this with Owen, in the hope of persuading him that this was the only realistic option. As might have been expected, Owen was highly diplomatic, in sympathy with our proposal but unwilling to embrace it, as he felt that public opinion wasn't ready for such a move. He was probably right in this, for organ transplantation was still at an early stage and its benefits not nearly as clear as they are now. It is a proposal that has recently been revived, for the shortage has, as organ transplantation has soared, become infinitely worse; and other countries such as Spain have introduced such a scheme with considerable success.

I drove Owen back to his home in Limehouse after another public meeting. Not once during the lengthy journey did he ask me what I did for a living, for he was totally preoccupied with his own affairs. On arrival he invited me in for a cup of coffee and there I met his very pleasant American wife. Some years later, when the SDP decided to merge with the Liberal party, Owen refused to go down that road and kept the SDP going with a small band of diehards who could not face the prospect of joining forces with a Liberal party that they despised. In doing so he did social democracy in Britain no favours and, to a degree, impeded the early success of the Liberal Democrats. His elevation to a peerage and, eventually, his United Nations role in Bosnia took him out of national politics. Ironically, his lecture in 2008 to the Royal College of Physicians had the title 'On the Hubris Syndrome'!

Borough elections in 1982 and the dire effect of the Falklands war

The Haringey SDP, ahead of its time, formed an alliance with three local Liberal associations to fight the borough elections in May 1982, and a joint manifesto was drawn up by the Haringey SDP-Liberal Alliance. It was a daunting task, as the Liberals often saw things from a different perspective, but after many lengthy meetings a very satisfactory nine-page manifesto was agreed and published. In its preamble it stated that 'Our programme is based on the belief that there must be equal opportunities for all and that it is the individual who matters above all when policies are decided. We also believe strongly in the rights of minorities and in the removal of racial and sex discrimination from our society.'

This manifesto, together with a small army of devoted canvassers, cut a lot of ice with the electorate of Haringey and our house-to-house canvassing indicated an extremely good response, which made us believe that a large number of our candidates would be elected. Then Argentina invaded the Falkland Islands on 2 April, and within a few days the Prime Minister, Margaret Thatcher, sent a task force to the South Atlantic to reclaim the islands for Britain. The effect this had on the electorate was predictable. The Union Jack appeared all over the place; people became ultra-patriotic and wanted to support 'their boys' and therefore the government; and interest in the new party largely evaporated. The SDP-Liberal Alliance captured a few seats on the borough council, and thereafter it was an uphill battle that was not won until recently.

In December 1982 we appointed a parliamentary candidate after listening to three short-listed candidates at a meeting of members. One of these was John Martin, who seemed to have the right background and for whom I had a marginal preference. In the event he was not selected, which was probably just as well, for years later I learnt from Carol that she had been married to him and that he had abandoned her and her three young children in the early 1970s.

I gave up the chairmanship after three years because it made too many inroads into my private and professional life. Much later, in January 1987, I wrote to David Owen urging him to consider the possibility of merging with the Liberals before the next general election and possibly making a limited electoral deal with the Labour party in order to break the stranglehold of Margaret Thatcher's Tory government. Owen did not bother to reply until July. I had sent a copy of my letter to Roy Jenkins, who very promptly sent me a note saying that he had read it with great interest and that he was in 'some considerable agreement'. When Owen eventually replied in July the notion of a merger of the two parties was being openly discussed, and he made it perfectly clear that he disagreed profoundly with such a move: not only would he decline to be the leader of a merged party but he would not even want to join it. He finished off a two-page letter with the following sentiments: 'There are moments when a decision is needed that requires self-confidence and courage. Such a decision is needed now and I hope that our members will see the promotion of an immediate merger for what it is – a takeover, and one in which the distinctive identity of the

SDP would be lost from British politics at the very moment when it is most needed.'

The Liberal Democrats: a new party is born

I think that history has proved Owen to be wrong though there can be no certainty of that; who knows whether the SDP on its own would have changed British politics. His attitude undoubtedly initially had a negative impact on the success of the new party, the Liberal Democrats, even though it had the strong support of Shirley Williams, Roy Jenkins and Bill Rodgers. I corresponded with Shirley in January 1988. Having expressed some impatience at the slowness of the negotiations between the two parties she replied immediately. (In those days politicians actually answered their letters personally; now one tends to get a general handout stating what is already well known.) 'I understand your impatience at some of the events of recent weeks,' she wrote, 'but I believe that the agreement reached virtually unanimously by the SDP and the Liberal negotiators on Monday night, 18 January, is a good, solid foundation on which to build the new party. The constitution is democratic and federal, has clear lines of accountability, and allows for a deliberate policy-making process . . . I believe that the necessity for an effective, constructive opposition party is ever more urgent. I hope that we can bend our energies to that objective, and I hope that we will have your help in doing so.' A handwritten PS said, 'Please don't abandon us – I do think it's beginning to straighten out at last.'

Ten days later she wrote again. 'I expect you will have read reports of the Liberal Assembly at Blackpool, which endorsed by a very large majority the agreement on the constitution and the policy statement. So did the Council for Social Democracy at Sheffield on 31 January.' She quoted the *Guardian* editorial of 1 February: 'Yesterday's decisive vote by the Social Democratic party in favour of merger with the Liberals means that there will be some form of effective third party politics at the next general election and beyond.' How right the *Guardian* proved to be. Although the electoral system is still heavily stacked against any third party, the Liberal Democrats have sixty-four members of parliament at the time of writing, and should do even better in the future.

Those who left the Labour party in the early 1980s to join the SDP have never been forgiven by Labour party zealots, and they have been blamed for the eighteen calamitous years ruled by Margaret Thatcher. She certainly did a huge amount of damage – the privatisation of vital industries, the running down of the railways, the destruction of the mining industry, the fatal erosion of the country's manufacturing base, her forceful reaction to the invasion of the Falkland Islands, to name but a few negative features. However, the formation of the SDP, and of the Liberal Democratic party that it gave rise to, galvanised the Labour party into setting its own house in order, and the rise of 'New Labour' can be largely attributed to it. I greatly welcomed the return of a Labour government in 1997 and there was a general feeling of hope that many wrongs would at last be righted. Alas, these hopes have only been very partially fulfilled, and on many issues the governments led by Tony Blair and Gordon Brown have been a severe disappointment. Some of their policies have been so extreme that even Margaret Thatcher would not have gone so far, for example the introduction of swingeing top-up fees for university students, and the relentless advocacy of the global economy. The Home Office under David Blunkett pursued some shamelessly populist and right-wing policies: when he suggested that it would be quite in order to take the children of failed asylum seekers into care, whilst returning the parents to their country of origin, I wrote to him in protest. I reminded him of a stirring speech he had given in September 2003 at the unveiling of a sculpture on Liverpool Street railway station, in memory of the 1938-39 Kindertransports. In recalling the spirit of compassion that led the then British government to allow 10,000 children from central Europe to enter Britain without visas, and praising the wonderful contribution these refugees had subsequently made to the British economy and culture, he added that he hoped that the current government would deal equally compassionately with asylum seekers. I did not receive a response until many weeks later, and this was a formal statement of Home Office policy: children would be taken into care only in exceptional circumstances. Tony Blair, to whom I had sent a copy of my letter, replied more promptly through his personal assistant to say that he had been 'interested' in my letter.

Letters to the press and politicians

In recent years I have not taken part in politics very actively, for I have felt that I have done more than my fair share of attending meetings and canvassing in elections. I am, however, a member of the Liberal Democrats and I allowed myself to be appointed by Islington Borough Council, which has a Liberal Democrat majority, as a governor of a local primary school. When Paddy Ashdown was the forceful leader of the Liberal Democrats I served on a parliamentary party committee formulating policy on animal protection. I found myself to be its only scientist with a personal knowledge and experience of vivisection in medical research, and had to argue forcefully to persuade others on the committee not to adopt a militant line against vivisection for medical purposes. The final document adequately reflected my concerns; but it came out strongly against vivisection for the development of cosmetics and put forward sensible proposals for the protection of farm animals and animals in the wild.

Paddy Ashdown was that rare party leader who answered letters personally. When, following a meeting of the committee, I expressed some concern at the highly emotional points made by some members, he thanked me for my own contribution and wrote: 'I share some of the despair expressed in your letter. But this is what happens when we get highly charged debates in which people take an entirely moral or an entirely pragmatic position. We had some good debates . . . My concern was not to allow either side to wreck it in one way or another. The points you make in your letter are I think extremely powerful and well made. I share your views on almost every point'. What modern party leader would reply in such terms? Paddy was in many ways a remarkable man and I often wish, when listening to his successors, that Ashdown was still at the helm.

As I read the *Guardian* regularly my letters to the press have usually been sent there. The topics have included the low pay and difficulty in the recruitment of laboratory technicians, vaccination for foot-and-mouth disease, the frightening hysteria that gripped the country following the notorious child killing of James Bulger, ethnic cleansing in the former Yugoslavia, the imminent attack on Iraq, General Pinochet's extradition, the Labour government's ambivalent attitude to the European Union, Ariel Sharon's attempt to influence terms of reference of the United Nations' enquiry into the alleged Jenin massacre, the crisis in the Middle East, the proposed immigration and asylum bill, human rights, and student 'top-up' fees. Quite a few were published whilst others were not. I will quote from one that was accepted on the subject of General Pinochet's extradition:

> I lost virtually the whole of my family in the holocaust. For me, the critical issue – one purely of justice – is whether, had Adolf Hitler survived the war, he could have been prosecuted for the slaughter of millions of defenceless people. Surely no one would have argued at the time that such a prosecution would have been illegal because Hitler had been head of state when these atrocities were committed, and it is unthinkable that such an argument should prevail in Pinochet's case. The precedent set by a decision not to extradite him would, in effect, legalise genocide.

Chapter Eighteen: 9/11/2001 and the attack on Iraq, 2003

9/11 and its aftermath

These do be times that take all you have to scrape up a decent laugh or so. I do not refer to the battlefields, but to this enormous pest of hate that is rotting men's souls. When will people learn that you cannot quarantine hate? Once it gets loose in the world, it rides over all barriers and seeps under doors and in the cracks of every house. I see it all around me every day. I am not talking of race hatred. Just hate. Everybody is at it . . . Once it was just Germany and Japan and Italy. Now, it is our allies as well. The people in the next county or state. The other political party. The world smells like an abattoir. It makes me very unhappy. I am all wrong in this vengeful world. I will to love.

Thus wrote Zora Neale Hurston, the Afro-American writer and journalist soon after the end of the Second Word War. It aptly expresses my feelings in the aftermath of 9/11 and the attack on Iraq, as well as the situation in the Middle East. I felt so deeply affected by these horrors that I was emotionally disabled much of the time. Indeed, the attack on Iraq (usually misnamed the war with Iraq) caused me to interrupt writing these memoirs for the best part of nine months, such was my despondency and depression brought about by this act of madness.

The attack on the World Trade Center on 9/11 was without doubt a terrible crime, which *nothing* could possibly excuse or condone. Nonetheless it is legitimate to ask what caused those Muslim fanatics to act in that way. I have long believed that the policy of the Israeli government, especially that of Ariel Sharon, had much to do with it, for it has fuelled a deep sense of grievance among Palestinians and their supporters throughout the world. This is a point that the American government under George W. Bush tragically failed to grasp; it is only the USA that could exert enough pressure on the Israeli government to moderate its policies and to seek a genuine accommodation with the Palestinians. No real attempt has been made – the 'road map' laid down by Bush seems no more than a gesture – and the steadfast support given by the USA to Israel has given Sharon and his successor *carte blanche* to do what they like.

The attack on 9/11 almost cost me my friendship with an American transplant surgeon, Tom Starzl, who is one of the foremost pioneers of organ transplantation. We were in active fax communication at the time and I was sent many of his manuscripts for comment. It was Tom who very generously nominated me, together with Rupert Billingham and Morten Simonsen, for the 1994 Medawar Prize of the Transplantation Society. The day after 9/11 I sent him a fax commiserating with him and his fellow Americans on the tragedy that had befallen New York and expressing my deep-felt sympathy. I added that, in my view, the unresolved situation in the Middle East had a great deal to do with it and that steps would have to be taken to curb the military activities of the Israelis against Palestinians. Further, I expressed the view that 'the world would never be the same again', for I had acute forebodings that human rights would be eroded massively in the ensuing fight against terrorism. Tom's reply was a passionate defence of the Israelis, entirely blaming Palestinian terrorism for the mayhem going on in the Middle East. In my response I playfully wrote that I hadn't realised that there were Jewish genes floating around in his genome. Whether or not Tom took offence at my pathetic joke, our correspondence came to an abrupt halt but was, happily, resumed eventually. Tom seemed to be unaware that anything had gone awry between us. In 2006 he published a charming account in *Annals of Surgery* of how I re-established contact with Professor Michael Trede – in somewhat bizarre circumstances in which Tom had played a pivotal role.

My fear about the erosion of human liberties has unfortunately proved to be more than justified. The anti-terrorist legislation introduced in the United States and in the UK has been draconian. It has made possible the incarceration of almost 700 detainees in Camp Delta in Guantanamo Bay, Cuba, who were largely taken as prisoners of war in Afghanistan, suspected of being terrorists. Many have now been held in barbaric conditions for well over five years without charge or trial, and could spend the rest of their lives there. The same could be said of the far smaller number of Muslims held at one time without charge in this country. In fighting terrorism we seem to have descended to the level of the terrorists, and I find this frightening.

Although it is often said that it was the dastardly attack on the World Trade Center that sowed the seeds of the attack on Iraq, it is now clear that President Bush and his neo-conservative advisors were intent on destroying the Saddam Hussein regime long before that cataclysmic event. This may have had something to do with a wish to do away with a regime that posed a threat to Israel but, more probably, it may have been designed to secure Iraq's oil supplies at a time when the world's oil reserves were shrinking. The notion that the war was intended to liberate the Iraqi people came much later, after the claim that Saddam had stocks of weapons of mass destruction (WMD) that could be used to attack strategic targets in the Middle East and Europe became totally discredited. It would seem that Iraqi émigrés living in the USA, principally Ahmed Chalabi, supplied the CIA with erroneous information about the WMD – information that was passed on to them by Iran: an attack on Iraq and the removal of Saddam Hussein were clearly in that country's interest.

Together with many people in the UK I already felt in the winter of 2002 that President Bush, supported by the British prime minister, was determined to attack Iraq no matter what and that the alleged WMD, the existence of which were in considerable doubt according to Hans Blix and his UN weapon inspectors, merely provided a pretext. In desperation I wrote to Tony Blair a few weeks before the attack took place. I expressed the view that he was making a huge error in aligning himself with the most right-wing president in modern history, that an attack on Iraq would make the attack on Egypt over the Suez Crisis in 1956, which led to the resignation of the then prime minister, Anthony Eden, look trivial by comparison, and that history would judge him very harshly if he went ahead. Not surprisingly I received no reply until a general statement, laying out the government's position in the most general terms, reached me many weeks later. Ironically, on 28 February, shortly before the invasion, Tony Blair roundly declared that 'history will be my judge' (the *Guardian*, 1 March 2003), and later, on the steps of a plane, he and Bush announced that 'history will be on our side'. Such a claim now rings hollow.

The big march

On Saturday 15 February 2003 an astonishing event took place in London. The Stop the War Coalition had called for a protest march through central London, with a rally in Hyde Park, and Carol and I, our neighbours Peter and Anita Rich, and my daughter Sue and her husband Dan had decided to join it. It was a cold but bright day and we had to wrap up well. So as to indicate that I was not a pacifist *per se* I had pinned my Second World War medal to my overcoat; it had never before seen the light of day, and it aroused quite a lot of interest. Approaching Tufnell Park underground station was an extraordinary experience, for people were streaming towards the station from every direction, as if the whole of London was *en fête*. The train was so packed that we could hardly get on. And so we joined the one and a half million people, from London and all over the country, on this historic occasion. The march was so massive and slow, even with twelve or fifteen abreast, that we never reached Hyde Park, where the rally took place, for after three or four hours of shuffling along we jumped ship in Trafalgar Square.

There were tens of thousands of banners – many home-made and thousands provided by courtesy of the *Daily Mirror*, which had consistently adopted an anti-war stance. The marchers cut right across the social and political spectrum. They included the trades unions, student bodies, schoolchildren, academics and university students, pacifists and socialists, artists, businesspeople, political organisations, religious groups, Jews for Justice for Palestinians, black and white, young and old, and a sprinkling of young Muslims sporting rather handsome blue pennants displaying the face of Saddam Hussein. The banners inevitably included some that were aimed at Sharon and the Israeli government, and a few anti-Semitic slogans could be heard very occasionally. However, it was generally incredibly good-natured, with a sense of togetherness that I had not experienced since the Second Word War. An impressive feature of the march was the auditory equivalent of the Mexican wave, which not infrequently began as a roar from the rear and swept forwards along the miles of marchers.

Early in January I had read in the *Guardian* that Charles Kennedy, who as the leader of the Liberal Democrats had expressed opposition to the war because he believed that the matter needed to be resolved by the United Nations, was doubtful whether he should join the demonstration. I wrote to him on 9 January urging him to do so and to join the speakers because 'It may be our last opportunity of halting this government's support for the policy of President Bush, and a shift in the British position could well make an impact on the Americans. Too often these mass demonstrations are taken over by the extreme left and by sectional interests. I would like to think that on this crucial occasion we, as Liberal Democrats, will play a full part.' He replied on 23 January, and was indeed there on 15 February, the only leader of the three major parties to voice his opposition to the war at the rally. This decision, quite apart from its moral impact, has stood the Liberal Democrats in good stead ever since.

We returned home from the march tired but feeling that we had taken part in an unprecedented display of protest against a looming war that would later prove to be illegal, immoral and unjustified and lead to the death of hundreds of thousands of civilian Iraqis and soldiers, and significant numbers of American and British soldiers. Sadly, the demonstration was belittled by the government and ignored by Tony Blair. I took part in a second march whilst the 'war' was at its height, this time armed with a Picasso-like banner (with an outline drawing of a child holding a dove) with the word 'Peace' emblazoned on it. Tessa Jowell, the culture secretary, had spitefully declared her intention to ban this demonstration from Hyde Park because it would damage the precious grass! I immediately wrote to her on reading about her ban, as no doubt did many others, and within a few days she had made a U-turn. Unsurprisingly the march was less well attended than the first, but it was thought that there were as many as 200,000 – a unique mass demonstration against a war that was actually in progress. All this should have given our prime minister food for thought. However, for reasons best known to himself – hubris, a conviction that he had to stand shoulder to shoulder with the Americans, megalomania, a misreading of history when comparing Saddam with Hitler or, as a devout Christian, a feeling that God was on his side? – public opinion was ignored.

Following the first mass demonstration David Aaronovitch, then a *Guardian* columnist, wrote a full-page article under the heading 'Dear marcher, please answer a few questions'. In it he belittled the marchers and challenged them to answer a series of questions. Had the absence of Kurds not bothered us? Were we worried about some of the slogans? Did we really believe that this 'parroted "war about oil" stuff' was really true? Did some of the speeches bother us? Did we really believe that Blair should act on our demands "because so many people turned out on Saturday"? Did the way the demo was reported in Baghdad bother us? What did we feel about the marchers wearing stickers bearing the Israeli flag and the words 'Fascist state'? Did we think that Blair 'should also halt plans for the housing of asylum seekers in Lee-on-Solent because, at the same time as you marched, one-third of Lee's entire population took to the streets to demand no asylum seekers in their town'? He even attacked Charles Kennedy for having said that he was 'yet to be persuaded that the case for war against Iraq has been made' and accused him of 'blathering'. And so on and so forth. The tenor of his article was set by the statement that 'it is now fashionable to pick up a placard with a slogan on it and walk for a few miles in the company of thousands of others. People want to say they "were there".'

It was a mean-spirited and tendentious article and I took Aaronovitch at his word in a reasoned three-page response, in which each of his 'questions' (essentially polemical statements) received a considered answer. For example, on the point of whether Blair should have taken note of the march I wrote, 'I believe that Blair is totally out of tune with the mood of the country and he is very foolish not to take the opinion of millions of people – cutting right across the community spectrum – into account.' On the question of asylum seekers, I wrote that 'Your comparison with political pressure concerning asylum seekers is rather a cheap one, if I may say so. That pressure comes from the far right and is being stirred up by the tabloids, and of course no governments should cave in to that sort of pressure. You seem to be assuming that the moral case of the marchers and the anti-asylum seekers is on a par. Do you really believe that?'

It is hardly to Aaronovitch's credit that he not only failed to publish at least part of my response, but did not bother to acknowledge it in any shape or form. I have ever since been reading his articles with more than a pinch of salt.

I also had an exchange of letters with Clare Short, the left-wing and outspoken minister for overseas development at that time. On 12 March I wrote to tell her that I strongly approved of her alleged opposition to any attack on Iraq and I expressed 'my profound admiration for your principled stand'. Clare Short had been reported to be on the verge of resigning from the cabinet over this issue. However, not many days later she changed her mind, and on the 19th I had occasion to let her know that 'It grieves me to have to withdraw my remarks'. Her resignation came much later and followed on the heels of that by the foreign secretary, Robin Cook, who had been a steadfast and principled opponent of military action without the sanction of the United Nations.

'Shock and Awe'

And so it was that on the eve of the horrendous 'shock and awe' aerial attack by the USA and Great Britain, on 19 March, I took part in a candlelight vigil outside Archway underground station. Some twenty to thirty people had assembled, among them my former *bête noire* Jeremy Corbyn, the Labour member of parliament representing my constituency. We stood there in silence, a rather forlorn group, knowing that B52 bombers would be taking off from RAF Fairford in Gloucestershire that evening to deliver the first devastating bombs to targets in Baghdad.

To use that old platitude, the rest is history, and it is history still in the making. The famous weapons of mass destruction have never been found and have been shown to be a myth. It was what the Bush and Blair governments needed to believe to justify the attack they had planned all along, and their rejection of the UN weapons inspector Hans Blix's report and his request to continue with the search for WMD is therefore readily explained. Suddenly we were told that the aim had always been to rid the world and the Iraqi people of an evil tyrant (which of course he was), but unfortunately he was a tyrant who had been set up and supported and armed in earlier years by the United States, when he appeared to be a convenient ally in the war against the Taliban. His atrocities against the Kurds and other opponents in his own country were at that time conveniently ignored. The Iraq-al-Qaida link that the Bush administration had claimed to have uncovered, allowing them to justify their attack on Iraq as a central part of the war on terrorism, was never substantiated and is now openly rejected by most commentators. Indeed, in 2004 it was shown by a congressional committee that Saddam Hussein had no direct links with al-Qaida. The United Nations, thanks to the French, Germans and Russians, was not prepared to pass a resolution authorising military action and according to many legal experts the action by the coalition was illegal by international law. Indeed, it is worrying that the British government has consistently refused to publish the report of the Attorney-General, Lord Goldsmith, on the legality of the coalition attack, and one can only assume that it came down on the side of illegality or, at best, that it was ambiguous. All these consequences of an ill-judged and, in international terms, illegal war are calamitous to say the least, and played into the hands of those who wish to destroy western democracy.

The consequences

Innumerable tragic consequences have followed: the widespread destruction of Iraqi cities, the appalling loss of life, the horrendous ill-treatment of Iraqi and Afghan prisoners-of-war both in Iraqi prisons and in Guantanamo Bay, the brutalisation of American and British soldiers, the insurgency of Iraqi factions against coalition forces, the brutal hostage-taking by various factions and the obscene killing of some of them, the continued fighting between coalition forces and the insurgents, accompanied by a heavy toll of civilian life, the huge weekly death roll and the vast number of wounded civilians brought about by internecine strife, the damage to oil refineries, and the loss of confidence by Muslims, throughout the world, in western-style democracy. Very serious, too, is the prejudice against Muslims in the USA and Britain, and the hatred the war has engendered in the hearts of many Muslims. It has deflected attention from one of the central issues that divide the Arab world from the west – the question of how to resolve the Israel-Palestine problem – and it has allowed the Israelis to pursue extremely harsh military and economic measures against Palestinians without incurring the wrath of America and Britain or even the UN. The war prevented the United States from focusing on the real problem of international terrorism as embodied by al-Qaida, and it almost certainly created many more would-be terrorists and suicide bombers ready to lay down their lives. Bin Laden, the head of al-

Qaida, has not been found, and if that was the prime objective then Iraq was self-evidently quite the wrong target.

More parochially, it has led to unbridled attacks on the admirable BBC, which the Hutton Report blamed unfairly for the errors that led to the death of Dr David Kelly, the British government scientist who committed suicide after having been exposed by the Ministry of Defence for having provided a BBC correspondent with information. Indeed, the Hutton Enquiry laid the blame for some of the errors made – unfairly – largely at the door of the BBC rather than on government departments such as the Ministry of Defence or even the prime minister himself. Both the Hutton and Butler Enquiries have failed to apportion blame where it belongs – the government. All this has proved to be destructive and divisive in the United Kingdom and the resulting public lack of trust the war has created will take many years to dissipate. The war – coupled to the failure to resolve the Middle East situation – has led to an upsurge of anti-Semitism in European countries as well as in the USA, with attacks on Jews and desecration of synagogues and cemeteries; and it has intensified attacks by suicide bombers against Israeli and coalition targets. The hatred that Zora Neale Hurston so deplored half a century ago and which characterises the first few years of the twenty-first century has been exacerbated, not diminished.

And finally, there is the cost of the war, which has so far (February 2008) cost the USA in excess of $3 trillion and Britain, Iraq and the rest of the world probably another $3 trillion, according to *The Three Trillion War* by Joseph Stiglitz and Linda Bilmes. This is serious in more ways than one, for it has deflected aid funds to developing countries and made the western countries involved in the coalition less willing to help solve the great human tragedies played out in Africa in terms of starvation and deprivation and AIDS, and it has undermined the urgent and promised task of rebuilding Afghanistan – as well as the much-needed fight against global warming.

Much has happened in Iraq since I wrote most of this. Elections have taken place but the country is no nearer to pacification. Lives are lost daily as a result of the internecine bomb attacks – mainly Iraqis, but American and British soldiers and airmen too. Over 4000 Americans have died since the invasion, and fifteen times that many are estimated to have been injured. Yet it is the massive death toll among the Iraqi population that gives rise to the greatest concern. General Tommy Franks has been quoted as saying that 'We don't do body counts', and the true death rate can only be estimated. Probably the most authoritative is the household survey highlighted in 2005 (and therefore out of date) by the medical journal the *Lancet*, although it is discounted by the Allies. According to the *Lancet* editorial, it is 'a dispassionate survey conducted in the most dangerous epidemiological conditions' and is unlikely to be biased because it is based on first-hand verbal autopsies and because it links the unclassified data with military offensives. The survey concludes that deaths exceeded 100,000 since the start of the war. Following the more recent, almost daily, suicide attacks, causing the weekly death of hundreds of innocent civilians, the total number varies from 200,000 to one million.

For President Bush and Prime Minister Blair the war may ultimately have one further consequence. Both were securely established in their countries and both seemed to be cruising to victory in their bids for re-election. Yet both have been rejected by their respective electorates for having led their countries into an unjustified and immoral war through serious misjudgements and misinformation. Although Bush was re-elected in 2004 the American people have come to regret it; and Blair retired in some ignominy in 2007.

Against all this one can point to the liberation of Iraq and the ending of a *highly* unpleasant and repressive dictatorship. It remains to be seen whether a return to civilian rule will enable Iraq to function democratically and peacefully, as is hoped. The omens are unfortunately not good. However, the election of Barack Obama as President of the United States is one of the hopeful signs in a world that seems to be falling apart.

I have devoted so much space to the Iraq débâcle because I believe that, together with global warming, it will prove to be *the* defining event of the twenty-first century.

Chapter Nineteen: Berbiguières: Vive la France!

Since the end of the Second World War I have had a love affair with France. This came about partly because for many years that other great European country, Germany, was out of bounds for me because of my antagonistic/ambivalent feelings towards it, and partly because I have always had much sympathy for the French, their troubled life under German occupation and their unique *joie de vivre*. When I visited Paris for the first time in the late 1940s, having been asked to escort Frau Kahn's daughter to friends there, I was immediately enchanted with French life even though I was an impoverished student at the time and stayed in the Paris youth hostel. I loved the city and the bohemian life of the boulevards. I later revisited Paris more than once: as a student, in my capacity as a scientist, as well as with my family. For many years I stayed in a modest hotel, Hotel des Montagnes, in the rue de la Huchette; I had read about it in the pre-war novel *A Narrow Street* by the American author Elliot Paul, which had captured my romantic imagination. French *haute cuisine* came my way when, in the 1950s and early 1960s, I was secretary to the international editorial board of the journal *Embryology* (Michael Abercrombie from University College was the editor, Peter Medawar a member) and one of the perks was the odd meal in a posh restaurant that would have been entirely beyond my reach.

My family holidays were mainly in Brittany, where we had several wonderful visits. Camaret (in the bay of Douarnanez) was a delightful, sleepy fishing port on the west coast. We found a small hotel right by the harbour, recommended by the local tabac – always guaranteed to be a mine of information – and Joanne and I felt privileged to accompany the brother of the voluble tabac owner on a trip to harvest lobster pots outside the harbour. Joanne soon regretted this venture, for the early morning swell was massive – it was impossible to see land when the smallish boat was at the bottom of the troughs – and she spent much of her time leaning over the side discreetly ridding herself of her breakfast. The trip had begun inauspiciously as the fisherman had already imbibed large amounts of liquor before our departure at 5 a.m. Quite against our expectations he was glad to take us along as his brother was indisposed, and he recognised in me an able-bodied assistant to help him haul up the lobster pots, by hand of course. Joanne's travails began when, on the way out, he baited the new pots with some foul-reeking fish, which he and I sliced in half: not exactly designed to discourage seasickness. However, all went well – I just about managed to avoid being sick – and on our return I was rewarded with a large crab, which we ate the next day in a restaurant close to the harbour. I haven't ever tasted a crab as delicious as this one, but then it was hard earned.

Two other summer holidays, this time with children and on one occasion accompanied by my recently widowed father-in-law, were spent under canvas in a camp near the coast. Both were highly enjoyable – Oates entered into the spirit of the thing with gusto – and we enjoyed the shoreline with its rock pools and the swimming, cold as it was.

Berbiguières

In the years in which my marriage to Joanne was already in tatters, Carol and I had spent a holiday in the Dordogne. Friends of hers had a cottage in Berbiguières, a 'beau village de France' near St Cyprien, and they kindly allowed us to stay there. Carol had been there several times when her children were still young and she was very attached to both the house and the village, which nestles under the walls of a seventeenth-century chateau and is totally unspoilt. Although it once sported a restaurant/café this has long gone and the only amenities are the Catholic church and its cemetery, a pillar box set in someone's wall and a public telephone. The houses, most of them built more than 200 years ago, are made from mellow yellowish stone and many had belonged to peasants working for the chateau owners. The village is situated on a hill and surrounded by densely wooded hills, and the river Dordogne, which snakes its way through the landscape on its way from the mountains of the Auvergne to Bordeaux, is about a mile away. Not a few of the houses are owned by foreigners, mainly English and Dutch but also American, Scottish, Belgian and German, resulting in the restoration of houses that had fallen into disrepair. This process of renewal has taken place throughout the Dordogne, which has been much favoured by the English and the Dutch – the former perhaps not only because they like the scenery, the weather, the wine and the cuisine but possibly also because they feel that, harking back to the Hundred Years War in the fourteenth century, they have a sense of affinity with an area that was once in English hands.

Like Carol, I too fell in love with the house and the village and its landscape, and on our second visit in the summer of 1990 we were idly speculating on how much the house would cost, for Carol had heard from her friend that she wanted to sell it after twenty years of ownership. It turned out that the sum we had in mind was just right. In that part of France one didn't bother to have houses surveyed, and although we knew that there was quite a lot of woodworm in the old beams we decided to buy it. And so, in 1991, we became the proud owners of the house with its pleasant front and rear gardens and its minuscule pond. As it was fully if simply furnished and it had all the essential kitchen equipment, it was the easiest of transitions.

One of the great attractions of the village is that it is utterly tranquil; coming from London, it is like stepping back into the nineteenth century. The tempo of life is simply different. Birds are numerous in our garden, the cuckoo calls across the valley from early in April, and in the summer the butterflies are an absolute delight. One species, the papillon colibri, buzz around our buddleias in great numbers in the summer, and it is wonderful to watch them hovering by a spray, with the aid of very rapid wing beats, to insert their proboscis with the utmost precision into each tiny flower.

We usually go to Berbiguières three times a year and, as the journey by car is in excess of 500 miles, excluding the night on the ferry, it is tiring. Fortunately we both enjoy driving, and although we can manage the journey in one day we sometimes spend the night somewhere *en route*. This has given us the opportunity of getting to know many towns, cathedrals and churches, and their charm and architectural interest has never ceased to amaze us. One couldn't possibly guess that France has been a battleground for at least a millennium and has suffered massive destruction at one time or another. The cathedrals are a wonderful testimonial to the human spirit, and although it may seem bizarre I have lit many a candle in memory of my family in churches that particularly took my fancy.

The last occasion was the towering twelfth-century cathedral of St Étienne in Bourges. We visited it on a Sunday morning whilst the Mass was in progress. The vast nave (no transepts) was packed with worshippers and the massive space was lit by two rows of giant chandeliers, with a semi-circular chandelier above the altar. The stained glass windows were magnificent and the organ, when in full cry, filled the space with ease. The dramatic effect was heightened by the presence behind the altar of some twenty huntsmen in full regalia, who from time to time blew their ancient horns in unison, thus creating a strange sense of excitement. All this made a deep impression on me and, before leaving, I once again lit a candle in memory of my Jewish family. Inappropriate and sentimental, maybe; but why not?

The villagers have without exception been friendly and welcoming, and we have made some good friends. These include a French couple, André and Johanna Galli (she is originally Dutch but has lived in France for many decades), who were both keen walkers, the life and soul of the now extinct Siorac walking club whose members were mainly French and Dutch, and with whom we have been on many delightful rambles. André is also my chief protagonist when it comes to playing pétanque (boules), and usually his long-practised wiliness and skill are sufficient to overcome my more basic approach. Other good friends in the village include Colin and Christine Scott, who have made it their permanent home. It was the Scotts who arranged for the regional Anglican church in Limeuil, where they worship, to offer weekly prayers for the restoration of health to my stepdaughter Siân, who suffered from a life-threatening non-Hodgkin's lymphoma in 2003. Happily their prayers (combined with the treatment, I have little doubt!) have been answered.

One of the great attractions of the Dordogne is the beautiful and fast-flowing river, which is clean enough to sustain a plentiful fish population, including trout, and which is attractive to swim in. There are many pebbly or even sandy beaches and on a hot summer's day the only way to cool off is to take a dip towards the end of the day, when the sun has lost its power. That is the time I most enjoy, as I do when I am by the sea too, with the beach emptying and the happy sound of children enjoying themselves providing a soothing background noise reminiscent of my childhood by the Baltic. The current is fast, and as it is hard work to swim against it we usually launch ourselves upstream and swim back to our clothes. Characteristic of the region are the many ancient chateaux, many of them high up on the rocky banks, commanding fine views that clearly stood them in good stead when they were used for the purpose for which they were constructed: warfare. A few miles upstream from St Cyprien is Château Beynac, which is north of the river and which was held by the English for many years during the Hundred Years War (1337–1453). Facing it on the other side of the valley is Château Castelnaud, which was in French hands! The incredible and unedifying story of the Hundred Years War is being exhaustively described (the third volume is in preparation) by our 'neighbour' in Chateau Berbiguières, Jonathan Sumption.

It is a story of unremitting mayhem, with both armies determined to defeat the other by force of arms, intrigue and deceit, with no thought for the local population, whose towns and villages were frequently sacked and whose lives were regarded as expendable. That a succession of English kings should have thought it feasible to conquer France is mind-boggling. It is a wonder that a hundred years ago the Entente Cordiale was established and that, despite some extremely rocky episodes, it has endured to this day, with France and England allies in two major European wars. Or has it survived? There continues to be suspicion and unease with each other, and the insults heaped on the French by the British during the Iraq episode were deeply offensive. Furthermore, the apparent unwillingness of most British people to welcome a united Europe, in which they would stand shoulder to shoulder with the French and their erstwhile arch-enemy, Germany, is deeply worrying.

The other fascinating attraction of our region of the Dordogne is provided by the numerous caves, some of great natural beauty such as Gouffre de Promeyssac and others with prehistoric wall paintings and engravings dating back to the Aurignacian culture of the Upper Palaeolithic Age (25–30,000 years ago). The most extensive and famous of these is of course the Grotte de Lascaux, near Montignac, which was closed to all but experts and scholars many years ago in order to save the paintings from deterioration. Lascaux II is a superb and near-perfect reconstruction that became possible with the help of modern technology, and for the non-specialist it is impossible to tell that this is not the real thing. Even the graffiti that can be found in the original cave, engraved on the walls by intruders in the mid-twentieth century, have been meticulously copied. However, there are smaller caves near Berbiguières, such as Font-de-Gaume, where the original 'art' can still be viewed and admired though the number of tourists is very strictly controlled. These paintings have survived because they have been at a very constant temperature and humidity for thousands of years. To see them is a truly awe-inspiring and wonderful experience. After all, they were executed, in relative darkness, by people who are considered to have been primitive cave dwellers and hunters. There are various theories as to what prompted these people to paint and engrave the walls of their caves and none strikes me as particularly convincing. However, the animals they portrayed were clearly of importance to them as prey, and their relationship to them must have been emotionally complex, perhaps pseudo-religious. When Carol and I visited Lascaux it struck me forcefully that the shapes and colours (mainly ochre and charcoal) and bold outlines we saw were reminiscent of Pablo Picasso: my facetious question to the guide as to whether there had been a period in Picasso's life that had not been fully accounted for met, perhaps not surprisingly, with incomprehension.

France under the Occupation

'Our' part of France has been traditionally socialist and its record during the German occupation, under Marshal Petain's Vichy regime, has on the whole been honourable. I became aware of the fact that this was by no means universal only when I saw Marcel Ophuls's astonishing film *The Pity and the Sorrow (Le chagrin et la pitié)* in the 1970s. It was shown on French television and raised a storm of protest in France because it showed for the first time that the Gaullist view of France, which maintained that nearly all Frenchmen and women had behaved honourably and even heroically during the occupation, and that the résistance was a mass movement, was a myth.

The Pity and the Sorrow was shown again in 2004 as part of the National Film Theatre's season of French films, and I was glad to see this immensely long film for a second time – intelligent, coolly analytical without being unduly academic, deeply upsetting (not least in showing the treatment meted out after the liberation to women who had formed relationships with German soldiers), and in praise of those men and women who did indeed work for the résistance, mainly in the Auvergne. By interviewing in depth both French and German participants in the Occupation, including an extensive and telling discourse by Pierre Mendes-France, who was Jewish and who had been wrongly accused of desertion from the army after the collapse of France, only to become prime minister in 1956, Ophuls managed to give the documentary footage and the dramatisation a remarkable immediacy and veracity. It showed the way things really were, and they weren't always pleasant: far too many people, especially among the bourgeoisie, were only too happy to go along with the victors and with Marshal Pétain's misguided and essentially spurious attempt to govern the southern part of France independent of the German occupiers.

This unhappy period in French history is discussed in great detail in Jonathan Fenby's book *On the Brink. The Trouble with France*. Fenby is critical of many aspects of recent French history, but his first chapter is a mind-boggling account of the country's many and wide-ranging political, cultural, artistic and scientific achievements. Whilst he is acutely critical of the treatment of Jews by the Vichy regime, which often anticipated the wishes of its German masters by mass arrests and deportation to detention centres, he is mindful of the fact that elsewhere, for example a town like Le Chambon-sur-Lignon, 'sheltered thousands of Jews from 1940 onwards. When the German army swept by on its regular patrols the refugees were hidden in the rough countryside of the windswept plateau that surrounds the town.'

Central to this heroic act was Lesley Maber, who died at the age of

234

ninety-two in 1999. Together with a friend she ran a *pension* for boys at the coeducational Protestant Collège Cévenol in Le Chambon-sur-Lignon, and many Jewish children were sheltered in *pension* Les Sorbiers. She did this at huge risk to herself. In 1943 a student hostel in the village, also sheltering Jewish refugees, was raided by the Gestapo, leading to mass arrest and deportations, and the hostel owner died in the extermination camp of Maidenek. Maber too was arrested in 1943 but released – apparently because 'in the 1930s she had legally adopted two abandoned babies of a child prostitute, and her release order reached the train *en route*' to an internment camp. 'Just after she left, the train was diverted straight to Germany; no one on board returned.' These quotes are from Lesley Maber's obituary in the *Guardian.*

Fenby reminds us of the deep-seated anti-Semitism that has long been prevalent in France, epitomised by the Dreyfus Affair towards the end of the nineteenth century, and Fenby is understandably alarmed by the recent outbreaks of anti-Semitism spearheaded by Jean-Marie Le Pen's National Front. Anti-Semitism has recently been superseded to a degree by prejudice against black people and Muslims, but the dire situation in the Middle East has encouraged Muslims in particular to attack Jews in the streets and to desecrate synagogues and Jewish cemeteries. However, successive French governments have made their repugnance of such actions very clear.

It was mainly through General de Gaulle's grandiose vision of France that some aspects of wartime France were swept under the carpet, and that people like Maurice Papon, who rose from being a senior civil servant at the regional prefecture in Bordeaux to chief of the Paris police (and, after the war, cabinet minister under Giscard d'Estaing), were not prosecuted for their part in sending thousands of French and non-French Jews to their death. According to Paul Webster in the *Guardian*, 11,000 Jews were deported from the Gare d'Austerlitz in Paris between 1940 and 1944. This is commemorated by a memorial placed at the station, not by one of the post-war governments but by a Jewish student organisation. The detention centre from which these deportations were organised was in the northern Paris suburb of Drancy, where up to 5000 people had to survive in appalling conditions at any one time until they were sent east to the extermination camps run by Nazi Germany. Indeed, the marble plaque at Drancy refers to the site as a 'concentration camp', where 'from 1941 to 1944, 100,000 men, women and children of Jewish religion or descendance were interned by the Hitlerian occupiers – then deported to Nazi extermination camps . . .'

Papon was belatedly put on trial in 1998, when he was eighty-eight years old. Having been given a ten-year prison sentence, he claimed to be too ill to remain in prison, and was released in 2002 after having served thirty months. During his trial he described the deportation of 75,000 French Jews as an 'inconvenience'; although he was complicit in the death of almost 1700 Jews from Bordeaux, he found it unnecessary to express regret for his actions. His trial and conviction were nevertheless a landmark, for they exposed the way in which some senior men, during the Vichy regime, dishonoured the name of France.

Charlotte Salomon

One of those deported from Drancy to Auschwitz was Charlotte Salomon, a twenty-three-year-old German Jewish woman from Berlin who had been sent by her parents to join her grandparents near Nice in January 1939, following Kristallnacht. It was thought that she would be safe there and her parents intended to follow her in due course, an intention that was never realised as they finished up in Holland. In May of the following year all German nationals were required to report to a detention centre in Gurs, near Pau in the Pyrenees, on the assumption that all Germans must have been sympathisers of the Reich. From Gurs, which was only one of several such camps in France and which housed up to 19,000 people in cramped barracks, Charlotte was allowed to return to Nice, only to be deported to Drancy in 1943. From there she was sent to Auschwitz, where she died.

Charlotte Salomon's case is of special interest because she was a talented painter, who created in the space of two years, before her deportation to Drancy, some 700 paintings illustrating her life and that of her family, and with it the rise of Nazism in Berlin. She gave them the all-embracing title of 'Life? or Theatre?', and they comprise a remarkable collection that survived the war in the care of an American woman, Ottilie Moore, who had befriended Charlotte in France. Their quality is such, and their interest so great, with their handwritten annotations and musical allusions, that many of them were exhibited at the Royal Academy of Art some years ago. The collection is housed in Amsterdam. Had Charlotte Salomon lived she might well have become a great painter.

My own and highly tenuous connection with her is twofold. First, the German-Jewish singing teacher in Berlin, with whom she fell in love and who played a very important (and somewhat ignoble) role in her story, developed a relationship after the war with the wife of an Old Bunce Courtian named Thomas Faraday, and the three of them set up a ménage à trois to provide a home for the child that resulted from that relationship. Thomas Faraday, now in his eighties, still lives in south-west France, only about two hours' drive from Berbiguières, and Carol and I have visited him on several occasions. Second, a few years ago my daughter Jenny took part in a dramatic portrayal of the Salomon story, put on very imaginatively and creatively by the Yorkshire-based Horse and Bamboo company. The play, which involved masks, miming, puppets and music, was called *Company of Angels,* and it was a riveting and deeply moving account of Charlotte Salomon's brief and tragic life as illustrated in her paintings.

The résistance

The shabby and inhumane treatment meted out to the Jewish population both in occupied France and in Vichy France should not be allowed to obscure the fact that many French people, like Lesley Maber, behaved extraordinarily well, often risking their own lives to protect and shelter Jews. The role of *la résistance* is well documented – see for example the excellent and moving book by Ian Ousby, *Occupation: the Ordeal of France 1940–1944.* Whilst it was particularly well organised in the region of the Auvergne – one famous exploit led to the disabling of the Michelin tyre factory in Clermont Ferrand – it was active in many parts of France, including the area behind the Normandy beaches when France was invaded by the Allies on D-Day in 1944. There was also a great deal of subversive activity in other regions of the south-east and south-west, that is in the Dordogne, Corrèze and Haute Vienne. This is where the infamous reserve Brehmer division held sway, named after its leader, Major-General Walter Brehmer. Following attacks by partisans on German military vehicles near Brantôme, south of Périgueux, which resulted in the death of several officers, a major reprisal involving summary executions, arrests, destruction of houses and deportations, began on a massive scale on 25 March 1944, and it extended throughout the three *départements.* Among those arrested, some 500 Jews were sent to Drancy and then on to extermination camps. Brehmer was later sent to Paris, became implicated in the Stauffenberg plot against Hitler, but escaped execution. He died in 1967. Operation Brehmer is set out in the greatest detail in a recent book by Guy Penaud, *Les Crimes de la Division 'Brehmer'. La Traque des Résistants et des Juifs en Dordogne, Corrèze, Haute-Vienne (Mars – Avril 1944).*

In the Dordogne as well as elsewhere one readily comes across streets named after heroes of the résistance and memorials to those who lost their lives in their fight against the German occupiers, and the careful preservation of the village of Oradour-sur-Glane, deliberately destroyed by the Germans as an act of revenge following a partisan attack, serves as a stark reminder of the brutality of those times.

It is only too easy to be judgemental about the French capitulation and their subsequent response to the Germans. A British person is hardly in a position to criticise, Britain never having been conquered and forced to live under the yoke of a foreign power. (I exempt the Saxon, Roman and Norman invasions from this generalisation!) Would Britons have responded any differently? I used to assume that they would, until many years after the end of the Second World War the well-hidden truth became known about the German occupation of the Channel Islands.

The German occupation of the Channel Islands

Jersey, Guernsey and Alderney – islands lying in the Channel between England and France – were left undefended at the outbreak of war and occupied by the Germans in June 1940. The population had a very small number of Jews. The response of the majority to the extreme danger that faced the Jews was mixed. Some denounced them to the German authorities, many turned away and pretended that what happened to these people was none of their business, and a few were conspicuously heroic and attempted to save Jews from deportation. For example, Albert Bedane in Jersey has been recognised as 'Righteous Among the Nations' by the Yad Vashem Holocaust Centre in Jerusalem for hiding a Dutch Jewess, Mary Richardson, for over two years from the German authorities and the Jersey police, and he also sheltered escaped Russian forced labourers.

Madeleine Bunting's careful research and the book that resulted from it, *The Model Occupation: the Channel Islands Under German Rule, 1940–45*, did much to expose the degree of collaboration and fraternisation by the local population with the German occupiers. 'When I began researching the German occupation of the Channel Islands – the only bit of Britain to be invaded by Hitler – in the early '90s, no one knew anything about Jersey's Jews.' The islanders generally feel that Bunting was merely intent on muckraking. It was claimed that there had been no Jews on Jersey, a view that was clearly false, and that no one had suffered. On Guernsey it was known that three East European women had been handed over to the Germans for deportation. The citizens of Alderney felt that there was no case to answer, for they 'simply claimed that the island was evacuated and nobody knew anything of the only SS camp on British soil and the French Jews and other prisoners who worked and died on the island'. Since Bunting did her research the situation has changed. On Jersey, monographs have been published describing 'what happened to the island's Jews and the 22 Jersey islanders who died in concentration camps. There's now a memorial to the island's Jews and another to the Jersey Twenty-Two on the harbour' and schoolchildren are taught 'about the thousands of forced labourers brought to build the huge fortifications on the island – many of whom died from exhaustion and malnutrition . . . What islanders have had to accept was the close involvement of island officials in implementing German orders against the tiny Jewish community. In Jersey, at least, material was found that showed that officials attempted to mitigate some anti-Semitic measures', for example, by refusing to implement the wearing of yellow stars and the selling of Jewish businesses to non-Jews with the intention of returning them to their owners after the war. 'However, officials on Jersey and Guernsey did quiz individuals about their Jewish ancestry and imposed a strict curfew . . .'

Guernsey seems to have had greater problems in coming to terms with its past, though a small plaque was erected in 2001 commemorating the three Jews who were deported and who died in concentration camps. As for Alderney, 'there is still no memorial on the site of the SS camp'. According to Vitali Vitaliev in the *Guardian* in 1998, 'there seems to be a peculiar pride in the islands about the fact that they were occupied by the Nazis . . . Jersey has more occupation museums than anywhere in the world . . . The beleaguered tourist boards of both Jersey and Guernsey are falling over themselves to stop the decline of the tourist industry' by focusing on the German occupation. 'Alderney is the only place on the Channel Islands that has not been turned into an occupation theme park', a fact that is in accord with the island's reluctance to face up to what happened during the war.

I have given the Channel Islands some prominence to show that inhumane and anti-Semitic acts might also have happened in Britain had Britain been occupied by Nazi Germany. We have no right to be complacent. Human nature being what it is, there will always be people who either bury their heads in the sand or exploit a potentially disagreeable political situation to their own advantage. Fortunately there will, also, always be men and women of the highest integrity, as was shown in both France and the Channel Islands.

Postscript

I continue to harbour very warm feelings towards France, which has been so much vilified in the UK for the role it has played – admirably in my view – in denying the USA and Britain a United Nations vote sanctioning the attack on Iraq. I can easily relate to the French people I have come across. (Carol's friend Rita is married to a Frenchman, Pierre Paycha, living in Paris and Brittany, and I have developed a close friendship with both of them.) I love the French countryside and architecture and cultural traditions and, it goes without saying, the country's cuisine and wines. France has a *joie de vivre* that is far less evident in the UK, as revealed in the many musical and cultural festivals everywhere and the fêtes and communal meals that can be found in most villages and towns in the summers. The atmosphere is always relaxed and friendly, no doubt helped along by the favourable climate, and Carol and I haven't come across the disturbing and frightening modern tendency of young people in the UK to go in for binge drinking and all that it entails in terms of boorish and antisocial behaviour. That is not to say that France, like other countries, doesn't have problems in community relations and its share of racial intolerance. But, on the whole, I say '*vive la France*'!

Chapter Twenty: On Judaism, Zionism and Anti-Semitism

My parents were observant but non-orthodox Jews, and I was brought up in that tradition until I left Germany in 1938. So far as I know they were never remotely interested in Zionism, and the thought of emigrating to Palestine would not have occurred to them. At least one member of my family must have visited the Holy Land, though, for I possess two little tourist books, with wooden covers, showing coloured scenes from that country. My parents regarded themselves not only as Jewish but also as German, and German culture, whether in literature, music or other spheres, was deeply ingrained in them. Despite clinging to their religion, and moving to a great extent, though not exclusively, in Jewish circles in Köslin, they felt thoroughly assimilated.

I shall provide a brief synopsis of the events that led to the creation of the state of Israel because so often strong opinions are expressed without an adequate knowledge or understanding of the historical facts. I have tried, to the best of my ability, to be objective, although I do not expect everyone to be in agreement in such a controversial and emotionally charged area.

The creation of the state of Israel

Numerous books have been written about the formation of the state of Israel (see, for example, *The Jewish State* by Alan Dowty and the website www.2000StateofIsrael.com). The events leading to the creation of the state of Israel, and the relationship between Jews and Arabs, are highly complex and tortuous, and they are interpreted in different ways by the protagonists. What I think is indisputable is that although relatively few

241

Jews had lived in Palestine since biblical times, the first wave of Jewish settlers from Europe arrived in 1882 – the so-called first Aliyah. Immigration continued in the last two decades of the nineteenth century and in the first half of the twentieth century, and the kibbutz movement took off, the first kibbutz having been established in 1909 when Palestine was still under Turkish rule. In 1914 alone as many as 24,000 mainly illegal Jewish immigrants arrived in Palestine, and by the end of that year Jews formed roughly 6 per cent of the population. At the same time Zionist leaders exerted pressure both in London and in Berlin for the establishment of a Jewish National Home after the war. Not a few of the early immigrants were socialists and intellectuals who had the ideal of living off the land, and the communities they formed, which were egalitarian and in which members worked for the good of the community, formed the springboard for the formation of the state of Israel.

After the First World War the League of Nations gave France and the UK control over the regions liberated from the Ottoman empire, and whereas France was allocated responsibility for the Lebanon and Syria, the UK was given Iraq and Palestine, including Gaza, the West Bank and Jordan. France and the UK were expected to prepare these countries for independence. It was Theodor Hertzl, an Austro-Hungarian writer, who published *Der Judenstaat* (The Jewish State) in the 1880s. His vision of a Jewish homeland in Palestine was profoundly influential, both in convincing members of the Jewish communities in Europe that it provided the only real solution, and in persuading the British government that such a course needed to be adopted. He was successful in both, for in 1897 the First Zionist Congress, held in Basel, called for a national Jewish home in Palestine; and on 31 October 1917 England committed itself to such a course with the Balfour Declaration (Balfour was foreign secretary at the time). It was thought that such a declaration would win over the European Jews to the side of the Allies in their war against the Austro-Hungarian empire, especially the Jews of eastern Europe, principally Russia. In 1901 the Jewish National Fund had been set up with the aim of acquiring land in Palestine and to 'make the country Jewish'.

Not surprisingly, the Balfour Declaration caused grave concern among Palestinian Arabs and to neighbouring Arab countries, who saw large-scale immigration of Jews as a dire threat. Arab nationalistic organisations were set up to oppose the British policy, and the Grand Mufti of Jerusalem did everything possible to enlist international support. Palestine having become a British Mandate in 1922, the British government found itself between the hammer and the anvil and, in an attempt to placate the Arabs, it imposed strict limits on the number of Jewish immigrants. However, following the assumption of power by Hitler and his National Socialist party in Germany in 1933, Jewish immigration became virtually unstoppable and had risen to about 60,000 by 1935. This triggered the Arab revolt (1936–39), which subsided with the outbreak of war. The Middle East then remained relatively quiescent for the war's duration.

At the end of the Second World War the British government (the foreign secretary was Ernest Bevin, who was not greatly in sympathy with the Jewish cause) refused entry into Palestine to the 100,000 European Jews who had survived incarceration in Germany's concentration and extermination camps or in hiding. Nonetheless, many thousands made their way illegally into Palestine, often after a harrowing voyage in unsafe and overcrowded vessels; for them Palestine offered the only hope of life without oppression and discrimination. In their attempt to stem the tide, the British made some terrible mistakes, such as preventing desperate immigrants from disembarking on arrival in Haifa and even sending some ships back to Europe. All this led to the establishment of not only the illegal Jewish army, the Haganah, but also of terrorist organisations such as the Stern Gang and Irgun Zwai Leumi, which ran terror campaigns against the British forces and against Arabs. Two of the worst outrages were thought to have been the work of the Stern Gang: the blowing up of Hotel King David in July 1946, in which 42 died, 52 went missing and 53 were injured; and the destruction of Hotel Semiramis in Jaffa, in which 300 people lost their lives. Many British soldiers and policemen were killed in the two years following the end of the Second World War, and by 1947 the British government was convinced that the mandate was no longer workable and referred the problem to the United Nations. In a six-week period (December 1947 to January 1948) alone some 2000 people are thought to have died – more than 1000 Arabs, about 800 Jews and more than 100 British soldiers. Towards the end of April 1948 Jewish soldiers had taken the town of Jaffa in a fierce battle that claimed 400 lives.

The state of Israel was declared on 14 May 1948, and five Arab armies immediately attacked it. Improbably, the Israeli forces managed to defeat them, leaving Israel with more territory than it had been allocated by the UN, whilst Jordan appropriated the West Bank and Egypt the Gaza Strip. For Israel this was the War of Independence; for the Arabs 'The Catastrophe' (Al Nakbar). One of the dire consequences of this war was the creation of nearly 800,000 Palestinian refugees. Roughly half had fled their homes in fear and the other half were compelled to leave. These refugees were accommodated in neighbouring Arab countries, many in primitive camps, and it is these refugees and their descendants who now constitute an insoluble problem. They feel dispossessed and want to reclaim their old homes, but if allowed to return they would almost certainly undermine Israel as a Jewish state. Some Palestinians stayed behind and now form a small minority, ostensibly with equal rights and representation in the Knesset.

In February 1949 Israel and Egypt signed a truce, following lengthy negotiations by Dr Ralph Bunche, the United Nations mediator. Israel retained most of the Negev and had troops stationed in Beersheba, but it had still not received recognition from Egypt, let alone from the other Arab countries. In April 1950 King Abdullah of Jordan annexed Arab Palestine, including East Jerusalem and Hebron.

The Six-Day War

By 1967 Israel felt sufficiently threatened by its Arab neighbours, especially Syria, to launch a pre-emptive strike against Arab air forces, destroying 374 planes and ensuring complete dominance in the air. This was done on day one of what became known as the Six-Day War, which also saw Israeli ground forces capturing the Sinai desert from the Egyptians and clashes with Jordanian troops in Jerusalem. On day two Israel was heading towards total victory, having crossed into the Sinai Peninsula and taken the Gaza Strip from Egypt and Bethlehem and Hebron from Jordan. On day three the Wailing Wall, Jericho and most of the West Bank were captured from the Jordanians, who then accepted the UN ceasefire. On day four Egypt admitted defeat, a large army having been encircled in the Sinai desert. On day five Colonel Nasser resigned as Egyptian head, and Israel launched an all-out attack on Syria, which quickly accepted a ceasefire. Finally, on day six Israel agreed to adhere to the ceasefire proposed by the UN. Overall, the war appears to have claimed some 100,000 casualties.

Israel was founded in the wake of the Holocaust, which left many thousands of surviving European Jews destitute and desperate to emigrate to Israel. Yet Zionist goals were achieved at the expense of the indigenous Arabs, who were displaced from their homes and forced to live in dismal refugee camps, and the loss of countless and mainly Arab lives. Having forged its statehood by the sword, Israel has disastrously continued in the same vein, without regard to the antagonism and hatred engendered by the use of brute force.

In 1968, at the end of a congress of the Transplantation Society in The Hague, I arrived early at Amsterdam airport in the company of an Israeli immunologist, Michael Schlesinger. We spent the best part of an hour in each other's company and I raised the Israeli-Arab problem. I said that in 1947 I would have been quite prepared to offer my services to the Israeli army as I would have been deeply unhappy for the Jews in Palestine to be 'driven into the sea', as Arab governments liked to proclaim. Since 1967 the situation had changed profoundly, and my attitude with it. I told Michael that the Israeli government had to show magnanimity and to offer to hand back all the captured territories. In return, Israel would be entitled to receive cast-iron assurances from the Arab leaders that they would never again attack Israel, with appropriate peace treaties underwritten by the United States and United Nations. Only with such a gesture – and it would have been a grand one and not without risk – could one hope to transform the turbulent Middle East into a peaceful region in which economic cooperation would be to the benefit of all the countries there.

Schlesinger replied that such a move would be far too risky; had the Arab nations not vowed to destroy Israel? He pointed out the small size of his country, and that it could be overrun with the greatest of ease by a determined enemy. Israel needed the new buffer zones for its own protection, and Israel could survive only as a strong military power. To make a gesture such as I had proposed would be regarded as a sign of weakness and be ultimately counterproductive. I disagreed with such a defeatist attitude, and everything that has happened since – the thousands of lives lost, the creation of yet more Arab refugees, the *intifada* with wave after wave of suicide bombers killing innocent civilians as well as soldiers, the creation of Jewish settlements on Arab land, the horrendous incursions into refugee camps, the wilful destruction with tanks and bulldozers of Arab homes and olive groves, the assassination of individuals by helicopter gunships (in which innocent bystanders as well as potential terrorists were killed), and the building of the infamous wall, often on Arab land and sometimes dividing Arab communities and even a university campus – all this has shown how counterproductive the use of force is in the long run. Like so many others – Jews and non-Jews – I am in deep despair when I watch this Greek-style tragedy being played out, apparently to the bitter end. I have never been more conscious of the biblical precept 'an eye for an eye', for this is exactly what has happened time and time again: a suicide bombing followed by the predictable revenge of the mighty Israeli army and air force. I cannot and will not condone the suicide bombers – even though they would argue that theirs is the only option left to them in their fight to establish the rights of Palestinian Arabs. But nor can I condone the brutality of the Israeli retaliations.

The incursions of the Israeli army into townships like Jenin and refugee camps like Rafah with tanks and bulldozers have led to a great loss of life and property, and they have not solved anything. Rather, they have bred a new generation of young Arabs ready to lay down their lives in what they perceive as a just fight. Likewise, the protective wall, the routing of which the Israeli High Court has declared to be illegal, has apparently reduced the incidence of suicide bombings but at the cost of giving further grave offence to the Arabs and to world opinion.

Another regrettable incident was the invasion of the Lebanon in 1982. It happened a day after the assassination of the Israeli ambassador to London by a Palestinian gunman. Whilst this served as an excuse, Israel had long complained about the fact that Yasser Arafat and the PLO had their headquarters in Beirut, and that a great deal of terrorist activity emanated from Palestinian groups sheltered in the Lebanon. The loss of life in Beirut was very great, and the subsequent incursion of the Christian Lebanese militia (the Phalangists) into refugee camps like Sabra and Chatila resulted in the massacre of hundreds of Palestinian refugees. Although at the time the Israelis denied having connived in this attack, an Israeli government enquiry a year later showed that an Israeli army unit, under the command of Ariel Sharon, had deliberately allowed the militia into the camps when they must have known that it would lead to a bloodbath. The inquiry, to its great credit, called for the resignation or dismissal of Sharon, who by then had become minister of defence, and it was also critical of the prime minister, Menachim Begin. Sharon was of course the prime minister who triggered the latest *intifada* by his ill-judged appearance in a disputed area of Jerusalem.

Is it surprising, then, that world opinion, including many Jews such as myself, finds it extremely hard to sympathise with successive Israeli governments, for which the use of force seems to be the main option in their attempt to protect their population? Fortunately there are also many Israelis, even though they continue to be a minority, who are critical of their government's policies, who demonstrate against government actions and who, as members of the Israeli army and air force, refuse to carry out military missions in Palestinian territory, at great risk to their liberty and livelihood. It remains to be seen whether the Israeli evacuation of the Gaza Strip will lead to a better *modus vivendi*. But here we are, in 2008, and the situation remains as unresolved as ever, with Gaza being economically and socially strangled by the closure of checkpoints and the absence of aid.

Jews for Justice for Palestinians

This British organisation, which relies heavily on its e-mail network, was formed in 2002 as a means of showing Britain and the world that there *are* Jews who are strongly opposed to the policies of the Israeli government. It also regards itself as a pressure group for a just settlement to the conflict, supporting those in Israel who openly defy their government, and counteracting the conservative views of the Jewish Board of Deputies. When I joined this organisation it had a membership of 23; now, in 2008, there are 1400.

Two years ago it sent an open letter to the Jewish Board of Deputies, which is the mouthpiece of British Jewry. It was signed by 849 people, including one member of the board, the director of the Jewish Council for Racial Equality, and notable people such as Harry Cohen MP, Rabbi John Rayner, Alexei Sayle, Janet Suzman, Jonathan Miller, Harold Pinter, Susie Orbach, Francesca Klug, and Professors Eric Hobsbawm and Mary Kaldor. I was happy to put my name to it, for it expressed my point of view exactly

Essentially, it condemned the repressive Israeli policy towards Gaza, especially the calamitous incursion into the Rafah refugee camp, and the failure of the board to condemn it. It ends, 'Silence discredits us all.'

Is a terrorist ever a freedom fighter?

I believe this to be a legitimate question even if it cannot be answered unequivocally. The difference between terrorists and freedom fighters can be a fine one. There have been a number of instances when terrorists have later been hailed as freedom fighters. Perhaps the distinction that should be drawn concerns the target of terrorism: if it is directed primarily against civilians, then it must be considered to be terrorism; if against an occupying army, then the perpetrators could be reasonably regarded as freedom fighters. Usually things aren't so very clear cut, for both civilians and soldiers can be the victims at one and the same time.

By this definition, the résistance in France during the Second World War must be regarded as freedom fighters, but the distinction becomes very blurred in the fight of the African National Congress against the apartheid governments, the IRA in its attempt to force the British out of Northern Ireland, the present insurgency in Iraq against the coalition occupiers (even though the Americans and the British see themselves as liberators), and the anti-Russian attacks in Chechnya, which are aimed at overthrowing what many people in the country regard as an oppressive occupying power. (The attacks by Chechnyan guerrillas against the occupying Russian army could be justified; the hostage-taking of hundreds of children and adults in Beslan, with its dire consequences, clearly cannot. Nor can the indiscriminate taking of life by the Basque nationalists in northern Spain.) The ANC is now in power in South Africa. The IRA, through its political wing of Sinn Fein, now shares political power in Northern Ireland. In Iraq the coalition-appointed government granted amnesties to those insurgents willing to give up their arms and to join in the democratic process, for a distinction was drawn between attacks on the foreign occupiers and the incumbent Iraqi government. The Stern Gang and Irgun are regarded as freedom fighters in modern Israel, though in the 1940s they were perceived as terrorists, even incurring the wrath of the Haganah. What role will history accord the Palestinian suicide bombers, with the terrible loss of life they inflict on the Israeli population? I don't know the answer to that question. The Palestinians would argue that it is the only option open to them to make their point, with the Israeli armed forces and government agencies so heavily defended.

The whole problem is compounded by the infliction of terror sanctioned by the state, as in Palestine and Chechnya for example, and very recently and most shockingly in the Sudan, where a million people have been turned into refugees, 50,000 have been slaughtered, and rape has been practised widely by the militia army, actions that seem to have had the tacit support of the Sudanese government as a form of ethnic cleansing. Whilst state terrorism may be explained as a necessary method of protecting the integrity of a country, its consequences are all the more shocking when it is directed against defenceless people or even relatively defenceless fighters who, in desperation, resort to methods of their own that have no moral or legal basis.

Since 9/11 Israel has justified its brutal treatment of the Palestinians as part of 'the war on terror', and because of the preoccupations of the United States government with that war it has been allowed to get away with actions that would normally have aroused revulsion. Indeed, the United Nations has censored Israel on more than one occasion but, without the cooperation of the USA, they have lacked the influence and power to do anything constructive. The American government's attitude is presumably dictated not only by the Jewish vote and the fact that several of the influential neo-cons in the Bush administration were Jews with strong links with Israel, but also because the USA sees in Israel the only democratic and reliable ally in the Middle East. Although it is true that Israel is a democracy I have to ask myself whether this democracy is not in danger of being eroded, as evidenced by its treatment of Arabs, its harshness towards soldiers and airmen who have refused to fight outside Israel's borders (the 'refuseniks'), and the unbelievable treatment handed out to someone like Mordechai Vanunu. This man is the former nuclear technician who was abducted from Italy and found guilty in Israel of having disclosed classified information to the *Sunday Times*, and who was held in prison for eighteen years (eleven of them in solitary confinement) before his recent release, though he has since been rearrested.

Is there a solution?

I fear that too much hatred has already been engendered for the Palestinian Arabs ever to accept a settlement, even if the proposals are close to their final objectives, but I hope to be proven wrong. Zora Neale Hurston's words about hate (quoted on p. 220) have never seemed more appropriate. There have been several occasions in the last two decades when agreement was close (the Oslo agreement, Camp David), only to founder on what seemed like relatively trivial outstanding problems.

Yasser Arafat was undoubtedly a weak and fickle leader who had not managed to transform himself into a statesman. Like Israeli leaders such as Ariel Sharon, he has been the prisoner of his militant extremists, afraid to give an inch. He died in November 2004 in a Paris hospital, having been confined to his Ramallah compound for two years. His death does not seem to have opened that 'window of opportunity' President Bush and Tony Blair have talked about.

Even that implacably right-wing politician Ariel Sharon came to the conclusion that it is safer for Israel to vacate the Gaza Strip than to attempt to hang on to it by force, and yet he came under threat of death from some of his former most vociferous supporters, and he was opposed by the religious parties and the extreme 'over our dead bodies' settlers. The repeated heavy-handed incursion of the Israeli army into Gaza, with heavy loss of life and the destruction of a large number of houses, are at odds with the government's declared intentions.

And yet, a meeting in London in 2003 between several senior Palestinians and Israelis, under the auspices of the *Guardian*, showed that there *is* a way forward provided both sides are prepared to give way on some issues. Following the 'agreement' reached between the unofficial negotiators I attended a discussion between Yasser Abed Rabbo, the Palestinian minister of culture and information, and Yossi Beilin, the Israeli architect of the Oslo Accord, with Jonathan Freedland of the *Guardian* in the chair. I came away with the optimistic feeling that a peace plan acceptable to both sides could indeed be achieved. Almost inevitably it was immediately condemned by the Israeli government, and was soon forgotten. Yet it has been reported that secret talks between Jewish and Muslim clerics are held in Jerusalem on a continuing basis, and perhaps one day these seeds, so far planted on barren soil, will germinate.

Positions on both sides of the divide are incredibly entrenched. I wrote to the editor of the *Journal of the Association of Jewish Refugees* in November 2002, complaining about the one-sidedness of one of his editorials which I felt had 'bordered on the perverse'. I wrote: 'Must it always be 'my country right or wrong' when it comes to Israel? After all, it isn't even your country, for you, like the rest of us Jews in the UK, have evidently chosen *not* to make it yours. Your apparent inability to comprehend that there is another side to the conflict in the Middle East and your (and the Jewish community's) unwillingness to criticise evil deeds by "one's own side" have, for me, extremely discomforting echoes from the past . . . We must be careful not to use the holocaust as a historical excuse for other acts of barbarism, whether carried out by Israeli forces or anyone else.' Whilst the editor remained silent, a correspondent later accused me of having advocated the destruction of the state of Israel!

As I see it, a solution to the problem of Palestine/Israel can be achieved only if both sides accept the notion of an independent Arab Palestine and an Israel with secure borders; Israel agrees to the unconditional evacuation of not only the Gaza Strip but also of the illegal settlements on the West Bank; the Palestinians and their Arab neighbours renounce acts of violence against Israeli citizens; there is joint sovereignty over Jerusalem; and, possibly, if there is a modification of the Israeli 'right of return', which entitles any Jew anywhere in the world (including those such as Robert Maxwell and Lady Porter) to enter Israel. This last provision would be emotionally hard to accept and politically difficult to negotiate, but whilst the unconditional right of return exists Israel will always be under pressure to appropriate Arab land. One could add to these issues the removal of the security fence, which is an impediment to good Israeli-Palestinian relations, though it would not be mandatory provided that its boundaries are redrawn to lie on the Israeli side of the border.

Despite all the pessimism there are hopeful signs, albeit on a small scale. For example, my friend, the late Tomi Spenser, an Old Bunce Courtian who moved to Israel soon after the Second World War and became a physician on a kibbutz, was involved in several initiatives intended to improve understanding between Israeli and Palestinian academics and clinicians. In 2001, soon after the beginning of the intifada, he helped to organise a meeting in Shfar-Am between twenty Jewish and Arab Palestinian physicians. In a memorandum sent to them the next day, Tomi outlined his thoughts on what had transpired and on possible future activities: 'Many people said interesting and wise things and offered suggestions. The best and most practical suggestion was to initiate meetings between the staff of neighbouring Jewish and Arab clinics . . . But the general feeling was that the sickness was incurable. This is not only depressing but untrue.' He went on to put forward a number of issues that he felt could be usefully discussed at future meetings: 'We will certainly keep in touch. I am an eternal optimist – I hope things will change', he wrote. I find his approach both admirable and courageous and, ultimately, hopeful. It is part of a wider movement among Israelis in search for a peaceful solution.

The new anti-Semitism

Anti-Semitism is of course as old as the hills. A minority group that is conspicuous by openly espousing a different religion and by differing from the majority in its cultural practices is a sitting duck as the eternal scapegoat, which virtually all societies seem to need when the going gets tough for one reason or another. In Eastern Europe it has been endemic for centuries and even now it is still alive, and in Germany it became a central tenet of the Nazi creed that led to the Holocaust. In the UK it was rampant in the Middle Ages, and British Jews achieved emancipation only in the nineteenth century. Emancipation does not, of course, lead to the disappearance of this prejudice, which is still alive and kicking.

In the 1930s anti-Semitism was deliberately and perniciously stirred up by Oswald Mosley and his British Union of Fascists. Mosley, together with his wife Diana and her sister Unity Mitford, was a huge admirer of Adolf Hitler. Many of the uglier manifestations of Mosley's political activity took place in the East End with its large Jewish population. It is not easy to understand how a politician, born into an aristocratic family and who began his career in 1918 as a Conservative member of parliament who later gravitated to the Labour party, could have become such a demagogue in a democratic society. His son Nicholas may have come as close as anyone to identifying the roots of his father's deviancy (see *Rules of the Game / Beyond the Pale: Memoirs of Sir Oswald Mosley and Family*). After the war there have been several pseudo-Fascist parties in the UK, most recently the British National party, which has had some political successes at a local level, especially in the north of England. Its racist targets are, however, in the main the Asian communities, who have over the years taken over the main role of victim from the Jewish community. Already back in the 1970s I remember taking part in a 'sit-down' demonstration in Brick Lane, which was by then inhabited by many Asian people, in protest against the militant activities of neo-Fascist thugs. The demonstration was organised by the redoubtable peace and social campaigner Pat Arrowsmith, who was arrested for her pains . . .

Jews have been displaced as the prime target for racial prejudice by the arrival of large numbers of people from the Caribbean and from India and Pakistan, whose minority status is so much more evident by their colour. These people therefore provide an easier target, and racial intolerance has led to attacks on black people in the streets and against shops owned by Asians, as well as to discriminatory behaviour on the part of the police. It is sad that the Jewish community has not played a more active part in fighting against this new racial prejudice and discrimination, which has been and still is a blot on life in the UK.

I must, alas, include the Chief Rabbi, Professor Jonathan Sacks, in this criticism. No doubt his heart is in the right place, but he seems to be the prisoner of his orthodox and inflexible congregation. This is clear from the Jewish community's reaction to his book *The Dignity of Difference*, in which he put forward the view that no single religion has a monopoly of the truth. One would think this to be pretty self-evident, but it led to his being accused of heresy by senior leaders of the Jewish community such as the president of the Union of Orthodox Hebrew Congregations, Rabbi Elchonen Halpern. As a result Sacks felt it necessary to promise to rewrite certain passages in the book for future editions. He is not the only major religious leader who has been forced to trim his sails to the wind: the Archbishop of Canterbury, Rowan Williams, whose views are admirably liberal, has also had to tread carefully in the schism that has engulfed the Church of England in relation to the ordination of women and gay priests. Although Sacks is clearly and rightly concerned about the growth of anti-Semitism in the UK (see his *The Dignity of Difference*), and complains about the failure of the left to protest against it, he must know that a fair and equitable solution of the Palestine problem would do more than any other single factor to undermine this ugly development, not only in the UK but worldwide.

Anti-Semitism has taken a turn for the worse since the military actions taken by the Israelis against the Palestinians from the beginning of the *intifada* and the subsequent illegal occupation of some of their land. (It is said that about 40 per cent of the territory of the West Bank has been absorbed into Israel by new settlements and the building of the protective fence/wall.) Many people seem to be unable or unwilling to distinguish between the Israeli government on the one hand, and on the other the Jews of the diaspora, who can hardly be held responsible for the actions of Israeli governments even though many do give their unquestioning support to Israeli policies. The anger generated in Muslim communities by the injustices inflicted on the Palestinians provides a major springboard for the new anti-Semitism.

If I have given undue prominence to these musings it is because, as an ethnic if secular Jew who escaped the horrors of the Holocaust by the skin of his teeth, I am deeply pained every time I read of excesses carried out by Israeli forces. As a soldier I witnessed the degradation of camps set up for 'displaced persons', with the best of intentions, after the Second World War, and I have empathy with Palestinians who have been displaced to similar camps in nearby Arab countries. It is a situation that *must* be rectified if human dignity is to be restored to them and to their descendants, and if peace is ever to break out in the Middle East and, indeed, in the world.

As for the 'war on terror', I find it deeply disturbing that the fear of terrorist acts is being used by the American and British governments to curb individual freedom and rights. The dangers this holds for western societies have been cogently discussed by Peter-Alexis Albrecht, a German Professor of Law, following a series of seminars with his students. We would do well to heed his warnings.

Since writing this there have been some major developments in the Middle East. First, the Gaza Strip has been evacuated, together with a few settlements on the West Bank. Second, there was Sharon's calamitous stroke on 3 January 2006, which has created a new political situation in Israel. And third, the election of Hamas with a crushing majority may yet force the Israelis to negotiate with their hated enemy. It remains to be seen whether these developments will lead to a just settlement; the omens are not in the least favourable.

Postscript

At the end of 2008 we witnessed the horrendous Israeli assault on Hamas and the citizens of Gaza, which was ostensibly triggered by the rockets, many handmade, fired by Hamas into Israeli territory. I do not on any account condone such rockets, even though they have killed only a very small number of Israelis. But nor can I condone the wholly disproportionate response by the Israeli army, air force and navy, which at the time of writing (13 January 2009), eighteen days into the action, is reported to have killed some 900 people, many of them civilians and children, and wounded almost 3000. This came after the virtual economic strangulation of Gaza resulting from the closure of its borders for many months, leading to a catastrophic situation. The letter I emailed to the *Guardian* early in the assault, on 2 January, and which was not published, is indicative of my sense of anguish that a Jewish state should be capable of such inhumanity.

Sir,

I am holed up in France and receive my *Guardian*, when I can, a day late. But I have looked in vain for any stringent attempts by the international community to halt the slaughter in Gaza. There has been head-shaking by the UN Director General, hand-wringing by our Foreign Secretary, positive support for the Israelis by Condoleezza Rice and the White House, a valiant but doomed attempt by the French to bring about a temporary truce – and a deathly silence from the UK Jewish community, from the Chief Rabbi downwards. The Zionist Federation is, I am told by its vice-chairman, in total support of the Israeli assault. Even that keeper of the nation's conscience, the Archbishop of Canterbury, has remained silent.

My family was murdered in the Holocaust, a fate from which I narrowly escaped. I have to ask whether it is the memory of the terrible events of the Holocaust that have induced a moral paralysis in the world at large – a willingness to ignore heinous crimes committed by a Jewish state. I have never felt comfortable with the biblical precept 'an eye for an eye', but in persuading the world that a hundred eyes for an eye and a hundred teeth for a tooth is acceptable the Israeli government has shown that it is morally bankrupt, a condition in which we must all share.

En désepoir de cause j'accuse . . .

Yours sincerely,
Leslie Baruch Brent (Emeritus Professor)

Chapter Twenty-One: The Holocaust: Feelings and Reflections

There is a vast literature on the Holocaust – the extermination of some six million European Jews as well as Roma, Sinti, gay people, the infirm, Communists and anyone who dared to oppose the Nazi regime. It is the defining and most horrendous event of the twentieth century and it has no parallel in history, even though there have been other genocides, such as that of the Armenians and, most recently, in Rwanda, the Sudan and in the former Yugoslavia. How and why it happened has been endlessly discussed. Here I want to focus on my own feelings about the Holocaust – the emotions connected with the loss of my own family, and on my attempts to make sense of these events in the light of present-day knowledge.

The fate of my family

I have in my bedroom photographs of my father, mother and sister, taken as passport photographs round about the time of my departure from Berlin. I also have a picture of my mother as a young woman, looking very beautiful in a huge, wide-rimmed and tasselled hat. I look at these photographs daily. That is how I remember them: my father almost bald and clear-eyed, looking a trifle stern but with just a hint of a smile, my mother soft and vulnerable and 'motherly', my sister beautiful and charming and rather sophisticated for a fifteen-year-old. When I look at them I want to weep for their terrible and cruel fate, and I try to imagine how life must have been for them in wartime Berlin and how they were savagely transported in sealed cattle trucks to their cruel deaths. They were not sent to Theresienstadt or Auschwitz, as I used to believe (and as seemed to be partly confirmed by the 'Gedenkbuch', book of remembrance, of the Jewish community in Berlin), but to Riga in Latvia. Documents I obtained from the Berlin Archives Office just a few years ago gave me precise details of the date of deportation, their destination, their personal details and the number of Jews on the transport. They were on transport (Osttransport) 44, together with 897 others, which left Güterbahnhof (goods station) Berlin-Moabit, on 26 October 1942. They were required to report to the collection point in Levetzowstrasse between 7 and 8 a.m. Their particulars were bureaucratically listed on the transport list: name, date and place of birth, occupation, married status, whether capable of work, age, last residence, identification number. Under 'occupation' it was stated that they had 'none', and this was consistently entered for everyone on the transport. The wagons must have been desperately overcrowded and the conditions beyond one's imagination. Thanks to the good offices of Dr Hermann Simon of the Centrum Judaicum in Berlin I now know that the transport arrived in Riga three days later and that all were immediately taken to the local woods and shot: according to the *Buch der Erinnerung* (*Book of Remembrance*) published in 2003 by W. Scheffler and D. Schulle, they were 'murdered immediately after arrival on 29.10.1942'. At least they were spared further incalculable suffering.

On a recent visit to Berlin Carol and I went to the station from which I had assumed that they were sent to their deaths, Bahnhof Grünewald. The disused platform (Gleis 7) has been turned into a moving memorial to the 50,000 Jews who were sent from there to their deaths, and the date (26 October 1942) and destination of my family's transport, and the number of people on it were engraved, among some sixty other transports, along the edge of the platform.

The vision I have of my beloved parents and sister on their last journey haunts me. Shortly before their deportation they were required to fill in a lengthy questionnaire about their assets and valuables, including clothes. I do not have the form for my parents but have one for my sister. It was completed in my father's handwriting: she had virtually *nothing* except the clothes she stood up in, and my heart bleeds when I think of the state to which these wonderful, cultured and sensitive people had been reduced and degraded.

Even when still in Berlin they must have suffered greatly and have been in utter poverty. I have several addresses for them between 29 December 1938 and the date of their transportation, and I imagine that they had to move into smaller and smaller accommodation; perhaps, eventually, into one of the so-called Judenhäuser (houses for Jews), where Jews were forced to live in grossly overcrowded conditions. It is from Viktor Klemperer's diary that I have learnt in astonishing and excruciating detail how the Nazi regime inexorably tightened the screw for German Jews; he lived in Dresden but it would have been much the same in Berlin. Klemperer was protected to a considerable extent from having been baptised by his parents, by his academic status and by his non-Jewish wife, but even so the numerous laws that made life such a misery for German Jews from 1933 onward eventually caught up with him, too. He and his wife Eva existed in straitened circumstances in a grossly overcrowded Judenhaus at the time of the controversial bombing raid by the RAF that destroyed Dresden in a ball of fire late in the war, on 13 and 14 February 1945. In the total chaos and confusion Klemperer and his wife and a group of other Jews escaped, removed the yellow stars that branded them as Jews and went into hiding until the end of the war. After much hardship and walking from village to village they eventually returned to Dresden on 10 June 1945. It is a remarkable story of survival and escape, and the Klemperers were undoubtedly among the lucky few. Klemperer's diaries have been abridged and translated into English.

Could the Allies have intervened?

This is an issue that has exercised my mind a great deal. What pressures could Britain and the United States have exerted on a wholly amoral Nazi regime that was fatally flawed by irrationality and determined to exterminate European Jewry? I have already alluded to the fact that two agencies, the Vatican and the International Red Cross, failed to live up to the high standards that one could have expected of them in upholding the right of Jews, Roma and others to life and human dignity by their refusal to apply moral pressure on Hitler and his henchmen. What about the Allies? I believe that something could have been done, for example the bombing of the gas chambers in Auschwitz and of the railway lines leading to the extermination camps, or the liberation of Auschwitz by volunteer parachutists, but there is in fact no simple answer.

W.D. Rubinstein thinks he knows; indeed, he called his book *The Myth of Rescue. Why the Democracies Could Not Have Saved More Jews from the Nazis,* and that title says it all. It is an apologia for Allied and especially American inaction, and considering that it was published sixteen years after Martin Gilbert's scholarly and objective review of the evidence on both sides of the Atlantic, *Auschwitz and the Allies. How the Allies Responded to the News of Hitler's Final Solution,* there is little excuse for such a one-sided picture. Apart from arguing that there is nothing the Allies could have done, Rubinstein is both facile and contradictory. His most potent argument against the notion of intervention seems to be that 'no person or group in the democracies . . . proposed the destruction of any extermination camp'. He goes on to say that just such a proposal was made in Britain in June 1944. According to Rubinstein, any such action, which would inevitably have entailed the killing of *some* Jews, would have been considered by today's historians as 'complicity in genocide and assisting the Nazis to kill the Jews'. What a bizarre argument.

A rather different view is expressed by Richard Breitman, who describes in some detail in his book *Official Secrets. What the Nazis Planned, What the British and Americans Knew* how much and when the Allies knew about the Nazis' policy of extermination. In Britain high-ranking Foreign Office officials, such as Victor Cavendish-Bentinck, dragged their heels and did everything possible to prevent positive action, even when the plight of the European Jews became known to them. (Extraordinary as it may seem, Cavendish-Bentinck became ambassador to Poland after the war and is recorded as having visited Auschwitz.) Both British and American governments were too preoccupied with winning the war, though Winston Churchill, who realised the horror of what was happening, told his foreign secretary, Anthony Eden, 'to get everything out of the Air Force you can'. However, action was ruled out on grounds of efficacy even though the secretary of state for air, Sir Archibald Sinclair, was willing to explore the possibility of bombing Auschwitz and/or the railway lines leading to it. When the first proposal to do that came from the Polish government-in-exile in August 1943 it is true that British bombers did not have the range to attack targets as far away as Auschwitz. Yet by early 1944 it would have been feasible with the help of an airbase in southern Italy, which had been captured by then. As for the USA, it doesn't seem to have been considered as a serious option even though the American Air Force was bombing factories and refineries not far from Auschwitz.

And so I come to Martin Gilbert's carefully researched and judiciously evaluated study, *Descent into Barbarism: a History of the Twentieth Century, 1933-1951*, which is probably the most authoritative analysis of the question of whether the Allies could have done more to save many Jews, Roma and others in, or about to be taken to, concentration camps. The Allies were clearly fully aware of the scale of the problem, in that the Allied Declaration of 17 December 1942 referred to these 'bestial crimes'. In Britain the reluctance of policymakers to liberate Jews tended to be justified by their fear that an influx of refugees into Palestine or indeed Britain would lead to a rise in anti-Semitism, an argument that strikes me as spurious and which may well have been indicative of their own anti-Semitism.

By the summer of 1944, when Britain and the USA were requested to bomb Auschwitz and a great deal was known both of its function and its geography, Winston Churchill gave his authorisation to a bombing scheme. 'Yet even then', writes Gilbert, 'a few individuals scotched the Prime Minister's directive because, as one of them expressed it at the time, to send British pilots to carry it out would have risked valuable lives.' But lives of volunteer air crews *were* already being risked during the Polish uprising, when supplies were dropped on Warsaw: 'these very pilots had actually flown across the Auschwitz region on their way to Warsaw'. Likewise, the American war department rejected all appeals to destroy the gas chambers at Auschwitz, 'although American bombers repeatedly overflew the camp in August to September 1944, had already photographed it from the air, and had even dropped bombs on it by mistake'. It would appear that the American War Refugee Board, set up specifically in June 1944 to examine methods of rescue, did not give its support for more than three months, 'by which time it was too late'. Assistant Secretary of State John J. McCloy was opposed to the whole idea, regardless of its feasibility.

Churchill undoubtedly emerges as the only statesman who both understood the horror and was willing to take action. According to Gilbert, he wrote in a letter to Eden in July 1944: 'There is no doubt that this is probably the greatest and most horrible single crime ever committed in the whole history of the world.' But, as Gilbert points out, though prime minister, Churchill was not always the final arbiter on policy decisions, and other counsels prevailed. Gilbert identified two reasons for lack of action. First, the main failure, 'shared by the Allies, were . . . of imagination, of response, Intelligence, of piecing together and evaluating what was known, of co-ordination, of initiative and *even at times of sympathy* [my italics]. The success lay elsewhere, with the Nazis; in the killings themselves, and in a series of bizarre deceptions which enabled these killings to be carried out on a gigantic scale, for more than three years, almost without interruption.'

Second, there was anti-Semitism, or at best a lack of empathy with the plight of European Jews. For example, when a Zionist request was made to the British government for the establishment of a Jewish military force to fight as part of the Allied army, this was rejected by the War Office and the Colonial Office even though it had Churchill's support. Churchill was moved to write to Lord Cranborne, then colonial secretary: 'It may be necessary to make an example of these anti-Semitic officers and others in high places. If three or four of them were recalled and dismissed, and the reasons given, it would have a salutary effect'. Both Herbert Morrison and Lord Halifax were antagonistic to a suggestion that the lives of some 400 old people and children in Vichy France might be saved by bringing them to England, ostensibly for fear of stirring up anti-Semitism. Following the publication in the *New Statesman* in January 1943 of an article entitled 'Our part in the massacre', the Archbishop of Canterbury, William

Temple, moved a resolution in the House of Lords (23 May) urging 'immediate measures on the largest and most generous scale' to give temporary asylum in Britain to all the Jews who managed to escape. But all to no avail and there was no change of policy, Lord Cranborne having warned that it would create problems of housing and food supplies.

There were dire failures of imagination even within the Jewish community. The head of the rescue department of the World Jewish Congress, Leon Kubowitzky, opposed the idea of bombing concentration camps because some Jews would be killed, and because it would allow the Germans to claim that it was the Allies who were responsible for the killings. He therefore did not even put such a plan to the State Department.

As I see it, by mid-1944 the bombing of the Auschwitz gas chambers and the railway lines leading to that centre of mass extermination *could* have been carried out, and even a drop of volunteer parachutists might have been feasible to liberate the camp. I and many other refugee soldiers would almost certainly have been willing to risk our lives. At the same time I do not underestimate the difficulties inherent in this kind of operation, especially the liberation of a vast extermination camp with sick and malnourished people without adequate food and medical supplies.

Ultimately, it must be said that the Allies were fighting a global war against a ruthless and determined foe, and it was therefore natural that winning that war should have been given top priority. Saving European Jewry was therefore not uppermost in the minds of the great majority of politicians and senior officers. Winston Churchill was undoubtedly heads and shoulders above the rest in terms of understanding, empathy and compassion. I am very glad that I paid my last respects to him when he was lying in state in Westminster Palace.

Who was responsible for the Holocaust – the few or the many?

Ian Kershaw has written what might well be the definitive account of the life of Adolf Hitler. Two decades earlier it was Sebastian Haffner, the *Observer*'s correspondent in Berlin after the war, who was the first to attempt to analyse what led Hitler to his rabid and irrational anti-Semitism that ended in the Final Solution. Neither of these authors regarded Hitler as a demented villain and, by tracing his life history and his development as a politician and demagogue, they discussed this man, who in twelve years 'changed the world' (Kershaw), with great detachment. Even so, Kershaw quoted Albert Speer, Hitler's architect and armament minister who spent many years after the war incarcerated in isolation in Spandau prison, who described Hitler as 'a demonic figure, one of the inexplicable historical phenomena which emerge at rare intervals among mankind'.

Kershaw rightly believes that to describe Hitler as 'a lunatic' or a 'raving madman' merely obviates the need for an explanation. And yet, ultimately, there is no clear explanation of how this man made the German people follow him blindly to their eventual destruction. Kershaw believes that the history of Hitler is essentially a history of power: Hitler saw it as his historic mission to save Germany, and he had persuaded himself from an early stage that this had to include the extermination of the Jews. I have sometimes idly speculated as to what might have happened if Hitler had not been turned down (twice) by the Vienna Academy of Art, where he had desperately wanted to study. It might conceivably have changed the course of history, unlikely as that may seem.

We shall never know. What *is* beyond doubt is that the fate of European Jews was sealed at the Wannsee Conference, which took place in a villa on the shores of a lake near Berlin on 20 January 1942. This meeting, which culminated in the 'Wannsee Protocol', is described and discussed in detail by Mark Roseman in *The Villa. The Lake, The Meeting. Wannsee and the Final Solution.* Clearly inspired by Hitler (the invitations were in the name of the Reichmarshal of the Greater German Reich), they were written and signed by Reinhard Heydrich, a protégé of Himmler and deputy protector for the occupied Czech territories. He was assisted in organising the Wannsee Conference by the notorious Adolf Eichmann. The invitations were sent to very senior officials, equivalent in status to under-secretary of state in the USA and permanent secretary in the British civil service. According to Roseman the participants fell into two groups – those responsible for 'the Jewish question', who came from ministries of the interior, justice, economics and the occupied eastern territories, and the majority from 'Party and SS agencies with a special interest in race questions'. The Jews, learned the Staatssekretäre, were to be 'evacuated to the East'. Although not everyone present had been aware of what was being proposed, the outcome of the day's discussions was 'the final solution', and Eichmann proceeded to send 'a circular to all the regional Gestapo centres concerning the new deportation programme'. From this moment, nine months before the deportation of my family from Berlin, the policy of extermination was pursued relentlessly and bureaucratically, even though it must have undermined Germany's war effort.

The question of whether the final solution was carried out in secret by élite units such as the SS, with or without involvement of the Wehrmacht, and with or without the knowledge and connivance of the German civilian population, has been much discussed. It has been tacitly assumed by many commentators that the population was unaware of what was happening. I have always found this idea incredible: surely Germans must have asked themselves why their Jewish neighbours had to report to special collection centres or railway stations and why they then suddenly vanished. Daniel Goldhagen created a furore with his thesis in *Hitler's Willing Executioners: Ordinary Germans and the Holocaust* that the whole German nation must bear responsibility. According to him, perpetrators of the Holocaust weren't just ordinary *people* who were pressurised into social conformity or forced to obey orders, thus becoming 'robotic carriers of the banality of evil'. They were ordinary *Germans* – true believers who were motivated by a historically rooted, widespread and virulent anti-Semitism that logically encouraged an 'exterminationist' ideology that existed well before the opportunity to act on it. In other words, they were 'willing executioners'. They *could* have refused to participate but they didn't; they not only acquiesced, but acted with zest and gratuitous cruelty. They did not need excuses to do what they already wanted to do. This is probably an extreme point of view, which takes no account of the overwhelming difficulties faced by a citizen wishing to protest against the all-powerful Nazi state.

Laurence Rees, in a book based on a BBC television programme, tends to support Goldhagen's thesis, based on a large number of eyewitness interviews and academic research. For example, one Adolf Buchner, who had served in an SS unit near Leningrad, stated that 'virtually all units were involved (i.e. in the atrocities) . . . it did not matter whether it was Wehrmacht or SS, both of them'. This was powerfully underwritten by an exhibition that toured Germany some years ago, in which letters of Wehrmacht personnel to their families were on display; it caused a great deal of controversy. Whilst, so far as the civilian population is concerned, specific knowledge was confined to relatively few people, *every* German must have been conscious of the fact that Jews had disappeared and something 'bad' had happened to them. By brushing this knowledge aside they had, in fact, acquiesced. According to one SS intelligence report (December 1942), even the Nazis became concerned about the effect news of the atrocities might have on the population at large.

A less extreme stance is adopted by Zygmund Bauman in *Modernity and the Holocaust*. He believes that obedience to authority explains why ordinary people are capable of doing terrible things if ordered and authorised to do so. They are not necessarily *naturally* willing, Bauman maintains, nor morally degenerate. 'Their denials of ideological motivations such as extreme anti-Semitism and their refusal to accept full responsibility for their actions are genuine.' The truth probably lies half-way between these viewpoints.

I do find it hard to accept that a massive operation such as the round-ups, the deportations and the killings – involving the police force, the Wehrmacht, railway workers, doctors, scientists, the chemical and pharmaceutical companies that employed slave labour and even financial institutions, as well as the SS and special units – could have been hidden from the civilian population. In *Nazi Policy, Jewish Workers, German Killers* Christopher Browning concludes that a minority, probably more than 10 per cent, evaded taking part in the killings themselves, but with rare exceptions did not hinder or protest against the killing process, mainly because evasion was tolerated by the authorities whereas protest and obstruction was not. The 'eager killers', writes Browning, 'were a minority, and some were transformed by the situation in which they found themselves. But many were ideologically motivated men ready to kill Jews and other so-called enemies of the Reich from the start . . . they formed a crucial nucleus . . . their influence was far out of proportion to their number in German society.'

Two notable exceptions were the non-Jewish women who took part in Berlin's Rosengarten demonstration, which led to the release of their Jewish husbands; and the subversive activities in Munich by a group known as 'Die Weisse Rose' (The White Rose), led by Sophie Scholl and her brother, who were eventually executed.

I conclude that most Germans were vaguely or implicitly aware of what was happening to the Jewish population, even if the killings themselves were kept secret.

Has modern Germany made amends?

My answer to that is in the affirmative. Not only has Germany paid the survivors of the Holocaust 'compensation' (never mind that no amount of money can actually compensate for the suffering inflicted or the loss of relatives), but it has commemorated the victims in many different and often moving ways. I have been impressed by the numerous plaques, memorials and sculptures that acknowledge German atrocities and persecutions, especially in the city that I know best, Berlin. Many of them have been in place for years but the most recent as well as the largest (it covers the area of two football pitches) is the Holocaust Memorial close to the Brandenburg Gate. The Jewish Museum, too, designed by Daniel Libeskind, is a cogent and poignant reminder of the nightmare of Nazi Germany; and Nazi policies and the Holocaust are widely taught in schools. Some of these memorials are also dedicated to non-Jewish victims, such as the Roma, Sinti, Jehovah Witnesses and political enemies of the Third Reich. Volume 1 alone of a list and description of these memorials in certain regions of Germany fills 840 pages.

Strangely, it is not in Germany but in Britain that the authenticity of the Holocaust has been challenged. The 'historian' David Irving has denied that the Holocaust took place on the scale that has been authenticated and accepted by all serious historians, scholars and the world at large, and he sued Professor Deborah Lipstadt, who had accused him of being a Holocaust denier, in a British court. He lost his case, having been branded by the judge as an active Holocaust denier, a racist and anti-Semite, and to be associated with rightwing extremists who promote neo-Nazism. He was later sentenced to a term of imprisonment in Austria.

Survivors' guilt

This is a well-known phenomenon, which can be observed in people who have lost their families in a disaster such as an earthquake or as the result of warfare. It hits Holocaust survivors particularly hard and I am no exception. Thus, I often ask myself why it is I who has been spared when virtually the whole of my family has been wiped out. What have I done to deserve this entirely fortuitous survival? It is a question that causes me much grief and that has no answer, for this guilt is an irrational emotional response. At a time when I subconsciously tried to sweep my past life under the carpet I was not affected by this guilt, but it has become acute as I have become older and confronted my early life and the fate of my dear ones. I like to think that my survival in this country provided my parents and sister with some solace – by knowing that I was safe and sound and able to grow up in an environment that was not overshadowed by the swastika. I wonder whether they ever thought of the possibility that I would join the British army.

Through my contact with younger Germans, mainly through my scientific contacts in Munich and the 'ski conferences', I have come to realise that not a few Germans suffer from a different kind of guilt, that associated with having had parents or grandparents who did not raise their voices during the Nazi era or who even took part in some of the anti-Jewish measures, or benefited from them financially. I have a great deal of sympathy with these people, and in some respects theirs is a harder guilt to come to terms with.

Will I ever be able to forgive those who perpetrated the Holocaust? I don't think so, for their actions were too bestial to justify forgiveness. However, I have no ill feelings whatever towards the modern generation of Germans, who cannot be blamed for what happened well over half a century ago, and I have developed close friendships with some of them.

Some notes on Holocaust literature

There is a vast literature, and I will confine myself to a consideration of a few authors who have made a deep impression on me. I have already referred to Viktor Klemperer's diaries. The author who has written the most poignant and moving description of what it was like to be a concentration camp inmate is of course Primo Levi, the Italian Jew who wrote so dispassionately and without bitterness about his own experiences and those of others. I first came across *The Periodic Table*, a collection of essays covering his interest in chemistry as well as his later experiences as a victim of Fascism. (The book was given to me by Carol.) Although he wrote a number of books following his release from Auschwitz, the most extraordinary is probably *If This is a Man*, in which he gives a detailed account of his life following his arrest by the Fascist militia in December 1943. He had joined the partisans in the mountains, was captured and taken to a detention camp, and when the SS became involved was taken, together with 650 others, to Auschwitz. He managed to avoid the gas chambers because of his skills as a chemist and survived as a member of the 'Chemical Commando'. This book includes a description of his liberation and the tortuous journey back to Italy towards the end of 1945. It is an inspiring testament to the human spirit, written in a matter-of-fact way, without apparent bitterness or rancour.

However, Levi's belief in God was evidently destroyed by his experiences. He describes one of the many 'selections', which involved men who had been ordered to strip and forced into an impossibly crowded space with two doors. An SS man ordered the men to exit from one or other of the doors – one leading to the gas chamber and the other to continued incarceration. It took the SS officer three to four minutes to seal the fate of 100 men. A fellow inmate called Kuhn was one of the lucky ones and prayed in thankfulness, wearing his beret and swaying forwards and backwards violently. 'Kuhn is thanking God because he has not been chosen . . . Does Kuhn not understand that what happened today is an abomination, which no propitiatory prayer, no pardon, no expiation by the guilty, which nothing at all in the power of man can ever clean again? . . . If I was God I would spit at Kuhn's prayer.' No wonder that Primo Levi is thought to have taken his life eventually: such memories would be hard to live with.

The other writer I want to single out was not Jewish and was born in Germany in 1944, therefore having no direct experience of the Nazi regime. W.G. Sebald moved to England in 1966 to take a lecturing post at the University of Manchester and later became Professor of European Literature at the University of East Anglia. His novels were written in German but translated extremely well into English, and all were subtly connected with the Holocaust. I use the word 'subtly' advisedly, for the reader is led to the Holocaust connection in a most oblique and intriguing manner, often quite late in the novel. I believe that Sebald has elevated Holocaust literature to a new level of artistry and sensibility, and his novels are characterised by the inclusion of grainy and often mysterious black-

and-white photographs taken by the author. *Austerlitz*, the story of a man rediscovering his past as a five-year-old Kindertransport child, is probably his greatest novel. He died in a car crash in December 2001.

Although first published in German in 1999, Sebald's assessment of the destruction of Dresden by the RAF late in the Second World War did not appear in translation until fairly recently. *On the Natural History of Destruction* is based on some lectures he gave in 1997 and discusses the Allied aerial assault on German cities late in the war, its horror, justification and morality. This book caused an outcry in his native Germany, where this topic had been regarded as taboo. Only someone of Sebald's integrity and sensitivity could have got away with it. He concluded, 'The majority of Germans today know, or so at least it is to be hoped, that we actually provoked the annihilation of the cities in which we once lived. Scarcely anyone can now doubt that Air Marshal Göring would have wiped out London if his technical resources had allowed him to do so . . . The intoxicating vision of destruction coincides with the fact that the real pioneering achievements in bomb warfare – Guernica, Warsaw, Belgrade, Rotterdam – were the work of the Germans. And when we think of the nights when the fires raged in Cologne and Hamburg and Dresden, we ought also to remember that as early as August 1942, when the vanguard of the Sixth Army had reached the Volga . . . the city of Stalingrad, then swollen (like Dresden later) by an influx of refugees, was under assault from 1,200 bombers, and that during this raid alone, which caused elation among the German troops stationed on the opposite bank, 40,000 people lost their lives.'

So far as Dresden is concerned, I feel that the bombardment so late in the war was inexcusable. Air Marshal (Bomber) Harris has been much criticised for it even in Britain, especially as the bombing of German cities, whilst inflicting huge casualties and damage, did not have the desired effect of bringing Germany to its knees.

Two other books – essentially examples of the many eyewitness accounts of the Holocaust – are worth a mention. Rich Cohen's *The Avengers. A Jewish War Story* tells the story of a group of young Jewish Poles who joined the ghetto in Vilna, Lithuania, where they organised the first underground movement in Europe, blowing up a German train, and then setting themselves up as resistance fighters in the forests of Poland. From their hideouts they blew up Vilna's waterworks and its power plant and paved the way for the arrival of the Soviet army. They survived the war and went to Israel. This story is a good antidote to the generally held assumption that European Jewry allowed itself to be slaughtered without any resistance. I don't think I need to mention the heroic and suicidal uprising in the Warsaw ghetto in 1943: that must certainly never be forgotten.

The other book consists of the personal recollection of Bert Lewyn, whom I got to know in the Jewish orphanage in Pankow, Berlin in 1937–38. We both loved football and played together in the same team. In his *On the Run in Nazi Berlin* he recounts how he survived the war years in Berlin, mainly underground. His experiences were absolutely hair-raising and his survival almost unbelievable, a tribute to his ingenuity and intelligence – and luck. The book reads like a thriller and, had I not met him several years ago at a reunion in the former Jewish orphanage in Pankow, I would have assumed that the story had been made up.

Chapter Twenty-Two: A Question of Identity

J was transplanted at the age of thirteen from a German-Jewish environment into England and, though mindful of my roots, I adapted to life in Britain with, ultimately, a British name. The question of identity, and especially perhaps Jewish identity, is of great interest to me. What kind of a person would I have become had I stayed on in a Germany that had not succumbed to rabid anti-Semitism? Would I have clung on to my Jewish religion? Why do I consider myself to be a Jew even though I do not practise the religion and have twice married non-Jewish wives?

At the 1999 reunion of those who had come to Britain in Kindertransports, organised by the redoubtable Bertha Leverton, whose great achievement has been to establish the ROK (Reunion of Kindertransports), I was asked to chair a workshop on 'Lost Jewish Identity and Assimilation'. Bertha Leverton had intended to publish the summaries of several workshops at the reunion in a booklet, but this did not come to pass until mine was published very recently. I reprint it here.

> At the end of the reunion I ran into a lady living in the UK and quite unknown to me. I asked her what she thought of the reunion as a whole and she replied: 'Well, I feel perfectly assimilated and all this introspective stuff doesn't really bother me!' I don't think that she had attended my workshop or others concerned with the same issues, but seventy to eighty crammed into a seminar room intended for forty to fifty, with as many again turned away. Evidently questions of identity and assimilation *are* of interest to a great many former 'Kinder', even now or perhaps particularly now; present were people living in the UK, USA, Israel, Australia and elsewhere.

I had drafted a number of questions that seemed interesting to me, and whilst we didn't get round to dealing with all of them we managed to stick to the framework pretty well. Even so, chairing this session was rather like riding a bucking horse for a couple of hours: the views expressed were very diverse, there were some quite acerbic – certainly lively and frequently passionate – interchanges, and whilst one or two speakers quoted Bea Green ('we are who we are') just *who* we were clearly wasn't a foregone conclusion for many.

I had given a short introduction in which I tried to explain what we mean by 'identity' and what one or two psychoanalysts have written about its development. There seems to be agreement that identity (Charles Rycroft, *A Critical Dictionary of Psychoanalysis*: 'the sense of one's continuous being as an entity distinguishable from all others') is developed in early childhood and that it depends on the interaction with parents or other loving carers, and that it has to be redefined in late adolescence 'in relation to the parents one is growing away from and the society one is growing into' (Erik Erikson, *Childhood and Society*).

The questions I posed ranged from a) the importance of genes versus environment (personal, social and cultural) in shaping our identity, b) the importance of economic factors, c) whether or not there is a British, American, Australian etc. identity available to refugees, d) the question of what is 'Jewishness' – whether it is possible to feel Jewish without a Jewish faith and without being a Zionist, e) the influence of the Holocaust and loss of family on our self-identification as Jews, f) whether assimilation necessarily carries with it denial of one's ethnic roots, and g) whether assimilation can be a force for the good or inevitably lead to renunciation of the Jewish component of one's identity, to intermarriage and thus to the demise of Judaism.

It was pointed out by an Israeli that not even Israelis have managed to come to an agreement about the nature of Jewishness, and it was thought that whether one felt to be a Jew was up to the individual. Whilst some thought that assimilation leads to a less Jewish coherence and identity, others believed that one's personality is enriched if *all* influences, Jewish and non-Jewish, are integrated. Thus a sense of identity develops through work, one's profession, through being an artist or a writer, or whatever. It should be possible to maintain Jewish (childhood) values in a non-Jewish environment.

Economic factors were undoubtedly important in shaping one's personality and identity, and especially the possibility of

268

undergoing higher education, if only to provide the confidence to take one's place in society. Often people other than the father or mother were a decisive influence. Thus, in one man's case it was the sympathetic headmaster of a preparatory school who decided that he was far too clumsy to become a shoemaker or something practical, and that he should be recommended for a 'public' (i.e. private) school scholarship – a decisive event in this man's life. Whilst the genetic factor was acknowledged it was felt by some that economic circumstances were more important. There was some discussion on whether this was more applicable to the United States, where opportunities varied in different regions, than to the UK.

Some questioned why it was necessary to search for an identity at all; surely, they argued, no-one can be without one! This reminded me vividly of someone I met at the reunion. Because of the particularly inimical environment into which she was plonked in this country (including schooling in a convent school) at the age of five, she felt that she had been deprived of her true identity until she discovered it following psychotherapy and later membership of the ROK. One participant described his unhappy childhood in a non-Jewish home, his escape and life in hostels, his state of confusion about who he was until he went to the USA, joined the Army there and learnt English and married. He felt that the search for his roots and the experiences resulting from that had helped him to develop a sense of identity.

Language – the ability to master it – was thought to be of great importance, and a landmark was thought to be the ability to dream in the language of one's host country. It was asserted by one person that, so far as he was concerned, no-one in the room spoke English like a native. This provoked some disbelief. The story was told of how one man felt linguistically totally absorbed into the English community; so far as he could judge he did not have a foreign accent. It was when visiting a citizens' advice bureau that he met a foreigner who commented on his 'funny accent'! Language was thought to be less important in the USA than in the UK, because there and in Canada in particular no-one cared about where one came from. The chairman explained why he and other wartime servicemen had changed their names, and why he didn't change back to his German-Jewish name after the war. Whilst one UK participant recounted his experience when applying for a job with a Jewish proprietor ('we don't take foreigners'), another (an Old Bunce Courtian) expressed the view that she was entirely happy to be thought of as a refugee and that she had no regrets about that.

Even when there was no overt adherence to the Jewish faith, some thought that adherence to Jewish values helped to shape one's identity. One man who felt unable to identify with any religion had daughters who had 'married out', but his love for his grandchildren was (naturally) undiminished. The chairman listed among the causes of his loss of religion the fact that the omnipotent Jewish God had not protected his chosen people, a point that provoked a somewhat noisy response (i.e. how naïve can one be . . .)! A passionate plea was made for the induction of our children into Judaism, and it was claimed that we must educate our children accordingly. But marrying out did not necessarily abrogate Jewishness. We must not be ashamed, but proud, to be Jewish; and yet it was recognised that it was almost inevitable that in countries outside Israel Judaism will diminish. Others thought that it was now chic to be Jewish.

The view was expressed that by allowing Judaism to decline we were achieving what Hitler had intended – perhaps rather an extreme point of view. A teacher in a Jewish school was amazed and outraged that people were so tolerant of assimilation: Jewishness to her was absolutely paramount and needed to be perpetuated. Someone else's attempt to define Jewishness was to say 'I am a Jew, period'); he felt that this should be enough. He happened to be a practising Jew, though.

Others saw no problem in being/feeling Jewish *and* assimilated. To them, Jewishness was a kind of ethics and, provided that was passed on to one's offspring, that should go a long way. How was it possible to prevent anyone from falling in love with a non-Jew? Well, said one vehemently, in that event you must ask him or her to become a Jew. Another participant's daughter was not religious but celebrated Seder and invited non-Jews to it: this passing on of the traditions of Judaism should be a requirement, and all schools should be taught about the Holocaust.

As for the future, it was felt that our responsibility was to ensure a climate of tolerance. Support for Judaism needed to be not only financial but also intellectual.

What became clear from the lively discussion is that there was no simple answer to any of the questions associated with identity, Judaism and assimilation. Everyone had to find their own solution, depending on their specific experiences. Many of those present at this workshop, and others I met during the course of the reunion, seemed substantially assimilated (whether in the States, Canada, the UK or Israel) but their presence showed that they were conscious of their roots and of the debt they owed to their Jewish past.

Who am I?

The answer to this question is largely embedded in the above report. Though I certainly was, once, a German-Jewish refugee I no longer consider myself to be a refugee. Seventy years of life in the UK, including wartime army service, an English education, mastery of the English language, a full professional life as a scientist, involvement in politics and community relations, my love for British culture (music, novels, art) and landscape, having had children and grandchildren born in this country – all this makes me feel that I am truly embedded in the fabric of British society. There seems absolutely no reason why I should cling to my refugee status, as evidently one participant at the workshop was only too happy to do.

Do I regard myself as British or English? The distinction between the two has been much discussed of late in the press, not least because of one home secretary's somewhat ludicrous tests of Britishness required to be passed by newcomers to the UK who apply for British nationality. (Many an English person would fail them!) The concept of Britishness is a relatively new one, formulated (and encapsulated in the Union Jack) to unify the English, Scots, Welsh and Irish, who had fought each other for hundreds of years. So the Scots, for example, can call themselves Scottish but also British, and the English are just that and British too. The term English is restrictive in that it usually conveys the notion of having been born in this country and being white; I would therefore not normally claim to be English and am content to describe myself as British, but born in Germany. The fact that I speak English with either no or only the slightest trace of an accent accounts for the fact that when, in 1989 (towards the end of my professional career) I appeared in the BBC documentary *No Time to Say Goodbye*, I received a number of letters from people who had known me but who were surprised by my origins. Not that I had ever tried to hide them, but neither had I flaunted them. Certainly all my friends knew about my past life, and childhood friends still call me Lothar. I know that American fellow immunologists, who heard me give talks at international congresses, used to think of me as the quintessential Englishman! I don't know how it came about that I developed a rather la-di-da accent; I don't particularly like it but it doesn't trouble me.

My friend Thilde Fraenkel once said to me, when I was still in the uniform of an infantry officer, 'so you are creating a new identity for yourself, Lothar?' Nothing could be further from the truth. My persona and my voice have developed subconsciously, no doubt strongly influenced by the different environments to which I have been exposed; and it is probable that, among these, the army was the most formative one. There I had to transform myself from a somewhat anxious adolescent refugee into a confident officer in charge of and leading men – Englishmen in the main – and I had to do so in a great hurry. In that sense Thilde was perhaps right after all, though I was, and still am, unaware of any abrupt change of personality.

According to Jerome Bruner, a psychologist and psychiatrist, in *Making Stories: Law, Literature and Life*, 'self is a perpetually rewritten story . . . and in the end we become the autobiographical narratives by which we "tell about" our lives'. I agree with Galen Strawson, who maintained in an article in the *Guardian* that this is not true, at least not for the majority of people: 'There is a deep divide in our species. On the one side, the narrators: those who are indeed intensely narrative, self-storying, Homeric, in their sense of life and self, whether they look to the past or the future. On the other side, the non-narrators: those who live lives in an essentially non-storytelling fashion, who may have little sense of, or interest in, their own history, nor any wish to give their life a certain narrative shape. In between lies the great continuum of mixed cases.' I have never kept a diary because I had it in mind to write, sooner or later, an autobiography. In no sense do I feel that I have created my 'self' through narrative, and the sort of person I have become, for better or for worse, owes his existence to a smooth continuous and natural process of growth and development.

Strangely enough, the term 'British' is now under attack for having racist connotations in our multicultural society. That is the conclusion reached by a commission sponsored by the Runnymede Trust, that bastion of racial equality and tolerance. Chaired by Lord Parekh, a Labour peer and political scientist, it concludes that the notion of 'Britishness' has been undermined by devolution, the (Irish) Good Friday Agreement and by globalisation. These arguments seem highly dubious to me, especially as 'Englishness' is rejected because 'to be English, as the term is in practice used, is to be white. Britishness is not ideal, but at least it appears acceptable, particularly when suitably qualified – Black British, Indian British, British Muslim and so on. However, there is one major and so far insurmountable barrier. Britishness, as much as Englishness, has systematic, largely unspoken, racial connotations. Whiteness nowhere features as an explicit condition of being British, but it is widely understood that Englishness, and therefore by extension Britishness, is racially coded.' This strikes me as political correctness gone mad.

The case of Andrea Levy, who was born in the UK of Jamaican parents, is of interest. Her father had come over in 1948 on the *Empire Windrush*, the ship that brought the first wave of Jamaicans to this country. She is a distinguished novelist and has made waves with her novel *Small Island*, in which she describes the antagonistic reception the early immigrants from the Caribbean were given in the UK. When visiting New

Zealand and asked where she came from she replied, 'England'. 'You don't look English', the white young man said. 'Well, this is what English sometimes looks like', was her retort. 'I am English', writes Andrea Levy. 'Born and bred, as the saying goes . . . England is the only society I truly know and sometimes understand. I don't look as the English did in the England of the '30s or before, but being English is my birthright. England is my home. An eccentric place where sometimes I love being English.' Bravo, say I, and much the same goes for me – despite the fact that I wasn't even born here.

There is hardly a need for me to point out that the English are 'mongrels' who owe their existence to many ethnic influences, from the Romans, the Vikings, and the Normans to East European and later West European Jews. As Peter Ackroyd argues in *Albion: the Origins of the English Imagination*, it is not so much the English resistance to foreign influences that makes them English, as their ability to assimilate them. 'Englishness is the principle of appropriation'. As a biologist I recognise the fact that mongrels (or hybrids) are indeed biologically 'fitter' than pure-bred creatures, and the success of the English in assimilating foreigners over the centuries is probably responsible for their huge success in science, medicine and the arts, out of all proportion to their numbers. Richard Eyre, in a very amusing and at the same time profound article about 'Britishness' in the *Guardian*, wrote: 'Now, if I belong to anything, it's to London or to Europe and the only things that I feel are indissolubly 'British' are my feelings about the language and the landscape.' I too like to think of myself as a European, and I regret the timidity, bordering almost on repugnance, with which British governments have sat on the fence for so long. The case against joining wholeheartedly in the European venture, made so vehemently and irresponsibly by the tabloid newspapers and the right-wing parties, has been left virtually unanswered. No wonder a majority of people in Britain are against accepting the European Treaty and joining the Euro currency.

As I said at the beginning of this chapter, I have wondered sometimes what sort of a man I might have become had I remained in Germany – in a Germany, that is, free of racial hatred. There cannot be a definitive answer. I might or might not have received a university education; if I had I would have been the first to receive that privilege in my extended family. The basis for my personality and character was undoubtedly provided by my parents in my childhood, and had I stayed I would presumably have continued to be influenced by them. I would like to think that I would have developed much as I have, with an overlay of 'Germanness' no doubt. I am reminded of my friend Michael Trede, who came to this country before the war and returned to Germany to become an eminent Professor of Surgery. In Germany he is thought of as being rather British, whereas in this country, where he is much respected, his fellow surgeons think of him as rather German. The best of both worlds, I suppose.

A person is often identified in terms of his 'Heimat'. I do not regard anywhere in Germany as mine, for Germany is a foreign country to me, with bitter-sweet associations. Rather, I would identify Bunce Court School and London as my Heimat.

So why do I think of myself as Jewish? Are there Jewish genes? Whilst there are some genes that are clustered more prominently in Jews than in other ethnic groups, I very much doubt it. I believe that my Jewishness is strongly linked to my childhood experiences and the fate of my family in the Holocaust, which I continue to feel so acutely and painfully. How could I possibly *ever* deny my Jewish roots? Furthermore, there is something in Jewish history and traditions that is admirable and edifying and with which I am happy to be associated.

There is no other country in which I would prefer to live. That does not mean that I feel uncritical towards my adopted country. There are times when I feel thoroughly ashamed – when, for example, my government blindly supports a very right-wing American president and follows him into an unjustified and illegal war, when I see yobbish behaviour in the streets, hear racist chants at football matches and read of racist attacks on black people or on Jewish cemeteries. But I am glad to be a member of a fairly tolerant multi-ethnic community, and glad to identify with the wonderful British achievements in science, music and the arts.

Chapter Twenty-Three: Music and Choral Singing

The man that hath no music in himself,
Nor is not mov'd with concord of sweet sounds,
Is fit for treasons, stratagems and spoils;
The motions of his spirit are dull as night,
And his affections dark as Erebus.
Let no such man be trusted.
> Shakespeare's *The Merchant of Venice*, Act V, Scene 1

Early musical influences

I can easily identify with Lorenzo's sentiments. Music has always been of great importance to me and I cannot imagine life without it. Apart from home music in my childhood, the sound of the organ in the synagogue and singing in the synagogue choir, my first serious exposure to music came at the age of twelve, when I was taken by the director of the Berlin orphanage, Dr Kurt Crohn, to hear Mendelssohn's oratorio *Elijah*. This made a deep impression on me and I have since sung it twice with the Crouch End Festival Chorus. In Bunce Court School we were exposed to music-making of a high order, with Helmut Schneider at the piano and Lotte Kalischer playing the violin. There we also heard opera in the shape of *The Magic Flute*, in which I had a tiny part as one of the Moorish slaves of Sarastro. Important, too, in my musical education was the collection of old 78rpm records that was available to some of us, especially later on, when I was no longer a pupil and the school had just closed.

On my release from the Army in 1947, as I mentioned earlier, I acquired a rather fine Philips wireless, housed in a handsome wooden

275

case. It cost £30, which was a lot in those days, and in the evenings, whilst studying or lying in bed, I listened until late at night to the Third Programme (the forerunner of Radio 3). It exposed me to a wide variety of music – the classics of course but also modern music. Brahms and Schubert became my favourite composers, and of the English composers I loved above all the music of Edward Elgar, especially his cello concerto, which was much later performed so passionately by Jacqueline du Pré. Through Annemarie Meyer I got to know and love Benjamin Britten's works, especially the *Serenade for orchestra, tenor and horn*, in which Britten has succeeded, against all the odds, to add to and embroider some of the finest poems in the English language. At University College, in the 1950s, I was introduced to Anton Bruckner and Gustav Mahler, two other composers I have come to admire greatly. Significant for me, too, were the chamber music concerts given regularly in the Barber Institute whilst I was at Birmingham University.

My interests were not confined to classical music. I was a great admirer of Ray Charles, the blind Afro-American blues singer and pianist, and on my forays into New York I usually managed to sneak into the legendary Jimmy Ryan's on 52nd Street, where authentic New Orleans jazz was played. Joanne and I also treasured several long-playing records of Yves Montand, the French chanteur. 'J'ai flané dans les grandes boulevards' lingers in my memory. It is only recently that I discovered that Montand was Jewish.

Music has sustained me throughout my life and Carol and I almost live in the Wigmore Hall, which lays on such sumptious chamber concerts year after year. There we have listened to a wide variety of music – from the Schubert song cycles sung by Ian Bostridge to piano recitals by Andreas Schiff, concerts involving the cellist Steven Isserlis and the performance by Steven Osborne of Messiaen's breathtaking *Vingt Regards sur l'Enfant-Jésus*. We visit the English National Opera from time to time and enjoy both classical and modern opera. Probably the most moving experience I have ever had in an opera house was when I heard Beethoven's only opera, *Fidelio*, for the first time in the 1960s, with Jon Vickers. I found that the dungeon scene in which the prisoners sing of their hope for freedom almost unbearably poignant, especially as they were dressed in striped pyjama-like costumes that recalled the uniform of concentration camp inmates. My hair almost stood on end and tears came to my eyes. For me, *Fidelio* is probably the greatest opera ever written.

The curious case of Richard Wagner

I must own up to having a deep-rooted prejudice against Wagner. I have made a genuine attempt to overcome it, with only partial success.

276

Wagner's reputation as a rabid anti-Semite is well known, as is the fact that he became Hitler's favourite composer. So, when Peter Medawar encouraged me to hear the four operas of the *Ring* cycle (*Der Ring der Nibelungen*) when the Royal Opera House staged it in the 1950s, I decided to give it a try and I booked tickets for all four parts, performed in the space of ten days. Peter was a very keen Wagnerian and I felt that I should be prepared to expose myself to his favourite composer.

Well, I did. My seats were in the 'Gods', high up in the opera house, and as it was a sweltering summer the temperatures up there were almost unbearable. As the operas last between three and a half and four and a half hours the experience provided both a musical and physical challenge. It was an outstanding production in which some of the best-known Wagnerian singers took part, foremost among them the great bass Hans Hotter, who was famous for his noble portrayal of Wotan.

My reaction to the *Ring* was complex: far too long, far too heroic and bombastic, and far too steeped in Germanic mythology, which not infrequently required a suspension of disbelief that I found well nigh impossible to achieve. On the other hand, I was entranced by Wagner's rich and complex orchestration and by his system of *leitmotifs;* this undoubtedly builds up a very potent and atmospheric picture, and of course some of the tunes are irresistible. I was impressed but not fully convinced, and not entirely able to shake off my prejudice against the man. I was glad to have heard the cycle but not to such an extent that I would want to hear it again.

This does raise an interesting question. To what extent should it be possible to distinguish between the private life of a person and his/her artistic achievement? In theory it should be possible to make this dichotomy but in practice it is often difficult, especially in the case of Wagner. Both the conductor Wilhelm Furtwängler and the soprano Elisabeth Schwartzkopf, who took Europe and the world by storm some years after the end of the Second World War, had been tainted by their associations with Hitler and his ideology by accepting honours and favours rather than distancing themselves. I remember when Furtwängler conducted for the first time in Birmingham: the Jewish community and some of the critics muttered about his Nazi past, but they were reluctantly won over by the brilliance of his interpretation of the great masters.

But Wagner *is* a special case. In 1850 he published a very nasty anti-Semitic polemic in which he scurrilously and vitriolically attacked the role played by Jewish composers in German music, principally Mendelssohn and Meyerbeer but also the poet Heinrich Heine. Having achieved notoriety, some approbation and some criticism, he went so far as to reissue the essay with minor modifications in 1869. This is all carefully described and critically analysed in Jens Malte Fischer's fairly recent book

Richard Wagner's 'Das Judentum in der Musik'. There can be no doubt at all of Wagner's vicious anti-Semitism, his pathological hatred of Jewish art and music in particular, and his wish to see all Jewish influence eradicated. Fischer believes that his dislike and pathetic underestimation of Felix Mendelssohn-Bartholdy and Giacomo Meyerbeer was based on jealousy of their achievements, but the roots of his anti-Semitism go deeper than that, possibly dating back to the years he spent in Paris (1839–42) where he was greatly impoverished and beholden to a Jewish music publisher, and where he was exposed to Jewish art. The most notorious portion of his polemic comes right at the end, where he seems to call for the annihilation of the Jews. The wording is not wholly clear, and much depends on the meaning he attached to the words 'Selbstvernichtung' (self-destruction), 'Erlösung' (redemption) and especially 'Untergang' (annihilation). What he appears to be doing is throwing out a challenge to the Jews: 'Take part in this self-destructive, bloody fight, and then we are at one and inseparable. But think: only the redemption of Ahasvers can absolve you from the everlasting curse – annihilation.' (My translation.)

Certainly some contemporaries, such as the composer, flautist and viola player in the Weimar Hofkapelle, Johann Christian Lobe, interpreted this sentence as a call for the destruction of the Jews. As Fischer points out, Wagner was addicted to dramatic, apocalyptic ideas, and the above sentence represents basic concepts in his mythology and fantasy. Ahasvers is a Jewish biblical character who denied Christ access to his house when, carrying the cross, he passed by in need of succour. Ahasvers was therefore cursed to wander through the world forever (the Wandering Jew?) until redeemed by his recognition of the return of the Messiah.

Wagner was a forerunner of Nazi ideology and provided Hitler with what appeared to be spuriously academic grounds for the persecution of the Jews, which Hitler was only too happy to embrace. He used and paraphrased Wagner's writings in his speeches and they were an important influence as early as 1929. According to Fischer, there is a direct line not only from Martin Luther to Hitler but also from Wagner. At the same time it goes without saying that Wagner could not have foreseen that Hitler would actually carry out his ideas about the destruction of the Jews . . .

In his last years (the early 1880s) Wagner moderated his anti-Semitism, if Cosima's diary is anything to go by. According to her he had said, 'If I had to write about the Jews again I would say that I have nothing against them, only that they came to us too soon, when we were not sufficiently secure to incorporate this element.' Hitler might well have made a similar statement had he survived the war.

The Israeli pianist and conductor Daniel Barenboim is clearly able to take a more objective approach, in that he had the courage, in 2001, to play Wagner's *Prelude and Liebestod* as an encore at a concert given by the Berlin Staatskapelle in Jerusalem. This was the first time that Wagner's music had been played in Israel. He first consulted the audience on whether they wanted him to do so, and after some forty minutes of discussion with the audience and the departure of twenty to thirty people the piece was performed, followed by a standing ovation. Barenboim, being of a younger generation, is able to stand back better than I can, but I am wholly with him in that I would strongly object to a boycott of Wagner's music. Some of it is indeed very beautiful. I also greatly admire the work Barenboim is doing in promoting Israeli-Palestinian relations by giving piano recitals in the West Bank and creating a Palestinian-Israeli orchestra.

The Crouch End Festival Chorus

Despite my love for music my early half-hearted attempts to learn to play the violin came to nought, and because my father was very keen that I should use the violin my parents had given me to take to England I have always had guilt feelings about this failure on my part. He asked me several times in his Red Cross messages after the outbreak of war whether I was practising hard, a question that I was careful to avoid answering. But no doubt he was right: music must have helped to sustain him through his awful experiences.

In the autumn of 1987 Joanne and I went for a walk in the Chilterns with our friends John and Lucy Roots, at a time when our marriage was already extremely rocky. It was a glorious day and Lucy, who was a music teacher, and I had walked ahead, singing a few phrases from Schubert's *Die Schöne Müllerin*. Lucy was a founder member of the Crouch End Festival Chorus (CEFC), which had been formed four years earlier, and she encouraged me to join the choir, whose conductor was David Temple. A few weeks later I stood in a queue at a checkout in our local Sainsbury's, quietly humming to myself, when a young woman behind me piped up with 'Oh, are you a singer, then?' I naturally denied any such thing, but she explained that she was an alto of CEFC; her name was Lucy Bailey. She suggested that I should consider joining the choir, initially attending a weekend workshop that was about to take place, in which parts of Bach's *B minor Mass* would be rehearsed. It seemed to me that fate had pointed its finger in the shape of the two Lucys, and I promised to make an effort to attend the workshop. I did, and never looked back.

There followed sixteen years of wonderful singing with a choir of about 150, and a new chapter opened up in my life. I couldn't have committed the time until late in my professional life, as the choir gave at least four concerts a year and the rehearsal schedules were fairly strictly enforced. I enjoyed the singing, under the inspirational baton of David Temple, who, though without academic qualifications, had a genius for delving under the skin of whatever music was performed and infecting the choir with his enthusiasm. Singing became something of an obsession, and as I never join an organisation without giving it my wholehearted support I soon became the choir's most prolific seller of tickets: my numerous friends were absolutely marvellous in supporting the choir and some of them came to almost every concert.

Although I had a reasonable voice that I was able to pitch fairly accurately, I could not read music – one reason that had previously deterred me from taking up an instrument or joining a choir. However, through osmosis with my immediate neighbour in the choir, Charles Murphy, who had a strong voice and who was a pretty good sight-reader, I gradually became more competent. I also practised at home, and in my department at St Mary's Hospital Medical School I had the expert help of one of our post-doctoral fellows, Keith Nye, who had an excellent tenor voice and was a perfect sight-reader. Quite a few lunch breaks were spent rehearsing difficult passages before a concert. My first concert, in the spring of 1988, included Stravinsky's *Symphony of Psalms*, Fauré's *Pavane*, Ravel's *Cantique de Jean Racine* and Poulenc's *Gloria* – truly a baptism of fire.

Singing became a passion, and my wish to sing in all concerts unless there was an overriding reason, such as an absence abroad at a scientific meeting, sometimes chafed with Carol when it came to making plans for weekends or holidays. I am immensely grateful to her for putting up with my obsession, and even coming to my concerts. She herself had sung with the Highgate Choral Society for many years before giving it up, and was therefore familiar with much of the choral repertoire. The quality of the CEFC increased steadily over the years, thanks to our ambitious conductor, and it is now nationally well known. The choir has given a number of concerts abroad, including Britten's *War Requiem* in the Netherlands and Tippett's *A Child of our Time* in Poland, remarkably enough, where it had its first performance to great acclaim. We also performed it on its fiftieth anniversary and in its original venue (the Adelphi Theatre), in the presence of an approving composer.

In the years I had with the CEFC I sang in about 170 works, which included some for which the choir had been asked to perform with professional orchestras. About 60 per cent were twentieth-century works and ten were commissions by the choir. Of the latter, the most memorable was to my mind Joby Talbot's *Shift*, a full-scale and somewhat jazzy celebration of the joys and dignity of nineteenth-century manual labour. Very special for me, apart from the Tippett work, was Mendelssohn's *Elijah*, with its recalled memory of the performance I heard in Berlin at the age of twelve. Of the English composers performed by us I particularly liked Walton's *Belshazzar's Feast*, Vaughan William's *A Sea Symphony* and Elgar's *The Apostles*, with its interesting slant on the role of Judas, who Elgar saw more as a victim than a perpetrator, and Britten's *War Requiem*.

The choir employed professional soloists and semi-professional orchestras of a high standard. The most impressive soloist was undoubtedly the Welsh bass Bryn Terfel, who is now world-famous and totally beyond the reach of CEFC. He sang with us on two occasions, the first time in 1988 in St Augustine's Church, when he was still a third year student at the Royal Academy of Music; we performed Walton's *Belshazzar's Feast* and Fauré's *Requiem*. His singing in the Walton was electrifying; beautiful as his voice was, I felt that it was almost too resonant for the Fauré. The second occasion was the Verdi *Requiem*, and that concert was sold out several weeks in advance, despite the fact that Hornsey Town Hall is able to accommodate a very large audience. Naturally Bryn Terfel brought the house down. I should also single out the participation of the legendary Willard White in our performance of highlights from Gershwin's *Porgy and Bess* in the Royal Festival Hall in 1999.

I was very fortunate, after the first few years with the choir, to have as my regular neighbour at rehearsals and concerts Geoffrey Kemball-Cook, a fine singer and outstanding sight-reader, and his presence was immensely helpful to me. He is a fellow scientist, a biochemist, and we enjoyed each other's company. Geoffrey was and still is one of the pillars of the CEFC.

In their ambitious aim to make the CEFC the best choir in the British Isles, David Temple and his committee arranged for a tri-annual voice test, and changed the concert venues from a local church to the principal concert halls in London – mainly the Royal Festival Hall and the Barbican Concert Hall. A test took place in the summer of 2003 and a number of singers who had supported the choir loyally for many years were asked to leave. My report said 'I would like you to sing with the choir for another year', a polite way of telling me that my time was up. Fair enough, I suppose, as I myself had become aware of some deterioration in my voice, though I would have preferred to have left on my own volition in 2005, on reaching the venerable age of four score years. The choir gave me a very touching send-off in July 2004. And so ended a very happy period in my musical life. Whilst I miss singing I do, at the same time, appreciate my new-found freedom to plan weekends and holidays without having to take the choir schedule into account, and so of course does Carol. Best of all, I no longer have to pester my long-suffering friends with concert leaflets!

Chapter Twenty-Four: The Nobel and Other Prizes

I have been as close to the Nobel Prize as it is possible to get without actually receiving it. My predecessor at St Mary's Hospital Medical School, Rodney Porter, was awarded the prize for his discovery of the structure of antibodies. And Peter Medawar shared the 1960 prize in physiology and medicine with Macfarlane Burnet, largely for work carried out jointly with Rupert Billingham (Bill) and myself on immunological tolerance and embedded in my PhD thesis of 1954. Medawar was the unquestioned leader of our team of three and I have never quarrelled with the wisdom of the Nobel committee in singling him out. In fact, I was intensely embarrassed when the French transplant surgeon and scientist Jean Hamburger, one of the great pioneers of kidney transplantation, introduced me at a congress in the USA in 1976 as the president-elect of the Transplantation Society. It was something of a disgrace, he said, that the Nobel committee had chosen not to include Billingham and Brent as prize recipients. I was on the podium with him and nearly died, and in my reply I assured him and the assembled members of the society that Bill and I had absolutely no problem with the committee's decision. Bill was in the audience and I felt that I had to speak for him as well as for myself, even though I had always felt uneasy that he, the second most senior member of the trio and the one who had been involved in the work leading up to the critical experiments in mice, should have been left out.

The Nobel Prize was set up by Alfred Nobel, the Swedish discoverer and developer of dynamite, and the first prizes in chemistry, physics, medicine, literature and peace were awarded five years after his death, in 1901. He had owned ninety-three dynamite factories and one commentator remarked at the time that Nobel's will 'challenged the humanitarian liberals among his personal friends to solve the problems his discoveries had created'. The prizes are wide open to scientists and writers throughout the world, and at least the early stages of the selection processes are democratic, in that the small Swedish committee sends out invitations to many eminent people in each field calling for nominations. In practice, much canvassing takes place and nominations tend to be highly concerted efforts, especially in the USA. The committee whittles down the nominations to a shortlist and then selects the winner(s) in secret session. Some of its decisions, especially in literature and in peace studies, can clearly be influenced by political considerations, and it is easy to think of laureates who, with hindsight, should never have been honoured.

Someone the Nobel committee should certainly have considered as co-recipient was Ray Owen, whose seminal studies on the blood groups of fraternal cattle had been of great importance. Medawar was very generous in the terms in which he wrote to Owen after the award, saying how much he regretted that Owen had not shared the prize with him. Owen in turn replied with great modesty that the thought had never entered his head. And so friendships were maintained and the whole matter was conducted in a most civilised manner, but this is not always the case. Nobel Prizes can be very divisive and cause much heart searching and chagrin and jealousy. With some who have been overlooked it can gnaw away at their psyche. It's very sad when it happens and makes one wonder whether such prizes are worth having. It is certainly legitimate to ask whether the composition of the Nobel committee, consisting of eighteen Swedes of greater or lesser distinction and elected for life, is adequate to the task. I wonder who would now consider Henry Kissinger as a worthy recipient of the peace prize – a prize that is, however, dispensed by a Norwegian committee?

On balance they probably are a force for the good, for they are now worth a great deal of money, which the recipients often put to good use to further their research. In 1960 Medawar received a relatively small sum by modern standards and he generously shared it with Bill and me: my first car was bought from Nobel money, and so was the resplendent Chinese carpet that adorned our living room. An award also leads to the lionising of the recipient – a double-edged sword – and ensures that there is never any shortage of money from grant-giving bodies.

During the whole of the twentieth century only eleven women have been awarded the Nobel Prize, starting with Marie Sklodowska Curie in 1903, who was awarded the Physics Prize jointly with her husband. Is this thanks to male prejudice or does it simply reflect the fact that few women rose to scientific eminence until fairly recently? Probably both are involved. There are certainly several women who might well have been awarded the Nobel Prize. Among them is Lise Meitner, a Jewish nuclear physicist who fled from Germany to Sweden in 1938. Although it was she who had helped to explain some of the unexpected experimental results obtained by her former German colleague Otto Hahn as having been due to the splitting of the uranium atom, it was Hahn who was awarded the Prize in 1944. Another surprising omission is that of Rosalind Franklin, the daughter of Anglo-Jewish parents. She was a crystallographer and, whilst at King's College London, worked alongside Maurice Wilkins, who later shared the Nobel Prize for the discovery of DNA (desoxyribonuclear acid) with Francis Crick and Maurice Watson. Franklin was left out, despite the fact that her data on X-ray crystallography of the molecule had been critically important.

Nothing should be made of the fact that both these women were of Jewish descent. The Italian biologist Rita Levi-Montalcini, who survived the war in Italy, largely in hiding, and emigrated to the USA after the war, shared the 1986 Nobel Prize for her work on nerve growth factors.

There are other, less prestigious prizes and one or two have happily come my way. I greatly treasured the Vice-Chancellor's Prize for the Most Outstanding Undergraduate of the Year at the University of Birmingham, which I received in 1951. I treasure it partly because I had a great admiration and affection for the Vice-Chancellor, Sir Raymond Priestley, and partly because it crowned a very arduous final year of my studies in which I managed to bring off a decent degree despite my involvement with the Students' Union as its president. My second prize – the Scientific Medal of the Zoological Society of London, came in 1963; and in 1994 I was awarded the Medawar Prize and Medal of the (International) Transplantation Society – a prize I was happy to share with Rupert Billingham and the Dane Morten Simonsen for the discovery of graft-versus-host disease.

I feel that my contribution to immunology has been quite adequately recognised, not least in my election to honorary membership of a number of immunological, medical and surgical societies – Scandinavian, Polish, British and American. I derived particular pleasure from having been singled out by the Royal College of Physicians, the American Association of Transplant Surgeons and the British Transplantation Society.

Fellowship of the Royal Society of London has passed me by, though. By the time Sir Peter Medawar nominated me in the late 1970s his health was in decline and he had lost his influence. Such nominations, unless they are made for the most earth-shattering discovery, often need a certain amount of canvassing and finessing. (See, for example, the furore about the *non*-election of the neuroscientist Professor Susan Greenfield, which received a huge amount of publicity when normally the society's deliberations are shrouded in secrecy.) I don't think that after the mid-1960s I pursued research with quite the single-mindedness required for that kind of success. When Sir Alexander Haddow, the director of the Chester Beatty Cancer Research Institute, was a visiting lecturer in my department in Southampton in 1968 he expressed astonishment that I had not been elected to fellowship and proposed to nominate me. I persuaded him not to do so, because I felt that such a move should come from my peers in the field.

Whilst scientific prizes can be divisive and cause bad blood I am, on the whole, in favour of them, for they provide encouragement, especially for the young. I feel differently about the British honours system, with its emphasis on celebrity and industry and the reward of people who, often having made pots of money, donate some of it to the political party in power. Now *that* is surely a particularly insidious form of corruption.

I treasure as much as anything a letter that I received from Dr Oscar Craig, then head of the radiology department at St Mary's Hospital and at one time president of the Royal College of Radiology. He is a genial Irishman who knew me mainly from our joint membership of the academic board of the medical school and informal meetings over lunch. In December 1986 he sent me a delightful letter, congratulating me on my award of honorary membership of the Royal College of Physicians. He wrote:

> 'Leslie, this acknowledgement is an enormous tribute to you for the contribution you have made to medicine, and we all appreciate how well deserved the award is. I must add however that your contribution has been over and above to that made in the field of medicine. You have made and do make a significant contribution to the Medical School and to your colleagues at all levels in the School and the hospital. Over the years you have been the champion of 'things that are right and proper' as opposed to those that are merely 'opportune'. You have a motivation that is grounded in honesty and never initiated by self-interest. You have rare qualities that are greatly appreciated. What a privilege to have had you as a colleague and may God grant that we spend many useful years together in the future'.

I would be very happy to let Oscar Craig's remarks be my epitaph.

Epilogue

These memoirs have been written over a period of years, and life has meanwhile come full circle for me in a number of respects. There does seem to be a distinct advantage in living to a ripe old age. I will therefore add brief accounts of some significant recent events.

Reunions in the Pankow orphanage

In the spring of 2001 the Friends of the Former Jewish Orphanage in Berlin arranged a reunion of former pupils. The occasion was the inauguration of the completely renovated building as a community centre, incorporating a library, a nurses training centre and a drugs rehabilitation unit. The original little synagogue or prayer room had been lovingly restored, though the ornately moulded ceiling had then not been completed, and the day's ceremonies and celebrations took place in this hall. It is now being used as a venue for talks, discussions and chamber concerts. Fixed to the wall at one end, behind the speakers' podium, was the original embroidered Thorah curtain of the synagogue, which had somehow survived the war. The renovation of the building had been carried out by the Cajewitz-Stiftung, a charitable trust primarily set up to provide housing for elderly people in Berlin-Pankow, under the careful supervision of Professor Peter-Alexis Albrecht, its energetic and charismatic director. Fifteen former pupils turned up from various parts of the world, including Bert Lewyn – the 'boy' with whom I used to play football and who survived the war years underground in Berlin. Some of us were accompanied by our wives and, happily for me, Carol came along too. Hilde Schoenfeld, who had been a day pupil in the orphanage school,

287

was there too; she died tragically the day after her return, but not before she had the thrill of seeing the name of her parents inscribed on a plaque in the building commemorating Jews who had been deported from Pankow by the Nazis. Ruth Albert, who had also attended the school, was unfortunately not able to join us.

It was a festive and moving three-day event, beautifully organised, with lovely music and interesting talks, and it revived many poignant memories. Our hosts – some Jewish, others not – were incredibly generous, thoughtful and charming, and some of them – for example, Inge Lammel and Peter Alexis and Julia Albrecht – have become good friends.

A second reunion took place in 2005. A smaller number turned up this time, but Carol and I were struck by the warmth with which the local organisers received us. The activities included visits to the Jewish Museum and to the recently completed Memorial for the Murdered Jews of Europe, right in the heart of Berlin. I published a full account of this reunion in the *Journal of the Association for Jewish Refugees*. In 2006 yet another reunion took place, but this time the number of participants was greatly diminished. It was of special significance for me because Inge Lammel took us to see the Jewish hospital, with its home for nurses where my sister had lived towards the end, and the small restored hospital synagogue. Incredibly, the hospital continued to function throughout the war, even though its cellars were used by the police as a collection centre for Jews about to be deported!

One woman who attended the first reunion was Renate Bechar, the daughter of the director of the Pankow orphanage before the war and who had lived in her parents' flat in the orphanage until it was liquidated in 1940, when she was eight years old. Three years later the family was deported to Theresienstadt, which she and her mother survived although, tragically, her father died in Auschwitz. Not long ago I received an e-mail from her in which she told me of a recently discovered letter sent by her mother after the war to the mother of my former friend Fred Gerstl, who as a non-Jew had survived the war in Berlin. (He died in January 2009.) In it she referred to a Lodenmantel (a German overcoat made traditionally from dark green cloth) from Lothar Baruch. Apparently they had taken this coat with them to Theresienstadt and it had returned with them to Berlin in 1945. It is a poignant thought that a coat that had once belonged to me should have helped Renate to survive the climatic rigours of the concentration camp!

The year 2008 was marked by two very significant events in Berlin. The first was the publication, on 9 November, of a book that comprehensively covers the history – architectural, social, educational – of the former Jewish Boys' Orphanage building in Pankow. I had the privilege of being one of the three co-editors, having commissioned and edited contributions from twelve former pupils, in which they poignantly describe their life histories, reminisce about the orphanage, and describe their attitude to the modern Germany. (This book, published in German, is *Verstoerte Kindheiten. Das Jüdische Waisenhaus in Pankow als Ort der Zuflucht, Geborgenheit und Vertreibung*, eds Peter-Alexis Albrecht, Leslie Baruch Brent and Inge Lammel, published by Berliner Wissenschaft-Verlag, Berlin, 2008.) The second event was the unveiling in central Berlin, close to Friedrichstrasse Bahnhof, of a memorial to the Kindertransports and the children who were left behind. I had been asked to contribute a speech (in German!), having been on the first Kindertransport to leave Berlin exactly seventy years ago.

The 'Stolpersteine' (stumbling stones): memorials to my family

It was during the last reunion that I learnt about the 'Stolpersteine'. These are small brass plates that are embedded in the pavements outside houses from which Jews were sent to their deaths; they can be purchased at low cost from an organisation comprising volunteers (such as Wolfgang Knoll) who perform their tasks as a labour of love. The Stolpersteine record the date and place of birth of the person and the date and destination of their deportation, and they are appearing all over Berlin and other parts of Germany in increasing numbers. Not everyone regards them with enthusiasm – the objection frequently raised is that people walk on them – but to me and hundreds of others they serve as a touching personal memorial. In 2007 I arranged to have them put in place for my parents, outside their last address in 7 Roscherstrasse, and for my sister Eva in the suburb of Eichkamp, where she had lived until she moved into the nurses home of the Jewish hospital. On a very recent visit to Berlin, arranged to discuss the publication of a book about the Pankow orphanage, I visited them and gave them a good polish . . .

A very different reunion

Another significant reunion took place in the summer of 2002, in the garden of Hans and Susanne Meyer on the North Downs of Kent, not far from what used to be Bunce Court School. They had invited as many Old Bunce Courtians and their spouses as possible for the day, and almost 100 people turned up from this country and from all over the world – the USA, Israel, South Africa, Australia, Spain, France and other countries. This followed a previous reunion a couple of years earlier, but this was quite the largest and probably the last. The feeling of fellowship among this disparate group of people – a fellowship generated by the common experiences of well over half a century ago – was striking. Whilst not everyone had been happy in the school – the circumstances of our arrival had often been too tragic for that – everyone had some pleasurable memories, and the names of Anna Essinger and those of many teachers were on everyone's lips. Many stories and anecdotes were retold – amusing, sad, touching and always interesting. It was a heart-warming day and it was wonderful to see Hans Meyer, one of the last surviving teachers, enjoy it all at the age of ninety.

Following this reunion Hans Meyer had the brainwave to invite everyone present to write a one-page account of what Bunce Court School had meant to them, 'warts and all'. The result is a privately published book (*Reflections: Bunce Court*), in which some seventy people reminisced about their experiences. To quote from a review I wrote for the *Journal of the Association of Jewish Refugees*:

> It is perhaps invidious to single out particular contributions, but undoubtedly the most famous of the ex-pupils is the painter Frank Auerbach. He concludes his handwritten eulogy by writing 'I cannot imagine a better home', and these sentiments are echoed by many. Samuel Oliner had arrived in Bunce Court in 1945; he was one of a dozen or so boys who survived the war in Poland, hidden or in camps. He became Professor of Sociology at Humboldt State University, California, and heads an institute doing research on altruism, heroism and forgiveness. Finally, Hans Meyer himself has written, at the insistence of some of his former pupils. He concludes: 'We knew of Bunce Court's precarious situation, we knew that it could not and probably needed not to exist for longer than its efforts required. But as long as there were children to whose wellbeing and thus future we could make a modest contribution, we hoped to stay on. Their trust and affection was the school's greatest gift to us.'

Hans Meyer recently presented me, very generously, with Anna Essinger's old and rather resplendent German bureau, which he had inherited after her death. It pleases me no end that these memoirs have been revised as I sat at this desk.

A remarkable tribute: Ulm celebrates Anna Essinger's 125th birthday

This was the title of a short article I wrote for the *Journal of the Association of Jewish Refugees*. I was fortunate to have been invited to the event, which took up the best part of a week. The city of Ulm celebrated its 1150th anniversary and chose to honour two people who had been born there: Albert Einstein and Anna Essinger, both born 125 years ago. Einstein had spent only the first few years of his life in the city but Anna Essinger had lived nearby until she went to the USA to study before the First World War. A week in March 2004 had been devoted to Einstein and his discoveries and Essinger's commemoration followed in October. It was an extraordinary week, meticulously and imaginatively organised by some teachers at what are now the Anna-Essinger-Schulen, primary and secondary schools on the same site.

Before the war Ulm had been greatly identified with Nazi ideology, and by selecting these two Jewish former citizens the city was clearly making an important point. Both are household words in Ulm: Einstein because of the revolutionary impact he made on physics and how we look at the universe, and Essinger because of her avant-garde educational ideas and her boldness in removing virtually a whole boarding school from nearby Herrlingen to England as early as 1933, when she saw the writing on the wall for Jewish education in Germany. It was extremely touching to hear 1200 children, many of them carrying banners with Anna Essinger's photograph, singing 'Happy Birthday, dear Anna'.

An official invitation from the city of Koszalin

I began these memoirs with an event in Köslin (Koszalin) and it is therefore not inappropriate to finish them with an account of some more recent stirring happenings in the town of my birth.

Here is quite the largest wheel to have come full circle. In July 2005 Carol and I spent a week in Koszalin, this time as honoured guests of the Lord Mayor and the city council. Evidently Zdzislaw (Zibi) Pacholski, the photographer who has befriended me, had told the mayor of my personal history and of my association with Medawar's Nobel Prize, and it was decided not only to invite me but to lay on some very extraordinary events in my honour. As I described these in the *Journal of the Association of Jewish Refugees* I will give the briefest summary here.

Carol and I were treated like celebrities and with the utmost consideration and courtesy, and wherever we went we were followed by journalists and radio and TV crews. Quite the most significant happening was the rededication of the old Jewish cemetery in a solemn ceremony in which the Lord Mayor, the Bishop of Koszalin, a Catholic priest (Henryk Romanik) and some Jews from Koszalin, Warsaw and Gdansk took part. The cemetery was bare, apart from the commemorative stone and a small cypress, but it was intended to move my great uncle's gravestone back into the cemetery from which it was so brutally removed in 1938. This has now been done.

Other events included the unveiling of a plaque in three languages on the wall of the building in which I had lived with my family in the 1930s; the gift of leather-bound documents from the State Archive concerning the births, deaths and marriages of members of my family; the award of honorary membership by the Regional Koszalin Chamber of Physicians; an evening's 'dialogue' between myself and some 120 people, who had crammed into a small theatre to question me about my past life; a symposium on the topic of 'Transplantation'; and a choral concert dedicated to me. No wonder that I entitled my account of this extraordinary week, which was emotionally very taxing, 'How I Came to Believe in Miracles'.

In May 2006 I was invited back to Koszalin. This time we were the guests of the University of Technology, and once again Zibi Pacholski and Henryk Romanik had acted as catalysts. The main reason for the generous invitation was the unveiling of a wonderful sculptured memorial on the site of the 'new' Jewish cemetery, which had been built over by the university. Again, the ceremony was conducted with great solemnity and dignity and there, on a lawn outside the university building, now stands the memorial with a suitable explanatory plaque. As I explained in the speech I was asked to give at short notice, that is where three of my grandparents were buried, and for me this commemoration was unbelievably poignant. During the week Carol and I spent in Koszalin I also gave a lecture on transplantation immunology to the staff and students of the university. Although knowing little immunology they proved to be very receptive and appreciative.

It is legitimate to ask why the Poles in Koszalin, who were in no way responsible for what happened in Köslin before the Second World War, have felt it appropriate to honour me in this way and to draw attention to the fact that the city had a small but thriving German-Jewish community before the war. I suspect that it has to do with a need on their part to confront their own anti-Semitic past and to reach out in a spirit of reconciliation. (In recent years Zibi and Henryk have organised candle-lit processions to the former Jewish sites, to commemorate Kristallnacht – an act of remembrance that I find particularly touching.) For Carol and for me the weeks there were an unforgettable experience; for them it was a case of 'let us remember the past and let us rebuild bridges' and therefore of the greatest significance. I was happy to play an emblematic role in all this, even if the attention I received sometimes seemed well over the top.

The future?

I used to be full of optimism, and in the fifties, following the war years, I believed that the world could only become a better place and that mankind was evolving socially and politically to be more compassionate and more tolerant. Certainly in the UK the policies of post-war Labour governments, with the Beveridge plan, the formation of the NHS, the creation of comprehensive schools and other social provisions seemed to point that way. I am not so sure now, for in some respects we seem to have gone backwards and poverty is still all around us. Looking at the world at large there seems to be nothing but mayhem. There have been and still are desperate wars everywhere, especially in Africa, where genocide is still being practised. There is widespread famine, disease, AIDS, global warming, tribal and national animosities, the calamitous invasion of Iraq, even in Europe the Balkans have shown how deeply ingrained national hatreds still are, the seemingly insoluble problems in Northern Ireland (now happily resolved) and in the Middle East; all these add up to a bleak and depressing picture. Has the world really learnt nothing from history? Has my generation failed the world? I fear that the answer must be in the affirmative. And, since 9/11 and several acts of terrorism nearer home, the intolerance and hatred of Muslims in Britain and elsewhere, and in many cases their inhumane and unjust treatment, threatens to bring about a major rift between the West and the Muslim world that could yet threaten the stability of the globe. Deeply worrying is the failure of the developed world, especially the USA, to tackle global warming. I feel sad that our grandchildren should be facing such a highly uncertain future. We have let them down badly.

Regrets?

Do I have regrets about my life? It would be unnatural if I had none. I wish I had spent more time with my children when they were small, for example. I wish that my first marriage had not come to grief. Yet a phoenix has risen from those ashes, and I am happy to be with Carol and to share the remainder of my life with her.

I undoubtedly had a difficult and sometimes painful childhood. But my father was right in pointing out that I was 'ein Sonntagskind'. I have been extraordinarily fortunate at various critical points of my life and I have succeeded in building my life on the foundations laid so lovingly by my parents in my first eleven years. I owe them a huge debt of gratitude, not least in letting go of me when it mattered.

Bibliography

Aaronovitch, David, 'Dear marcher, please answer some questions', *Guardian* (18 February 2003)

Ackroyd, Peter, *Albion: the Origins of the English Imagination* (Chatto & Windus, London, 2002)

Albrecht, Peter-Alexis, *The Forgotten Freedom: September 11 as a Challenge for European Legal Principles* (Berliner Wissenschaft-Verlag, Berlin, 2003)

Amis, Martin, *Koba the Dread: Laughter and the Twenty Million* (Jonathan Cape, London, 2002)

Bailey, Alison, 'Who was . . . Rosalind Franklin?', *Biologist*, vol. 50, pp. 92–3 (2003)

Barnett, Antony, 'Final agony of RAF volunteer killed by sarin in Britain', *Observer* (18 September 2003)

Bauman, Zygmund, *Modernity and the Holocaust* (Polity Press, Cambridge, 1989)

Beatrix, Doris, *Heimat oder Zuflucht – die Landschulheime Herrlingen und Bunce Court School/Kent* (Universität-Gesamthochschule, Paderborn, 1999)

Beevor, Antony, *Berlin: The Downfall, 1945* (Viking, London, 2002)

Belsen. Supplement to the British Zone Review, 13 October 1945 (Chief, Public Relations and Information Services Control Group for Germany, BAOR, 1945)

Bergas, Hanna, *Fifteen Years - Lived Among, With and For Refugee Children* (unpublished, Palo Alto, 1979)

Billingham, R.E., Brent, L. and Medawar, P.B. 'Actively acquired tolerance of foreign cells', *Nature* **172**, 603 (London, 1953)

Billingham, R.E., Brent, L. and Medawar, P.B., 'Quantitative studies on tissue transplantation immunity. III. Actively acquired tolerance', *Philosophical Transactions, Royal Society B Quantitative studies on tissue transplantation immunity* **239**, 357 (1956)

Billingham, R.E. and Brent, L., 'A simple method for inducing tolerance of skin homografts in mice', *Transplantation Bulletin* **4**, 67 (1957)

Billingham, R.E and Brent, L., 'Quantitative studies on tissue transplantation immunity. IV. Induction of tolerance in newborn mice and studies on the phenomenon of runt disease', *Philosophical Transactions, Royal Society B* **242**, 439 (1959)

Black, S., Humphrey, J.H. and Niven, J.S., 'Inhibition of Mantoux reaction by direct suggestion under hypnosis', *British Medical Journal* **1**, 1649–53 (1963)

Boyd, Valerie, *Wrapped in Rainbows. The Life of Zora Neale Hurston* (Virago, London, 2003)

Brambell, F.W.R. and eight others, *Report of the Technical Committee to Enquire into the Welfare of Animals Kept Under Intensive Livestock Husbandry Systems* (HMSO, London, 1965)

Breitman, Richard, *Official Secrets. What the Nazis Planned, What the British and Americans Knew* (Hill & Wang, New York, 1998)

Brent, Leslie, 'Obituary: Sir Peter Medawar, OM, CH', *Independent* (5 October 1987)

Brent, Leslie, 'Quiet Hero of Berlin', *Guardian* (20 November 1989)

Brent, Leslie, *A History of Transplantation Immunology* (Academic Press, London, 1997)

Brent, Leslie, 'Billingham, Rupert Everett (1921–2002)', *Oxford Dictionary of National Biography* (Oxford University Press, Oxford, 2004–8)

Brent, Leslie Baruch, 'Obituary: Professor Rupert Billingham: pioneer in the field of organ transplantation' *Independent* (25 November 2002)

Brent, Leslie Baruch, 'A remarkable tribute: Ulm celebrates Anna Essinger', *Journal of the Association of Jewish Refugees* (November 2004)

BIBLIOGRAPHY

Brent, Leslie Baruch, 'Rupert Everett Billingham', *Biographical Memoirs of Fellows of the Royal Society* 51, 33–50 (2005)

Brent, Leslie Baruch, 'Reflections: Bunce Court – book review), *Journal of the Association of Jewish Refugees* (February 2005)

Brent, Leslie Baruch, 'Berlin Jewish orphanage for boys: a second reunion', *Journal of the Association of Jewish Refugees* (August 2005)

Brent, Leslie Baruch, 'How I came to believe in miracles', *Journal of the Association of Jewish Refugees* (December 2005)

Brent, Leslie Baruch, 'More miracles from Poland', *Journal of the Association of Jewish Refugees* (July 2006)

Brent, L. and Berrian, J.H., 'Cell-bound antibodies in transplantation immunity', *Annals of the New York Academy of Sciences* 73, 654–62 (1958)

Browning, Christopher R., *Nazi Policy, Jewish Workers, German Killers* (Cambridge University Press, Cambridge, 2000)

Bruner, Jerome, *Making Stories: Law, Literature and Life* (Harvard, 2003)

Bunting, Madeleine, *The Model Occupation: the Channel Islands Under German Rule, 1940–45* (HarperCollins, London, 1996)

Bunting, Madeleine, 'Our part in the holocaust', *Guardian* (24 January 2004)

Burleigh, Michael, *The Third Reich – a New History* (Macmillan, London, 2000)

Campbell, Duncan, 'Long Walk to Freedom', *Guardian* (15 November 2004)

Campbell, James, 'The great literary lottery', *Guardian* (6 October 2001)

Cohen, Rich, *The Avengers. A Jewish War Story* (Jonathan Cape, London, 2000)

Cohen, Stanley, *States of Denial. Knowing About Atrocities and Suffering* (Polity Press, Cambridge, 2001)

Corbett, Anne, 'Obituary: Harry Rée', *Guardian* (20 May 1991)

Cornwell, John, *Hitler's Pope: the Secret History of Pius XII* (Viking, London, 1999)

Diggins, Francis, 'Who was . . . Almroth Wright F.R.S.?', *Biologist* 49, 280–2 (2002)

Dowty, Alan, *The Jewish State* (University of California Press, Berkeley, 1998)

Dunnill, M., *The Plato of Praed Street: the life and times of Almroth Wright* (Royal Society Medical Press, London, 2000)

Equiano, O., *The African: The Interesting Narrative of the Life of Olaudah Equiano* (Black Classics; X Press, London, 1998; first published 1789)

Erikson, Erik, *Childhood and Society* (Triad/Pelican Books, London, 1977)

Eyre, Richard, 'Landscape as language', *Guardian* (20 March 2004)

Fenby, Jonathan, *On the Brink. The Trouble with France* (Little, Brown, London, 1998)

Finkel, Sidney, *Sevek and the Holocaust – the Boy Who Refused to Die* (S. Finkel, Illinois, USA, 2001)

Freud, Sigmund (transl. James Strachey), 'Review of August Forel's *Hypnotism*', *The Complete Psychological Works of Sigmund Freud* (The Hogarth Press, London, 1968)

Gilbert, Martin, *Auschwitz and the Allies. How the Allies Responded to the News of Hitler's Final Solution* (Michael Joseph, London, 1981)

Gilbert, Martin, *A History of the Twentieth Century, vol. 1: 1900–1933* (HarperCollins, London, 1997)

Gilbert, Martin, *The Boys: Triumph Over Adversity* (Phoenix, London, 1997)

Gilbert, Martin, *Descent into Barbarism: a History of the Twentieth Century, 1933–1951* (HarperCollins, London, 1999)

Goldhagen, Daniel J., *Hitler's Willing Executioners: Ordinary Germans and the Holocaust* (Little, Brown, London, 1996)

Gottlieb, Amy Zahl, *Men of Vision; Anglo-Jewry's Aid to Victims of the Nazi Regime 1933–1945* (Weidenfeld & Nicolson, London, 1998)

Gutterman Bella and Morgenstern, Naomi (eds), *The Gurs Hagaddah. Passover in Perdition* (Devorah, Jerusalem, New York, 2003)

Haffner, Sebastian, *The Meaning of Hitler* (Weidenfeld & Nicolson, London, 1979)

Hamilton, Nigel, *The Full Monty: Montgomery of Alamein 1887-1942* (Allan Lane, London, 2001)

Heaman, E.A., *St Mary's: The History of a London Teaching Hospital* (McGill-Queen's University Press, Montreal, 2003)

Jeffries, Stuart, 'Undercover cop', *Guardian* (2003)

Josephs, Zoe, and members of the Birmingham group, *Survivors: Jewish Refugees in Birmingham* (Meridian Books, Oldbury, 1988)

Kershaw, Ian, *Hitler. 1889–1936: Hubris* (Penguin, London, 1999)

Kershaw, Ian, *Hitler. 1936–1945: Nemesis* (Penguin, London, 2001)

Klemperer, Viktor (abridged and transl. Martin Chalmers), *I Shall Bear Witness. The Diaries of Viktor Klemperer 1933–1941* (Weidenfeld & Nicolson, London, 1998)

Klemperer, Viktor, *Ich Will Nicht Zeugnis Ablegen Bis Zum Letzten. Tagebücher 1933–1942, and 1942–1945* (2 vols) (Aufbau-Verlag, Berlin, 1998)

Klemperer, Viktor, *To the Bitter End* (Ibis Editions, Jerusalem, 1999)

Lammel, Inge (ed.), *Jüdisches Leben in Pankow: Eine Zeitgeschichtliche Dokumentation* (Edition Hentrich, Berlin, 1993)

Lammel, Inge, *Jüdische Lebenswege. Ein Kulturhistorischer Streifzug durch Pankow und Niederschönhausen* (Hentrich & Hentrich, Berlin, 2007)

Leverton, B. and Lowensohn, S. (eds), *I Came Alone – The Stories of the Kindertransports* (The Book Guild, Lewes, 1990)

Levi, Primo, *The Periodic Table* (Abacus, London, 1985)

Levi, Primo, *If This is a Man* (Abacus, London, 1987)

Levy, Andrea, 'This is my England', *Guardian* (19 February 2000)

Levy, Andrea, *Small Island* (Review, London, 2004)

Levy, J.A., *HIV and the Pathogenesis of AIDS* (American Society of Microbiology, Washington, 1998)

Lewyn, Bert and Saltzman Lewyn, Bev, *On the Run in Nazi Berlin* (Xlibris, USA, 2001)

Lovell, Bernard, 'Obituary: Professor Sir Fred Hoyle', *Guardian* (23 August 2001)

Lowenthal Felstiner, Mary, *To Paint a Life: Charlotte Salomon in the Nazi Era* (Harper Perennial, London, 1995)

Maddox, B., *The Dark Lady of DNA* (HarperCollins, London, 2002)

Malte Fischer, Jens, *Richard Wagner's 'Das Judentum in der Musik'* (Insel Verlag, Frankfurt am Main, 2000)

McPherson, Klim, 'Counting the dead in Iraq', *The Lancet* **365**, 550–1 (2005)

Medawar, Jean and Pyke, David, *Hitler's Gift – Scientists who Fled Nazi Germany* (Richard Cohen Books, London, 2000)

Medawar, Peter, *Memoir of a Thinking Radish. An Autobiography* (Oxford University Press, Oxford, 1986)

Mercer, D. (ed.), *Chronicle of the Twentieth Century* (Longman, London, 1998)

Meyer, Hans (ed.), *Reflections: Bunce Court* (H. Meyer, Kent, 2004)

Moorhead, Caroline, *Dunant's Dream: War, Switzerland and the History of the Red Cross* (HarperCollins, London, 1998)

Morris, Jan, *Trieste and the Meaning of Nowhere* (Faber & Faber, London, 2001)

Mosley, Nicholas, *Rules of the Game/Beyond the Pale: Memoirs of Sir Oswald Mosley and Family* (Pimlico, London, 1998)

Newsletter (1ˢᵗ Battalion, Worcestershire Regiment, January 1947)

Nicholls, S.C.J., Some *Jewish Soldiers and Officers* (Burnett's Printers, Burgess Hill, 2004)

Oakes, John, 'Obituary: Jeff Crawford', *Guardian* (10 January 2004)

'Obituary: Colonel Bill Bowen', *The Times* (15 March 2001)

'Obituary: Alex Comfort', *Guardian* (28 March 2000)

'Obituary: Martha Gellhorn', *Guardian* (17 February 1998)

'Obituary: Richard Maber', *Guardian* (11 February 1999)

'Obituary: Sir Peter Medawar', *The Times* (5 October 1987)

'Obituary: The Marchesa Iris Origo', *Independent* (1 July 1988)

Origo, Iris, *War in Val D'Orcia* (Jonathan Cape, London, 1947)

Ousby, Ian, *Occupation: the Ordeal of France 1940–1944* (Pimlico, London, 1999)

Patkin, Benzion, *The Dunera Internees* (Cassell Australia, North Melbourne, 1979)

Paul, Elliot, *A Narrow Street* (The Crescent Press, 1943; reprinted by Penguin, Harmondsworth, 1954)

Pearl, Cyril, *The Dunera Scandal* (Angus & Robertson, London, 1983)

Penaud, Guy, *Les Crimes de la Division 'Brehmer'. La Traque des Résistants et des Juifs en Dordogne, Corrèze, Haute-Vienne (Mars–Avril 1944)* (La Lauze, Perigueux, 2004)

Potten, Dorle, *Des Kindes Chronik (A Child's Story)* (Privately published, in English, 2004)

Priestley, Raymond E., *Antarctic Adventure* (T. Fisher Unwin, London, 1914; republished by C. Hurst, London, 1974)

Puvogel, U., Stankowski, M. and Graf, U., *Gedenkstätten für die Opfer des Nationalsozialismus. Eine Dokumentation* (Bundeszentrale fur Politische Bildung, Bonn, 1995)

Rees, Laurence, *The Nazis. A Warning from History* (BBC Books, London, 1997)

Rollyson, Carl, *Beautiful Exile. The Life of Martha Gellhorn* (Trafalgar Square Publishing, London, 2002)

Roseman, Mark, *The Villa. The Lake, The Meeting. Wannsee and the Final Solution* (Allen Lane, London, 2002)

Rubinstein, William D., *The Myth of Rescue. Why the Democracies Could Not Have Saved More Jews from the Nazis* (Routledge, London, 1979)

Ryan, Nick, *Homeland: Into a World of Hate* (Mainstream, Edinburgh, 2003)

Rycroft, Charles, *A Critical Dictionary of Psychoanalysis* (Penguin, Harmondsworth, 1972)

Sacks, Jonathan, 'The hatred that won't die', *Guardian* (25 February 2002)

Sacks, Jonathan, *The Dignity of Difference – How to Avoid the Clash of Civilisations* (Continuum, London, 2002)

Schachne, Lucie, *Education Towards Spiritual Resistance: the Jewish Landschulheim 1933-1939* (dipa Verlag, Frankfurt am Main, 1988)

Sebald, W.G. (transl. Anthea Bell), *Austerlitz* (Hamish Hamilton, London, 2001)

Sebald, W.G. (transl. Anthea Bell), *On the Natural History of Destruction* (Hamish Hamilton, London, 2002)

Snowman, Daniel, *The Hitler Emigrés* (Chatto & Windus, London, 2002)

Spiro, Michael, 'Women and the Nobel Prize', *Journal of the Association of Jewish Refugees* (London, November 2002)

Starzl, T.E., 'Leslie Brent and the mysterious German surgeon' *Annals of Surgery* 244, 54-7 (2006)

Stiglitz, Joseph and Bilmes, Linda, The Three Trillion War (Allen Lane, London, 2008)

Strawson, Galen, 'Tales of the unexpected', *Guardian* (1 January 2004)

Sumption, Jonathan, *The Hundred Years War, vol. I: Trial by Battle* (Faber & Faber, London, 1990)

Sumption, Jonathan, *The Hundred Years War, vol. II: Trial by Fire* (Faber & Faber, London, 1999)

Transplantation Society, The, 'The shortage of organs for clinical transplantation: document for discussion', *British Medical Journal* 1, 251–255 (1975)

Travis, Alan, 'British tag is "coded racism"', *Guardian* (11 October 2000)

Trede, Michael, *Der Rückkehrer. Skizzenbuch eines Chirurgen* (Ecomed Biographien, Landsberg, 2000)

Trott, Uta-Elizabeth. 'Anna Essinger (1879–1960), educationist', *Oxford Dictionary of National Biography* (Oxford University Press, Oxford, 2004–8)

Turner, Barry, *And the Policeman Smiled* (Bloomsbury, London, 1991)

Vitaliev, Vitali, 'Showing off the sites of shame', *Guardian* (10 December 1998)

Wagner, Richard, *Das Judentum in der Musik* (Neue Zeitschrift für Musik, 1850)

Webster, Paul, 'Vichy criminal too ill to stay in jail, court rules', *Guardian* (September 2002)

Wright, Sir Charles, 'Sir Raymond Priestley: an Appreciation', *Polar Record* 17, 251 (1974)

Whymper, Edward, *Scramble Amongst the Alps: in the Year 1860-69* (Thomas Nelson & Sons, London, 1900) Young, David, 'When Hell Froze Over', *Guardian* (9 October 2001)

Interviews with the author: Gwynne Angell (2001), Dr Dennis Brind (2000), Lucie Kaye (née Schachne) (2001), Hans Meyer (2000); personal communication with the author: Renate Bechar.

Radio and Television: BBC radio programme: *Children in Flight*, producer Robert Kemp (3 January 1939); BBC television documentary: *No Time to Say Goodbye* (1989); Schubert Filmproduktion documentary: *Anna's Kinder*, producers Angelika Schubert and Gabriele Krober (Munich, 1995). An English version, *Anna's Children*, was made soon afterwards.

Index of Names